MASS MOVEMENT:
THE DIGITAL YEARS VOL. TWO

Tim Cundle

Published by Earth Island Books
Pickforde Lodge
Pickforde Lane
Ticehurst
TN5 7BN

wwww.earthisland.co.uk
© Copyright Earth Island Publishing Ltd

This collection first published by Earth Island Publishing 2020

The moral rights of the author have been asserted.

All rights reserved.

No part of this publication may be reproduced, distributed or transmitted by any means, electronic, mechanical, photocopying, or otherwise, without the prior permission of the publisher.

ISBN 978-1-9997581-7-2

Printed, bound and distributed by Ingram Sparks

*"Say what you must, do all you can
Break all the fucking rules and
Go to Hell with Superman and
Die like a champion..."*

Do What You Want – Bad Religion

Copyright Brett Gurewitz / Universal Music Publishing Group

*"You're the underdog
You're just like me
There's something deep inside
That tells you to be free..."*

Back to Back – Underdog

Copyright Richard Birkenhead & Underdog

All content copyright Mass Movement Magazine and may not be reproduced in any medium with prior consent or permission. All photographs and imagery originally published in Mass Movement Magazine (2009 – 2015) and have been reproduced based on prior permission being granted. Respective credit or all imagery has been acknowledged were possible.
This collection first published by Earth Island Publishing 2020

Contents

CHRISTOPHER FOWLER	2
CINEMATIC BLOOD – COLOUR FILM OR BLACK AND WHITE?	8
DANNY DYER	12
JOEY CAPE (LAGWAGON / ME FIRST & THE GIMME GIMMES)	18
EMILY BOOTH	22
MARK "BARNEY" GREENWAY (NAPALM DEATH)	28
SCREEN DAMAGE – APOCALYPSE WOW!	36
SIMON GUERRIER	44
THE OLYMPIAN SPIRIT IN 28MM	50
BRIAN SLAGEL (METAL BLADE RECORDS)	56
DR. LIVING DEAD!	62
JAMES LOVEGROVE	66
JUSTIN MELKMANN	74
MARK OF THE VAMPIRE – THE LITERARY TRACES OF A BLOODSUCKER	82
NOW THEN GADGIE…THINGS THAT SCARED ME SENSELESS WHEN I WAS A BAIRN…	86
SCREEN DAMAGE – HURTS TO BE DEAD	92
CHARLIE HIGSON	98
MICHAEL BIEHN & JENNIFER BLANC-BIEHN	102
STEVE NILES	108
JAY BENTLEY (BAD RELIGION)	114
BAFFLEGAB	120
KEN CASEY (DROPKICK MURPHY'S)	126
THE GREEN HORNET – A DIFFERENT KIND OF SUPERHERO	130
WHAT MAKES A COMIC SCARY?	134
NEAL ADAMS	138
SCREEN DAMAGE – RIVERS OF BLOOD: GOING TO HELL IN A BABY CART	144
DUNCAN REDMONDS – (SNUFF / GUNS 'N' WANKERS)	154
JAMES TYNION IV	160
THE MASKED MARVEL – THE KING OF COOL SUPERHEROES	168
JOE R. LANSDALE	172
MICHAEL ALAN NELSON	180
SPY SMASHER – THE SLICK MOTORCYCLE RIDING CRUSADER	186
JEFF "SWAMPY" MARSH	190
PAUL MAGRS	194
PIMP MY WRITE	200
STERLING GATES	204
LECKY VOORHEES (VOORHEES / WALK THE PLANK)	212
DEAN BEDDIS (BAD SAM / LAS VEGAS ELVIS / COWBOY KILLERS)	216
BL'AST!	220
CAPTAIN MIDNIGHT – THE MANIC ACE OF THE AIRWAYS	226
GREGG HURWITZ	230
INJURED EYEBALLS	236
OUT COLD	242
ROBERT VENDITTI	246
SHAI HULUD	250

THE SPIDER'S WEB – THE RUTHLESS TWO-GUN SUPERHERO	256
TOBY HADOKE	260
C.J. RAMONE	266
HOPS & BARLEY – WENSLEYDALE BREWERY	274
VINNIE FIORELLO (LESS THAN JAKE)	280
MATT FITTON	284
THE MYSTERIOUS DOCTOR SATAN – A MAD SCIENTIST READY FOR WORLD DOMINATION	290
THE WEIRD WORLD OF BILL ALEXANDER	294
THE CRIMSON GHOST – THE NEATEST COSTUME IN SERIAL HISTORY	300
CRUMBSUCKERS	304
ENGLISH DOGS	312
EXCEL	322
LUDICHRIST	328
ROTTING OUT	334
SCHEISSE MINNELLI	340
GARY NUMAN	346
LESS IS NEVER MORE - MORE OR LESS	350
THE FIGHTING DEVIL DOGS – THE FORERUNNER TO DARTH VADER	354
GARY DANIELS	358
DICK BRIEFER'S FRANKENSTEIN	362
WELLY ARTCORE (ARTCORE FANZINE / FOUR LETTER WORD / VIOLENT ARREST)	366
MANHUNT OF MYSTERY ISLAND – THE SWASHBUCKLING VILLAIN WITH AN ATTITUDE	374
ROGER MIRET (AGNOSTIC FRONT)	378
ANDY WEST – (KILL YOUR IDOLS)	388
CHAKA MALIK – (BURN / ORANGE 9MM)	392
FREDDY ALVA	398
GARY BENNETT II (KILL YOUR IDOLS / SHEER TERROR / BLACK ANVIL)	406
EDDIE SUTTON (LEEWAY)	412
JORDAN COOPER (REVELATION RECORDS)	418
SEAN TAGGART	424
PAUL BEARER (SHEER TERROR)	430
TONY RETTMAN	436
RICHIE BIRKENHEAD (UNDERDOG / YOUTH OF TODAY / INTO ANOTHER)	442
ACID REIGN	448
I WAS SATAN'S SLAVE TO THE MUSIC!	452
NIGHT BIRDS	456
THE BATMAN – A WARTIME SUPERHERO	460
MASS MOVEMENT 32 + 33	464
MASS MOVEMENT 34 + 35	465
MASS MOVEMENT 36 + 37	466
MASS MOVEMENT 38 + 39	467
MASS MOVEMENT 40 + 41	468
MASS MOVEMENT 42 + 43	469
MASS MOVEMENT PRESENTS…	470
MASS MOVEMENT 44	471

Foreword

I've always been a sucker for the printed word. It's great to read anything, anywhere, but you cannot beat a good book or a good fanzine. Which is why I'm so pleased to see all this online material from Mass Movement finally bound up as a real book. Especially as I can now read it on the toilet, which as everyone knows is actually the place that fanzines were invented to be read. That and the back of a van – on route to a gig, of course, because the internal light never worked for you to read on the way home.

What made Mass Movement so much fun was how eclectic it was. Still, eclecticism in itself isn't always a good thing if all the influences are completely disparate to your own, but by happy coincidence the things that Mass Movement loved were all things I loved. Punk, hardcore and thrash metal for starters, but also horror films and books – I've been a fan since I was old enough to read and/or turn on a TV. I was a teenager during the whole video nasty controversy in the early Eighties, which was enough to cement a lifelong fascination with gruesome films, but I have a general taste for the weird and macabre. I also loved comics when I was a kid, and superheroes, and wrestling... just escapism really, sometimes dumb admittedly, but anything that triggered my imagination and got me day-dreaming.

Back then there were fanzines and magazines that covered all these things, not least of all Maximum Rock 'n' Roll and Fangoria, to name but two, but none that combined them into one randomly bulging whole. Mass Movement had a modus operandi that almost mirrored my own interests, so it was always going to be a winner. In fact, the only thing MM liked that I didn't was Dungeons 'n' Dragons roleplaying, but my aversion to that is wholly traceable back to sharing a house when I first left home with a few lads who took it all a bit too seriously for their own good...!

Tim tells me that we first met when my old band Decadence Within played somewhere up the Welsh Valleys in the early Nineties, and I'm sure this is true, because we played round those parts a lot and met lots of lovely folk – and a few nutters – when doing so. But the first time we really sat down and had a good chat was in 1996 when he interviewed myself and our singer at the time, Heath, when I was playing in the UKHC band Stampin' Ground, and we played Bogiez in Cardiff. Tim and the 'MM crew' were regulars at most of our gigs in South Wales – in fact, they were regulars at all gigs in South Wales, not just ours, and very supportive of the local, national and international scenes.

Tim was knowledgeable and supportive and enthusiastic. He was also an anomaly in that he was the most amicable miserable bastard you could ever hope to meet! But that was just fine with me, because I do like a deadpan sense of gallows humour. And whilst that doesn't always come through in some of the pieces that ran in MM, it was most very definitely there in Tim and his team if you were stood outside a virtually empty venue in the freezing drizzle waiting for either the PA, the main band or a crowd to turn up.

Anyway, what you have here is a printed compendium of fascinating online interviews and articles from the period when MM became a digital magazine. And where else could you possibly hope to find an interview with Barney from Napalm Death rubbing shoulders – completely comfortably, I should add – with a Danny Dyer interview? Or an overview of the Warhammer Olympics cosying up with Brian Slagel, the founder of legendary label, Metal Blade? Or an analysis of vampirism in literature next to Marv from the wonderful Gadgie fanzine talking about what scared him as a child? Or a frighteningly detailed look at the bonkers

'Baby Cart' films butted up against Duncan Redmonds from Snuff and Guns 'n' Wankers? Or local scene vet Beddis from the Cowboy Killers, and more recently Bad Sam (probably the two best bands you've never heard of, so look them up!), looking terrifying compared to comic writer Robert Venditti over the page? From Doctor Who writers to the Ramones to DIY breweries, from crossover to Gary Numan to martial arts, nothing was off the table for Mass Movement. Which was what made it so unpredictable and entertaining.

And I for one can't wait to dive back into this forgotten treasure trove, that also serves as a neat little time capsule of underground, pulp and counter culture circa 2012 – 2015.

The thing is, even though the digital format is always there, and you can return to it whenever and from wherever you like, it's also completely disposable. You didn't pay for it, you didn't pick that particular title off a bulging shelf of other publications because it caught your attention. If you're reading something online, you've often stumbled across it by accident, or you're passing through because you need a particular piece of information very quickly. You'll skim-read it, take what you need, and leave. There's no immersion or love there like there is with a book.

Like I said at the start, I've always been a sucker for the printed word. And there's plenty to suck on here.

Ian Glasper, June 2020

Introduction

If you've already read the previous volume, then you might want to skip this introduction and dive straight into the content as it's pretty much the same as it is in the other one. In fact, it's exactly the same, so don't worry, you're not missing anything. That said, if you haven't read Part One because you're one of those don't play by the rules types who likes to do things the way you want to do them, didn't fancy it for whatever reason or just liked the look of this book instead, then read on Macduff...

It was never supposed to last or be anything other than an underground punk rock fanzine. All Mass Movement was ever meant to be was a stop gap to fill the hours while, after losing my job as a Drugs Counsellor and gaining my journalism accreditation, while I tried to figure out what the next step on my journey was going to entail. However, these things, no matter how much we'd like them too, rarely work out the way that we think, hope or imagine they will. Which is why, twenty two years after I started mailing out the first illicitly photocopied issue of Mass Movement, it's still a thing. Granted, it's now entirely online and a denizen of the World Wide Web, but Mass Movement is still a thing.

Swept up by, and engulfed in, the nineties tsunami of zine culture and having written for a variety of publications, that included everything from the local newspaper to a veritable who's who of UK based DIY magazines that no-one except the handful of rabid devotees who gladly and fastidiously consumed them faster than they could be produced remembers, since the age of fifteen, I decided, with more than a little encouragement from my wife, to strike out on my own. And on, and following a phone interview with Tim Barry from Avail that was the first procured article for MM (which is how Mass Movement has commonly been referred to by the plethora of writers and readers who have sustained it for more than two decades), an unusually warm for that time of year April evening in 1998, Mass Movement was born.

Taking its name from an Underdog song after I'd been talked out of, having been made to see reason by both my long-suffering other half Emma and MM's co-founder Ian, calling it Hail Satan, Mass Movement took off faster than I ever thought it would. From an original, late night, illicitly copied on the office machine after hours run of a hundred copies, by the time it reached its tenth issue, Mass Movement was topping a thousand copies and being produced by a real life, honest to goodness professional print company.

Every copy that we had, we either sold or sent out to a record label that requested one; we didn't keep a single issue. It never failed to amaze me that people wanted to not only read Mass Movement, but were willing to spend their money to do so. Twenty years after Mass Movement started shifting copies, I'm still a little flattered and flabbergasted that every issue sold out. Maybe if I'd charged more for Mass Movement then, I wouldn't be broke now. But that's another story for another time and one that's probably best left to my accountant to tell. Or at least it would be if I actually had, or could afford, an accountant. Which I don't, and can't, because punk rock and comics don't pay and writing about them pays even less.

Where was I? Oh yes, Mass Movement... Slowly, but surely, Mass Movement started to expand its remit, as even the most holier than though and punkest of punks can't live on music alone, to include all of the things that I, and the rest of the miscreants responsible for creating its content, loved and were, and are, passionate about. Comics, wrestling, genre fiction and film and all manner of associated franchises, RPG's (that's Dungeons & Dragons and its ilk for those of you not familiar with these things) and everything in between began to appear in its pages and Mass Movement became something else. It became a zine, and later a magazine, that was devoted to all aspects of fringe culture, and the more facets of said culture that we featured, the more copies we sold. There was, and still is, far more to punks and punk than just punk rock. The underground popularity of Mass Movement proved that.

Then Beer City Records came knocking and offered to make Mass Movement a global entity by increasing its print run and giving it something that it had never had; a distribution network. It seemed almost too good to be true, so we leapt at the chance. Unfortunately, for one damnable reason after another, none of which I hasten to add were Beer City's fault as they were nothing but absolutely professional and we remain best buds to this day, it took nearly eighteen months for the first issue of Mass Movement produced by this joint venture to appear. And by the time it did, my personal circumstances had changed dramatically. My step father had discovered that he was terminally ill which meant that I wouldn't be able to put the time and effort that Beer City required into Mass Movement as I'd be spending whatever time I could looking after, and out for, Pops. Family always comes first, so Mass Movement and Beer City parted ways. We were on our own again.

All told, we (the "royal" Mass Movement we that is) made a bloody good fist of it too; being on our own that is. Having had a taste of the "big time", we decided that we liked it and went all posh and glossy. We looked good, we had great content – even if I do say so myself, and we were printing and selling the same amount of magazines as our super-market shelf distributed contemporaries. Mass Movement became the one of the biggest selling magazines that no-one in the mainstream, and a worryingly high percentage of folks involved in the underground and geek culture, had never heard of. Then the bottom fell out of the print market, production costs almost doubled over night and faced with the certainty of having to vastly increase our advert and cover prices, something that we were unwilling to do, Mass Movement ceased print publication and became a free, digital magazine distributed by an online platform.

For twenty issues, a number of one off specials and five years, Mass Movement existed solely as a digital magazine. We didn't have to worry about distribution or production costs and we weren't limited by a page count. We did what we wanted to, featured whoever we felt like featuring and reached a far wider audience than we ever had. It was fun, we were busier than ever and not only were we covering all of the bills, we actually making a little profit. A teeny, tiny, almost negligible amount, but it was profit nonetheless. The future was, all things considered, looking pretty good for Mass Movement. Right up until the moment that Microsoft and Adobe had a behind the scenes falling out which rendered all of our production and publishing software obsolete in the space of a single Bill Gates update. After seventeen years, Mass Movement Magazine lost the magazine part of its name, went completely online and our entire digital back catalogue became a thing of the past. Until now.

The book that you're holding in your hands is a compilation of the best interviews and features from the second half of Mass Movement's digital period. Some of you have probably seen a lot of it before, but I'm willing to bet that for the majority of you, this is the first time that you've seen most, if not all, of this content. And you know what? It's good. It's really, really good and while I'm happy, well as happy as a miserable old bugger like me can be, that this content is finally available again, what I'm genuinely thrilled about is that it shows how varied Mass Movement Magazine was and captures the spirit and essence of everything that Mass Movement is and probably, always will be.

Are you ready? Then let's begin. It's Mass Movement time… Again

Tim "Mass Movement" Cundle

South Wales, May 2020

MASS MOVEMENT:
THE DIGITAL YEARS VOL. TWO

Tim Cundle

CHRISTOPHER FOWLER

How often do you get a chance to chat with one of your favourite authors? Since reading *Full Dark House* about seven or so years ago, I've been a rabid Bryant & May (the heroes of the novel) fan, consuming each book in the series as and when they've been released.

Following the release of *Hell Train*, Christopher Fowler's brilliant love letter to a bygone age of classic British Horror Films, I tentatively (Yeah, I still get kind of nervous when interviewing my favourite artists, irrespective of the medium they work in) approached his publisher about the possibility of an interview with Chris. A couple of hours later it was set up, and it was time to discuss Bryant & May, *Hell Train* and more...

Interview by Tim Cundle

MM: For the benefit of those who came in late, would you like to both introduce, and tell us a little about yourself Christopher?

Christopher: Sure – I was born in Greenwich, London and attended Colfes, the Royal Leathersellers Guild School. I joined J Walter Thompson as a copywriter.

At the age of 26 I founded The Creative Partnership to create film marketing, and worked in film, creating movie posters, trailers and documentaries. I'm a movie-obsessive. I handled films like *Reservoir Dogs*, *Trainspotting*, *Goldeneye*, *Moulin Rouge* and *28 Weeks Later*, working with directors like Mike Leigh, Martin Campbell and Peter Greenaway, and on a lot of duff Hollywood blockbusters. I ended up writing for everyone from Kenneth Williams to Michael Caine, the Spice Girls, Pierce Brosnan, Leslie Nielsen, Julie Walters and most of the Pythons. I've written comedy and drama for the BBC, including Radio One's first live broadcast drama in 2005.

I'm the author of over thirty novels and twelve short story collections, and the author of the Bryant & May mystery novels. My first thriller was *Roofworld*. Others include *Spanky*, *Disturbia*, *Psychoville* and *Calabash*. My books have been optioned by everyone from Guillermo Del Toro (*Spanky*) to Jude Law (*Psychoville*). My graphic novel for DC Comics was *Menz Insana*. My short story *The Master Builder* became a feature film entitled *Through The Eyes Of A Killer*, starring Tippi Hedren and Marg Helgenberger. Last year I wrote and produced the play *Celebrity* at the Phoenix, London, and wrote the War Of The Worlds videogame for Paramount, starring Sir Patrick Stewart.

MM: What, initially, made you want to be a writer? Where you drawn to the written word and the world of literature through a love of the medium, or did something else spark your interest?

Christopher: My mother was a mad reader, and the local library was pretty much where I lived through my formative years. We didn't have a TV for a long time (my family hated the idea of just staring at stuff) so curiosity drove me to discover books.
Oddly, there are a chain of rather shabby, sleazy secondhand bookstores across the city called The Popular Bookstore. They stocked porn on the top shelf, and all manner of great books on the reachable ones in comic-style racks. At this time Pan was bringing out very sexy paperbacks in every imaginable genre, and they cost just a few pence, so I stocked up fast.

**NON STOP.
ONE WAY.
STRAIGHT
DOWN!**

HELL TRAIN

CHRISTOPHER FOWLER

There was an additional problem for me; I grew up in a house with no books, which is why I started hitting the library with a vengeance. You can read about this time in *Paperboy*, my memoir, and in the sequel *Film Freak*, due out soon.

MM: Which authors, if any, have influenced you as a writer, and how, if it all, do you think their influence(s) manifest themselves in your stories and novels?

Christopher: At the library I found Jules Verne, HG Wells and Dickens, while at the Popular Book Stores I found the Pan Books of Horror, featuring a huge array of brilliant writers, and JG Ballard. He became my god, and I still use his ideas and tropes. In crime, I loved the almost-forgotten writer Edmund Crispin, who combined comedy and thrills beautifully.

MM: When did you realize that you'd become a professional author?

Christopher: I started writing at around 8 years of age, and had amassed a huge amount of really bad writing by the time I left school (where I ran a magazine). But it was while I was living in LA and had time on my hands that I finally found the confidence to write professionally, and sold my first short story.

MM: At what point in your career where you finally able to make a living as a writer, and how did it feel when you were finally able to "give up the day job"?

Christopher: That didn't happen until I'd written well over thirty books! I was running my company, and only went full-time when my business partner died and I sold up. Writing around the working day was not a problem, but I started when an author only had to write and not handle their own publicity, blogs etc. Everything else was done by the publisher.

MM: Where did the idea for Bryant & May come from? Did the detectives or the Peculiar Crimes Unit come first – that is, did the idea for their work place, or the characters themselves emerge from your cerebellum first?

Christopher: I had an idea to use elderly detectives many years ago, and tested them out in other books first to see what the response was like from readers. But the stories were all going to be set in wartime. Then my then-publisher turned the book down. I went to Transworld and they 'got' it.

MM: What was the initial reaction, from both your publisher and fan-base, to their (Bryant & May) first adventures like?

Christopher: The reaction was terrific, but from a very specific fan base, so I didn't become supermarket-popular like Lee Child, say. My readers tend to be very literate and quick-witted, which is just as well because I pack a lot of stuff into my books. I planned to develop the characters and use them in a variety of different mystery tropes – locked room, thriller, chase, whodunit, whydunnit etc.

MM: Did you always plan on creating a series of books around the characters, or were they initially supposed to just feature in a couple of books? Is it more difficult to create characters for a solitary novel or a series?

Christopher: Once you get the characters right, you can throw anything you like at them and know what they'll do, so that was the real key. A series allows you to develop and deepen their stories, and fool around a bit, but it's tricky because you need to bring new readers up to speed and keep old ones. I used a trick from SF TV, having a big story arc and individual cases.

MM: Having now appeared in nine books, is there any situation or mystery that you think wouldn't fit a Bryant & Mystery, and if so, what is it and why wouldn't it work in their world, or with the characters?

Christopher: Each book tests out a different type of mystery novel on them – I don't think they'd get on with the kind of gritty procedural serial-killer stuff you find clogging the arteries of airport bookshops.

MM: Regarding the adventures of Bryant & May, do you have a favourite story? If so, which is it and why? If you had to recommend one book in the series to a new reader, which would you recommend and why

Christopher: It's odd but I really don't. I'm more pleased with some than others, but each new book twists everything around, and it's a challenge to keep it all fresh. That's the bit I love most. I would recommend *The Water Room* (the second in the series) as a good starting point though. The first book is very much an 'origin' story. If you like two you'll like the rest. And they're not designed to be read in any special order at all, except seven (*On The Loose*) and eight (*Off The Rails*), which form one big story.

MM: I know *The Memory of Blood* is still fresh on the shelves, but what, if anything do you have planned for the tenth book, and what (if anything) can you reveal about it?

Christopher: It's almost finished. *Bryant & May and the Invisible Code* is about class war, witchcraft, madness and Hell Fire Clubs. It's serious stuff, but there are some very silly jokes.

MM: Time to move on to *Hell Train*... Where did the idea to create the lost Hammer classic come from? Why Hammer and not Amicus? Why use a factual studio instead of an imaginary one? At times, *Hell Train* almost feels like a love letter dedicated to the bygone age of classic British Horror...

Christopher: And that, of course, is precisely what it is. It was about creating the film that Hammer SHOULD have made but didn't. Amicus were the third-rate knock-off of Hammer, producing horror portmanteaux because you could pay the actors by the day, not because of any creative decision. Hammer was the gold standard; they had the Queen's Award for Industry and were better scripted and shot than most mainstream films.

MM: I'm guessing that Hammer, and latterly Amicus (who were more famous for their portmanteau creations) had a large influence on you as grew up, as they did and maybe still do, on anyone and everyone over the age of 35. What, do you think, made Hammer and Amicus special? Why are so fondly remembered and well regarded? What drew you to both...?

Christopher: Starting at *Dracula, Prince of Darkness* I saw every single Hammer movie at the cinema, not on TV, all the way through to the end. Then I worked with Vic Fair and John Stockle, who drew all the posters. Then I actually ended up working on the Hammer relaunch. So yes, I was pretty embedded in the subject from the outset. They're also proof that ideas should reach fruition not by committee, but by the decisions of a handful of quirky individuals. Hollywood, take note.

MM: Although *Hell Train* has the loose feel of a portmanteau style collection, in that each character has their own tale to tell and hell to face, but it also works as well rounded, brilliantly executed and written slice of good old fashioned Horror, which in turn made me wonder if you'd thought about selling the film rights….? Maybe to Hammer now that they've re-emerged from the grave? Hammer making a Horror film that's wrapped in a fold around story about glory days of the studio…? Have you thought about optioning the film rights, and while we're on the subject, have you ever thought about optioning the rights to Bryant & May?

Christopher: The TV rights to Bryant & May have been sold for nine years now, with tentative casting of Michael Gambon and Derek Jacobi. *Hell Train* got helpful notes from George A Romero, John Landis and other directors. I'd love Hammer to do the film, obviously! That would complete the circle nicely.

MM: I've mentioned the almost Portmanteau feel of *Hell Train*, and as we're sort on the subject, I thought I'd ask you about it?. Why do you think the portmanteau horror genre, or films, were so successful? From *Dead Of Night* through to the Amicus classics like *Asylum, From Beyond The Grave, Doctor Terror…* and *The House That Dripped Blood*, and the final, well known and not as well regarded (although it is pretty good) soon-to-be-classic, *Monster Club*, for three decades the ideas behind, and the films themselves, seemed to flourish, but almost as quickly as they appeared, they seemed to fade from the spotlight. Why do you think the genre burned brightly for that all-too brief (in terms of cinematic history) period and then faded away? Would, in your opinion, portmanteau horror films appeal to the hack-n-slash fans of modern horror? Why, or more accurately maybe, why not?

Christopher: I don't think the portmanteaux were only there briefly. They started with *Dead of Night*, continued through the Somerset Maughan anthologies, were taken up in Italy and France, and were killed by Amicus, who undermined audience faith by making too many cheap, lazily-written anthologies. When they used established horror writers like Ron Chetwynd-Hayes (*From Beyond the Grave*) the results were exemplary.

MM: Is *Hell Train* the start of a new literary direction for you, travelling down the tracks (I know, I know, I should be ashamed and believe me, I am…) of, and bringing back the classic horror story?

Christopher: Oh, it's a return to where I began! I love the genre, and it's been a pleasure to jump back in. When I started writing, this style of book was just beginning to fall from fashion, so I welcome the chance to do more in the same vein. As it were.

Originally published in Mass Movement #32, April 2012

CINEMATIC BLOOD
COLOUR FILM OR BLACK AND WHITE?

The blood-splattering gore that exemplified horror films of the 70's and early 80's launched many directorial careers and gave the world a host of gruesome, iconic figures, the likes of which still remain in our cinematic consciousness. Who can forget Freddie's pyro-enhanched countenance from the thriller *A Nightmare on Elm Street* (1984)? Or how about Leatherface in the *Texas Chain Saw Massacre* (1974)? Speaking of chainsaws, there's Ash from *Evil Dead* (1983) using one to cut up everything including the scenery. You can't leave out Jason of *Friday the 13th* (1980) with his hockey mask and Jim Bowie butcher knife and, of course, Michael Myers from *Halloween* (1978) fame.

Directors Wes Craven, John Carpenter, San Raimi and Tobe Hooper, among others, became well-known filmmakers whose success continues to this day. These individuals' utilized blood and guts in beautiful colour, along with a dash of black humour, to sell their wares to an anxious, gore-minded audience of horror fans.

Across the pond, Hammer Studios produced a plethora of first-rate horror flicks and earned the moniker of "The Studio that Dripped Blood." Hammer directors made spectacular use of period costumes and lavish sets to recreate the ambience of Victorian Europe, when the legends of Dracula and Frankenstein were forged. Most of all, their efforts were greatly enhanced with the use of colour cinematography.

But there has always been the argument among students of the horror genre as to whether or not black and white celluloid is a more effective device in establishing atmosphere as opposed to the sheer blood and guts approach of Technicolor. And while it's a good argument, it all comes down to personal preference.

During the Expressionist movement of the early Twentieth Century, black and white film was an ideal medium for creating mood and atmosphere. With the loss of the First World War and the massive debt associated with defeat, Germany was faced with the possibility of never again being a major super power. Of course, all of that would change when Hitler seized control of the political scene just a few years later. But in the early 1920's and 30's the country's bleak outlook was the perfect artistic backdrop to convey misery, depression and an altogether nihilistic approach on life itself.

The German cinema would reflect and exploit this low point in the country's fragile condition with a number of dark productions such as Fritz Lang's silent, futuristic classic *Metropolis* (1927). Centred on the struggles of working class serfs against the powerful capitalistic hierarchy, the film's effectiveness is portrayed in contrasting elements of light and darkness as they apply to the different stratums of existence—the dark and dreary underworld of the workers in opposition to the well-lit opulence of the ruling class. Although not a horror film, the success of *Metropolis* as an all-time classic is in no small part due to the brilliant use of black and white cinematography.

Those aficionados of the silent film era defend the use of black and white cinematography with such moody, horror classics as: *Nosferatu* (1922), *The Cabinet of Dr. Calagari* (1919), *The Golem* (1920) and *The Phantom of the Opera* (1925), to name just a few, because of the shadowy stark quality of the finished product. And I guess it's somewhat of a moot point, since colour photography was still several years in the making (although some creative auteurs painstakingly experimented with hand painting or colour shading individual frames of film, a process that was used very sparingly).

Even with the introduction of Technicolor in the 1940's, black and white cinematography was still the choice of most studios, primarily because it was more cost effective to produce. And, since most horror films were considered low budget quickies, it made perfect sense to use this standard fare approach to filmmaking.

At the forefront, Universal Studios was perhaps the most prolific producer of black and white horror films as they established the prototypical device for box office success. It's the stark, surreal, rather pristine contrast of black and white photography that is unmatched for the conveyance of life to death — shadows to light. Murkiness resides, hidden, amidst tones of grayscale and modicums of brilliant white light, which add a morbid serenity to the scene. As shadows slowly span across the cinematic landscape, the viewer is reminded that something inherently evil dwells on screen. And whatever evil lurks "in frame" can easily evoke terror in the human mind. The motion of shadows playing against the light is a major factor in how atmosphere is perceived by the viewer.

So, if shadows and light help to establish black and white photography as an effective conveyor of atmosphere, what does colour photography utilize? As one can easily surmise, it's simply the colour itself. But beyond the obvious, the granular, faded quality of a seventies horror movie is actually the result of several different factors, one of which is faster film speed. Prior to the seventies, Eastman used the standard ASA 100 speed film (ASA is an arrhythmic scale used as a guide to determine film speed). Theoretically, an ASA 200 speed film is twice as fast as 100, resulting in more contrast and granular quality to the negative.

Another factor for that seventies "look" is due to the film being underexposed. The more it is underexposed, the more faded it will appear. This combined with the side washing of studio lights creates a rather subdued setting, typical of most films from that time period.

Double-Fogs were a popular filter of the time, which is hardly used anymore. Plenty of seventies films were unfiltered as well; for example, *The Godfather* only used Chocolate filters for the Sicily scenes, no diffusion. (*Godfather, Part II* used Low-Con filters for the flashbacks.) *The French Connection* or *The Exorcist* did not use diffusion filters; any softening was more from these older lenses being shot at wide apertures combined with underexposure and push-processing. Compare *The Exorcist* to *The Exorcist II*, which used a LOT of filters, particularly in the African scenes (Mitchells, Low-Cons, Fogs, Corals, etc.)

The end result is a stylized approach to filmmaking that helps to establish colour cinematography as a viable expression of atmosphere   Once again; it all comes down to personal preference.

Doug Crill

Originally published in Mass Movement #32, April 2012

DANNY DYER

Danny Dyer. He's a bit like Marmite, you either love him and his films, or you don't. Personally, I'm a fan. I think he embodies the everyman quality that's increasingly rare in film these days, and has also been in some of most important, British genre movies of the last decade, films such as *Severance*, *Age Of Heroes*, *Doghouse* and *Adulthood* that have proved that the UK film industry can compete with the 'big boys' and more than hold its own. We caught up Danny as his latest film, *Deviation* went on general release...

Interview by Tim Cundle

MM: First of all Danny, congratulations on *Deviation*, it's a great film...

DD: You've seen it yeah? Thanks for that I'm really proud of that, really fucking proud...

MM: You should be. What attracted you to the film initially..?

DD: I think it was just the idea of two people in a car you know? Pure dialogue and the idea that the victim and the predator are in that close proximity, and how that plays out. I loved the idea of that you know? The fact of these silent moments; they are really powerful. I just think it was a real test for me and I was looking for a decent script because the last few films I've made have been fucking shit mate, I'll be honest with you, I think I lost my way a little bit.

MM: *Age of Heroes* was good...

DD: Yeah *Age of Heroes* was fucking great but it didn't get the release it should have got. At the moment these are tough times and people don't want to take any risks. They put it out in about 4 or 5 cinemas then couldn't wait to get it out for DVD. I think they missed the boat there a little bit...

MM: Frank (in *Deviation*) isn't the usual kind of character you play, so I wondered how difficult you found it to get into the right mind-set to capture a personality like that?

DD: I just wanted to go down this childlike route you know? I didn't want to be obvious with it. People think they know me and it's all going to be the same, you know, smiling and being nasty whatever. I thought that that's not really what he's about; he is a lunatic, he is a bit schizophrenic, he's never grown up you know? He's a bit useless around women, he's a bit shy and an all-round oddball really, he's never grown up. It's a joy because you can go where you want with it, go as left field as you want and you can't really be accused of overacting because you're playing a psychopath. So I tried to go with the flow, I don't like to think about it too much. The big key for me was whether I got on with Anna (Walters who plays Amber in *Deviation*) because it was like, just me and her in the car. When I got to know her I fell in love with her though, she's lovely... taller than me though- about 6 foot three she is, she plays it ever so well...

MM: I was going to ask you about that, because it's essentially a two person film, with the two of you working that closely together, did that affect the way you work or the way you approached the work?

DD: Yeah it did, it's all that dialogue you know? It's a risk, just to have two people in a car for most of the movie, just talking, it's got to have something about it you know? There's not any effects or repeated car chases, just the basics. So that was the challenge, keeping it interesting, keeping people riveted I suppose. So I'm hoping we did the job. I'm hoping that from the first five minutes people get it and get into it.

MM: The success of the film relies entirely on your performances…

DD: Yes, and so, obviously, there is a lot of pressure. It was hard because it was all night shoots as it's all set over one night, so you've got to keep in character and your home life's suffering 'cos you're getting in at 6 in the morning. The missus was getting up with the kids, going to school and I was on this weird night shooting mode. It was tough you know? it was all filmed in London as well; usually you're far away in a hotel and you can concentrate on the job, but I didn't have that this time.

MM: You mention London, and watching the film it's almost like the city is a third character in the film, so how important do you think the location was, and is, to the film?

DD: Really important, just the idea of her sitting there in the front seat and she's only a metre away at some points from safety, but London's such an impersonal city. People go around getting on with their lives with their heads down. It's such a strange town like that. In the film people are oblivious to what's going on in the car. Then obviously as it gets dark and late at night and I take her out into the suburbs on the outskirts because I think it's safer, but nowhere is really safe in London…

MM: What was the overall feel like on set when you were making the film? Did you know that this was going to be a good film that the end product was going to good…?

DD: Well you try to. I love the energy you're giving it, you really enjoyed it but I read a review in Total Film last week and they gave it one star. You never know. I think it's a good film, I think it stands up. What are films? They're entertainment. So, does it hold your attention for an hour and a half? That's the bottom line. I think Total Film are up their own fucking arseholes a bit, with the Hollywood actors and the fucking poncey cunts. But if we're working in independent films just trying to make a bit of entertainment then they rip it to shreds. Each to their own I suppose, it's the business I'm in….

MM: The audience, in your portrayal, feels what Frank's feeling when he's around the women…

DD: It's about what happens when you kill a person, all the pain. There's a surge and rush of pain through his body when it happens and I remember reading in the script that he would be making weird animal noises and I thought "What the fuck am I going to do here?" I just thought that the more you go for it the better. If you hold back you make it a lot harder. I just wanted to make it as weird as possible..

MM: It is weird. It's like he can't help himself when he's doing it, then he just reverts back to normality and gets on with life and it brings...

DD: Yeah, but there are people like that out there, on the street. Complete fucking raving lunatics...

MM: You always seem to be working and you must see hundreds of scripts. What made this one stand out?

DD: I took a little bit of time out actually. I thought, in one year I made about eight movies and I just thought it was fucking ridiculous you know? I wasn't really seeing my missus, and I wasn't really seeing the kids, I was just thinking about the cheque really. I started to lose my way a little bit, so I just thought I'd take some time off. As I'm getting older I think the most important thing to me is being a dad and bringing up my two daughters.

The biggest gift I can give them is my time and my attention. Doesn't matter if you're rich and covering them with gifts but if you don't see them for week, it doesn't work. It's been tough doing loads of jobs because I love being on a film set you know? But I need to spend time with my family. It's been great being around the kids, but you start getting paranoid thinking that if you keep saying no, then the phone will stop ringing. Then this script came along and it was really low budget, it wasn't about the money, it was about me just purely doing something because I love acting and I'm really fucking serious about it, and this had that character that appealed to me.

I met the director and he was a really lovely guy and I loved the fact that he was trying to make it with no money, and I loved the fact that he'd written it with me in mind, so I said "Fuck it mate let's do it". We did a bit of guerrilla filming and it was just like going back to basics and sometimes, as an actor you need that.

MM: I was going to ask you, as you've done TV documentaries as well, which medium do you prefer – film or TV?

DD: I love film all day long, that's my game. I've been off the beaten path a little bit, went and did these documentaries, they weren't my idea. I wasn't really comfortable doing them, but it bought me a house mate, you know what I mean? You just want to do cool and cult films, but when you have kids; you have a mortgage and bills to pay, your view changes. Some of the best films I've done I've hardly got paid for you know? Then you do that shit, and it pays all the bills. I won't be doing any more documentaries though. The UFO one really caught people by surprise. Some people slagged me off for doing it, some people got it, got what I was trying to do. I'm really into that fucking stuff you know? I'm a bit of a sci-fi geek and I really enjoyed it.

MM: How does the public perception of Danny Dyer differ from the real you?

DD: I'm quite a sensitive soul really, not like most people expect. I think I divide people quite a lot, some people get me and back me quite a lot, then another group fucking can't stand me and never fucking watch any of my movies. That's part of the game I'm in really but like I said to you the most important thing to me is my daughters, my family. As long as I'm keeping them happy. That's what life's about.

You open yourself up for criticism in this game and I won't lie to you it does hurt, some of the comments you read on the internet and shit- although I don't always read all that bollocks. But if my kids are happy, they get to go to private school and they get all they need then that's all that matters...

MM: You've got another film, *Freerunner*, coming out in the next few weeks as well haven't you?

DD: Yeah, I haven't seen that yet. Look that's another job I did, took the cheque and my daughter who's 15, she's always wanted to go to America and the film was shooting in Cleveland and that, so I took her with me to make the film. Afterwards we went to LA and stuff and it was a bit of a holiday really. I haven't seen it yet, it's a bit of a cliché fucking film, I'm a bit of a Bond villain in it. Quite a good idea though, I'm a billionaire and keep inventing all these games to bet with other billionaires...So I capture these free-runners and put bombs around their necks and basically they have to race to get to a checkpoint and the last one who gets there has his head blown up. So it's a bit of a mess, but my daughter got to go to America, I got to work with Cameron again, so like I say I haven't seen it yet but I hope it's not as bad as it could be – it has a really low budget – and that it works okay...

MM: What's next for you?

DD: There's a movie about me getting stalked, and it's a bit different kind of thing for me, I play a writer you know? I'm shooting that in April. Then I've got a movie called *Billy Roundtree* where I play a West Ham player – it's a comedy with me and Johnny Vegas. Then there may be something with Ray Winston and Helen Mirren called *The Most Dangerous Girl in the World*, it's different, it's a different thing, so they are just waiting on getting the money then hopefully we'll be shooting it in the summer.

Danny Dyer stars in *Deviation*, available now on DVD through Revolver Entertainment. He can also be seen in the film *Freerunner*, out on DVD 23rd April.

Originally published in Mass Movement #32, April 2012

JOEY CAPE

(LAGWAGON / ME FIRST & THE GIMME GIMMES)

We (we being myself and the ever elusive Mr. Pickens) first stumbled across Lagwagon in 1994. They were playing TJ's, supporting the recently released *Trashed*, the band they were supposed to playing with (Face To Face) hadn't been allowed into the UK, and about thirty people turned up to the show.

But that didn't stop Lagwagon. They dropped the door price, played two sets (every single song they knew including covers) and hung out afterwards. From that night on, I've been a fan. There's been a load of Lagwagon moments since then, my old band supported them, there were a couple of drug and alcohol fuelled road trips to see them play and a load more stories that I can't go into without fear of being arrested for gross indecency and crimes against humanity.

And doubtless there's a load of Lagwagon moments yet to come, and thanks to them being at the centre of some of most incredible times, I can honestly say that they are a band that changed my life for the better. Bearing that in mind, on a cold winter's evening, I managed to keep my nerve and prevent my inner fan boy doing too much damage and spoke to Joey Cape about all things Lagwagon and more...

Interview by Tim Cundle

MM: Bring us up to speed on what's been happening in the Lagwagon Camp since *I Think My Older Brother Used to Listen*...

JC: That was a while ago. We did a lot of touring then took a bunch of time off. That's kind of what we do I guess... Nothing. We took some time off after we made that record; what year was it 2008? Then I think that in 2010 we did a three week tour of Europe that had nothing to do with the EP as that was really old then; we just went out there. But we really haven't done that much in the last few years until we started working on the box set.

MM: What made you want to release this box set? Why the first five albums?

JC: Anything after that was recent enough that there wasn't the same need. Part of the point of doing this box set was that a lot of the older records were poorly mastered for vinyl and for digital By today's standards they are not really competitive with tracks designed for mp3 download and just the sound of the files is not right. Making it work for digital download is a good reason to re-master or re-record. Also in the early days we were producing a lot of music so there were many, many outtakes and there was a lot of material. The decision was made later to do them all at once, which is good and bad. It was great, but it made the project much more difficult and longer. It was interesting because every time I found something for that record; I found a track or found some other thing that we had and we kept adding it, then we got to a point when we kind of had to stop because it was too much. I've kept almost everything I've ever done with Lagwagon, all the memorabilia, boxes of stuff, tapes of tracks in different formats, I have all of it. It was fun though, a labour of love.

MM: I'm sure doing all of that stuff dragged up a lot of memories. What do remember most about the recording of each particular album?

JC: I think that probably the best and most surprising memories that came back were the really early years before we made our first record, the demo. It was just fun to go back and listen to it because we've changed so much since then. We put the entire original demo on the new release because it was so much fun to hear it again. When we got together and collaborated and talked about what we were going to do for the first demo, I didn't write that much music – most of the lyrics and some of the tunes, but most of the music was actually written by our original guitar player Shawn Dewey. So coming back to that was fun for me because it was something I hadn't heard in 25 years since we made it. Especially because the mixing on that was so bad and I got those tapes transferred, then we transferred them to digital and I got to remix them.

MM: With the gift of hindsight, looking back at the records how do you think Lagwagon have changed, evolved and developed over the years?

JC: I think we've got a bit more comfortable over the years. In a way you get more comfortable with who you are and don't try to second guess everything which gives you a bit more flow and ease when it comes to putting the music together. That in some ways is a mark of how you mature as a band. Also I think as you get older there is some of that youthful energy – when you're young you'll practise 20 hours a day, 7 days a week and never get tired- that's not there anymore. Right about the time we made *Hoss* we lost Derek, our first drummer and with the new drummer the chemistry of the band was changed, so some of that evolution was forced. I don't really think about song writing really, I think you just become more comfortable with who you are as a songwriter and early on it took a bit more effort and was more calculating, whereas when you get older you just write. I learned fairly early on that it was better to write about the human nature rather than the politics of government.

MM: The bands popularity seemed to soar between *Trashed* and *Hoss*. Was it a sudden upsurge or more gradual growth?

JC: I've done so much touring since then really I don't have that good of a memory. Really though I don't think we had much in the way of down time in the early days. We were doing upwards of 280 shows a year, we were always on tour. I think it was early enough that there weren't really that many bands doing what we were doing so there was an advantage there. But we had a good work ethic and that's all we wanted to do and there wasn't that much competition. So maybe that's why things built so quickly for the band. Then we just stayed the same for ever. It had to do with not doing radio or videos or that kind of thing, so we didn't stand out too much. But we made a good steady career, it's been good.

MM: When the band became more popular did anything change for you on a personal level? How did it affect you?

JC: It wasn't that sudden. We toured so much for quite a few years so each time we came back there were more people, but at that time we were coming back often. Yes there were spikes, but it didn't affect me at all. I don't think it affected any of us as we were just happy to be in a band that people were interested in. Bands like ours are different to bands who become an overnight sensation and achieve some kind of fame. I imagine it gets to a point where they can't even buy groceries; we never experienced anything like that other than at some point I was able to not have a job and that was great. That simple fact that we were earning enough money to play music and tour all the time, and that we could afford to have houses and keep apartments.

MM: As you go back to the five albums, do you have a favourite?

JC: Not really. Each one of the records have different reasons why there are regrets. I can say that the record where I opened up the most was *Double Plaidinum* it was all heartache and I was a mess. I wrote the record in about a week and I wasn't very happy. Some of the other records, some of the early records, there were some lyrics that when we went back to re-master literally make me cringe. I can't imagine why I thought at the time, it was good to write it.

I think *Hoss* was the most diverse record that we made, I think we just had the courage to do what we wanted. Although the record phonically, consistently sounds one way there is no production value there. I think the best one is *Let's Talk About Feelings*, but I think the record as a whole is too short. We were trying to record about 10 more songs but we reached some kind of deadline which we finally gave in to. It was the only time in our career as a band that we did. We so rarely get into a situation where there is pressure to deliver a record, but when we did *Let's Talk About Feeling* things were going really great with the band and we really had to get it done. As a result we put out a 10 song EP, but if we'd waited another two months we could have got a much better record done. It would have possibly been our best. It's hard to be objective, but it's difficult to remember how you felt at the time. Listening to all those records now, there was no one clear record that I thought was the champion. There's different things about each record that I like.

MM: What's the current state of play with Lagwagon is there going to be another record?

JC: I don't know about that. My feeling is that a better idea than an album would be to find a way to release a few songs at a time because of the way people buy music now. It's just the concept of an album doesn't seem to work for me right now and that's really hard to say because I grew up with vinyl, I'm 45 years old. Vinyl died and now CD's are almost dead, so I really don't see the point of making a record. If you think of the amount of work that has to go into it and everybody's schedule; even if you put everything into it, something's going to get missed and I just think it's much better to concentrate on producing one or two songs at a time and achieve what you want to with it. So I'm not sure about making another record, certainly I don't have any material for it; I think I have one song. We're doing a tonne of touring though this year, 2012 is a Lagwagon year. We need to get out on the road and be a band again and work out how that works before we try to start creating again I think.

MM: With 2012 being so busy how will that affect your solo projects?

JC: Well the reason I have so many side projects is that I don't like a lot of down time, I like to be busy so if my band isn't doing anything for a long time I can't just sit around and suck on a bong, so my answer is just to do other projects. So it won't affect anything, I'll just be into Lagwagon this year.

Originally published in Mass Movement #32, April 2012

EMILY BOOTH

Bela Lugosi, Boris Karloff, Peter Cushing, Christopher Lee and Ingrid Pitt. At one or another, during the last eighty years, each has been named as the face of Horror. The actor or actress who embodies the genre, and as the twenty first century slowly starts revealing its ghastly surprises to us, Horror has a new face. Emily Booth. Actress, presenter and face of the Horror Channel, Emily recently launched her new show, *Horror Bites*, which presented us with a perfect opportunity to catch up with her and talk about her career and new show.

Interview by Tim Cundle

MM: Right, for the benefit of those who came in late…Would you like to both introduce, and tell us a little about, yourself to the folks out there in Mass Movement land….?

Emily: Okay! I'm Emily Booth and I'm a TV presenter and actress working largely in the Horror industry, I've been in a few cult British horror films like *Evil Aliens* and *Doghouse* as well as presented horror shows like *Out There* and *Shock Movie Massacre* on Channel 5 – more recently (well in 2007!) I became the face of the Horror Channel!

MM: I guess, like most folks, we know you from your involvement in all things Horror related, and as such, wondered what initially drew you to the world of blood, guts, gore, scares and more? Has your abiding love of, and the way you view the genre in general changed over time, and if so, how has it changed and why?

Emily: I came to love horror because I watched them loads as a young girl with my older brother! I guess he wanted someone to watch them with! So I was watching 80's horror when I was about 8 or 9 and got hooked! My love for the genre has not really changed, though it's hard to find classic gems like the ones from my childhood now – but that's probably because I am not a child, naïve and gullible – those were the days! I work in the genre now so I do see it quite critically I suppose – but basically I am still just a fan – whenever I take a film out from the video store – it's always a horror.

MM: How did you make the transition from being a fan to working in the genre, as both an actress and presenter? What do you remember most about your first day on a film set? Was it how you thought it would be or was it vastly different? If it was, how did it differ…?

Emily: I got my first break doing *Pervirella* – a film, whilst I was still at college, and to be honest on a lot of strange low budget movies – people working on them are fans as there is no money so you do it because you love it! Initially at least – then you need to make money from it! My first day on set? Can't remember the exact first – I think I was shooting a really hard scene for my first as I was topless – my entrance in *Pervirella*! So I drank a can of Diamond White – classy!

MM: Everything changes in an instant….Film and TV are evolving at an unprecedented speed, which in turn means that Horror as a genre is also changing at an incredible pace and as such, I sort of wondered how you think the genre has changed since you made you first film, and whether those changes have been positive or detrimental for the genre as a whole?

Emily: Gosh that's something I'd need to research and really think about! Well things have changed in lots of ways - in terms of the 'industry' since '96 when I made *Pervirella* I would say more horror films are being made due to the digital revolution as its much cheaper, easier and accessible - *Pervirella* was made on 16mm, but also the genre has experimented a lot more - there was the huge dawn of the 'found footage' film due to *Blair Witch Project* - although in truth that movie just reinvented it and made it mainstream - the first film to do that was really *Cannibal Holocaust,* since then we've seen so many docu-horrors *Paranormal Activity* being the mega success story too.

Then of course there's the internet and marketing (again *Blair Witch* paved the way for how to successfully market a horror movie online really!) - Horror now has a very strong community thanks to the internet - where you can also sell your idea, meet other film makers and actors and even beg for money from 'joe public' to finance your film! So it's all a lot more 'out there!' More films are now being made, many of them are rubbish but there's more chances for gems to get made and discovered!

MM: Which of your films, that is the films that you've been actively involved in as a member of the cast, is your personal favourite? Why? And, which is your least favourite? Why?

Emily: I think *Evil Aliens* and *Pervirella* are the ones I had the most fun on - but also *Doghouse*! They were just the most amazing atmospheres and the people involved were all wonderful quirky creative people, just unforgettable experiences that are very unique. I can't say what my least favourite is! I don't really have one!

MM: You seem to have a pretty good working relationship with Jake West, as you were in both *Evil Aliens* and *Doghouse*, and as both are Mass Movement favourites, I was curious about how you became involved with both films and what you remember most about making them? Do you think that you'll work with Jake again, and /or, do you have any planes to work with Jake again?

Emily: Yes I love Jake! Though I've probably exhausted that working relationship! I would work with him again in a second as his films are always unique and fun and he just gets things done - a hard feat in this country - and his films get cinema releases too! He's always been very honest with me and said that IF there is a suitable role in a film for me - he would cast me - but often there isn't - so while we are really good mates now - I would not expect him to cast me in a film just cos he knows me - we're professional like that - I was good casting for *Evil Aliens* as I played a Horror TV presenter who liked shagging cameramen! I suppose I initially got involved with Jake West cos he got to know me through Eileen Daly off *Pervirella* and asked if I'd play her lesbian lover in *Razor Blade Smile* which I turned down at the time! So he cast me in *Evil Aliens* instead - I'm very grateful he persisted! I owe a lot to him really.

MM: What was making both *Out There* and *Shock Movie Massacre* like? What, in your opinion, were the strangest things that you were asked to do for both shows? Why?

Emily: Both shows were great to do! I loved them - very different though, there were LOTS of strange things I had to do for *SMM* - I had to become a Drag King, strap my tits down and put a sock as a cock in my pants and pretend to be a man whilst undercover in a nightclub trying to 'pull' - really difficult and testing! But fun, I was de-girlified for the night - very strange being the one giving the sexual attention not getting it!

MM: Which sort of brings us your latest project (congratulations by the way, damn fine job on the show), *Horror Bites*... Do you want to tell us all about? How, when and why did the project come into being, and how did you become involved? Is it going to remain a "bite" sized show, or are you planning to expand it from its ten minute run time to something a little more, uh, substantial, say thirty minutes...?

Emily: Thanks! *Horror Bites* is my latest project with the Horror Channel - I've been 'the face of' since 2007 so it was just a natural progression for me to host this new show - I've wanted to do this for years and been banging on at them to give me a show!! So finally it's happened! At the moment it's a preview show rounding up all the premieres on the Horror Channel but we include director interviews and hopefully soon some on set reports to make the show that much more meaty! Yes I'd love it to run to 30 minutes - hopefully soon when we're into the swing of it all!

MM: How involved are you in determining and helping to shape the content of *Horror Bites*? Assuming that it's filmed in advance, what can you tell us about what's going to appear (interviews, features etc.) in the show in the near future?

Emily: Well the content of the show depends on what is on the channel that month - so that's not down to me – that's the schedulers and channel managers. But we have a Heritage of Horror Season showcasing new and classic British films, as well as a Zombie season which has some major TV premieres in store! The quality of the films on the Horror Channel is just getting bigger and better - with critically acclaimed as well as mainstream movies and independent gems!

MM: Which do you think is more challenging, working on films, or on TV shows like Horror Bites? Why?

Emily: Films are probably more challenging - especially if you have to get into character and do really long shoot days - it depends on the project - but films are all consuming - you live and breathe that film till the shoot finishes - usually 4 - 6 hard long weeks. TV is a bit more every day and normal and you get to be yourself.

MM: Sticking with the theme of *Horror Bites*, if you were asked to recommend five of your personal Horror movie favourites for the show, and given an evening in which to show them, which five films would you choose and (yeah, you guessed it, our favourite add on), why?

Emily: Five of my favourites?!!! Well I like all the classic ones and my personal favourites are often ones that involve creepy childhood fantasies. In fact two of my faves are already on the channel! *American Werewolf in London* and *Company of Wolves*!

So that's two down - my other more recent favourite is *The Orphanage* - it's just really emotional and clever and sad and atmospheric - really rare things for a horror film to possess. I'd love to see *Cat People* premiere on the channel as I think that's an unusual animalistic film…. hmmm what else?! I have also ALWAYS loved *The Wicker Man* – 'cos I'm dirty old pagan at heart and for some old skull 80's fun you can't get much better than *Nightmare on Elm Street*!

MM: Every Horror fan has a favourite director, studio and decade (in which their favourite films were made), what are yours? And, yeah, here it is again, why are they your personal favourites?

Emily: Actually I don't think I have a favourite director as there are so many one off horror gems! Though I think Stanley Kubrick is just the most intelligent one, he's the only one who can create off key dream like atmospheres, Neil Jordan too is brilliant. I suppose for me my face decade is the eighties, there was still a kind of innocence and naivety to horror films then - we hadn't yet 'seen it all!'

MM: What's next for you Emily? What else do you have lined up and planned?

Emily: Well I just had a baby recently and already feel pretty busy juggling motherhood and my Horror Channel commitments, so for now that's it for me! Making *Horror Bites* for the Horror Channel - hopefully when things settle down (if they ever do with a baby?!!!) I'll try and get back into some film work soon.

MM: If there's anything that you'd like to add, now's the time…?

Emily: Hmmm nah - my baby's calling me! But thanks for the interview and big shout out to all my 'fans' they really are the best.

Originally published in Mass Movement #32, April 2012

MARK "BARNEY" GREENWAY (NAPALM DEATH)

Like the Great Red Spot on the planet Jupiter, Napalm Death are an eternal force of nature. Relentlessly beating humanity about it's own stupidity and ignorance. Having been at the forefront of the metal and hatrdcore scenes for thirty plusyears, without becoming worn down, jaded or stale, the band seem to live by a simple code, loud music has to be made, and a message has to be spread. *Utilitarian* is their latest masterpiece in brutality, and we caught up with vocalist Mark 'Barney' Greenway to discuss life, the universe, *Utilitarian* and everything...

Interview by Martijn Welzen

MM: As you're always out on the road with the band, and are politically very outspoken, how do you, personally, see the UK's place in Europe and the rest of the world?

Barney: I'm always trying to keep a human prespective, rather than look at some policy. The UK is going through it's own just like every country on its own. The UK has to deal with cut backs on public services which will only benefit those who don't need these services in the first place and I'm currently involved, as a person, in trying to retain those services. And I, and a lot of people in England, feel that the police have too much power. They can just 'stop and search' you without any specific reason or without any specific goal. That's the tactics they use, and these are there to be challenged, and as a human I intend to challenge them.

MM: And does your prespective on your own country change when you're travelling the world with Napalm Death?

Barney: I think as a human, or humanitarian if you will, I think that certain basic conditions need to be in place. That's the general rule of thumb. Human rights is the very first direction for me, before anything else. It's quite simply freedom from oppression, intrusion, surveillance and all the other things that come with it.

MM: So in that respect, countries don't really differ from each other?

Barney: No, well things are more pronounced in certain places. If you go, for example, to China you'll see a policeman on every corner watching your every move. If you go to Russia, you're required to register either at a hotel or at a police station, or at a local government office. Why can't you just travel freely? All these restrictions go against the very idea, the very essence and core, of humanity.

MM: Are you, in that respect, also opposed to globalization, where everything apparently needs to give way in order to create a global village?

Barney: Globalization as we know it, which is an, almost, free market, which can be ruthless. Of course I'm opposed to that. One of the aspects of globalization is the placement of processing plants in areas where it's not appropriate and local communities require actual social interventions, not an industrial intervention. One way to demonstrate it, is the rate in which

Pepsi or Coca Cola open plants in South America. They kick people, litterally, off their land, and these are the poorest people you can think off. The very little space that they got gets cleared. That can't be fucking right. Do something about that! And another one that doesn't get talked about very often is what Royal Dutch Shell are doing in Nigeria. It's a huge British company, with Dutch involvement, and they're basically raping that country for it's natural resources. The people that resisted them within the country are being labelled terrorists, when they're just asserting their rights to not be exploited like that. Of course I'm not going to condone kidnapping or extreme violence. I just don't like violence you know. For some time I've been really opposed to it. Having said that, this doesn't mean that what is going on can easily be excused....

MM: I am trying to link this idea with what the utilitarian theories actually mean...

Barney: Ah, there's a multitude of aspects involved here, as with any philosophical theory, there are a hundred different interpretations. I mean you may haveve seen that if you looked into it...

MM: Yes I have, and there was one thing that really stood out for me: "How to produce the greatest amount of good for the greatest number of people?" Doesn't that mean globalization?

Barney: It does, and that's the thing. Utilitarianism is about people who are, on one hand humanitarians, and also animal-rights defenders, or animal activists and they still believe in the quality of life for sentient beings, whether human or otherwise and all should be treated equally. At the other end of the spectrum you have these ultra-brutalists or capitalists whose sole desire is to amass as much as they can and many people suffer because of that. For them is doesn't matter because total happiness is the objective. That's the real paradox. And I think it's a good thing to do, to use those paradoxes and what I'm actually doing with the album, is not just saying, "I'm writing about utilitarianism, and here it is", the actual point I'm trying to make is, and it's been very hard for me to do this with only the physical album, I could not find out whether I am a utilitarian or not. I just don't know. But I do see a certain parallel with myself and many other people as well. I live very ethically. If I think that my action is going to cause any negative impact on somebody down the line, I won't do it. That to me is the good side of the consequences of one's actions.

I've taken this a bit futher, and that's where it got very hard, portraying it on the album. There's a human trade beyond that of self doubt, and we'll all have to go through self doubt at some point. My self doubt is in the fact that I'm living that kind of life. "Why am I doing this with my life? What's the fucking difference that I'm making? Where is the result?" We always want solid, tangible results. Now!, Now!, Now! We can never be patient and wait for it to progress, progress that necessary ethnical actions consequiences. It's a very gradual developement. No matter how much we would like it to change then and now, that's not a reality. So it makes me wonder: "Should I not live just like everybody else does?" Go through life, just living and not worry about it. That's sort of the conclusion to it. Yes! You should persevere in your opinions, if you don't it will leave a gap, that can't be filled by the very things you're critical of, or protesting against and that, in turn, will allows things to be manipulated even more. So living that way, ethically if you like, is a low level form of protesting.

It's another form of going out on the streets and expressing your dissatisfaction. Now you can see where the difficulties lie. It's this subtle chain of progression which is very difficult to portray. So what we did is to take the centre-piece and expand on that, with the artwork and lyrics following that idea...

MM: Your new album touches a wide variety of subjects, from the environment to the weapons trade. Are all these topics as important as each other?

Barney: At the end of the day they all tie in with the idea about utilitarianism. Where I see the parallel is that good actions result in good consequences. This all involves a certain social attitude. Society in general has a very hierachical structure and when you have such a structure you'll also have a philosophical approach to that hierarchy, and as with all ideas there's a beginning and and end, and we should look past these two points to make life better. It's just too hard for society to achieve that...

MM: And how do you prevent certain subjects from clashing? Most obvious is, of course, the ongoing struggle between protecting the environment and economic growth...

Barney: The thing is I've never really argued for economic growth. It's not economic growth as such, but the way we've tried to reach that growth. This has put us in the mess we're currently in. Maybe I should back track a bit on this. There's only so many aspects I draw from the utilitarian theories. There's only certain sympathies I have with it. I don't feel connected to the other end, where you go overboard to reach happiness. I don't promote that stuff. To me there's been too much emphasis on economic growth. That's what really perpetuates this inequality and if there's just one positive thing that came from this, it's that people understand the gap between those who have the resources and those who have the power over them is ever widening. At least we now recognize this. Will it ever change? I think it will, because it HAS to. It's unsustainable. You can't have this chasm of inequality.

MM: Can we ever correct this inequality without violence? You're firmly opposed to violence, but people often resort, or feel they have to resort to it...

Barney: I think we have to! We have to find another way. And I know it might sound a little naieve. In many aspects I am a very cold and logical writer, I rely on logic. Where the emotional part of me lies, is that I think violence is self-perpetuating. It's one person attacking another person, and he then attacks another person. They'll then leave each other alone for a while and then attack each other again and when you set that standard in society, it's a free for all basically. You set a precedent, which can't be stopped, but if we can move away from that, maybe violence will become so stigmatized, that it won't be used anymore. Maybe that's the hippy in me talking, but I believe in peace and I've never shyed away from that. I would defend myself if I was in danger of being severly hurt, I'd use defensive measures against anybody, and I'm quite capable of doing that. I used to fight all the time, but I just don't see the sense in it. I just try to pratice what I think are the right things to do in life...

MM: In what way can you seperate cold, hard politics, from basic human emotions? People get furious about something, use violence as an emotional response...

Barney: As you get older, your views might not necessarily change, but they do get refined. I can see that within myself. I might be even selfish in the way that I think people can live up to, and by, the same standards that I do.

Everyone is different, but you have to start somewhere. If you don't do anything, you're just insuring that nothing will ever be resolved. I used to be quite nihilistic about things, but now I think there is hope. It's not a morality thing, as morality itself, I think, is one of the basic, fundamental problems we face...

MM: Aren't you sometime overwhelmed by all these subjects and the negativity that comes from, and with, them?

Barney: You know, thinking about it makes my head fucking spin at times...

MM: How do you keep your sanity?

Barney: I just do. I'm very self conscious concerning that. I mean, I'm a human being and I'm doing all this stuff because that's how I feel, and especially during the last few years I'm not really bothered by what people think of me. They're quite entitled to think of me what they like. Still things often go around my head like crazy, so I don't know, I think I've just accepted it in some way...

MM: Is being the singer of a band your way of keeping your sanity?

Barney: I never thought this was going to be a lasting thing. I was a lot younger, and, like I said, my thoughts weren't as refined, but I was certainly heading in that direction anyway. And you're totally right on what you just touched on there. Let's not forget that Napalm Death is a band, and not me just standing on a box on a street corner. There's a musical angle to it too. There's an entertainment side to it all. When we play gigs we have the desire to make it memorable and not only because of the things I say on stage. We also have fun, and a laugh while we're doing this. There's always room for jokes, even about the stuff that I'm talking about, and that's the thing. This might sound a little bit trite, but we're a serious band and the end result has always been, the quality, about the planet that we live on, but also about laughter, happiness and fun...

MM: And not taking everything too seriously all the time? That might leave you bitter and frustrated...

Barney: I'm very much in control of who I am, and what I do. I honestly believe that I can control that fine line between things. But then people always say that about themselves, I suppose...

MM: And whilst touching a wide variety of subjects on the new album, I also get the idea you've broadened your prespective musically. Does one follow the other?

Barney: No that's not the case. We could make any kind of album really. The lyrics could be applied to any style of music. We're a band, and we do have a certain creative drive, but the new elements you're talking about, we've actually had them for a very long time. You can even go back as far as 'Scum'. There were influences from the Jesus and the Mary Chain. What we did was extreme, but nobody was talking about the extremity at the time. Yes, we do employ different influnces, but the difference with this album is that I applied them to the fastest stuff on the album, whereas before they found their natural home with the slower stuff. It's been something like, let's try this and if it works; great and if not we'll change it. The bariton kind of vocals on the fast parts really worked....

MM: If you would take for example an anti-war song, does it have to be fast or aggressive, or can it still utilise, not only the same message, but also the same emotion when it's a slow song?

Barney: It can be anything!

MM: But people might feel, or see it, differently...

Barney: No, for me personally, I can convey the same emotion through whatever style we play. It can be very bleak and morose, like this Joy Division kind of thing, and be amazingly fast. I don't think the emotion changes...

MM: Well if you take for example a song like *War Ensemble* by Slayer, you can feel the energy and aggression, a doom song with the same content might not have that....

Barney: Ah yes, well I think Napalm has different qualities. Slayer are, and I don't get me wrong, I'm not saying this in a negative way, but they are quite one dimensional and unapologetically so. Napalm has more dimensions. If you are talking about Slayer and take a song like *Mandatory Suicide*, which is pretty slow, that could have easily have been aplied to *War Ensemble*...

MM: Are you interested in conspiracy theories? And with that I mean, we can't change the world on our own, because some very powerful people are pulling the strings of humanity. If that's the case, Utilitarianism will not work....

Barney: Conspiracy theories are just a label that you put on things. It's actually the things that are underneath that we have to examine. Some of these things I see, and there's definitely a reason and a rationale for it. The power mechanisms on this planet are so incredibly huge there's just no reason to disbelieve that some of the things I've pointed out aren't true. It could be the case, it could not be the case, but there's certainly the possibility. Just look at these conglomerates. They are fucking powerful. We have had this financial crisis, as they call it, and the banks and investors really were responsible for it, they've really brought the house down, when they started messing with countries abilities to actually feed their people, especially when their resources are already low. They might have had one meal a day, and now they'll have one meal every three days. That's scandalous! And we all know that no-one has answered for this. Are you aware of anybody that stood up and felt responsible in any significant way? Lots of fingerpointing and lots of bravado, by the usual politicians, but nothing has been done. Again it's down to the power of the conglomerates, who are so powerful, the can just tell any government to "Fuck off". "Come at us and make trouble and see what you get."...

MM: It's often been said that banks are above any government...

Barney: I wouldn't doubt that. That's no far-fetched conspiracy theory, that something that really rings true.

MM: And talking of that, the cover of the new album, is that linked to the Occupy Movement?

Barney: Yes, it is. Perhaps there's even a more simpler link to it. We've had lots of movement down the generations, the decades and even millennia. They always seem to be quite probing and after a while they just dissipate. Determination isn't always constent. It's all about the desire to make a changes. These movements tend to be very immediate, but then die out. This Occupy movement seems to have a certain momentum to it, especially now, after the events we just talked about, there's a realization from people that we don't have to take it anymore. It's about not taking authoritarian supression, and when there's no reponse to what has happened...

MM: And are things changing?

Barney: Again, that's a gradual thing. We want results now, and never ever know if we're ever going to get results. I'm quite happy that this Occupy movement is still alive, and has grown to the size it has, with all it's tentacles. Let's just see where it goes from here. You have to remember that when 'Utilitarian' was written, and the art was actually conceived, this hadn't happened yet...

MM: That's interesting because on the cover there is, what seems to be, a protester, on the ground, getting kicked by these bankers, or businessmen...

Barney: It's actually quite symbolic. What it is, to me, and Shane might tell you differently; the guy in the middle is the 'would-be' utilitarian and the guys around them, although they're dressed in suits, are not necessarily businessmen, they're the embodiment of the power mechanism and they're stamping on him. It's about the doubt the guys on the ground has, whether he is effective, and the things you see outside of the main image are the thoughts that are in his head. So, it's quite simple...

MM: As you said you're trying to live your life ethically, would you, personally be able to cope with the power(s) that come with being extremely rich?

Barney: I don't seek it, but if I were to become extremely rich by accident... One of the big things for me, is that I would like to think that I would redistribute my wealth. If we really talk about extreme wealth, the large sums we're talking about could actually prop up the world. Then I would gladly give it away. I would personally also benefit from the redistribution of this wealth. So why would I need to hang on to it? I know there are plenty of people who would say: "Yeah, yeah, you can say that now." I can only say what I feel now. Having said that, I don't seek it. Wealth has never been the thing for me. As someone who thrives on logic, I can see that my time on earth, just as much is yours, or anyone elses, is finite. Only the universe is infinite, nothing else is. What I want from this life, is that I'd like to be able to look back, and have the benefit of knowing that, at certain points, I was happy. Happiness in its simplest form; contentment. Contentment is a very simple thing. And that's what I want to be able to say. And I don't think wealth will give me that.

Originally published in Mass Movement #32, April 2012

SCREEN DAMAGE
APOCALYPSE WOW!

Fear of the bomb has long been a Hollywood tradition. Back in the 1950s, films like *Them!*, *The Amazing Colossal Man* and *The Incredible Shrinking Man* helped keep the paranoia alive in our collective consciousness, and over the years it has been revisited in movies ranging from *Dr Strangelove* to *Waterworld* and *The Book Of Eli*.

For a short, fertile period in the early to mid-1980s, it seemed as if every country was taking a low budget stab at the genre, and the likes of *Def Con 4*, *City Limits*, *Radioactive Dreams*, *Stryker*, *Land Of Doom*, *The Ravagers*, *Survivor*, *The Aftermath*, *Battletruck* and *Steel Dawn* were duly trotted out to fill up video shop shelves around the world.

Without a doubt, the country which made the greatest effort to keep the post-nuke tradition alive during this golden age was Italy. If I have learned anything from the endless hours that I racked up as a teenager hiring low budget Italian movies, then it's that among the many threats that we will have to contend with in a post-apocalyptic world are book-burning nihilists in pimped-up dune buggies, rat-battling Hare Krishna survivalists, tap-dancing street gangs, futuristic gladiators and robots that have been designed to look like the Frankenstein monster for no discernible reason.

As with most of the Italian film industry's output back then, the majority of these movies were cheap and cheerful knock-offs of foreign hits – titles such as *Escape From New York*, *Rollerball*, *The Warriors* and of course, the all-powerful *Mad Max 2*.

Not many of the post-apocalypse movies could hope to match the budget or marketing hype of the films that they were imitating, and the Italian movies were no different. I'm sure that for many of them, part of the attraction was that films set in an atomic wasteland were cheap to make – you only needed a backdrop of dirt and rock, and maybe some steel plate welded over the windows of a junkyard car or three.

What really sold these films was the strength of their incredible marketing artwork, the majority of which managed to be hugely exciting while at the same time only rarely bearing any accurate reflection of the actual content of the movies - a quick glance at eBay reveals that the stunning posters for cheap epics such as *Wheels Of Fire* or *Fists Of Steel* continue to command steep prices.

Some of the best artwork was produced for Enzo G Castellari's *Bronx Warriors* and *Bronx Warriors 2* (aka *Escape From The Bronx*). Both of these films are among the most well-known and successful titles that the Italian post-apocalypse genre produced. Taking *The Warriors* and *Escape From New York* as their template, the first film concerns gangs fighting it out for territorial rights in a society that is well and truly on the ropes. In an odd touch, it predates the plot of the later *Escape From LA* by having the daughter of a powerful politician run away from home and take up with a goofball named Trash. Boasting tough names like the Zombies, Scavengers, Tigers and Sharks, each gang has a visual gimmick of some kind – big George Eastman, the 'Anthropophagous Beast' himself, plays Golem, the leader of a bunch of pony-tailed roller skaters, while exploitation stalwarts such as Fred Williamson and Christopher Connolly play Ogre and Hit Dog respectively.

Top billing goes to Mark Gregory/Marco De Gregorio as the aforementioned Trash, a well-muscled pretty boy who rides around on a motorbike with a plastic skull mounted on the handlebars. For the tough leader of a biker gang, Trash is incredibly effeminate, and has an unfortunate habit of flip-flopping his hands in a limp-wristed manner whenever he runs anywhere. Legend has it that the actor was spotted while waiting tables in a Roman restaurant, but if the producers picked up on their star's fey manner, it didn't stop him from returning in *Thunder I-III*, a trilogy of cheap *First Blood/Rambo* clones.

The true villain of *Bronx Warriors* is Vic Morrow as Hammer, a Government agent sent in by what is left of the ruling elite to rescue the politician's daughter and orchestrate a programme of genocide against the gangs. Morrow has a ball in the role, which was shot not long before he was decapitated in the infamous helicopter accident on the set of *Twilight Zone: The Movie*. Trash unites the gangs to defeat Hammer, and the climax sees him climbing on his bike and dragging the villain's corpse away. After the film notched up decent sales, it left the way open for *Bronx Warriors 2* in which the plot was much the same, but with Henry Silva stepping in to play the villain ordered by property developers to clear out the Bronx gangs to make way for luxury condos.

If the brace of Bronx Warrior films prepped audiences for what was to follow, then Castellari's follow-up, *The New Barbarians*, surely set the rules for the shape of subsequent entries. This totally insane film features the Templars, a gang of gay, predatory rapists who, with their silly haircuts and matching white and grey uniforms, look like members of some awful prog rock band. The Templars spend their time driving around the post-nuke wasteland in dune buggies and modified golf carts, most of which sport lethal flamethrower, cannon or blade attachments. When they are not killing people for pleasure or tormenting male survivors, the Templars dedicate themselves to burning books as they reason that "It was damn books that caused the apocalypse!" Hmmm, no arguing with that kind of logic...

When the Templars learn that Scorpion (Timothy Brent), a former member of their happy brigade, has joined a caravan of survivors, they declare war and set out in their silly looking vehicles to take them on. Maybe they are jealous of Scorpion's totally awesome car, decorated as it is with an enormous plexi-glass bubble on the roof and vacuum cleaner hoses draped across the hood. Fred Williamson turns up again as Nadir, an archer who favours explosive arrows and big black rubber outfits, and he comes to the rescue after Scorpion is 'punished' for leaving the gang by One (George Eastman - you'll see a lot of the same names cropping up in these movies). Scorpion gets his revenge in a thrilling 15mph buggy chase sequence which ends when he impales One on a huuuge hood-mounted drill... I think you can get the symbolism here without any help from me. With exploding heads aplenty, there's lots of fun to be had with *The New Barbarians*.

Sergio Martino stepped up to bat next with *2019: After The Fall Of New York*. This time out, the silly names ran to Wagnerian references – Michael Sopkiw plays a Snake Plissken lookalike called Parsifal, coerced by what's left of the post-nuke government into searching the ruins with his buddies Bronx and Ratchet for the last fertile woman on Earth (the French model Valentine Monnier, who also starred opposite Sopkiw in the half-squid-half-shark travesty *Devouring Waves*). Having ruined one planet, the powers that be have their eyes set on a replacement world, and need her to help them recreate the human race. But a bunch of bad guys have other plans - the gag here is that once Parsifal has delivered the girl and the two of them are fired off in a rocket to reseed mankind, it is revealed that she has already been impregnated by Big Ape, a Neanderthal throwback again played by George Eastman (imagine how much money they saved on the make-up for this role!). One of the very best of its type, *2019: After The Fall Of New York* actually has some decent production values, and the model work of a ruined New York city in the opening scenes is especially impressive.

A talking computerised motorbike that calls bad guys 'dickheads' and answers to the name Einstein was the main gimmick in David Worth's *Warrior of the Lost World*, an American-Italian co-production that starred Robert *The Exterminator* Ginty in the titular role, Donald Pleasence as the villain and Fred Williamson as his evil henchman. The story behind this production is actually far more interesting than the so-so film – director Worth was hired blindly by the producer, flown to Italy, told that no script had been written and handed a poster that had already been painted for the film with the instruction to 'make this'! Those crazy Italians…

Talking of which, Ruggero Deodato, the dark genius responsible for *Cannibal Holocaust*, pitched in with *The Atlantis Interceptors*, a breakneck tale of how unspecified pollution and the raising of a stricken Russian submarine causes the lost island of Atlantis to rise up from the bottom of the sea where it has been hidden away inside a giant glass dome all these years. Pretty soon, downtown Miami is being plagued by the rampaging hordes of Atlantis… yeah, about those hordes. Not only do they appear to have had access to the American motor industry during their time at the bottom of the sea, their effectiveness is also severely handicapped by the fact that there only seems to be about 15 of them in total. But it doesn't matter, because supercool adventurers Christopher Connolly and Tony King are on hand to fly over to Atlantis, crack some jokes and take on the 'horde' and their leader, Crystal Skull – presumably named in an attempt to make the plastic bowl he wears over his head seem much tougher than it really is.

If all of this sounds ludicrous, it is – but it's not as nutty as *Exterminators of the Year 3000*. This one features a hero called Alien who roams around the wasteland in his stinky car, the Exterminator, fighting with bandits and rogue cops who like to prove their bravery by occasionally venturing out from whatever remains of civilisation. An unashamedly cheery rip off of *Mad Max 2*, this time out water is the most valuable commodity, something which the survivors need in large supplies for their underground plant and crop nurseries which they plan to use to make the Earth green again. Alien agrees to accompany an expedition out into the forbidden lands in search of a secret reservoir, acting as muscle whenever bandits attack – their leader, Crazy Bull, drives his men on with morale-boosting encouragement such as "Into battle, my merry mother-grabbers!" and "'Hit their flanks, you lousy blobs of abomination!" Working an armour-plated tanker into the mix, the film wears its influences on its sleeve, but just as you think it's going to surprise you with a downbeat ending which sees the reservoir destroyed, the skies open up and it starts to rain, all of which leads to much merriment for Alien and his pals. Did I mention there's a kid with a detachable bionic arm?

Arms also part company with torsos in the equally insane *She* by Avi Nesher. This v-e-r-y loose adaptation of H. Rider-Haggard's classic pulp tale has a family of traders visit a typical post-nuke town which is quickly attacked by a band of raiders known as the Norks from Norksville - no, really! With their sister kidnapped by some big Norks (snigger!), the two brothers head for a city ruled over by She (Sandahl Bergman, here a VERY long way from *Conan The Barbarian*). Refused help, they kidnap She and force her to lead them to the Norks' lair. Along the way the three encounter such delights as a mummy who drops body parts everywhere and sports sunglasses, a gay vampire, a tutu-wearing giant, werewolf orgies, mad scientists, a psychic communist and Hector, the hatchet-faced leader of the Norks.

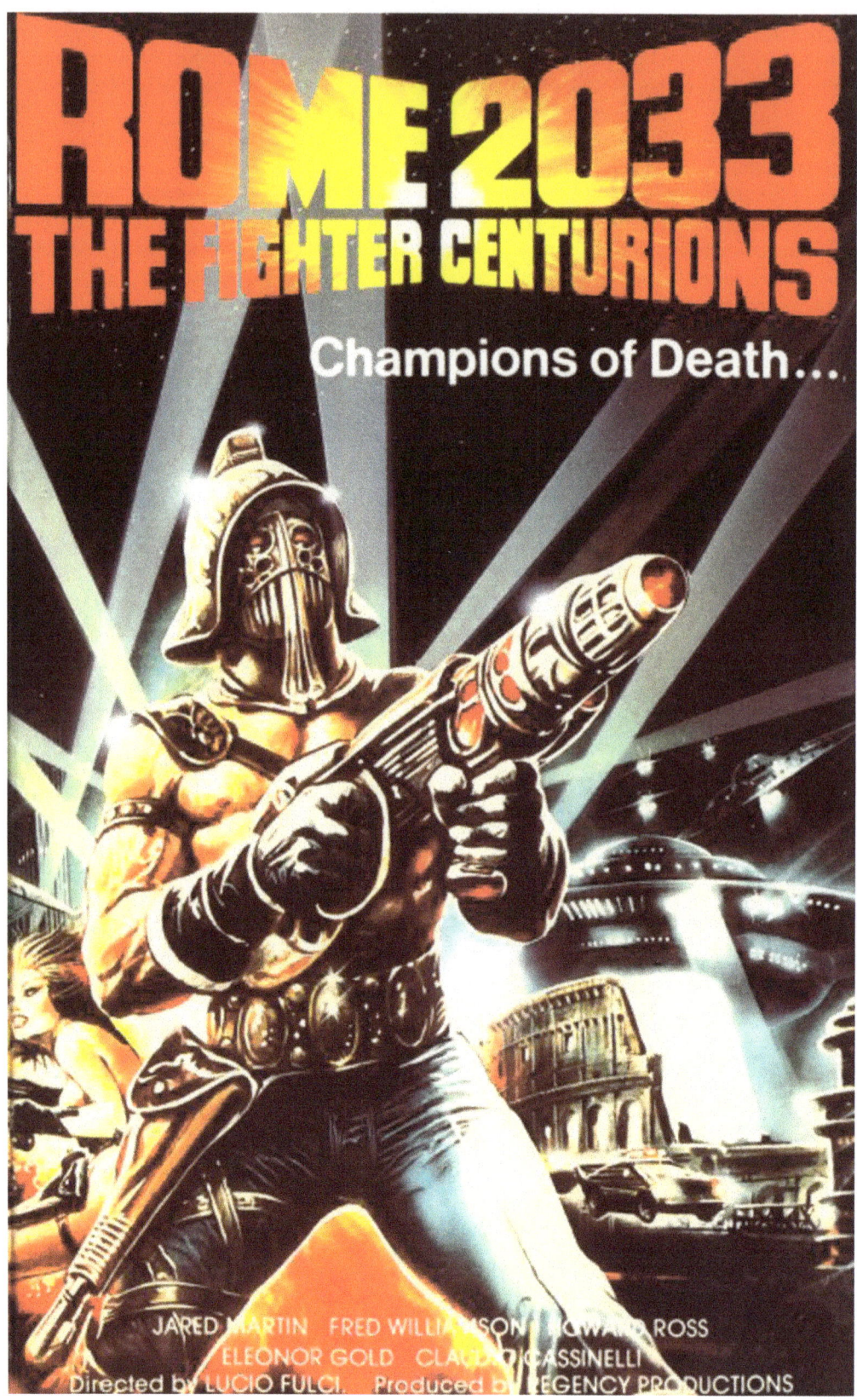

With its practically free-form plot, I've heard tell that some folk use *She* as their background viewing of choice while partaking of certain mind-altering substances, but if you ask me, you don't really need to do much else other than simply watch the trippy visuals of the film - as She herself says at one point, "This has nothing to do with sense."

Joe D'Amato's *Endgame* is a far more serious affair, but I have quite a soft spot for it as the old VTC precert video boasted the very best sleeve art of the lot, and it opens with a genuinely scary (because it's real) close-up shot of a huge mushroom cloud billowing up into the sky. This time it's the turn of big Al Cliver to play hero against George Eastman's villain – they are both stars of Endgame, a televised gladiatorial deathmatch played out in the nuclear ruins. Having humiliated Eastman, Cliver agrees to escort a band of telepathic mutants to a safe zone in exchange for gold. Putting together a squad (the audition process for which seems to mainly involve chucking knives at candidates and seeing if they can duck out of the way in time), they set off on their journey and wander from one battle to the next until the mutants are safe and only Cliver remains. But Eastman has followed him to settle who is the toughest once and for all, and the film ends on an enigmatic freeze-frame as the two enemies rush at each other, teeth bared.

Staying with the gladiatorial theme, Lucio Fulci gave us *Rome 2033: The Fighter Centurions*. This had a bigger budget than many of its peers, but sadly focused on a boring conspiracy plot instead of motorised coliseum carnage. In a storyline that Fulci would later claim was the inspiration for *The Running Man,* a brutal TV syndicate in future Rome keeps the population sated with ultra-violent gameshows. Jared Martin plays a Kill Bike champion who is framed for a crime he didn't commit, and is forced to fight alongside death row prisoners who include among their number a by-now obligatory Fred Williamson (Al Cliver is in there somewhere, too).

Joe D'amato's *2020 Freedom Fighters* tried to mix its after-the-bomb antics with western and war movie stylings as wannabe nazis lay siege to a Texan town, but it's a bit of a mess by anyone's standards. It stands out in my mind only for the early scene where the heroes track down a gang of mutant scumbags, then stand by and wait while the bad guys finish raping and murdering a bunch of nuns. Only after the last nun is dead do they leap into action! I mean, WTF? By the time that the townsfolk join forces with a tribe of red Indians to fight off the nazis, you'll be hitting yourself over the head to check that you aren't dreaming.

Another flick that will have you doubting your sanity is Bruno Mattei's *Rats: Night Of Terror*. Here, survivors of a nuclear war search the ruins of a small, empty town in search of food. Finding a huge stockpile, they decide to hold up for a few days, and we are treated to odd scenes of them joyfully sampling bags of flour and sugar. As they feast, thousands of rats start to emerge from the sewers beneath the town, and a tape-recording is found which warns that in the aftermath of the bomb, the vermin have become a super-intelligent menace - the food stockpile is merely the bait for their trap. The group are slowly whittled down by the hungry rodents until only two remain. Managing to escape, they are confronted by strange figures wearing yellow hazmat suits. In a classic twist ending, the figures remove their hoods to reveal furry faces, long whiskers and sharp teeth – yes, the radiation has caused the rats to evolve into mutant rat-men! If this isn't enough to persuade you to see this demented gem, it also boasts scenes such as one where a man remonstrates with a swimming rat by shouting "You dirty beast! That's why our water gets polluted!"

Sadly, *Rush The Assassin* and its semi-sequel, *Rage* were nowhere near as much fun. In the first film, Conrad Nichols is Rush, the leader of a resistance group opposed to dictator Gordon Mitchell. Mitchell controls the last piece of fertile ground in the world, and uses a private army to force his fellow fallout survivors to labour in sterile plastic greenhouses. Discovering that the whole thing is a scam designed to keep the toiling masses in their place and that life is starting to return to the wastelands, Rush initiates a rebellion and overthrows Mitchell in a hilarious fight scene which doesn't bother to hide the actor's blatantly obvious stunt double.

Nichols returns in *Rage* to play a guy called Captain Strike. As his superiors obviously feel that Strike isn't a macho enough handle, he's also known by his code name, Rage. Strike/Rage (what a great name for a band) agrees to lead an expedition to find a store of uranium, mainly because what a post-nuke society really needs is even more radioactive material. They fight off the usual mutant and bandit attacks and confront Strike/Rage's old enemy, a guy so badass that his codename is Slash. Strike/Rage wins the day and announces to his colleagues that "It won't be easy, building up a new world – but there's no harm in trying." Eat your heart out, Shakespeare...

However, the single most entertaining example of the Italian post-apocalyptic genre has to be Antonio Margheriti's *Yor: The Hunter From The Future*. If you want an insight into just how amazing this film is, go and search for the Yor theme tune on YouTube, the opening lyrics of which consist of "Yor's world! He's the man!" repeated over and over. As played by the legendary Reb 'Captain America' Brown, Yor wanders a prehistoric world fighting violent cavemen and killing huge dinosaurs before he gets the hots for Corinne Clery. When she is kidnapped by troglodytes, he has to figure out a way to get into their mountain-top cave. Yor's problem is solved when he kills the Beast of the Night, a giant flying bat-monster, and – honestly now, I'm not making this up – uses its corpse as a hang-glider while the soundtrack screams "Yor's world! He's the maaaaan!"

If you haven't already seen the film, you may be wondering how any of this nonsense fits into an article about post-apocalyptic movies. Well, the climax (not to mention the film's full title) reveals that, in a twist lifted from *Teenage Caveman*, Yor's prehistoric world is really the result of a nuclear holocaust, and apart from a few small hi-tech enclaves, society has regressed back to the Stone Age. With this revelation comes an attack by Darth Vader-alike robots and an amazing ending where Yor learns how to fly a rocket ship in five minutes flat. Wow.

By the time that Romolo Girolami's *The Final Executioner* arrived on the scene, the post-nuke boom was starting to fizzle out in Italian cinema, so it was nice to see the genre end on a relative high note. The film takes a leaf out of *Turkey Shoot* and presents a post-apocalyptic society where the rich live in comfortable bunkers and the poor are classed as target material – in other words, sport to be hunted down and killed by the elite of this brave new world. When his girlfriend is raped and slaughtered by a gang of privileged hunters who leave him for dead, Alan (William Mang) is found by Woody Strode's Sam, a man who claims to be the last surviving member of the former New York police force. With Sam's help, Alan learns how to fight back, and sets off to track down the rich scumbags. The film ends with Alan and Sam agreeing to set up a new police force to bring order to the ruins. Unfortunately, Girolami followed this decent action flick up with a muddled sequel of sorts in *Bronx Executioner*, a nonsensical mess which uses huge amounts of footage from the previous film to pad out the slim running time – truly a case where the less that is said about this one, the better.

They were cheap, they were tacky, they were downright stupid, but I find it fascinating that so many people of a certain age now look back on these weird little B-movies with such nostalgic affection.

Sadly, with the Italian film industry still in a state of stagnation, it doesn't look like we can expect to see resurgence in the post-apocalyptic action genre anytime soon. Until the situation improves, I'm afraid that it's a case of apocalypse - ciao!

Liam Ronan

Originally published in Mass Movement #32, April 2012

SIMON GUERRIER

Having created one of the most memorable Doctor Who companions, Oliver Harper, for *The Companion Chronicles* in the shows long history, I thought it was about time that I sat down to talk to Simon Guerrier about Oliver, Doctor Who, Blake's 7 and more. Without further ado, I give you Simon Guerrier…

Interview by Tim Cundle

MM: The best place to start is always at the beginning. Would you like to both introduce, and tell us a little about yourself, Simon?

Simon: Hello. My name is Simon Guerrier (rhymes with 'terrier') and I am a tallish, balding writer of sci-fi nonsense.

MM: Have you always wanted to write and be a writer, or was it a career choice that you discovered you had an aptitude for in adulthood? What made you want to be a writer, and does that initial inspiration still motivate you, or have the forces that impel you changed over time, and if so, how have they changed, and what are they?

Simon: Yes, I've always wanted to be a writer. I've always written – and have boxes of terrible stories in even more terrible handwriting from when I was small. But for a long time writing didn't seem a real job – it was a pipe dream, like being an astronaut or pop star (both of which I also wanted to be). Then I read an interview with Paul Cornell in a 1991 edition of *Doctor Who Magazine*, where he explained how you could pitch to Virgin for their Doctor Who books – even if you'd never written anything before and didn't have an agent. It suddenly made writing a real possibility, and I took that interview in to my careers advisor at school. Who told me I'd never make any money as a writer. I pitched my first novel idea to Virgin when I was 18, and finally got accepted to write a Doctor Who novel (with BBC Books) when I was 28. By that time I'd already gone freelance and had some Doctor Who short stories published, but it did take a long time and a lot of perseverance.

I think the tricky bit is working out what you want to do. Once you've decided, everything else is practicalities: how do you do this thing while still being able to eat? There's no great secret to becoming a writer. You write things, you send them to people you hope will like them enough to pay you for them, and while you wait for them to reject it you write something else. At the same time, I looked for jobs in publishing that I thought might give me an 'in', and got my first paid credits writing for corporate magazines. I'm still trying to write stuff I enjoy and at the same time pay the bills. I think the big thing that's changed over the last few years is that I'm much more interested in writing my own stuff than other people's. I love working on Doctor Who and Blake's 7 or whatever else, but ideally I'd be doing my own stuff all the time, if I could make that pay. There are also people I know I really like working with, and would find it difficult to turn things down if they were involved.

MM: You're most closely associated with your work in, for and around Doctor Who, so I was curious about how, when and why you initially became a fan of the show? What's your earliest Who related memory, what was it about The Doctor that made you a fan and what, as both a fan and a Who writer, do you think the show's appeal is?

Simon: My earliest memory of anything is a cliffhanger from *Full Circle* (1980), as Tom Baker crouches with K-9 in the reeds and watches Marshmen emerge from a lake. My older brother and sister watched Doctor Who, so I watched it with them. And I was terrified. It terrified me for years – I think it's that raw, emotional response of terror that made me so devoted to it.

After the Doctor regenerated in *Logopolis* (1981), my brother gave me his copy of the Doctor Who Monster Book from 1975, which explained about there being other Doctors than Tom Baker. I think that's what made me a fan – that book is so simply, vividly written and I wanted to read all the Target books advertised on the back. And as I grew up, I started seeing more in the show: it wasn't just terrifying, it was smart, too. As a writer, I think Doctor Who is a brilliant format for creating stories. You can think of any setting, any scene, any mad idea, and then land the TARDIS in the midst of it. The Doctor arriving changes whatever's going on in your initial setting – people are surprised to see him, monsters attack him or he spots something's wrong – and your story is already moving. Starting a Doctor Who story is easy: the bit we get paid for is sustaining it and paying it off.

MM: Another fan related question, Simon, sorry - what's your absolute, definitive, favourite Doctor Who moment, and why is it your favourite?

Simon: Oh hell, there are loads! I love the space pig in *Aliens of London* (2005), which manages to be mad, silly, exciting and moving all at once.

MM: How did you make the transition from being a fan to being a part of the Whoniverse, one of the people who help to shape and develop the canonicity and mythology of Doctor Who? Is being a fan a help or a hindrance when it comes to expanding the Doctor's history? Why?

Simon: Um... It sounds a bit mercenary, but I got into organised fandom because I wanted to write. I knew from reading *DWM* that there were fans who'd helped and encouraged each other to write books, and wanted to be part of that. I went to a Doctor Who convention in 1997 where I got to meet Paul Cornell and various other people – and the only autographs in my programme are writers. Paul was very patient when I told him I really wanted to be a writer. 'Then write,' he said – which made a massive difference to me because I think I'd been waiting for permission or for someone to hand a career to me on a plate. If you want to do it, just get on with it. And if you can, make your own work. (Paul later encouraged me to write my own fanzine as a way of showing people who I was and what I was into.) I think the main advantage of knowing the history of Doctor Who so well is that it saves a lot of time. I already know which stories have been done before, so I don't get pitches turned down because they're too much like *The Claws of Axos*. I can also include references and allusions to old stories – and even old monsters like the Vardans – which will mean something to other fans. But it doesn't make me all that special. Lots of writers – and editors, producers, artists etc – know lots about Doctor Who. I'm very aware that there are lots of other talented people my bosses could employ in my stead. The most important thing is that I can deliver a good, exciting story. I'd like to think people enjoy my stuff because it's a good story well-told, and not because it mentions Liz Shaw's time working for PROBE.

MM: As both a novelist and audio writer, which medium, as an author, do you prefer? Why? How do the mediums, from the writer's point of view, differ?

Simon: I like the variety. I find prose slower going, though you can do a lot of different things with it. Prose is a bit lonelier too. All writing is lonely – you spend a lot of hours alone in your own head, which is why writers can be so peculiar. Scripts are at least written with the performance in mind. At the moment I'm enjoying writing scripts for TV (not ones that have been commissioned, ones I'm doing in an effort to get some work). The different media allow you to do different things and tell your stories in different ways. Jonathan Morris gave me a great piece of advice when I was starting out, to use the medium you're telling the story in as part of the story. If you're writing a comic, do a story you could only tell as a comic. If you're doing an audio story, use the fact it's on audio. I *love* the Companion Chronicles format, which allows you to really get inside a companion's head.

MM: Focusing on your audio work for a while - having contributed to the main Doctor Who range and the Companion Chronicles, I wondered if writing for each differed vastly, or at all, and if so, how? Do you prefer either, and if so why, and is one more difficult to write than the other? Why?

Simon: I think the main difference is that the Companion Chronicles are two-handers, so they're much more intimate and have a lot more straight narration where you can get a character's innermost thoughts and feelings. But then I did something a bit like that in my main range story *The Judgement of Isskar*, where an episode begins with a piece of narration by the Doctor. Without spoiling what happens, I did that to change the pace and also build a bit of scale and flesh out one of the characters, and I think that worked quite well. But a lot of writing is about practicalities: how do you tell a story with X number of characters? Sometimes there are additional practicalities: maybe Actor Y is only available for one day of the recording, so can only be in so many scenes. Often you're asked to work in things to help the series as a whole. I wrote the narration for *The Settling* after hearing Gary Russell's plans for the future of Ace and Hex – plans that never then happened as Gary left Big Finish. No, the main difference between the main range and the Companion Chronicles is that more people listen to the main range and (so) the pay is better. :)

MM: I have to ask you about Oliver Harper. How did you feel when you found out that you were going to be responsible for creating a new companion? How easy or difficult was it to bring Oliver to life, and how difficult was it to write his eventual fate? It was, I'm not ashamed to admit, an ending that was responsible for a few minutes of 'grit caught in my eye'-related mayhem at Mass Movement HQ...

Simon: That's very kind of you to say so. That trilogy was a real pleasure to work on. But Oliver Harper was really the creation of producer David Richardson: he devised Oliver's character, name, background and secret – and also the end of his story. I'd pitched David a story that became *The Cold Equations* and in discussing that, David proposed this new character and also his first adventure. He recommended I watch the Dirk Bogarde film *Victim* as a pointer towards the character he had in mind, so I did that and also talked to my friend Matthew Sweet, who knew a lot about Bogarde and the context of that film. He lent me a couple of other Bogarde films, too. So I wrote a part with a 'young Bogarde' in mind. Once we'd recorded the first one, I wrote the next two with Tom Allen in mind. He was perfect casting as Oliver, and his dynamic with Peter Purves worked really well. Peter asked David if he could do more comedy scenes – hence the comedy in *The Perpetual Bond*.

And then, when we were recording that, he asked me to write more straight drama so he could do a bit more acting. I think those are what make *The Cold Equations* and *The First Wave* so effective. So it was really quite an easy job with Oliver – everything was handed to me. After we'd recorded *The Cold Equations*, David and I did have second thoughts about the way we'd end the trilogy. We suggested a couple of alternatives to our original plan, but they all seemed to be cheating. Better, we thought, to go for the most dramatic version.

MM: I know that for writers it's often difficult and sometimes nearly impossible to choose a favourite personal work, but I wondered if you had, or have, one? Which of your Who-related creations is your personal favourite? Why?

Simon: You're right: it's very hard to choose. And the reasons I'd choose something are very different from anyone else's – I'd choose the one that was most fun to work on, that I've got the best memories of, rather than whether it was particularly successful. I was a bit surprised when people heard the first series of Graceless and thought it was dark – my memory of it was how much fun it had been to make. So I'm not a very reliable judge. My wife likes my BBC book *The Pirate Loop* best – she thinks it's the most 'me' – so probably best to pick that one.

MM: You also served as editor on some volumes of Big Finish's Short Trips anthologies, didn't you? Was that hard? Again, making the transition from writer to editor; how did you find it? Was there anything about the editorial process that you didn't like, or were uncomfortable with, or did you find it an easy role to fulfil? Why?

Simon: I'd edited a couple of Bernice Summerfield anthologies before I was offered my first Doctor Who one. If I remember rightly, Paul Cornell's *A Christmas Treasury* (2004) had sold very well, so Big Finish were keen to do another Christmas book for 2005 but didn't have a lot of time to produce it. I'd edited a Benny book at high speed, so I was offered the job. Again, that was a fun time. We were all writing it as the first series of the new Doctor Who was on TV, so there was a real buzz about it. I think my main advantage as an editor was that I'd written for lots of different editors by that point, so had an idea what worked and what didn't when dealing with writers – or at least, what I'd responded to myself. Simple things like, whatever you think of a story, whatever you want to see changed, always begin 'I loved it,' say the good things first, then 'but I've some ideas how we can make it better'. I think – though you'd really have to ask the writers – that it was a good, fun job for everyone, and I even threw a party when the book came out. My last book as editor was completely different. *How The Doctor Changed My Life* was the result of a competition for first-time writers, and it was a hell of a lot of work. Again, I'm really pleased with that book – it's a real credit to all the writers, many of whom have gone on to have lots of other things published. But by that time I'd stopped being a producer for Big Finish (I ran the Benny range for two years) because I knew that for all producing and editing were fun and had taught me a lot, I really just wanted to be a writer. I'm not exactly sure why it is; just that, having done the jobs, I know which I find the most rewarding.

MM: You've also written a number of Who-related and unrelated (Sapphire & Steel, etc) projects for Big Finish, so what attracted you to each of the non-Who projects, and which of the non-Who related projects you've been responsible for (again!) is your personal favourite (and yes, you guessed the next part correctly), why is it your favourite?

Simon: I generally try not to turn down work, and spend a lot of time pitching for stuff that either doesn't happen or I don't get picked for. So I'm not sure you can draw many conclusions from the things that I've ended up doing – they're just the ones that worked out, rather than any conscious plan on my part. I guess you'd have to ask the producers why they chose me. I pitched an idea for Sapphire and Steel to producer Nigel Fairs when we were at a convention. I'd only recently discovered the original TV series and also loved what I'd heard of the Big Finish version – I think the first two stories were out at that point. After that, I suppose people already knew my work – and that I could do what I was told, on time, which make producers' lives easier. Mark Wright told me he was producing the Iris Wildthyme range when we sat together at a curry night out, and the next morning I sent him an email with the rough idea we'd come up with between us. I'm generally pretty good at following up on things and quickly when there's a sniff of work, so perhaps that's why I got the jobs.

As for favourites... I'm really pleased with Richard Armitage's reading of my Robin Hood story, and think Big Finish's Robin Hood series has been sadly underrated. And I was thrilled by Matthew Waterhouse's performance in my Dark Shadows play. Working with James Goss and Joseph Lidster on that was really rewarding – I didn't know Dark Shadows at all, but they made the whole thing very easy.

MM: What's next for you, Simon? What new and exciting projects are you working on, and what can you tell us about them?

Simon: I'm in the midst of writing another Companion Chronicle that I can tell you nothing about other than it follows on from one of my previous ones. And I've just had an email this afternoon from Big Finish executive producer Nick Briggs asking me to write something exciting for 2013 – which of course I can speak no more of. I'm also busy taking the short film I've written, *Cleaning Up* – starring Mark Gatiss and Louise Jameson – to film festivals and trying to get interest in doing a longer version of it. And I've got a novel of my own that I keep meaning to write more of...

MM: If there's anything that you'd like to add, now would be the perfect time to do so...

Simon: Bourbons are my favourite biscuit.

Originally published in Mass Movement #32, April 2012

THE OLYMPIAN SPIRIT IN 28MM

As the sporting world basks in the afterglow of London 2012 Olympic and Paralympic Games, new heroes heralded and records smashed, drugs cheats named and shamed, another titanic struggle will begin. In a sweaty hall in Poland over 200 athletes will battle with the Corinthian spirit that the Olympics - in all their mass market commercialism - singularly lack.

Yes, unbeknownst to all normal people, the 'World Cup of Warhammer' takes place and, in 2012, when the eyes of the world will be on our capital city and the finely-honed physiques of the Olympians, there'll be men wielding spells and dice for the greater glory of their countries. The European Team Championship (ETC) is an annual event that pits national teams of the best competitive players of Warhammer against each other.

Thankfully the ETC is open to all body types, when the most important things are brain-power, strategy and knowledge. Mass Movement decided it was about time this apotheosis of wargaming was writ large across our pages, so we caught up with two of the UK's top competitive Warhammer Fantasy players, each of whom are leading their country into battle. Dan Heelan is the newly-elected captain of Team England, and Matt Yeo is his Welsh counterpart.

I heartily recommend Dan's Warhammer podcast in which he and a regular cast of fellow players talk enthusiastically but humorously about their hobby and the competitive scene in the UK. He's one of the most high-profile competitive players on the UK scene, and is relishing the challenge of leading England. I ask him to explain in layman's terms what the ETC is.

"The ETC is a team tournament for teams [28 in 2011] of eight players. Each player has a race/army and only one race/type of army per team may be taken. In each round all players' scores are added together to give the team score. Match-ups per round are determined via a 'Swiss' system where winners play winners, losers play losers etc, using the scores as a differentiator. Individual players are then matched up in a specially-designed system which in itself is a game. Player versus player match ups are a key part of the round where you can literally win or lose if you get the process right or wrong."

Got that? It's clear even the mechanics of the ETC are part of the gameplay and as strategically-important as the actual on-table action. The choosing of team members and their particular army to play opponents to their best advantage is paramount.

Dan was voted as 2012 England captain by the outgoing 2011 team - a system that happens each year. He sees his role as different prior to the event and during: "This year and last we had a playing captain and a non-player coach who basically carried out the role of 'ETC captain' during the rounds so the captain can concentrate on his game. For me, the role of captain in the England set-up is to guide the selection process, plan and guide the preparation and practice and generally keep the team focused and working together. At the event the actual captain's administration and other tasks will be carried out by the manager/coach."

He attended ETC 2010 and 2011, having failed to make the cut in 2009. I wonder if the team selection is a cut-throat affair, so I ask Dan how team members are selected. "The English team is selected via committee. The committee is appointed via a strict charter that ensures

a mix of ETC experience and community presence. This committee then take applications and pick the eight players based on a set of thorough criteria. These criteria can be seen on www.warhammer.org.uk in the Tournament News section. It is a mix of having a proven track record at tournaments, ability to practise/play/attend events, enthusiasm, knowledge and being a team player amongst other things. You are going to be playing against probably the best players in the world so you have to be good on the table."

Matt Yeo, Team Wales captain, has also attended for the last two years, so how does the Welsh system differ? Suffice to say, the difference in the size of the countries and their gaming communities is stark: "[In 2011] We took anyone who was Welsh, was a reasonably good player and was actually able to afford the trip [to Switzerland]. We then filled in the one remaining slot with a ringer who lives by the Swiss border in Germany." That's what having a population of 3million instead of 45million does for you. Read on to find out where Wales came in 2011...

Regardless of eventual position, each team and their captain is competing with a sense of pride. Psychologically speaking, the act of donning a 'national' identity must be a factor. Dan explains: "Without doubt there's a sense of pride in representing your country. You ask anyone who has put that England shirt on what it means and they all feel the same. National pride can be seen no more obviously than when it's been crushed after losing a game. It is a horrible feeling knowing you have let your team-mates down by losing a game."

There must be many tens of thousands of Warhammer players in the country, out of whom just a few are representing England, so does he feel any pressure or nerves? "I think you can't help it," he says. "There's so much expectation and also I think everyone likes to justify or prove why THEY have been selected over others. I think the nerves get better after the first year; I certainly felt fewer nerves this year than the previous ETC (my first). The one game where everyone feels it more I think is against the 'big teams' and in the 'Warhammer Ashes' against the Australians. We have a 100% record against the Aussies so no-one wants to be part of the team that is the first to lose!"

I wonder if Matt feels the same way about national pride and pressure. "In a way there is pride in representing your country," he says. "Perhaps not so much in my case, as I'm not Welsh by birth, although I qualify due to living here a long time! I'm originally from Cornwall though, so the Celtic blood does run deep. We feel a bit of pressure, but not as much as the bigger countries. We weren't overflowing with people for this year due to the costs involved, and a lot of the many thousands of players in the country don't know of the existence of this tournament or maybe even the whole independent tournament scene in general. We set out with our goals for this year and did achieve them, so we have something to build on for next year."

Matt has put his finger on the strange split between the tournament 'scene' and the 'hobby' scene. The vast majority of Games Workshop (GW) fans are garage gamers, playing with mates and with, at best, knowledge that GW run their own tournaments at their Nottingham HQ and at stores. This independent, ultra-competitive, top-level battle of skill and knowledge is a strange beast. Things aren't all sweetness and light within the scene itself: in the period after the announcement of the England team for 2012, Dan had to deal with a lot of online bickering about the selections and the process. The insularity of the scene can have the negative effect of blowing problems out of proportion, but I guess it's the same in any niche activity.

It can seem cliquey and impenetrable, but Dan feels that things may be changing, especially with the increasing presence of tournament players on social media. He says: "There is some criticism, if we are honest, every year with regards to the team selection. There are always a few individuals who feel disappointed and/or aggrieved they did not make the team, but overall the support is great. Tournament regulars are definitely aware the ETC is going on and with the aid of Twitter and podcasts it has continued to raise its profile as an event." I can't help but feel, listening to the Heelanhammer podcast in which Dan addressed these issues, that people just ought to get out more.

Earlier, Dan mentioned the 'big teams'. I'm intrigued to find out which countries are the Warhammer versions of Spain, Germany and Argentina in football. Who are the biggest challenges? "The traditional big hitters are Italy, Poland, Denmark and Germany. They are the traditional big four. England have never quite made the top 10, although personally I believe this is mainly down to the score system in which a bad or good result can drastically change your position and can exaggerate or hide your true performance. In 2010 we had a fourth place finish on offer if we won, but the loss put us outside the top ten. 2011 was a similar result although we were not in as high a position. We still have a long way to go with our preparation before we can really start to compete with those four. We are obviously hoping to sort that this year!"

There's no reason why England can't smash into those 'Big Four', given the size and health of the scene, but what about Wales? "Last year we finished dead last," says Matt Yeo. "This year we were second from last and much more in the running, although we had a slightly disappointing day two which dropped us down the table. We were aiming at not being last this year and achieved that so we were pleased."

The difference between the expectations of the two countries is, of course, large, but as with any amateur participatory activity, the desire to win, while strong, is ameliorated by the fact that teams go to the ETC to also have fun. It's people sharing an interest, taking that interest to a high level. The thing is, there are potentially more than 20 languages in that one room. So how does the dynamic work at the ETC? Matt says: "There's lots of banter between the home nations teams of Wales, Ireland, Scotland, Northern Ireland and England. Games are generally played in a firm but fair manner, but communication issues and rules disputes can occur though, due to different ways of playing things or interpreting rules in different countries."

Dan agrees: "I think with this many cultures and languages in a system that is not that 'tight' as a rule set there are always going to be some communication problems. Luckily most teams speak English (or at least one of the team does!) so problems don't usually last very long. The atmosphere is something that is hard to describe. Having hundreds of wargamers plus supporters, coaches etcetera all in on one place from all over the world and from different cultures is a spectacle that is hard to describe. Many teams will give gifts to their opponents before the games or to their favourite team they played over the weekend. Banter is certainly present as well!"

No doubt the 'banter' is at its most ripe in the games between our home nations and the Australians. Dan:"For me I have enjoyed playing the Australians in both years. I think it is because they play the game in a similar style and are easy going, fun guys. I don't think there are any teams I don't like playing. You get the odd tense game or rules discussion but that is to be expected when everyone is under so much pressure to not let their country down!"

Don't let your country down. Play firm but fair. Strive to be the best you can be. For Dan, for Matt and for their English and Welsh teams the Olympian spirit is alive and well. It's just the small matter of scale isn't it?

James McLaren

Originaly published in Mass Movement #32, April 2012

BRIAN SLAGEL
(METAL BLADE RECORDS)

Whether you realise it or not, if you're read Mass Movement, chances are that Brian Slagel has, indirectly, had a huge impact on your life. As the founder, owner and operator of Metal Blade, Brian has been responsible for putting out some of the greatest records of the last half century, and has, arguably, had a greater impact on the overall global metal scene than any other single individual. Plus, the dude gave Metallica and Slayer their first breaks and unleashed them on the world! As Metal Blade is thirty years old this year I decided that the time was right to try and catch up with Brian for a chat about Metal Blade...

Interview by Tim Cundle

Photographs by Stephanie Cabral

MM: For the benefit of those who came in late....Would you like to both introduce, and tell us a little something about yourself Brian?

Brian: Ha, I run a label called Metal Blade Records for the last 30 years. I live in Los Angeles and I was born and raised there as well. I also travel a lot and am a huge sports fan, especially ice hockey. Mostly I am a big time metalhead.

MM: Let's go back to the beginning of what's become a life long journey... What kick started your love of metal and heavy music? Do you still feel the same way about metal and music today, that you did when you first became a fan and do you still get that same insane buzz every time you hear a classic riff, mind shattering vocal attack or blistering rhythm section, or has the music changed for you? If so, why, and if not, why do you think your passion for metal has remained undiminished?

Brian: When I was 11 my cousin played me Deep Purple's *Machine Head* and I was hooked. I still love metal and listen to it all the time. I think I am still the same fan now as I was over 30 years ago. I love hearing new stuff as well as listening to the classics!

MM: You started a zine, *Metal Revue* and then started writing for other metal publications didn't you? How difficult was it to make the transition from just being a fan to being a critic who could potentially, within the smaller metal scene at the time, make or break a band? Having started as a writer, how do you feel about the modern music, and especially metal, press, given the power they wield when it comes to your own bands and releases?

Brian: I just started out trying to turn people onto new music that really is still the same today. When I was writing I tried to mostly do stuff I liked and not stuff I did not. Most writers today are metal fans, so I think they do a great job. As far as the power goes, I suppose it is there but also they help the bands out as well more than the opposite.

MM: Right, let's get down to basics. Its thirty years since you compiled and released *Metal Massacre*, so what you remember most about putting the record together? How did you pick and choose the bands for the album? Did you know, think or have any idea that what you were about to unleash would change not only your destiny, bit the destinies of the bands involved forever? And, how does it feel to be known as the guy who "discovered" Metallica, arguably the biggest Heavy Metal band in the world?

Brian: I was really just trying to help out the bands in LA who had no way to get any exposure. I knew all the bands on the album and just went to them and asked them to be on the album. None of us back then ever thought things would get this big for sure. It is amazing to have had a small part in helping Metallica start, they are still great friends of mine. It is really insane to see what they have done! It was interesting putting an album out back then, not as easy as you would think!

MM: Following on for the last question, do you have any plans to reissue the classic *Metal Massacre* albums, especially in this era of download sales which are more cost effective for the label than printing CDs? Metal Blade introduced more legendary bands than any other label (all other labels combined almost!) with these compilations: Metallica, Slayer, Voivod, Metal Church, ... Ratt, Black 'N' Blue etc.?

Brian: Maybe, but the agreements have all run out on the early albums. We re-licensed some of them for our 20th anniversary box set. So you never know!

MM: How did the advent of thrash metal and crossover during the mid-eighties affect Metal Blade? What kind of lasting impact, if any did it have on Metal Blade, and which of the bands that originally emerged from the thrash scene did you think (at the time) would make it but never did? Was, in your opinion, a thrash resurgence inevitable, and if so why? Talking about musical resurgence, why do you think metal, more so than any other music tends to have a cyclical resurgence with its subgenres? By that, I mean sub-genres arrive, dies, then are "reborn" for a new generation of fans…?

Brian: Well Thrash, like all the genres of metal have certainly had a big influence on us and metal as a whole. It was just a great scene and it was really fun to be a part of. I think the elements of thrash are really around today in so many of the current bands. There are some "true" thrash bands out there and we will see how it all comes together. Metal is just a great form of music and like all forms it is cool to see the older stuff creep into the new bands.

MM: When did you realise that Metal Blade had become a full time label rather than something you were doing for fun and to help bands out? How did you feel when that moment of realisation arrived? Have your feelings about and toward the label that you started since that moment? If so, how have they changed?

Brian: The first three years was just me in my mom's garage. So I think when I was able to afford an office and one employee. I think at that moment I figured this might go somewhere, but it was a gradual thing and not any one moment really. I still love doing this, so I think my feelings have not changed much over the years. It still is a lot of fun.

MM: Is there such a thing as a 'Metal Blade band'? What do you look for in a band before signing them? Are there any bands that you wish you had signed but didn't and if so, who are they, why do you wish you had signed them and what prevented you from doing so at the time?

Brian: We have a very diverse roster, so I don't think there is a typical Metal Blade band. I like stuff that is a bit different from what is going on and I think that is one of the reasons we have been able to stick around so long. So for new bands, we like to try to find stuff that is not the current scene. Always trying to fine the next scene if we can. I had an opportunity to see Guns N Roses many times when they first started out and never went. Then I heard *Appetite For Destruction* and thought, oops!! I think I should have gone. Certainly I would have loved to have done the first Metallica album, but I had no money.

MM: Wasn't there some controversy with GWAR and *America...* following the albums release? Do you want to tell us about it?

Brian: Yes there was a song on the album that a lot of people had some problems with. Basic censorship, which we have dealt with a lot over the years. I always want the bands to say what they want and I will not ever censor them.

MM: What, in your opinion, are the biggest changes that have occurred in the music business, and especially within metal, in the last three decades, and have they been positive or detrimental for the business as a whole, and how have these changes affected, if at all, Metal Blade and the way that it operates?

Brian: There have been so many, from vinyl to CD, and now to digital. We embrace change and new technology so I think we try to use all of these to help us. Certainly the current music business is much different now, but we have been able to do well. Metal fans are very supportive and we love that. We also really try and put out the best product and packaging as we can. I do think the internet has changed the business more than anything. As I mentioned we use that to help us as much as possible. There is always change in any business and if you can adapt you will be successful. We try and do that as much as we can.

MM: Talking about change, what kind of impact has the advent of the internet and digital delivery and formats had on the way Metal Blade operates? How do you think (time to play soothsayer and seer) the, seemingly, ever increasing reliance on, and growth of digital platforms will affect the label in the future?

Brian: As I mentioned before this is certainly a big thing. The internet and all it brings has made music more available than ever before. So more people are listening now and that is a great thing. However, CD's are still by far our biggest format. Even in the USA our new releases are 80% CD and 20% digital. The catalogue is more digital than CD though. Long term I think both formats will continue to exist together (at least for metal). At least we can have all of our our catalogue available digitally now so that is cool.

MM: Many comparable labels have "diversified" in a sense - Roadrunner took on Nickelback, Victory is far from its roots as a straightedge East Coast Hardcore label - what are your thoughts on the competition, and what - if anything – do you foresee Metal Blade doing to take things in a different direction if the winds pointed you that way? Maybe an imprint or imprints to separate the metal from the death metal from the comedy from the metal-core, something like that?

Brian: We have always tried to sign different bands, so I think that will continue and hopefully we can also sign some cool new things. I think we are already doing that as we have all along. So hopefully our tastes will go the right way. We used to do imprints, but now I think it will all just be on Metal Blade no matter what since our catalogue is already so diverse.

MM: On a similar note, do you ever feel pigeonholed by the name? (for the record, if I woke up in a world without Metal Blade records I would cry - I'm just saying)….

Brian: We used to feel that way a bit in the early days. At this point since we have done so much I think we are ok with the name…

MM: Okay, time to get incredibly specific, but this is Mass Movement, and sometimes we need to get really specific….So, what are your recollections of first signing, then working with, King's X after their split with Atlantic/Megaforce? How did that coincide with Metal Blade also working with Galactic Cowboys and Atomic Opera, both of whom came from the same Houston scene that was run at one time by Sam Taylor?

Brian: I am a HUGE Kings X fan, so being able to work with them was a real honour and dream of mine. Same with Galactic Cowboys. I was a huge fan of both and I was friends with them even before they were on the label. It did kind of all happen at the same time which was cool for me. Since I was friends with them when they needed a label we talked and it worked out. I really love the albums we did with those bands and like I said it was a true honor to work with them. They are still all good friends too.

MM: I guess that's about it Brian, so if there's anything that you'd like to add or tell us about that's coming up on Metal Blade in the near future, now would be a good time to spill the beans…

Brian: Thanks to everyone for supporting Metal Blade, the bands and metal for all these years. We would not be here without all of you, so again thanks so much! You can follow me on twitter @brianslagel. Thanks!!

Originally published in Mass Movement #33, August 2012

DR. LIVING DEAD!

Crazy bunch that we are, we need to visit a Doctor on a regular basis. Not the boring pill peddler around the corner, but the more interesting physicians, like Doctor Who, Doc Strange or Dr. Know. The ailments that we have; the crazy love of sci-fi, thrash and punk rock need special treatment. We've now found a new health care provider, from Sweden, by the name of Dr. Living Dead, who shares a love of all the things that epitomise Mass Movement. Bassplayer Dr Rad, called me in from the waiting room, for an initial consultation. I hope it won't hurt....Too much...

Interview by Martijn Welzen

MM: So Doctor, you're heavily influenced by bands like Suicidal Tendencies and Nuclear Assault, who on paper, don't really seem too alike. How did that come about? Do both bands have more in common than we might suspect?

Rad: We don't really think too much about what exactly it is we're doing, the song ideas come from various places. Sure, bands like ST and Nuclear Assault influence us a lot but so do bands like Slayer, Vio-lence and Anthrax. But the basic concept is just to play thrash that has plenty of attitude and power so whatever fits that that bill, we'll use, may it be death metal, hardcore or something completly different. The most important thing for us so far has been to cut out the boring stuff but still keep it catchy. Usually we know pretty fast what is going to work and what isn't. Lately we've been experimenting a bit more though, in order to keep things interesting. I think we've progressed as a songwriters, so try to not paint us into a corner from the beginning....

MM: At first glance I thought your band was all about fun and having a good time, but when I read lyrics like *My Brain For Sale* I thought there's a lot more depth to you guys than I expected there. What can you tell us about how you balance having fun with more serious topics?

Rad: I guess most people don't know what to make of us at first sight but that may be a good thing as well I think, as it creates a bit of mystery and hopefully some interest. We have different kinds of lyrics, some are meant to be taken more seriously than others, but it's all part of who we are in a way. We like to have a good laugh but at the same time we're serious about the whole thing, I think people can see that if they look closely.

MM: Are lyrics like *My Brain For Sale* or *Dead End Life* also influenced by Mike Muir, who writes about feeling lost in a world he doesn't understand?

Rad: Well I guess you can say that in a way they are influenced by Mike, otherwise I would be lying, but the actual lyrics are written by our singer Ape and they deal with his feelings. It would just be kinda stupid to write something like that out of the blue just because it's supposed to be a certain way. But all in all I think Mike has written some of the most powerful stuff out there so I guess that in itself is an inspiration to not just fall into the same old cliches. It's also a nice contrast within the concept of the band. We can go from the comic book style lyrics about the Doctor to singing about some funny movie and on to more personal stuff without sounding weird. It's like they're all a part of our personalities....

MM: How important are films for the band, in the sense that they're an escape, and as far as movies are concerned, do ou think that the stranger the films are, the better they are... Whether that be Sci-Fi, Horror, Action etc?

Rad: We totally love movies, yeah. I think Sci-Si is the most important genre for the band and concept as a whole. We're nuts about *Alien* and *Bladerunner* and things like that. We also enjoy the cheesy action movies that you find in our lyrics, mainly because they are extremely entertaining and quite frankly, we just had to do a song about *Kindergarten Cop*. But we watch all kinds of things from horror to comedy to documentaries, even though we don't write about it all...

MM: As your music is firmly influenced by the eighties, would you say it's also that era which gave the world the best films?

Rad: A lot of the best ones are definitely from the eighties but there are so many from the seventies and other eras that are just total classics too! Hard to say really. Gotta love the pre CGI-days!

MM: Who are your film heroes? Jean-Claude van Damme, Sylverster Stalone, Arnold Schwarzenegger, are linked to some of your songs, even though they're not always the best actors though, or doesn't acting ability matter...?

Rad: Ha, ha, I just find those guys hilarious. I wouldn't say that they are heroes but classic actors nonetheless. Personally I don't really have a favorite, depends on the movie and the character.

MM: Any recent films or actors that really caught your attention?

Rad: I'm absolutely stoked about seeing *Prometheus*. That's all I care for at the moment. It seems like Swedish actress Noomi Rapace is going to deliver the goods! I also liked the film *Moon* from 2009, that was really good.

MM: Speaking about Schwarzenegger, do you know the band Austrian Death Machine? If so, what do you think of their take on the Governator's work?

Rad: I've heard a song or too. Not my cup of tea, I think it gets a bit too much to be honest. Our songs that deal with films are usually pretty stupid and spontaneous which helps them not get old too fast, I think.

MM: I also really like the *Ancient Revelations* on the lyric sheet, which is obviously a link to Iron Maiden's *Piece of Mind* album. But there's also some truth in it. Does that actually sum up what Dr. Living Dead is about? You know, how fucked-up the world can be, but at the same time not taking it all to seriously?

Rad: Thanks! Yeah that's the way we like to do it. We're not ignorant fools and I like to think that people can actually make out the messages and themes that are in there and think about them, but still be entertained by the music and concept.

MM: Your imagery also has a firm link to comics, is that something you might like to expand on in the near future? It would be amazing if you could create a comic with accompanying sound track....

Rad: Yeah, we've thought about that. We'll see what happens...

MM: Speaking of which, do we take things too seriously? Do you offer an escape for people who truely feel lost?

Rad: I don't want to get too philosophical here but I think it's fairly easy to say that a lot of people take the wrong things too seriously, but I think it's important to be serious about some things. If we do offer people an escape that would be great but I guess it has more to do with if the fans can connect with the music or not. Our goal is to make music that kicks ass and that we feel represents us as individuals and for us, the band is an escape in a way so I guess that other people might feel the same way, if they are into what we do. But I don't think we're that much different from other bands who are totaly dedicated to what they're doing in that sense. I just think that honest music is going to get recognized in one way or another by the listeners.

MM: Sticking with a similar theme, is that also a part of thrash and crossovers success these days? The links to the eighties, in that, we're now in the same kind of economic, social and political mess as we were back in thrash's hey day...

Rad: I don't know. The way I see it there doesn't seem to be much connection to politics in todays scene. But I think that the boredom that spawned most of the bands way back when may be the same that people today feel when they start up. Personally I've felt that something was missing for a long time and I wanted to fill that void. I think a lot of the new thrash bands feel that way, so now all of a sudden there are all these thousands of bands from all over the world doing shit and promoting it on the internet. The thing is that I still think that there is something missing and part of it has to do with the way people record stuff nowadays. I'm totally fed up with trigged drums and the plastic guitar sounds that totaly ruin everything that was good about the old stuff that influenced you in the first place. We're just trying to be a band that we would want to be able to see ourselves and that includes none of the above....

MM: Have you had any reaction from bands, you're influenced by, or even played with, like Suicidal, Nuclear Assault, and Anthrax? There's a photo of you with Kerry King on the inner sleeve of your album - what did he think about the band?

Rad: We did open for Slayer back in '08 when we were still a pretty new band and that's when we took the picture with Kerry. He was nice to us and introduced himself as Kerry Burger King since he had heard that we had a song named after him. We explained that it was supposed to be taken as a tribute and I think he got that. We gave him our demos and that was it basically. They didn't watch our show or anything like that. I remember one time we got this e-mail from a guy who played in Neighbourhood Watch from Venice Beach in the 80s and he was super stoked on what we were doing, so that was fun. It's also great to be working with Fred Estby since we have all grown up on Dismember and that sort of stuff!

Originaly published in Mass Movement #33, August 2012

JAMES LOVEGROVE

There are times, admittedly few and far between, when I really, really love this job. I mean, how often do you get to interview two of your favourite authors in a row? Last issue, Christopher Fowler, and this issue, James Lovegrove. What could be better? Uh, I guess maybe having my own intergalactic warcraft crewed by scantily clad, buxom Amazonians would be better, but not by much. Anyway, I'm drifting off topic. James Lovegrove, in case you're unfamiliar with his work is the man responsible for the *Pantheon* series, a collection of alternate history /world novels in which the Gods, and associated mythology, of Aztec, Greek, Egyptian and Norse culture are a reality, and how their existence has shaped and defined the world and the lives of the mortals destined to live alongside them. So, when the chance to interview James appeared, I seized it, and this is what he had to say...

Interview by Tim Cundle

MM: I've always found that the best place to start is at the beginning, so would you like to both introduce, and tell us a little about, yourself?

James: I'm James Lovegrove, I'm 46 years old, I have been a published author since I was 22, I live in Eastbourne on the south coast of England, I am a father of two and a husband of one, I have a penchant for jam doughnuts that is both unforgivable and, at my advanced age, probably unwise.

MM: What made you want to be, and influenced you decision to become, a writer?

James: I never intended to become a writer, in that when I was young I was firmly convinced I was going to grow up to be a rock megastar. Deep down, however, I think I realised that writing was the thing that came most naturally to me and that I was temperamentally suited for. I always loved writing stories, especially as a set part of an English lesson at school, since that seemed to me fun rather than work. At university, having tried to pop-music career route and found it inordinately difficult, I got more into writing. I entered a college short-story competition and won, which encouraged me. I also paid to have the story typed up rather than doing that myself, and this cost me more than the prize money.

A harsh but necessary lesson in the economics of writing there, I feel. Then, as I was about to graduate, I discussed my future with my tutor, and when I told him I fancied the idea of writing a novel, he said, "Then you must do so, darling!" That expression of confidence from someone I respected was exactly what I needed, so I sat down and did just that, wrote a novel. It was *The Hope*, it was accepted for publication immediately by Macmillan, and I was on my way. I don't believe there was any one book or eureka moment that told me I should try and write fiction for a living. I think it was just there all along, encoded in my genes. I love reading, I love writing, so why not?

MM: Staying with the idea of influences, who and / or what has influenced you as writer, and how do you think these influences manifest themselves in your work? Someone quite famous, but whose name eludes me at present, once said that "A man is the sum of his influences", and I wondered if you thought it was more important to "find you own voice" as a writer or to accept your influences and incorporate them in what you write? Why?

James: I suppose my first and most significant influence was Stan Lee. People might find that absurd – "A comic book writer!?" – but I devoured Lee's Marvel work when I was a kid, and he taught me more about storytelling, characterisation and use of language than probably even I realise. After him comes Ray Bradbury. A teacher read his *The Veldt* to my class when I was about 9 or 10, and that was the first time it dawned on me that science fiction wasn't just pulp or trash – not that there's anything wrong with that – but could aspire to being great fiction, even art. Then it was Stephen King, who hit me in my teens with his combination of powerful narrative sweep and fine ear for dialogue. Plus, you know, cool scary scenes. After that they all came in a crowd: Ballard, Vonnegut, Colin Wilson, Alan Moore.

The people you should read in your teens and twenties, when you have the luxury of plenty of time to read and think about what you've read. I no longer attempt to emulate or slavishly copy any of these guys. I've been doing this long enough to have developed my own working methods, my own style, my own approach to my craft. But they're there, layered in, indecipherably, inextricably. If you don't start out by wanting to be, or at least be like, your favourite writer, you'll never get anywhere. And when you do get somewhere, you should strive to be as little like him or her as possible. That's the deal. Find a literary mentor, learn from your mentor, outgrow your mentor.

MM: Your novels tend to dip in and out of different genres, or literary subjects and fields and as such, I was curious about whether you saw yourself as a writer of general fiction or genre author, and if you do consider yourself to be a genre author, which genre you identify with in particular as a writer? Likewise, are you drawn to any particular literary genre as a fan, and if so, which one and why?

James: You're saying I have a short attention span, aren't you? Well, you're right. I'm appallingly promiscuous when it comes to genre. I care little for the distinctions between genres and certainly wouldn't want to be pigeonholed as *this* kind of writer or *that* kind of writer. Too restrictive for comfort, that. I love all different kinds of fiction and read in every conceivable genre, though I do draw the line at chick lit and teen vampires. I write whatever kind of story I feel like writing at the time, or whatever kind of story the publisher or commissioning editor is looking for. It's all narrative, isn't it? All storytelling? So why make distinctions?

I suppose one thing you can describe me as *not* being is mainstream, but that's perfectly acceptable to me, and explicable in that while I enjoy mainstream fiction well enough, my heart is always in the genres. If I have any particular inclination at the moment, it's towards thrillers with a science-fictional bent, authors like Michael Crichton, Douglas Preston, Lincoln Child. They're kind of a guilty pleasure, but that doesn't mean they're not good.

MM: Let's talk about *Redlaw*, which is your vampire novel that it isn't just about Vampires. Let's just say that it wouldn't appeal to the average reader of the nausea and boredom inducing Twilight series. Would you care to elaborate a little on the plot, and why did want to write a Vampire novel, and why did you choose, apart from the blindingly obvious of course, to use blood sucking parasites to satirise modern political and business models?

James: The idea for *Redlaw* had been kicking around in my head for quite some time. It started originally as a comic strip which I and an artist friend, Adam Brockbank, put together in the mid-90s and pitched to *2000AD* and Marvel. Nothing came of it, and the character of John Redlaw, a cop who polices vampires, went into the mental cupboard. A couple of years back, I took him back out of the cupboard, dusted him off, fixed a few things that needed fixing, and hey presto, I had a concept for a novel – a series of novels, in fact.

Very little of the original comicbook *Redlaw* remains, but the newer version is a much sharper and wiser entity. Using vampires as a way of commenting satirically on our world isn't exactly new, but I felt that the whole notion of bloodsuckers and their metaphorical realworld equivalent, politicians and businessmen, was too ripe with potential to resist. And in an economic downturn, caused by banking malpractice and just plain greed and stupidity, what better time to write a novel about it? Adam, by the way, has gone on to huge success both as a storyboard artist, working on movies like *X-Men* and the Harry Potters, and also in the comics world with his brilliant, beautiful strip *Mezolith*, which first appeared in the late, lamented *DFC* comic.

MM: Following on from the last question, why do you think, having written *Redlaw*, that Vampire fiction has seen a surge in popularity? What is so appealing, both to writers and fans alike, about the Nosferatu?

James: It seems that these horror tropes go in cycles. Werewolves, zombies, vampires, mummies, they all have their turn, fade away for a while, then experience a resurgence. Each is a fundamental expression of how we see ourselves and how we see the Other, the Outsider, the Not-Us. They're creatures of the id, so we can never really be rid of them, even if we wanted to be. Now is the vampires' time and – discounting *Twilight*, which is bilge, and boring bilge at that – I would think their predominance has a lot to do with the suspicions and uncertainties of the era, the general feeling that somewhere out there is an elite who care nothing for the rest of us and see us as just cattle to exploit and milk, a sinister cadre of beings who consider themselves superior in every way and are eternal in as much as they never go away, they just get replaced with more of the same. And how wonderful it would be, wouldn't it, if we could destroy them with righteousness – a stake through the heart, a crucifix in the face, a dousing of holy water?

MM: Time to move on to The Pantheon, your alternate /parallel world series…Where did the idea come for the series come from? Do you believe in parallel universe and world theory, that divergent decisions create different realities and that our reality is one of untold billions that exist simultaneously, or do you think it's just a load of scientific hokum?

James: Sometimes theoretical scientists come up with stuff that just makes you think, "What the hell are they smoking in the lab at Princeton?" I mean, seventeen dimensions? Superstring theory? Quantum foam? It's almost as if they get together and decide what could be the most absurd concept they could foist on the public and still make it sound somehow plausible? Equally, just the very idea of infinite multiple universes, each springing off from

the tiniest of points of divergence, makes one's mind boggle so much, one can hardly think straight. But then again, it's weirdly reassuring to think that somewhere out there in the multiverse is a version of you who hasn't made all the mistakes you've made and has gone on to live the perfect life you always dreamed of yourself living. In many ways it seems that scientists keep coming up with ideas which suggest the enormity and significance of human existence but don't have to couch it in a religious framework, and I like that.

It's somehow more satisfying than faith. But, to answer the initial part of the question, the idea for *The Age Of Ra* came about simply because George Mann, who at the time was publishing director of the Solaris imprint, got in touch one day and asked if I'd like to pitch them an idea for an alternate-history novel. I came up with a proposal for a book about a world where the Ancient Egyptian gods held sway and had divided our planet up amongst themselves. It was vaguely steampunky but with the added bonus of deities. I didn't think that had been done before, and George liked the proposal very much, and that was that.

MM: Did you, when you began writing *Age Of Ra* envision The Pantheon becoming a series of novels, or was the original idea for a single novel? Why deities? What made you choose and pursue mythology and folklore as the central premise for the series?

James: It didn't even occur to me that *Ra* would be anything more than a one-off. I'm not that farsighted or calculating. However, once I'd done it, and enjoyed doing it, I realised that there was plenty more mileage in the pantheons of various cultures. Each is as different from the other as is imaginable, and yet they all have a common thread, this sense of gods as sprawling, dysfunctional families, forever squabbling and infighting and doing all sorts of bad things like tricking humans and sleeping with their siblings.

I suppose I quite fancied the whole thematic uniformity of it, too, having separate unconnected stories linked by the same subject, humans' relationship with the beings they worship and vice versa. What I've found, now that I'm working on the fifth book in the series (sixth if you count the novella *Age Of Anansi*) is that the nature of each pantheon determines the nature of each book. The mythology drives the narrative, so that I never know from one book to the next what I'm going to write about, until I start to research the folklore and the characters of the gods themselves. That's the fun part, figuring out how I can work the various different aspects into a plot and devising new ways of retelling old, old stories.

MM: Is there an order to the cultures you've so far chosen for The Pantheon? If so, why follow that particular order, and if not, how do you choose which culture each book will be based in, on and around?

James: I'm approaching the series one book at a time, so I have no particular pecking order in mind. I started with the Egyptian pantheon even though I knew little about it at the time. It intrigued me because, even by mythology standards, the Ancient Egyptian myths are truly bonkers, and then also there was the whole fantastic visual appeal of gods with different animal heads and the kitsch fun to be had with Egyptian burial practices and pyramids and all of that. The Greek pantheon came next, and it was the one I'm most familiar with, from having studied Classics at school to having loved Ray Harryhausen movies and having read Hawthorne's *Tanglewood Tales* when I was little. Thereafter, I just pick on whichever pantheon or religion seems the most interesting at the time, whichever suits my mood or looks like it'll be a laugh to delve into and exploit.

MM: Are you going to limit The Pantheon to real world cultures and their resultant mythology and folklore, or have you ever thought about expanding it into the realms of fictional mythology, such as the Cthulhu Mythos? Why / why not?

James: For me, the appeal of existing cultures is that they have a reasonably solid framework already in place, a set of rules to work with. They're already fictional, based on stories ancient peoples told one another to explain the workings of the world and their place in it. That, I suppose, makes them little different from Lovecraft's mythos, but what has happened yet with that is that it's become extensive enough and detailed enough to provide a broad range of material to work with. It could be, though, that that's only a matter of time.

Perhaps a couple of centuries from now, Cthulhu could be worshipped as openly and publicly as any other deity. What started as a kind of literary in-joke has spread, become a meme, and taken on its own life, even its own reality. That would be truly funny, and an emblem of how unseriously and ironically we should treat religion. I mean, Scientology calls itself a religion, and yet it was invented – dreamed up out of whole cloth – by a pulp-fiction author. It's the proverbial "lie big enough" that became a truth.

MM: I know this will be a tough question to answer, and I really shouldn't ask it, but I'm going to anyway. Which, so far, Pantheon title is your personal favourite, and why is it thus? What makes, for you, your chosen titles stand out from the others and why?

James: Really can't answer that. I've enjoyed writing each one but for different reasons. I think *Zeus* comes closest to my idea of a nice, fat paperback thriller and comes out punching and just doesn't stop. Plus, it has monsters. But then *Aztec* has the copious bloodshed, the endless guts and gore, and *Odin* I love just because the narrator character, Gid, took over almost from page 1 and I hardly had to tell the story, I just sat back and let him do the work.

MM: You're also part of the team responsible for Comic Heroes, and being a four colour fan myself, I wanted to ask you a few questions about the medium… Have you ever though about maybe making the transition to the world of comics and working on a book or two, and if so, which existing titles would you love to get your (writing) hands on and why? If you were given your own book, which artists would you like to be paired with? And, yeah, you guessed it, why…?

James: I would love to write a comic, but I would also prefer to be asked rather than pitching for it. At this stage in my life and career, I don't have the time to go around knocking on editors' doors with a proposal and then having to follow it up and keep getting their attention in order to secure the commission. There are very few existing comics titles that I'd like to write, since most of them are already being scripted by very able, sometimes even brilliant people and I wouldn't want to have to follow in their footsteps. I'd be too scared. However, what I would like is to be given the opportunity to revisit some of the Marvel characters I loved in the seventies – the esoteric left-field ones like Killraven, Deathlok, Howard the Duck, Man-Thing, Omega the Unknown, Skull the Slayer, Gabriel the Devil Hunter, Sons of the Tiger – and revive them without jettisoning the things that made them great at that time. As for artists, the aforementioned Adam Brockbank would be one of my first choices, but I'd also love to work with George Pérez, Bryan Hitch, Tonci Zonjic, Jock, Alberto Ponticelli, D'israeli, Frazer Irving, Frank Quitely... and if he were alive, Kirby. I don't have to explain the last, but as for the others, I think each is brilliant in his own way and brings more than just artistic skill to his work – brings passion and inventiveness and true vision.

MM: Okay, pinning you down James. If you had to pick five comics to recommend to someone, which five books would you choose and why would you recommend them?

James: *Watchmen*, obviously. *All-Star Superman*, because it's both respectful and sublime. Dan Slott's current run on *Spider-Man*, which is the best Spidey's been in, oh ages, and probably the best superhero title on the shelves. Kirby's *Fourth World* saga, for the pure, unbridled imagination of it and the melancholic sense of incompletion that hangs over it, the feeling of a work cut down in its prime. *Planetary*, just because it is both writer (Warren Ellis) and artist (John Cassaday) in their prime; they put everything they had into it, and it shows.

MM: What's next for you James?

James: I'm busy with *Age Of Voodoo*, which welds a men-on-a-mission plot to, well, voodoo. It's coming along nicely, and since voodoo – *vodou* as it's properly called – is a working, living religion I'm being as respectful as I can towards it while at the same time using it shamelessly as a source of pulpy thrills. *Redlaw: Red Eye* is coming out this autumn, a sequel which sees John Redlaw bringing his vampire-policing skills and absence of personal tact to the east coast of America. I've also just been commissioned to write a couple of Sherlock Holmes novels for Titan Books, the first of which features a steampunk-superhero and the second of which is to be set in my hometown, Eastbourne, since Holmes is reputed to have retired to a village nearby to keep bees. In fact, you can go visit the cottage where he spent his last few years. It's in a village about two miles west of where I am right now, and there's a blue plaque on the wall commemorating its famous resident. Because Holmes really existed, of course...

MM: If there's anything that you'd like to add, speak now or forever hold your peace...?

James: Blimey, I think I've blathered on plenty, don't you? Let the rest be silence.

Originally published in Mass Movement #33, August 2012

JUSTIN MELKMANN

Folks, meet Justin Melkmann, guitarist with, and founding member of World War IX and cartoonist, writer and comic publisher extraordinaire. I could tell you all about Justin, about his incredible comics that incorporate the sense of fun, mischief and honesty of Robert Crumb and The Freak Brothers, cranked to eleven as they document punk rock life in NYC, his obsession with GG Allin and the raging tunes that World War IX kick out on a regular basis. I could do that, sure, But I won't. I'll leave that to Justin…

Interview by Tim Cundle

Photographs and artwork courtesy of Justin Melkmann.

MM: It's always best to start at the beginning - Introductions time. Who is Justin Melkmann and what makes him tick?

Justin: I like long walks off of short piers, hang gliding and Mexican food. I once saw an alien after partying too hard and I love television. I have over 4000 records and I hate thinly veiled cries for help on Facebook. Music makes me tick. Anything from the heart. Punk rock, country, soul…I love it all.

MM: Let's talk comics. When did you first become interested in comics? What attracted you to the medium, and what made you want to write and publish your own comics?

Justin: The moment I pulled a *Ghost Rider #1* out of an Atlantic City dumpster at the age of 6 I was hooked forever. A flaming skull riding a red hot chopper? Come ON! What could be better? What I liked most about the medium was that I could enjoy it by myself at my own pace. I'm a bit dyslexic. I had to write and publish my own books because I was running out of things to read. I got sick of the glut of "woe is me" indie books, and let's face it, most super hero comics blow.

MM: Most writers and artists can trace their "careers" back to one early, important break. What was your "break", how did you feel when you got it, and how did you feel and react when your work was first published?

Justin: My break was having some of my worst shit ever published in a high end/low culture magazine called *Eye*. Looking back I can't believe ANYONE would have published my one panel, poorly drawn junk. But they did. Thank God. I felt like I could die happy. I didn't play in a band yet, so the only creative outlet I had was comics. But it was the NYC downtown music and art paper of record, *New York Waste*, agreeing to publish the series I was doing about my love for GG that really kind of changed my life. At least at this point I had some confidence in my ideas. The drawings were still weak, but the writing came very easy to me.

MM: We've got to talk about GG Allin. Why, on reflection, do you think you became obsessed with the man and his music, and what made you want to document both his life and your life documenting his in a comic book? Your initial strip, as we've already mentioned, changed direction and focus due to Merle (Allin) right? Do you want to tell us what happened? How did your relationship with Merle change from your initial encounter with him, to later working with him?

Justin: Oh GG let me count the ways I love you. I always liked music that fell on the uh...wacky side of the spectrum, and what can I say... He's the king of wacky? Honestly, I was in a VERY bad place in my life when I was turned on to GG and he made me laugh and want to punch holes in walls. His songs are nothing less than genius, something hard to convince people of (and I've been trying for years...most of the time succeeding). He was one of the few people that seemed as angry and unhappy as I was, and he was doing something about it. The man was a doer.

Yes, it's true, at first I was doing a straight biography of GG. Merle and I worked on the definitive GG bio for about 6 months, but fifty pages in, it fell into the abyss. About two years later, I decided to take that research and do a comic. Merle was not happy about that. It was one of the worst days of my life when he "asked me to stop." I was JUST starting to get a following as a comic artist and here, and I've got to worry about my safety? What could I do? I wanted to honor Merle's request because he and I always did get along, and I always had the utmost respect for him. So fuck, I just changed a biography into an autobiography. I went from writing about GG, to writing about my love for GG. That decision was the best thing that I could have done. I mail my book out every week to all parts of the globe, and it's MY story. Cheers to that. I gave a copy once to the singer of GWAR and he said, "Wow, there should be a Dave Brockie biography." I'm sure it would be a good read, but I have no interest in telling someone else's story ever again... Better to live a life worthy of its own biography. Merle and I have made up. I'm seeing the Murder Junkies in a few weeks and can't wait.

MM: What is it about GG that attracted, and still attracts people to his music, as, more than any other "underground musician", he's achieved this 'cult of personality' type fame that continues to drive his legacy nearly twenty years after his death? You knew the man, so how did the GG you knew differ (if at all) from the widely held view that he was, quite literally, mad, bad and dangerous to know? A shit flinging, sex and drugs obsessed rock-n-roll terrorist...?

Justin: He's as far as you can go if you like punk rock and wild behavior. If you don't care about these things, you will NOT like him...Well, except for the Jabbers, everyone loves them. And they are incredible. I only knew him a little bit, but I will say the thing that a lot of people might not know is how fucking funny he was. And if he wasn't "on", he was plenty nice and easy to talk with. I wanted to publish a book of all of the absurd rumors I've heard about him over the years. "Is it true that GG used to dig up graves?" No. "Dude, is it true that GG used to drink the blood of AIDS patients?" Yes....well, no, but some kid out there needs to believe that. Kinda like a reverse Santa Claus.

MM: Are you still working on the definitive GG biography and will it ever see the light of day? Or is that a thing of the past, and if so, do you think you'll ever go back and revive the idea?

Justin: The only way I'd ever finish what I started is if Merle wanted to do it, and I'd be shocked if that happened. Not to mention, I just got all uppity in question #4 about writing someone else's story, and I can't go back on my word now. Oh god, what have I done!!!!

MM: Moving on to *Earaches & Eyesores* your comic. The book documents the life and times of an NYC punk rock band, World War IX (your band) and its members (in particular your own life) and their constant struggle to put the punk back into the lives of punks everywhere. It's truthful to a fault, completely honest and pulls no punches, so I was wondering if by barring your soul and putting it all out there, you've ever upset anyone or anyone has ever reacted negatively to being included in its pages, as everyone is the hero in their own story and when confronted by their own behaviour from another's perspective, rarely act appropriately or pause to think that their actions may have affected someone else. On a lighter note, what's the overall reaction been like so far? How do most people react to the book, and how do you think it's evolved since the first issue?

Justin: "Truthful to a fault", that's funny. As far as I know I've never upset anyone, not yet at least. Most of the time I'm fully aware of my role in the bad shit that goes down, and that's what I choose to write about. People are so complicated and I know EVERYONE has their own reasons for acting the way they do, and I take full responsibility for my actions. That said, about a year ago, our drummer, THEE Jon Kleinman, reminded me of a great Hell's Angels' saying: "Treat me good, I'll treat you better. Treat me bad, I'll treat you worse." And that's kind of the subject of my new book I'm about 75% done with.

The overall reaction to my work has been incredible. I'm genuinely touched by some of the letters I've gotten. I guess people do like shit that's "Truthful to a fault". For example I straight up wrote about how scared I was of GG and Merle...that sentiment got to a lot of people. I suppose it would be easy to act tough, hiding behind a pen and paper, but fuck that. That's fantasy, and I don't do fantasy...yet. I do like knights and cowboy crap though.

MM: Sticking with *Earaches & Eyesores*, it almost feels like a punk rock version of Gilbert Shelton's *The Freak Brothers*, but with less drugs and more booze, and has a counter-culture vibe running through its pages, so I was curious about what influenced you as a writer and artist, and how you think these influences manifest themselves in your books and how they've changed, inspired and affected your output since you began publishing your books?

Justin: In terms of my comics what influenced me the most was early John Waters, Woody Allen, and R. Crumb...typical smart-ass white guy shit. But from my own life? Hanging out in dingy NYC bars for THE ENTIRE DECADE OF THE NINTIES! I used to go home drunk and try and draw some of the nuts I'd befriended just hours before, but I couldn't do it of course, I was too drunk! I'm inspired every day I ride the train to work. Talk about your freak parades! Sometimes it's frightening, but mostly it's a riot. I'm influenced by the other bands and artists I see and work with on a daily basis. My buddy Sergio Zuniga is a constant source of inspiration. He brings low-brow to a new high in his artwork. Steve Vincent and all the guys at Angry Drunk graphics make life worth living.

MM: You're planning an animated film based on *Earaches & Eyesores* right? Do you want to tell us about it?

Justin: Sure! It's more like an ongoing series of animated shorts based on my comics. Mr. Kleinman and I are putting together a 1 to 2 minute short, every couple of months that features the music of some of the incredible bands we play with on a regular basis. People always say "It's not like it used to be." Well, we are SURROUNDED by GREAT artists and musicians, and we want to celebrate that fact.

MM: Which brings us to World War IX. When, where and why did the band come together, and what made you want to make the transition from fan and someone who documented the life of a musician to becoming a musician yourself? What made you want to play?

Justin: The band started when old friends of mine kinda nudged me aside from their new band only to be saddled with one of their boyfriends. He was a HUGE talent and wanted to start a band called The Diarrhea Family. I told him I too wanted to be in a band, but not one called The Diarrhea Family. I'd been in one band that was just about done when this guy approached me. I knew I didn't want to go back to a life of not rocking, so we decided to give it a whirl. He's long gone, along with a bunch of others. WWIX is almost as much an art project as it is a band, and I didn't want it to stop because one guy can't handle his shit, or another guy loses his nerve. Hey, it's not for everyone, but that's not my problem. As far as what made me transition from being a fan to a musician? Turning 28 and realizing that I didn't want to keep talking about OTHER people's bands. I wanted to contribute something of my own to my record collection, and at 28 years old, I was staring the rest of my life in the face and unless I got off the couch and out of the cooler, it wasn't going to be pretty.

MM: How easy or difficult is it to be in a punk rock band in the city that gave birth to punk rock? What makes you keep playing?

Justin: It's a piece of cake. The Ramones invented it, and didn't really know how to play, and that's what it's all about, for me at least. I can only play bar chords and I'm ok with that. I see a ton of much better guitar players, but who cares? I don't. I'm just happy I can write songs that I like to listen to. Also, Kleinman and I are now working with a great couple of mega talented, good people, and if you can get along in the rehearsal room, on the road, and at the show…that's the most important part to staying together. What KEEPS us playing? Why compliments and drink tickets of course…what else is there?

MM: What are your, so far, favourite and least favourite memories / stories associated with World War IX? Would you like to share both with us….?

Justin: Least favorite memories? Too many to count. Most favorite? Double it! I hate having to kick people out, but it's never done until the situation has gotten that bad, and the rest of the band agrees with each other. Having to deal with ex band members publicly wetting themselves on the internet is never fun, but always seems to yield good publicity, so that's great. What else is great is plugging in my guitar at every show we've ever played. I don't think I've ever NOT wanted to play. I was once told by someone that band practice should be as fun and exciting as playing a show, and I would agree with that. I never get bored of playing our songs, and I suppose I'm lucky. Most people I know don't like playing the same songs over and over, but I love it. Honestly, I still can't believe it's me doing it. I like playing the old stuff just as much as coming up with new masterpieces! I like the fact that I'm losing track of the shows we play, and I no longer obsess about our gigs. I always envied people who could hold conversations and actually be somewhat relaxed before they play. Now...after some time I feel like I'm there. I still get nervous, but that feels good. Good Nervous.

MM: You guys, that is WWIX, have a new EP out right? Do you want to tell us about it? How, if at all, do you think it differs from your previous records?

Justin: It's true! We do have a new 5 song EP out. It features the new line up that has Philly Phill on vocals and Brian Jackson on bass. Also what's new is that there's only ONE tune about drinking. It's the title track called Bender Royale and it kinda sums up the misery of having TOO MUCH FUN. Phill came up with some fantastic lyrics for the record, and Brian is a god-damn MONSTER on the bass. The mofo plays lead guitar on his four string, which works great with my dumbed down, pile driver, guitar playing inabilities.

MM: How, in your opinion, has the punk rock scene, both on a local and global level, changed since WWIX started playing out, and do you think those changes have been beneficial or detrimental to the scene as a whole? Why?

Justin: That's hard to say since we're all so self-absorbed! HA! Seriously though, and I touched on this before...there's so much talk about how it's not like it used to be, but what are you going to do? Time machine's haven't been invented yet and I like my life right now. I don't wish WWIX lived in a different time, or long for days of yore when there was a "better scene". Things were better because you were 15 and life was MAYBE (if you were lucky) not as oppressive. I love most of the bands we play with and all the people who come to our shows. I've been reading that punk is dead since I was 12, but if you go to an all ages show in say Queens, and you see a TON of kids AND adults of all ages, going bonkers, jumping off pool tables and only giving each other the highest of fives, the current state of punk rock seems to be doing just fine. Sure, commercial punk sucks, but I suppose people often forget that the Sex Pistols started as a way for Malcolm McClaren to sell his fucking clothes clothing. I don't care what shit bands do or have to say or how silly they look. I do know that since we've started it is, thanks to the internet, much easier to hear more great bands from around the world, and there's nothing wrong with that. Sometimes I miss the hunt, for a great record in a music store, but now the hunting ground has just changed to the inside of my computer.

MM: Okay, time to start wrapping things up I guess, so if you were forced to (which I guess you sort of are), which five comics would you recommend to anyone and everyone, and why would you recommend them? What makes them, in your opinion, stand out from the rest of the pack?

Justin: Like I mentioned earlier, anything by Sergio Zuniga or the guys on the Angry Drunk Graphics site is worth checking out for SURE. One of the funniest things I've scene recently is a drawing Sergio did of a tourist eating Chinese food in front of The Leaning Tower of Pisa. Fucking perfect. No words needed. *Alcoholic* by Johnathan Ames will tare your heart out. *My Friend Dahmer* by Derf is the best new thing I've read. A buddy of mine Julie Condon has some KILLER stuff out now. I got a book of hers called *Strabismus* which is pretty great. Personal stories that make me laugh and put a lump in my throat.

MM: What's next for you and WWIX Justin?

Justin: Well, we've got band practice on Thursday. Oooooh, you mean "Big Picture" What's next? RIGHT. Well, we're working on the title track to a new horror movie, new tunes for a new EP, and we really want to tour Europe next summer. We've crossed the U.S. before so Europe seems like the logical progression. Let's see, breast reduction surgeries all around, keeping away from brown liquors, and generally causing a mess where and whenever we can.

MM: If there's anything that you'd like to add, now's the time. Speak now or forever hold your peace...

Justin: Anything else? Shit, ain't you sick of reading about me yet?! Thanks so much for letting me talk about myself for so long.

Originally published in Mass Movement #33, August 2012

MARK OF THE VAMPIRE
THE LITERARY TRACES OF A BLOODSUCKER

Will there ever be an end to the undead? I mean, it's quite a stretch that the sixteenth president of the United States would be slaying an army of bloodsuckers with an axe. Leave it to Hollywood to capitalize on such a bizarre storyline. It seems that no matter who's playing the role of a Van Helsing-type character, the foe is always the same.

As far back as ancient Babylon, vampires have been a part of native folklore in one way or another. The Babylonian's fascination with the bat and their belief that to drink human blood could extend one's mortal existence is a very interesting concept, indeed. Perhaps this is the basis for the folklore about vampires being able to assume the shape of a bat, even though there is no mention made of the fact in Babylonian culture.

Along the same lines, the early Greek civilization had a penchant for a female vampire known as a Lamia. Legend suggests that the creature would seduce members of the opposite sex and drink their blood by way of the mouth. Sucking the man's tongue from its placement, the Lamia would siphon his lifeblood and continue until he was drained dry. This gives a whole new meaning to the term "French Kiss."

As disgusting as this sounds, however, it only goes from bad to worse. The Lamia would then tie the victim's tongue to her collection of past unfortunates to create a whip, and she would flagellate prospective victims into submission.

Another creature closely associated to a vampire whose name is derived from the French word "revinir," to return, is the revenant. More like a ghost than a vampire, the revenant would rise from the grave and harass past associates rather than harm them. There are historical accounts of encounters with such a creature by so-called reputable individuals.

One such individual was the 12th century English historian, William of Newburgh (1137-1198). Newburgh was emphatic about the existence of revenants that walked the earth, claiming to have unfinished business with mortal beings. Newburgh, himself, is said to have witnessed one of these creatures roaming in the streets of a near-by village and calling out the names of the local inhabitants. When asked to prove his chance meetings, however, Newburgh, like so many other believers, could not produce a shred of evidence. In reality, these accounts have long been ruled out as individuals with overactive imaginations.

But the true test of a vampire's strength is in the popularity of the written word. *Varney the Vampire* was a fictional, gothic horror story printed in serial form that made its debut in 1845 and sold for a penny a copy. Also referred to as a "penny dreadful," the sheer volume of the serial was extraordinary, reaching 700,000 words in total and amassing 220 chapters. Eventually in 1847, the entire series was printed in book form.

Sir Francis Varney is the central character who, for dubious and inconclusive reasons, has an extreme dislike for the Bannerworths family. Author James Malcolm Rymer is unable to clearly develop Varney's character in terms of motivation and intention.

Although Varney displays many of the same legendary Vampiric characteristics of Eastern European folklore (he has two fangs, leaves puncture wounds on his victim's throat, has hypnotic powers, and has superhuman strength), he is driven more by monetary greed rather than his need for blood. The author is also very vague as to the time period of the story.

Over the course of the book, Varney is presented with increasing sympathy as a victim of circumstances. He tries to save himself but is unable to do so. He ultimately commits suicide by throwing himself into Mount Vesuvius, after having left a written account of his origin with a sympathetic priest. According to Varney, he was cursed with vampirism after he had betrayed a royalist to Oliver Cromwell and accidentally killed his own son afterwards in a fit of anger, although he "dies" and is revived several times in the course of his career. This afforded the author a variety of origin stories.

Of all things, Varney is an interesting collection of Vampiric lore, no matter how exaggerated and undefined the storyline seems to be.

All things considered, the character of Varney no doubt had an influence on Bram Stoker when he decided to create the most famous of all literary vampires – Dracula.

Doug Crill

Originally published in Mass Movement #33, August 2012

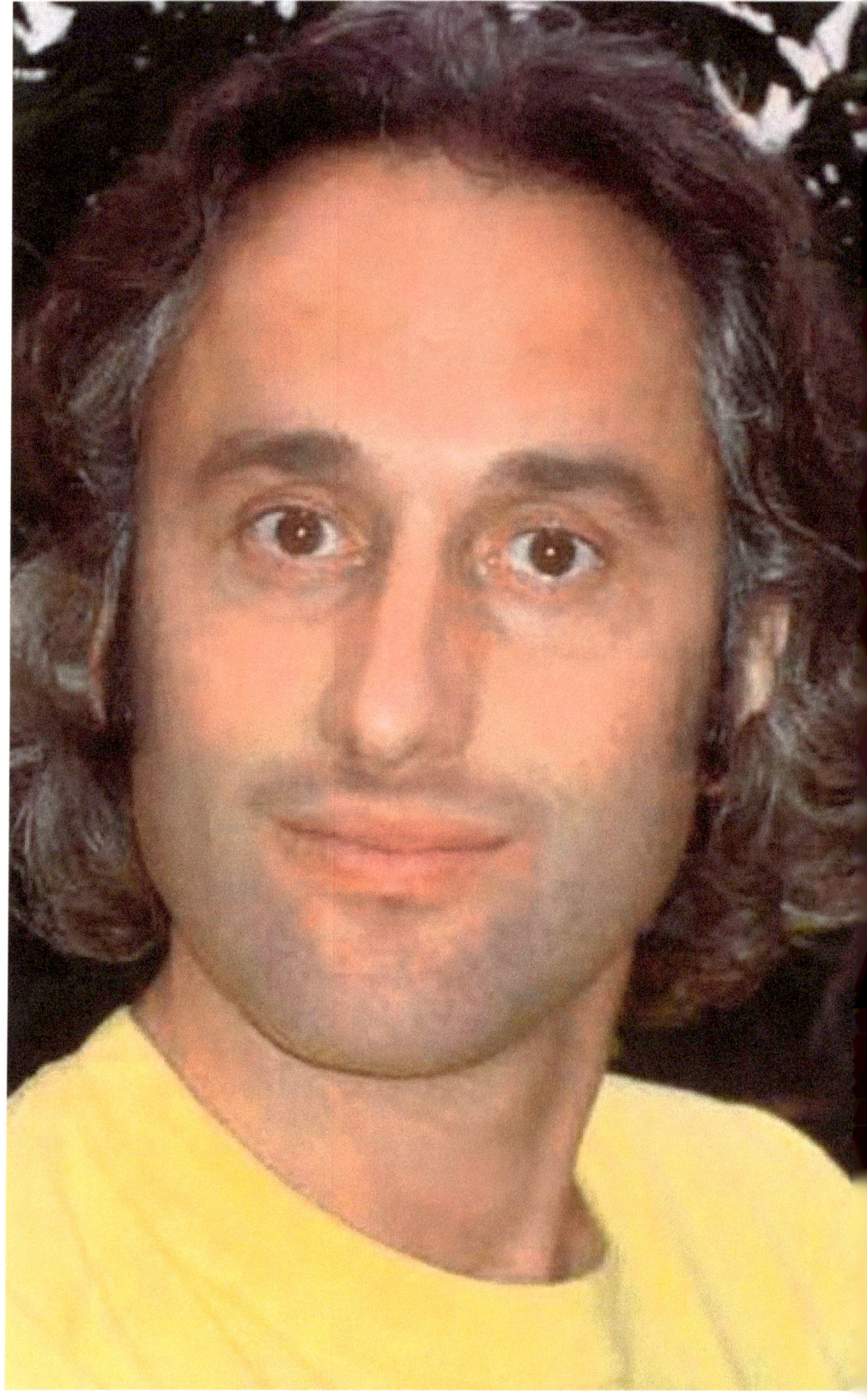

NOW THEN GADGIE...
THINGS THAT SCARED ME SENSELESS WHEN I WAS A BAIRN...

The long mooted and will they, won't they, return of the Hammer Horror studio a few years ago was, of course, cause for great celebration in Gadgie Towers. Along with *Monty Python's Flying Circus*, Hammer Horror flicks with their lurid boobs and blood adolescent hormone baiting were staple ingredients of post-Match of the Day Saturday night viewing on the BBC back when I was a bairn. Whether it was the Pythons or yet another entry in to the eternal Christopher Lee vs Peter Cushing conflict one thing said to me Marv, you have to sit and watch this my lad, you'll be a better person for it!" One simple thing meant these two monolithic slabs that appeared to my impressionable monkey mind were must watches.

My Dad didn't like them. Not being a fan of footy, our Dad would disappear for a bath or summat when I sat glued to the telly watching the likes of Frank Stapleton, Kenny Dalglish and never Middlesbrough before descending the stairs to lock up and send everyone to bed. One night though ... one night ... as Match of the Day's fanfare faded the spinning globe BBC voice over thing appears and informs us that classic British comedy *Monty Python's Flying Circus* was starting before the station shut down for the night. Suggesting I may give a go, Father decreed "You aren't gonna watch them idiots are you? That's as old the hills!" Needless to say that was a recommendation and considering *The Young Ones* was banned in our house, I gave it a go and life was never the same again ... but my obsession with Python is another story for another day ... a similar experience happened one glorious evening when after Dr Who. or *The Tripods* (it might even have been after 3.2.1.) when the evening's roster was announced with little clips of everything: "... and rounding off the night some classic horror with *Dracula Has Risen From The Grave*!" One flash of Count Dracula's menacing eyes and a glimpse of fang was enough to send me and our lad bonkers. We have to watch that!

And, again, the patronising, world weariness that only adults have, was visited upon us. "You won't like that, it's as old as the hills!" No Father. You were wrong. Very wrong. For we did sit up and watch Match of the Day and then instead of climbing sleepy mountain to bed, we sauntered down shit scary street to Transylvania or where ever Hammer Horror would have us believe it was set. Innocent and naive travellers would chance upon villages rapt in fear of some silly superstition, warnings given would go unheeded, tavern wenches would mysteriously disappear, Christopher Lee would rise from the grave and Michael Ripper was always the bar tender. I was completely and utterly smitten with being absolutely terrified and sought as much horror as you could in the days when there were only three channels and before video rental shops became our Mecca. There are from this strange period of time (a sort of "waiting room" before *Zombie Flesh Eaters and I Spit On Your Grave*) however a number of telly related things that utterly scared the living doodles out me and to this very day have left a lasting impression. I reckon if I saw 'em now I'd think nowt of it but to a pre internet, pre video nasty, pre George Romero, pre punk, little fella like me, who was yet to see Sadako climb out of the telly on *Ringu* late one night on Channel 4, who hadn't even seen *The Exorcist* let alone the bit where the nurse gets followed in *Exorcist III*, I will never forget the following terrifying telly terrors ...

At number five in this most pant filling of recollections is *Jaws*. Everyone's seen *Jaws*. It was one of the very first "Big Summer Blockbusters™" that I can recall. I saw a trailer for it at the cinema before Sammy's Super T Shirt or The Battle For Billy's Pond or something but we were too young to get in to see an X certificate even though everyone at school pretended they'd seen it. So when it finally came round to being on telly one Friday night, everyone watched it, even though "Yeah, think I will watch it, even though I've, you know, seen it a load of times and it's not actually that scary, 'cos I'm so nails". Time has dimmed my opinion of Spielberg's classic, and because it is considered one of the all-time greats, its power as a scary movie has somewhat been forgotten. It certainly wasn't forgotten that night. We all asked if we could leave Meccano Club early when it was on to go home and watch *Jaws*. It really was an event when there was a big movie premiere on in those days. Our Meccano Club leader wasn't particularly impressed with our mass exodus ... and yes I did go to a Meccano Club, another time, I promise ... there's plenty of column inches in that one ... but anyway ... we'd seen a leg fall to the bottom of the sea which was pretty disturbing, we'd heard the iconic dur dur "sharks coming to eat you to death" theme, but when an upturned boat is investigated and a head, yes a fucking head, falls out of the crack in the boat I almost had an accident and I'm not talking about falling off me Chopper bike! The film was great, and still is, but that head falling out of the boat, with its glassy stare and sudden, jarring appearance haunted my dreams for days and days, and even though they wouldn't admit it, most of my class mates, judging by the multitude of conversations starting with "Did you see that bit whine that man's head falls out the boat?" were rather scarred by it 'n all.

Number four in our horrifying highlights is a bizarre one. Bear with me but *Watcher In The Woods* is a Disney Horror. Yes, you are reading that right. A Disney Horror. Set in England with an aging Bette Davis playing a batty old dear in a stately home that harbours a terrible secret, this oddity in the House of Mouse's output proved genuinely unsettling to me as a nipper. An American family – mother and two kids who failed the audition for the *Red Hand Gang* – move to a mansion in England. Of course this is "England" as in the stiff upper lip, butlers, house maids, mansions, china tea sets and everyone talking with a plum in their gob as only the Americans do and Bette Davis is the enigmatic woman in the window every good haunted house flick has. The teenage daughter starts seeing strange lights in the woods next to the house and investigates. There's a missing child story that unfolds and the obligatory assortment of gentle "bump in the night" shenanigans which all build up to a pretty wimpy, nice ending that you'd expect with Disney. Come on, the whole cast were never in any danger of being slaughtered were they? A scene with a mirror however, proved to be utterly devastating to my innocent and easily influenced mind. Looking in a mirror in the vast mansion our heroine sees herself as you'd expect but with a blindfold on! I'm sure the mirror cracked or something but the idea that you look in a mirror and see a different reflection was enough to give me the heebie jeebies about brushing me hair for a fortnight! Mirrors were to be avoided from then on! What's that you say? Quite a good policy with my looks ... you cheeky get.

Our third macabre moment is something of a long lost piece of petrifying programming. I've never, ever, seen it again and for some years actually believed that it didn't exist and was all part of some dream I had. Holy shit though *The Bells of Astercote* was real and made the Daleks look like Rod, Jane and Freddy. It appeared on our screens one Christmas, the day before Christmas Eve in fact, though festive cheer was in very short supply after watching this spookfest! I seem to recall it even being on at tea time in the kids telly slot but may be wrong. Anyhow, it all focuses on a couple of kids, the girl called Mair stands out as it's an odd name, who move to a sleepy village where peculiar things do happen. A buried chalice, a mute kid, a haunted wood, a host of superstitious British bumpkin caricatures and ghostly bells ringing that only

Mair can hear ... or something. It turns out that a long extinct village once stood here but was decimated by the plague back in the mists of time. Superstition abounds and the chalice is some sort of potent warder off of evil and so long as it isn't moved from ... blah blah blah you get the picture. So far so kids telly but then ... Mair, bless her, is atuned to some sort of supernatural portal to the past and she sees the plague sufferers, the white crosses on doors of the afflicted and worse off all, a chilling scene where a rotting plague victim reaches towards her with the awful incessant moaning "The sickness ... the sickness". This scene absolute froze the blood in my veins and for months I lay in bed imagining a plague carrier stumbling up the stairs reaching out to me with decaying digits and the macabre mantra "The sickness ... the sickness ..." Me and our lad would wander in to each other's bedroom on a morning, arms out in front of us moaning this awful adage for weeks. I have never seen it again and my brother is the only other person I know who has seen it, but the indelible mark it left on me is to this day, a vivid memory of that wretched plague victim and the sickness ... the sickness.

Penultimate petrifier, and probably the first slasher movie I ever saw: *Dark Night of the Scarecrow*. If *The Bells of Astercote* was a sort of pre zombie obsession primer, then this nasty little TV movie definitely set me up for a lifetime of watching gangs of decision making-ly challenged teens getting offed by a masked killer in a series of gruesome set pieces. All I remember is a huge fella called Bubba who was a mahusive red neck in dungarees with a body of a grizzly bear and the mind of a three year old child getting stitched up for killing a little girl. I seem to recall him holding her lifeless body and saying "Bubba didn't do it!" and then hiding in a scarecrow (I kid you not) before a possie of rootin' tootin', double denim, mesh cap and tobacco chewing chunder heads take brutal retribution and Bubba is summarily executed. While disguised as a scarecrow. Or summat. It may seem contrived but yep, you guessed it, the mob of murderers get their comeuppance as a scarecrow stalks the farm yards and barns dispatching them with an assortment of heavy machinery and tools. My abiding memory is of someone falling in to a threshing machine of some sort and the camera cutting away as his screams give way to a splatter of blood and grue flying up in the air. My memory is hazy on this one but the sight of a scarecrow killing folk stuck in my mind and try as I might, every other exploration of the "scarecrow killer sub-genre" has never lived up to that first barn yard bloodbath and corn field carnage!

... And finally, my most shreddies shredding, wabs worrying, cushion grabbing, waking up screaming moment of telly based kiddie nightmares is the original BBC adaptation of faux Victorian horror *The Woman In Black*. This brings things full circle as I started out talking about the re-emergence of Hammer and their new, not as good as this one, take on the novel/play/film is just out on DVD now. The latest version sees Harry Potter himself being spooked and chased around a stylised haunted house with nods to J-Horror's lights down the corridor, creepy kid routines aplenty and to be honest it has its fair share of predictable but fun scares. When compared to the adaptation the BBC screened one Christmas in the eighties however, Master Radcliffe gets off lightly. A solicitor is sent to deal with the estate of a deceased woman who lives in a huge house at the end of a causeway that gets cut off from everywhere whenever the tide comes in. We all know the plot by now as the new film has been heavily hyped but this older take on it is far more chilling because it doesn't lay it on thickly. The house isn't a clichéd old house with cobwebs and rickety furniture. Scares happen in daylight or a normal looking building and because it's not in a "ghost train" of a set like you'd find Scooby Doo on, it appears more "real". The woman in black is just that as well. A pasty faced woman in black but not a horrific vision like we get in the latest movie. The fact she is "just a normal woman" who everyone seems to want to deny is there is a far more enigmatic and mysterious device and sets us up for an ending that will just fucking kill you. Alright we all know the new, Hammer one has an

awful wimpy ending that borders on the Christian (for fucks sake) but no such luck back in the eighties. Sitting up late to watch a spooky Victorian ghost story, maybe a bit Turn of the Screw, maybe like those Christopher Lee narrated *A Ghost Story For Christmas* type things they used to show ... yeah right. As we think we are watching a happy ending unravel there she is ... the Woman in Black standing on the fucking river and everyone dies! Holy fucking shit! The icy glare on her face and the fact she is stood on a river as our hero rows his family around before a huge tree falls over and drowns the lot of 'em made me shout out loud something like "Fuck!" waking Dad up and incurring his wrath for watching that rubbish. It's as old the hills you know...

Marv Gadgie

Originally published in Mass Movement #33, August 2012

SCREEN DAMAGE
HURTS TO BE DEAD

When I first saw *The Return Of The Living Dead* as an impressionable young teenager, it wasn't the outrageous gore that caught my attention. The self-referential pitch black humour and full-frontal nudity had a certain appeal, true, but what really spoke to me was the amazing punk rock soundtrack. Or as the character Suicide puts it: *"You think this is a fuckin' costume? This is a way of life!"*

My experience of most eighties American movie soundtracks at that point had taught me that they were the dumping ground for any number of bloody awful AOR bands (I'm looking at you, 'Karate Kid'). But thanks to music consultant Steve Pross, *The Return Of The Living Dead* offered a veritable who's who of cool alternatives to the bland, mulleted keyboard-rockers doing the Hollywood rounds back then. Some of the names in the credits were better known to me than others, but there wasn't a bad song to be found among them.

For the – ahem - record, the movie soundtrack offered up *Surfin' Dead* by The Cramps, *Party Time* by 45 Grave, *Nothing For You* by T.S.O.L, *Eyes Without A Face* by The Flesh Eaters, the demented *Burn The Flames* by Roky Erickson, *Dead Beat Dance* by The Damned, *Take A Walk* by Tall Boys, *Love Under Will* by Jet Black Cherries and *Tonight (We'll Make Love Until We Die)* by SSQ, plus its eerie refrain, *Trash's Theme*.

But it could have all been so different – the movie was well into pre-production when the producers decided to change the soundtrack deals for the bands, meaning that they would lose the rights to their featured songs.

More than one group refused to co-operate with this and jumped ship, most noticeably Sid Terror's self-styled kings of gore-core, The Undead. They had produced no less than four songs for the movie – *Undead Anthem*, *My Girlfriend*, *Everybody's Dead* and *Zombie Army* – which left a large hole for Pross to fill (The Undead later released their missing songs as *Return of the Living Demos: THE ORIGINAL Original Soundtrack* – check them out on YouTube and MySpace, you won't be disappointed).

Their departure was good news for 45 Grave as it meant that the reworked version of their signature tune, *Party Time*, moved up to take centre stage, eventually becoming even better known than The Cramps' track which everyone expected would be the album's main talking point.

The original version of *Party Time* drew controversy for its depiction of the real-life rape and murder of a five year old child, but singer Dinah Cancer has also said that the song depicts how the little girl discovers that for her, heaven is an eternal birthday party – thus qualifying it as rather sweet by 45.Grave standards. The lyrics were heavily reworked for *The Return Of The Living Dead* to give the song more of a zombie theme, and it served to underscore the start of the onscreen mayhem.

And there's certainly plenty of that - nobody comes out of *The Return Of The Living Dead* feeling like they've been short-changed.

The film began as a novel by John Russo, the co-writer of *Night Of The Living Dead* who intended the screen version of his book to be a straight sequel to the 1968 George Romero ground breaker. Originally announcing that it was to be filmed in 3D by Tobe Hooper, the producers employed Dan O'Bannon to polish the script, then offered him a shot at directing the film when Hooper backed out to make *Lifeforce* for Cannon (which, ironically, was also scripted by 'O'Bannon).

O'Bannon agreed on the condition that he could rewrite the script from scratch – he really didn't want to encroach on what Romero had done with either the original film or his own sequel, *Dawn Of The Dead*. The producers agreed, and anyone who has read Russo's original novel will know that O'Bannon really ripped the guts out of it, and took the film in a whole new direction. By the time that the movie was released, Russo retained only a 'Story By' credit, but the only similarity to what he had originally planned was the title. Such is Hollywood...

O'Bannon's concept was simple but brilliant: he crafted his version of the film as one long sick joke which would play on what Romero had achieved while remaining visibly different.

To this end, he created a film-within-a-film scenario in which Romero is revealed to have based his own movie on real life events after the army created a chemical, Trioxin, which had the ability to bring the dead back to life. The undead corpses were packed into barrels and sent to a storage facility, only for a shipping error to misdirect them to a medical supplies warehouse where they were quietly stored in a dusty corner of the basement. Before the opening credits have even begun, the barrels have been breached, the chemicals are released and the local cemetery and morgue is soon beset by hordes of hungry zombies...

Arguably one of the best of the early 'splatstick' films that emerged in the eighties, *The Return Of The Living Dead* helped popularise later horror comedies such as *Bad Taste*, *Evil Dead II*, *Black Sheep*, *Frankenhooker*, *Evil Aliens*, *Shaun of the Dead*, *Severance*, *Zombieland* and *Tucker and Dale Vs Evil*.

Like *An American Werewolf In London* a few years before and *Reanimator*, *The Return Of The Living Dead* demonstrated the right way to mix horror with comedy. It broke new ground in that it used zombies as both its instrument of terror as well as laughs – for example, the classic scene where the hungry dead ambush the ambulance staff, then tell the radio dispatcher to "Send... more... paramedics!"

The film contributed a number of themes to cinematic zombie lore. For a start, it was one of the first to abandon the stiff, slow attacks generally associated with the living dead, instead letting them sprint and fight with gusto – a lesson not lost on the likes of *28 Days Later* or the *Dawn of the Dead* remake.

Then there was the issue of what exactly the zombies were after – no mindless gut-munching would satisfy these vicious ghouls, only fresh brains. The scene where the survivors snag a female zombie – well, half of her, anyway – in order to interrogate their enemy reveals that the zombies want brains in order to ease the pain of rotting away. Or as Ernie the mortician (a sublime Dan Calfa) puts it: "It hurts to be dead."

Zombies with an agenda, the ability to speak and, in the case of the principal flesheater known to fans as the Tar Man, the intelligence to use tools to get to their prey - all fresh concepts that have since been assimilated into the genre in various ways.

The Return Of The Living Dead also beat *Wes Craven's New Nightmare* and *Scream* to the punch by delivering a self-referential horror film with its tongue planted firmly inside its rotting cheek, too. It's telling that when first confronted by the zombies, the characters call on what they know from the movies to try and dispatch them. One pick-axe through the head later, they realise that destroying the brain simply isn't enough, leaving them to whine incredulously that the movies must have lied.

Besides the warehouse staff (led by Hollywood rebel Clu Gulager) and the mortician, the other main characters in the film are a group of young punks who are hanging out in the graveyard when the zombies crawl out of their graves. The production demonstrated just as much care with the look of the punks as they did with the authentic style of the bands on the soundtrack.

Special mention must be made of the late Mark Venturini, who played the intense, angry Suicide – a guy who is so tightly wound, he takes his hands off the steering wheel to start in-car fistfights and greets people with lines such as "Fuck you, ballbuster!" Ironically, his aforementioned comment about his pierced, bechained and shaven-headed look was exactly that – a costume – but the realistic feel helped the former high-school athlete shine in a memorable role before he sadly later succumbed to leukaemia.

Surprisingly, Linnea Quigley as the death-obsessed punker, Trash, was the only cast member with any kind of rock 'n' roll background in real life.

"I was playing in the band, The Skirts, but had that on the back burner since I was doing a lot of horror films and auditions," she said. *"With a band, you have to do a lot of work. We recorded and played gigs, but I wish I'd had the time to be more active. It was between stuff, we would record or play and rehearse, and you always have, y'know, the disappearing drummer."*

Given her fresh-faced roles in the likes of *Savage Streets* or *Night Of The Demons*, Quigley's career in such music may come as a surprise to many fans.

"I was more into the punk scene since I played underneath the Pussycat Theatre, but I couldn't go all the way. With acting, you can't go around with mohawks or you're really limited, and the girl-next-door was very popular then."

Despite her hilarious dead-pan delivery of her lines, Quigley was not the first choice for the role.

"I got the part of Trash because Stanzi Stokes, a casting director who had cast me in 'Silent Night, Deadly Night' called me to audition for a bunch of people," she said. *"Then I was called to audition for Dan and Graham with the character Spider (Miguel Nunez, who also appeared with Mark Venturini in 'Friday The 13th: A New Beginning' and who was allegedly homeless and sleeping rough when he got the role). I guess they had cast someone, then they had some money problems, and she had gotten pregnant in the meantime. Thank goodness - I never knew how it would change my life."*

The famous scene where Quigley performs a naked dance on top of a tombstone certainly changed *my* life.

"I didn't rehearse," Quigley said of the scene. *"I remember just getting up and doing it on the spot. I danced to Vanity's 'Nasty Girl', not the song that is in the movie (by SSQ)."*

Legend has it that the producers were so shocked by the full-frontal nudity and unabashed relish with which Quigley dances that they ordered O'Bannon to make her wear an invisible prosthetic over her vagina. But Quigley has a different take on this.

"I'm not sure if they were shocked by the footage," she laughed. *"Before we even shot, they made that prosthetic piece for me to wear. I heard Dan wanted me to look asexual, like a Barbie doll, but also it served to not get an X-rating."*

Quigley spent the remainder of the film running around in the rain wearing only a waistcoat and legwarmers.

"It was really hard for me," she said. *"Oh man, I wanted to say, stop, I'm cold and tired and want to go home! But you can't on a film, you gotta tough it out. I'm sure glad I did, I just tried to stay calm and know it was getting done, and I'd do it."*

Given her vegan lifestyle, Quigley wasn't around the night that O'Bannon gave the zombie extras a personal demonstration on how to eat the cow brains that were used in some of the gore scenes.

"I heard people turned a bit green. Dan was stressed since they were watching every penny, and he had a really clear vision and wanted to do it right the way he saw it. He lost weight and all and was pretty uptight, but did great. I had no problem with him."

Some of the other cast members had mixed feelings about their director, who passed away from Crohn's Disease in 2009.

"I didn't get along with Dan at all," remembers Beverly Randolph, who played Tina, the straightlaced good girl of the gang. *"I was young and he terrified me. I know that he wanted to get even with me for running out of his house after he requested that I 'run lines' with him. When I showed up at his home, he had a gun on the coffee table and porn on the television! When he went to answer the phone, I ran out claiming that I had forgotten about an appointment. From then on, he made my job very difficult."*

Randolph credits this fraught working relationship with why she dropped out of the movie business not long after making *The Return Of The Living Dead*.

"I quit soon after, I think, because I didn't have the best experience on 'Return' and thought I would go back when I wanted to. Other things caught my eye and I just never went back...I truly didn't know how lucky I was."

Some might wonder how a nice girl like Tina fell in with Hardcore punks with names like Trash, Scuz and Suicide, but Randolph has a simple answer to this.

"She fell in love with a bad boy," she said, referring to her onscreen boyfriend, Freddy, played by Thom Mathews.

Mathews appeared in *The Return Of The Living Dead Part 2* with his co-star James Karen, who played the doomed Frank here, but like Randolph, he also decided to leave the film industry.

"We keep in touch mostly via email and the occasional texting," Randolph said. "His texts can be very funny - he runs a construction company and builds high end 'Hollywood' homes now." John Philbin, who played horny nerd Chuck, didn't have any problems with his director, but was concerned with the length of time that the film took to get made.

"The casting process was toooo looong!" he said. "I was getting worried I might rehearse myself right out of a job. Dan was great with me, he did not have much to say and I don't think I would have understood him if he had. He was working on a much higher and deeper plane than me."

Chuck's attempts to woo Jewel Shepard as the stunning Casey provided the film with a lot of laughs – such as where he asks if she likes sex with death and she tells him "Yeah, so fuck off and die."

"Much like myself, Chuck was a poseur looking to hang out with the cool kids, avant-garde sexy tough chicks and scary badass dudes," John said. "I don't know Dan's intentions for Chuck, but I'm forever grateful that he let me get close to the stunning Linnea in the cemetery scene."

What about the scene where Shepard as Casey, faced with a zombie apocalypse, turns to Chuck and says "I never did like you - oh, but God, hold me tight!"?

"The foreplay was successful, the mission was eventually completed," John said. "We're still getting along famously, but I got no love on the set. She is a real badass chick."

One of the best scenes – in which Frank climbs into a crematorium to avoid becoming one of the living dead – came about because actor James Karen didn't want to film any of the cold, wet night shoots where the zombie hordes spread out into the city. He suggested the alternative demise seen on film to O'Bannon, who liked the idea and readily agreed to incorporate it into the script. With the added accompaniment of *Burn The Flames* by Roky Erickson, it stands out as a black highlight of the movie's tone and an example of O'Bannon's overall approach to the project – something which Quigley has confirmed.

"It wasn't decided, oh, you will play it this way or that," she said. "I guess they let everyone do their thing."

Such ad-libbed invention demonstrates the one thing that *The Return Of The Living Dead* has above most other films in the zombie genre: an abundance of talent, enthusiasm – and, of course, plenty of fresh brains.

Liam Ronan

Originally published in Mass Movement #33, August 2012

CHARLIE HIGSON

Interviewing Charlie Higson is very much like making... No. I'm not going to do it, I'm not going to utilise a catch phrase that has nothing to do with Charlie's career as an author in order to try and establish some sort of common ground in order to ease you in. You don't need to be eased in. This is Charlie Higson, one of the most recognisable faces to have graced the millions of television screens that exist in and throughout the length and breadth of the UK. Having achieved mainstream success via the cathode ray, Charlie also established himself as a successful (and bloody good), best-selling author thanks to both Young James Bond and The Enemy. On the eve of the release of, the quite frankly brilliant, *The Sacrifce*, the fourth instalment in The Enemy'series, I caught up with Charlie for a chat about his latest novel, The Enemy, his previous books, Zombies, 007 and, the agent provocateur himself, Swiss Toni...

Interview by Tim Cundle

MM: You're about to launch the fourth book in The Enemy series. For those who haven't read the series, how would you describe The Enemy and the story so far without revealing any spoilers?

CH: The idea of the series is that there is a disease that hits the planet that only effects people over 14. They become so badly infected that they begin to act like the classic text book zombie. The books are about various groups of children around London scavenging for food and shelter whilst desperately trying not to be eaten by marauding gangs of diseased adults. There are a group of kids near Holloway and they set off for somewhere they hear is a safe place – Buckingham Palace and on the way they get split up and a character ends up on the wrong side of town; so in this, the fourth book he sets off back across London in search of his sister.

MM: So how does *The Sacrifice* differ from *The Enemy*, *The Dead* and *The Fear*?

CH: The series is an on-going story but each book is reasonably self-contained. The books sort of go forward and backward in time a bit...

MM: How do you think the evolution of the series so far affected the way you approached *The Sacrifice* in terms of both story and character development?

CH: I originally envisaged it as a trilogy and I planned it out as a trilogy and had it all worked out; but as I developed the books I realised that I had a lot of other stuff I wanted to write about which required it to be expanded to a seven book series which meant I had more space to work on characterisation and story. I suppose with this fourth book I had to start giving some information about what the disease was and how it works, I think the audience wants to know that.

MM: Were you at all influenced by this huge new wave of zombie film and literature?

CH: I first had the idea about five years ago to write this series, to write a horror series. I figured if I could really, really scare the kids, they would always remember where they were when they read that book and always remember reading it. I sat done and wondered which of all the horror nonsense, which scared me the most? And what always scared me when I was a teenager was zombies. I remember watching night of the living dead which freaked me out in a really big way. They've been popular since *Dawn of the Dead* really but that's part of the fun of it. So I suppose I was on the front end really of all this wave of zombies stuff. They were around, and they were popular, my kids were into it through comics, then it just sort of exploded about the time my books came out so it looks a little bit like I was cashing in on a lovely wave but it was just lucky timing. As you know it takes a long time to bring a book out. And I've wracked my brains because people keep asking me why are zombies so ubiquitous now? And I don't know, maybe it's just that things become popular because they're popular and it seems to be that teenagers, and adults too for that matter, just love the idea of zombies. There are zombie walks, zombie costumes, Halloween now is full of zombies. I went down to a local cinema the other night and there are about four upcoming kids horror films coming out on the animation front. Zombies feature heavily in most of those films because they are completely ubiquitous now and I don't really know why. One theory I had the other day is that we actually are living in times where there is this general feeling of doom and gloom and things going wrong, that the planet is falling apart because of global warming and there is nothing we can do about it. Perhaps making up stories about monsters who can be stopped is a way to deal with the helplessness of not being able to do anything about the real world. It's a small theory but I'm working on it.

MM: So, James Bond and Zombies, you must pinch yourself sometimes. Did you ever dream when you were growing up that you would be so closely involved with the worlds of espionage and horror?

CH: Well no I never realised that I could have a career writing horror. Whatever has happened to me has been pure chance. I've never had a career plan or a career path. When I was at school there was no such thing as media studies, I didn't know anyone who was a writer or an actor or who worked in television or anything like that; but I was lucky enough when I went to University, I met Paul Whitehouse there when we did our degrees. Eventually, after working as a decorator for a few years, people I'd met started working in TV so I kind of tagged along with that really. It had never been anything I thought I might do, but then it started to go quite well, to take off. Then with these books as well it was purely by chance, I was approached by a writer who asked if I wanted to write some books for kids. It was fantastic to be offered to do something completely new for a year as a kids writer. I'd always loved horror and thought I might write something horror based one day, but to do it for kids was great fun.

MM: Did you find it difficult to make the transition from writing for adults to writing young adult fiction? Are the rules different for each audience and genre?

CH: No, not at all really. And kids don't like to be patronised. I've always been a fan of that American way of crime writing: very stripped back, very direct and quite colloquial and there aren't huge long pages of description. That was the style that worked for me when I was a kid, so I knew immediately that I would use a style to reflect that.

MM: Have the film rights for any of the books been optioned?

CH: The area of James Bond film rights are incredibly complex and have for years been fraught with legal conflict and it's all tied down. The only way to really access Bond rights is through an actual novel. So any film rights, exploitation rights or anything really is automatically owned by Eon, so I knew from the start that was always going to be tricky if not impossible. When the books came out everyone including Speilberg seemed to want to make a film of it; in fact the only people who seemed not to want to make a film of it were Eon themselves and they automatically owned all the rights. With the Enemy series I've been holding out. To do these stories you need a proper budget. We've all seen ITV and BBC try to do a post-apocalyptic series but they've never really had the budget to do it properly. The books are for young teenagers; and the fact of the matter is that you can get away with a lot more in a book than you can with a film or on TV. My books are quite grown up. They're very scary and violent and if you were to try to do that on film and stay true to the book you'd be looking at an 18 certificate and there is no way it would be accessible to the kids who follow it. There's a challenge there. Could you do a pretty full on zombie story and keep it at a 12 certificate.

MM: Sorry Charlie I have to ask. Could you be tempted, if you were offered fine wines and Belgian chocolates to return to the role of Swiss Tony full time?

CH: I love playing that character and it only came at the end of the *Fast Show* so it wasn't one of the ones that had been around for as long as some of the others and hadn't got as stale as perhaps some of the other ones. I really loved doing the sitcom but it never quite – it was always designed as one of those mainstream BBC1 type programmes but we never seemed to break out of the confines of BBC3. I was thinking recently that we should think of a film idea for it. I love *Anchorman*, I've seen that so many times and I think there are a lot of parallels between the characters but we'll have to see if we come up with a good enough idea.

MM: What's next for you Charlie?

CH: I start on the next book in the series it's never ending, and I'm popping out to South Africa to start filming on a new Miss Marple…

Originally published in Mass Movement #34, December 2012

MICHAEL BIEHN
&
JENNIFER BLANC-BIEHN

When you get offered the chance to speak to Michael Biehn (I mean, c'mon, the guy was in *Aliens* and *Terminator*) and Jennifer Blanc Biehn, you don't turn it down, and so on the back of their latest film - their first together, *The Victim*, and via a transatlantic phone line in late September, I found myself speaking to Michael and Jennifer about *The Victim*, independent film, Hollywood and more…

Interview by Tim Cundle

MM: As the producer of, as well as one of the main leads, *The Victim* is obviously a labour of love for you. How difficult was it to bring it to the screen? What were the toughest challenges you faced from inception to final edit?

Jennifer: First of all I think I found something that I really wanted to do, that I thought was a great concept, plus I have a very busy brain so it helps for me, it works for me to be producing as well as acting, to be spread thin because I think I work well that way. As for bringing it to the screen, Michael has had to work his arse off to be honest, because it's hard to get people to watch an old time movie, they always concentrate on blockbusters. So we kind of did the Kevin Smith tour with it, went to festivals, got some good reviews on it then people started taking notice. Then Inca Bay got involved and now it's just fantastic because through social media and through festivals and the support of the fans it got a lot easier, but it took a while.

MM: The title sort of has a double meaning because Mary is the original victim, then there's the sub-plot concerning the missing women, then Harrison refers to life in general and says that you can go for what you want and grab it by the balls or spend your life being a victim. It suggests that all the characters in the film are victims and that everyone is a victim of life itself…

Jennifer: It's interesting that you said that because I have to tell you that this was my feeling about that and people always miss that. This film is a little more sophisticated than you'd think, so people often miss that. Some people though really get it and the fact that you've just picked up on that – to me that's what it's always been about, I think for Michael that's what it's always been about. The decisions that people make about sex make them a victim, women being victims having to use their sexuality to get by, and I agree, every character in that movie is a victim of circumstance.

MM: It's referred to as a Grindhouse film but it's a real character driven piece, so I was wondering how you managed to walk that fine line so it didn't fall too far into either camp?

Michael: I think that when I described this movie as a Grindhouse movie, I'd sort of labelled it that from the very beginning, it was because I'd worked with Robert Rodriguez and Quentin Tarantino so basically I think of a Grindhouse movie as nothing more than a really

low budget exploitation movie. I think that in this situation, I took a small amount of money and decided to make the movie that automatically makes it a Grindhouse movie. To me it's no different to what we used to go and watch in the sixties and seventies and called B movies. We'd go down to the drive in movie and our parents would want to watch *Cat on a Hot Tin Roof* and that would start at eight, but at six, when it hadn't even got dark yet and the kids were still out playing, they'd put on a movie and it would be a biker movie starring Vic Morrow or something like that, and that would be a Grindhouse movie. It's kind of like a Roger Corman movie, he kind of worked in that area – low budget and exploitation. With this film there's more of a thriller feel, it's probably got a bit more plot than some of those movies do, but I tried to have fun with this and make a real movie. So that's why I did all this stuff like "not based on true facts" at the start of the movie, just to let people know that we don't take ourselves too seriously, we don't have any money, we're just fun. We quote Quentin Tarantino movies, we quote Clint Eastwood movies, the character I play is basically my most famous character, in the *Terminator* movie, its just fun, a fun movie. There is a serious side to it as well of course, because basically the whole of humanity are complete slaves to sex; it doesn't matter how powerful men are women control sex and can use their sexuality to create a different situation for themselves, whereas men will spend 30 years building up their influence and reputation but throw it all away for a blow job.

MM: Was it difficult for you to make the transition from actor to actor/director?

Michael: What was difficult about that was that I'd had it eight days, and began shooting it in 3 weeks. Usually when people tell me they have the money, they don't have any money, I say Okay, I'll work on the script you have then don't think about it. Then all of a sudden the cheque cleared and I was stuck having to do a page one re-write – it was originally written by a kid and was called *The Victim* and it did have a loner in it, a kind of *Saw* like killer, it was a kind of *Saw* like film and it was kind of written like a novella – it was the first screenplay he'd ever written. So once the cheques started clearing it was clear it was the real deal. So we did pre-production, crewed up, did locations and everything without a script at this stage and started shooting in three weeks. So we did the practical stuff in the day and I wrote the script at night. So from clearing the cheque to finishing the film was 5 weeks because we shot the film in 12 days. We did 45 set ups a day, and the thing is that when we were making it, it never dawned on me about the power of the media and the power of film, that this movie would be reviewed by the New York Times. I thought it would just slip over to Netflix and be a bit of fun. But it's gotten so much attention that I've spent the last year with it because people liked it so much I realised that I could make some money off it, and I never in a million years thought it would be the case with this. It was just some fun. I had friends and family working on this film for free.

MM: One of the things that struck me was that Annie and Kyle aren't typical heroes, they are more like anti-heroes. How do you ensure that the audience identifies with both of them?

Michael: When you first see Annie at the beginning of the film it's just in a couple of flash backs and she's no different from a lot of women we know, not evil, not criminal, young girls getting by, what they are doing is no different to what go-go dancers were doing in the sixties and seventies, they are just getting by. Kyle was always supposed to be a character that you just don't know. He's out in the woods, he's reading and he's obviously trying to change himself and he's just trying to get away. He's just a guy who is stuck in bad circumstances like you or I would be until he gets that crow bar out. There's something about movie making where you think "I wouldn't get a crow bar out and torture that guy" but he does so is he a serial killer? I think in the sequel the stick man opening to the film would be Kyle saying "No I'm not a serial killer, I know all about these guys I know what they do, I'm not like them". I meant that to be more ambiguous than it turned out to be...I wanted it to be a real question mark: is he or isn't he? I think it turned out pretty much the way I wanted. But the thing that happens to Kyle is that he drawn into through a sexual situation and that's the overriding theme really. You know about all those sexual scandals in the sixties, I know Val Kilmer's first wife played that beautiful Christine Keeler in *Scandal* and politicians and anyone in a position of authority, they just don't know what to do with themselves with a pretty girl around.

MM: At the end of the film did you leave that door open for Annie and Kyle to return on purpose?

Michael: I was joking when I said about the stick man, but if this movie is successful I already have a whole sequel mapped out in my head, where I want to shoot it and everything. If I had the money and it was all in place, I'd basically like to do what Jim Cameron did with *Aliens*, kind of like a walk through a dark house and every once in a while something jumps out at you then turn it into a full on action movie.

MM: With such a small cast and crew I'm guessing there must have been a lot of fun on set – what was it like working on the film?

Michael: I think that most people had a lot of fun doing it. Myself I'm quite a passionate person about my acting alone and I was described as a drill sergeant and a raving lunatic by a journalist of the set so I've worked with Jim Cameron, I've worked with Michael Bay, I've worked with Billy Friedkin and if you take all three of those guys on their worst day I was worse than them put together. But we were having to do 45 set ups a day. It was all about the process for me and nobody quit, nobody got fired. There's a bonus feature on the DVD that follows the making of the film and I think it gives you a really good insight into what it was like making the film. We shot it day for night so we didn't have to light it and it was 12 hour days and we ran from set up to set up.

MM: *The Victim* is proof positive that you don't need a big budget to make a great film. Do you think that days are numbered for the big budget overblown blockbuster films?

Michael: The thing about the massive overdone films is that they have these great marketing machines behind them – I have a son and he's nine and he sees trailers and advertising and I take him to see these films – anything he wants to see, always have always will, I don't care what it is and it's the $100million they spend on marketing that makes my son say he wants to see something, and that's okay. They need to have those huge budgets to make any money. I don't think it matters what the film is as long as they spend that money to market it. That's not to say that there aren't a lot of big budget films that aren't a pretty good effort as films, but when you've made *Aliens 1,2,3,4,5,6* then it's let's start again 1,2,3,4,5,6,7 and so on I just don't think – when you first do a movie there's something magical, like *Pirates of the Caribbean*, when that came out it was truly magical and a lot of fun and it's really hard to replicate that it's hard to make a good movie and when you get *Pirates 1,2,3,4* I think it makes it difficult to keep the quality consistent. Or what I consider to be good. But then what do I know, what does Michael Biehn know about anything, it's not about quality it's about money. It's always been about money.

MM: How would you describe *The Victim* to someone to make sure they picked it up or went to see it?

Michael: I would say it's an exploitation movie and that it is meant to be fun and something that you go to and don't take too seriously. I tell people when I introduce the film to leave their phones on you know? It's just a movie, just a bit of fun, there's really not that much to it.

Originally published in Mass Movement #34, December 2012

STEVE NILES

I'm going to keep this simple and straight to the point. Steve Niles played in two of my favourite bands in the eighties, Gray Matter and 3, and now he writes two of my favourite, ongoing, books, *Criminal Macabre* and *30 Days Of Night*, so when I found out that he was planning to cross both titles (the books that is) over, I knew I had to speak to him. Luckily, as well as being an incredible writer (not smoke blowing kids, it's a fact), Steve is also an incredibly nice guy and having sorted out schedules, it was time for me to speak to one of the new Masters Of Horror. Here's Steve…

Interview by Tim Cundle

MM: Which came first for you, punk rock or comics?

Steve: Punk rock. Actually no, because I read comics when I was a kid. I was playing in bands when I was a teenager, so my two lives overlapped.

MM: Was it difficult making that transition and the decision to move from music to writing?

Steve: Not really. In so many ways – the way I do it at least, I try to do everything myself – it's very much the same. It was something I used to do to show to my friends I never thought of making money from it. Then my friends, who later on went on to be Fugazi and Foo Fighters went off and made mega money from it…

MM: You were in Gray Matter during the Revolution Summer weren't you?

Steve: Yeah…

MM: So what was it like being part of the DC scene at that time, and how do you think it changed things?

Steve: It was so strange then. It was like punk rock had hit a rut, and what nobody realised was that the next step was getting political. At that time, everybody had new bands, and if you didn't have new bands you had, like we did, a totally new sound and it was just this big joke. All of a sudden the old bands just sort of faded and all the new bands like Rites of Spring and Grey Matter, then later Fugazi, and it was incredible you know because it was just an explosion. We were as excited about it then as we are looking back at it now. It was a really cool, crazy time, there were gigs virtually every weekend. It was a really amazing time.

MM: When you made the transition to comics, what drew you to horror? You seem to have chosen the medium rather than the traditional world of capes, meta's and the standard all American hero types…?

Steve: I always wanted to tell stories. I wanted to make movies; I used to make Super 8 movies with my friends, but it got incredibly hard to make movies as I got older because I just wanted to make them better. Then I experienced one of those moments when I just looked at my storyboards and looked over at a wall of comics, and it was one of these moments when I just slapped my forehead because I hadn't even thought that I could do something like this, something that I loved so much. Luckily I came to this in the mid-eighties at the height of the explosion of all those indie companies. This was good for me because I knew

how to do something myself, I didn't know how to approach publishers so it kind of happened that way. The punk rock thing really helped out the comic thing. I just loved the medium, it's just a great, great medium, but it did choose me.

As for horror, I just love the genre and thinking about it, it makes the characters really honest. There's no room for bullshit when you're being chased by a monster. I don't fully understand what it is I love about it, I just love being scared and I love scaring people…

MM: You're crossing over two of your most famous books: *30 Days of Night* and *Criminal Macabre*… Is that something you've wanted to do for a while, bringing those two separate worlds together?

Steve: It's something I never really thought about it till about six months ago when I had a deadline and I had to do two scripts in one day and I suddenly realised how McDonald in *Criminal Macabre* is always talking about the coming monster wars and how it's always growing and there are always new attacks, sort of like in the *X-Files* with the alien conspiracy, it's always there. Then in *30 Days Of Night* I had this total shift in the characters where the lead character, Eben, just decides he's going to become an evil fucking vampire, no more trying to be nice; and he wanted to start a war with humans. I thought "Oh my God, these two series are heading on a collision course" so I called IDW and Dark Horse and asked if I could do it. It's such a cool thing to have two different things that you own, with two different companies come together like this. I have high hopes for that one.

MM: I wanted to ask you about Creator Owned Heroes, because you're a driving force behind it and it seems like it's very close to your heart. Do you think the future of comics is creator owned or do you think the status quo with the big publishers will remain in place? And where did the idea for Creator Owned come from?

Steve: Basically there was me Jimmy Palmiotti and Justin Gray – they are my writing partners – we were at a comic convention in Baltimore, me and Jimmy, and we had tables next to each other and we both had lines all weekend but they didn't overlap at all. We talked about it and wondered if we did something together if we could possibly bring our two audiences together. But me and Jimmy don't actually do anything that different, so that's where the idea came from.. If we combined audiences, could we get to more people and bring more attention to what we were doing? As we moved forward we started talking about making it more like, not a magazine, but more like social media where there would be lots of titbits about what we were doing, what we're reading, talking to other creators and just putting some time into this thing. It was just luck.

MM: It kind of brings to mind the whole DIY ethos from the 80's. Do you think that ethos from the punk scene has influenced the outlook you have in, and on, the comic world?

Steve: Yes, absolutely. The thing about it that people don't realise is that all these people who created these amazing properties that are making millions of dollars don't get any recognition and certainly aren't making much money. So part of the idea behind Creator Owned Heroes is creating awareness of that. I'm not saying it's a bad idea to go off and work for Marvel and DC, but just be aware of what will happen to what you create for them. They need to understand that there is a different dynamic in the world of creator owned comics, and if something happens to a character you created, the creator benefits too. Unfortunately history has proven too often for that not to be the case. People mistake my enthusiasm for being anti Marvel and DC but that's just not the case.

MM: You've also started something with Brett Gurrewitz – Black Mask Studios?

Steve: Yeah, we're moving pretty slow with that, with Brett and also with Matt Pizzolo, because we're trying to work out the financing. But it's a very simple concept. You know Brett runs Epitaph Records and it has a very different audience and an audience that may have some interest in comic books so what we really want to try to do- we're not trying to reinvent the wheel – but to get comic books in front of people who may not realise they even like them. This is another thing I'm always harping on about. I grew up in a time where there were comics everywhere, it was before the direct market and literally you couldn't go to a store without there being a comic rack there. So I often got dragged out by my mom and sisters to go shopping and so I developed a sixth sense for spotting the spinner racks and I would gravitate to it. That's something that we don't have any more, as you can only get comics in special stores so people have to make an effort. And you know what happens when you ask people to make an effort – they don't show up. So Black Mask is just a way to get comics in front of more people.

MM: So talking of which, on your site you're offering the complete *Edge Of Doom* for free download. Why did you make that decision? Some people may think it's counterproductive for a writer to give their work away for free...

Steve: I don't see how (*I'm 100% behind Steve on this, if you make something readily and easily available or people, it automatically draws them toward it and it could be the thing that changes their lives, makes them a tiny bit better, but better nonetheless – Tim*) . With that property, it was always one of my favourites, and when it came out it sold okay, but it didn't sell great so it's one of those ones that just kind of passed by. But it was a good, complete little project that deserved a wider audience, and making it available as a free download makes it a great way to give people a whole story as a sampler. Most of this stuff is available on bootleg sites anyway, so I kind of think, if someone's going to be giving away my work for free, I want it to be me. I had a great conversation with Neil Gaiman about this a few months back. He's had a positive experience with piracy, if you look at numbers; more of my stuff is pirated than sold, with him the numbers are reversed because of giving people free samples. What a daunting task it is to walk into a comic book shop for the first time and choose a book. Hopefully, by doing this we're making the job a bit easier.

MM: You mentioned films before, in terms of you making them; but now that people are adapting your work how do you feel about the films of your work that have appeared so far?

Steve: Some I love, some I don't, but the one thing I learned from being in Hollywood, and I didn't have this perspective before, is that the same hard work goes into the worst movie. I'm a lot more reluctant to really slam anybody's movies because I may not like what they did with all of them, but like I said, people worked really hard on them, and if I'm not out there slamming them, people really like these things. People come up to me and say they like the DVD sequel to *30 Days Of Night* is better than the theatrical original ; I don't know what happened, but mostly I just think I've been very, very lucky, especially with *30 Days Of Night*. I haven't watched it in years, but all I wanted was a good, solid horror movie, and I think I got a flavour of that. And to make a scary vampire movie... You've got to go back *to Near Dark* or the black and white version of *Nosferatu* to find really scary vampire movies. So they did well. I'm very happy. It's been a strange ten years, lots of ups and downs but overall I'm very happy.

MM: Which of your books is your personal favourite, and is it the same as your readers' favourite?

Steve: That's so hard because I have *Macabre* and *30 Days Of Night*, those are two huge ones that I've literally been writing since I was a teenager. But if I had to pick one, one that changed me and my approach to how I write, it'd be *Freaks of the Heartland*. When I originally wrote it, it was heavy with captioning and lots of description and character stuff. Then when Greg delivered the first pages I literally scrubbed out all the captions except the first panel and the last panel. Because the drawings were so good and the expressions on the characters' faces were so perfect that it made all my internal monologue redundant. I'd never had anything like that happen before. So that's one of the ones that stands out, mostly because of Greg Ruth and what he did.

MM: Tell us something about the books you're currently working on...

Steve: the big one is that I'm doing a sequel to the *Frankenstein* novel which is mind blowing on so many levels to me. It's coming along slow, we've got the second issue coming out now, and the art looks so gorgeous. Also I'm working with Wes Craven now on a project of his called *Coming of Rage*. I've got *Confusion* at IDW which was one of those little projects that I did on the side last year and people just seemed to dig it, so a lot of stuff. Those are the big ones right now.

MM: If you had the chance to write any books in comics, what would it be?

Steve: My first instinct is Hulk or Batman, but I wrote a cartoon for the Spectre a few years ago and I really fell in love with the character. He's perfect because he's a cop who is also a vengeful spirit, so two of the things I loved to work with. So that's one I've always got on my radar..

MM: So what's next for you Steve?

Steve: I've got a new series coming out for Dark Horse which hasn't been announced called *Breath of Bones* and it's a big departure for me. You could let your kids read this one, it's a World War II monster story. Then I have to keep all the other things going as well. It stems from being a freelancer who doesn't have enough work; now that I do have work I'm scared to say no to anything because I'm honestly worried it will run out...

Originally published in Mass Movement #34, December 2012

JAY BENTLEY
(BAD RELIGION)

on the eve of the release of Bad Religion's new album, *True North*, I spoke to bassist Jay Bentley (one of the nicest guys in punk rock, period) about the record, life in the band and Bad Religion's past, present and future. Here's what he had to say...

Interview by Tim Cundle

MM: The new album *True North*; what do the album name and title track refer to? Is it about people following their hopes and dreams, or the place to which they need to travel to feel most comfortable?

JB: Both. I think that it's basically a direction. Using a compass guide, how I got it when I talked to Graffin about the song is that *True North* is not north on a compass, not physical north, but it's about treading the path that you think is right. *True North* could be a few degrees off, when it comes to your true north it's the direction that you need to be.

MM: The album, like all BR records, combines the melancholic and almost wistful, with an upbeat, direct and almost confrontational feeling So was there an overall emotional context which helped to shape the record? And if so, how would you describe the emotional input that influenced *True North*?

JB. Wow. I can give you parts of the song-writers ideas when they were writing... When we sat down to talk about making this record, one of the things we all said was let's just make a record like we know how to make, that's not overblown and go back to what we know how to do. Brett said that he sort of learned from the last record that he was writing on an acoustic guitar so as not to wake his baby daughter and that wasn't any way to write a Bad Religion record. I think for Greg, he's made some major moves in his life and he's been trying to find a place to settle down. I think that when you start to think about the end of the band, the end of this thing happening and basically moving on with your life, I think that that's where Greg is right now in his life. So I think he was asking: Did I do everything that I wanted to do in my life? Did I try everything that I wanted to try and what are the mistakes I've made? But we wanted to make it in a way that everybody could relate to too, so that's kind of where we were at with this record.

MM: I don't know if you've spoken to Greg about all the songs but there is a line in *The Department of False Hope* that I wanted to ask you about *"Hold your head up high forgotten man, tomorrow's not for me and you"*. It conjures up an image of inevitability and finality. Who is the forgotten man?

JB: I think that with Greg and Brett it was everybody – all of us – everybody. I kind of have to go back to the ironic part, because when Brett was writing the song we were already in the studio. When Greg was singing it, it sounded like "forgot and man there's nothing left for me and you". So for us it was like, you come here you live you die you're gone. There is no everlasting because today doesn't mean anything. When you're gone you're gone.

MM: There is also a sense that it's also about ageing and losing your sense of optimism, like you're passing something on to the next generation...

JB: That's kind of normal for us; it's a pretty standard Bad Religion thing: "We're not teenagers any more, this sucks"

MM: I also wanted to ask you about the first song off the album you released *Fuck You*. Is it a song born of built up frustration that acts as a sort of release or is there something more to it than that?

JB: Here's the ironic part about our song *Fuck You*. The song isn't about us saying fuck you. We don't say fuck you to anybody. It's a literary diagram of how you get to that point; why you would get so frustrated to say that. But people are like "Yeah fuck you man" but that's not us at all. It's just an interesting thing as to why a human being would get so frustrated as to say that. You should think "Yeah, that was really refreshing!"

MM: Likewise with *Dharma and the Bomb*. The title seems to link natural order and natural law and one is an inescapable part of the former, but lyrically it veers away from it completely...

JB: There are two ways of looking at this whole *Dharma and the Bomb* thing. Firstly, the terrorists having a dirty bomb in a suitcase scenario. That's the genie in the bottle. Two is like India and Pakistan having this almost nuclear abrasion and tension right now and this is getting out of hand. You or I could think of these people as being driven by religion but they're not all like that. I don't care what your philosophy is but we're going to end up bombing the shit out of you if you keep fucking with us...

MM: The whole song-writing and recording process, with you guys spread out all over the country now, how does it work? Do you set deadlines for yourselves? Do you just go with the flow and get together when you need to get together?

JB: Every record is different and every record has a different reason how it comes about. With this one Brett did some demos and we all had these templates to kind of riffle through and get started; I live about an hour from Brett, so Brooks and I got together to meet up with Brett and work on some songs. We knew we wanted to make the record we just didn't know how or when. Then our drummer Brooks had been on tour with Tenacious D and he had this little tiny window of about two weeks where they were taking a break, so we said that's when we're making our record. We got together and Brett was still writing, so we started recording and writing and it all came together like this. We've done records like this in the past and it's really good for us. We have a philosophy that if you work too hard in pre-production you suck the life out of it and the longer you're in the studio the worse your record's gonna get. So it's great for us, we can chop into it, record it and get the fuck out of there and that's what we wanted to do.

MM: Do you think that the global socio-economic and political situation has had any influence on the band as musicians and the way you write as a whole?

JB: I think in the beginning, we were like fifteen years old; then with *Suffer* it was the first time we actually left the country and went on tour and became more aware of the world, What I'd like to say is this: America's impact on the globe has had a profound impact on the way we write, but really what it is, is that as we have an opportunity to see more of the world when we tour and we see the negative influence our country has around the world. It's not that America is the only bad place, it's just that it has such a bad influence on the rest of the world. Other countries may have a similar impact in terms of what they do, but if you look at what is seen, whether it's a global corporation like Kentucky Fried Chicken or whatever, or whether it's a Hollywood movie going bang, bang, bang and shooting everyone up.

MM: How do you think the 15 year old you would have reacted if you'd told him that 16 albums in the band would still be going strong?

JB: I don't think I would have believed that. At all…

MM: You've spent almost your entire adult life in Bad Religion. How do you think the band has changed, and how do you think these changes have been mirrored by changes in your own life?

JB: The biggest change in the band is that it went from being the creative force of kids and the ultimate outlet; it still is, but it's like a hobby that's got out of control. With the recording and all the touring that we do you can ignore it, but you can't really ignore it because you end up just having to face up to it in the future. The other change in the band is with the punk rock lifestyle in general. When we started your aspirations to get big were to play to 30 people in the club down the street, and now it's part of mainstream culture, so it's different, you can see that. And okay it is what it is. I see guys like Frank Carter as being more influential than the more popular "punk rock" bands.

MM: Do you still think of Bad Religion as being a punk rock band?

JB: I do but only because I think of myself as a punk. There is something about the ideology which I learned at 15 which was: question everything, everyone's a liar and never trust a hippy and it sort of sunk in and that changed my life. Being in the band with real smart people and having hour long conversations to speed up van drives across the country has been my education. I dropped out of high school but I never stopped learning. Hard rock and this band has really been my school so shaped everything about what is my world view and what I think about everything.

MM: You guys celebrated your 30th anniversary in 2010. To what do you attribute the band's longevity? And do you ever envisage a time when there won't be a Bad Religion?

JB: I don't have to envision it, I'm sure there will be a time when there is no Bad Religion. As far as longevity I would say that like other bands we've had our ups and downs, we've broken up, but when we all started to pull back into the band we all realised that we enjoyed doing it. It's not the most important thing in the world, nobody puts a lot of pressure on the band to make their life perfect or happy or anything. It's basically like playing poker with the guys on Wednesday nights and if you treat it like that you never really have that overwhelming sense of despair that the band is not what you want it to be. As long as you're just creating the thing together and you're having a good time why wouldn't you keep doing it?

MM: Do you think there are any preconceptions that still persist about the band. Perhaps people read too much into the band's name?

JB: Yeah, but surprisingly, less than you think. And even less are those who actually want to have any dialogue with us about the name. We've had the odd confrontation where people say "Oh Bad Religion you're Satanists" we're not Satanists at all, not at all. Misconceptions about the band have been rampant since the beginning: we're vegan, from Washington DC, anything because no-one really knew that much about us We were just going out on tours and doing what we do and I always kept pretty much under the radar. Generally the majority of the population ignored us and that's just the way we liked it.

MM: With the new album out do you have a tour organised and when can we expect to see you in the UK?

JB: I'm going to say August. We have a US tour set up, and half of a European tour set up for June and then we were coming back for August and as we don't have any UK dates in June it's definitely in August.

Originally published in Mass Movement #35, May 2013

BAFFLEGAB

Mention audio drama to anyone in the UK, and they'll invariably (and justifiably) start talking about Big Finish, but hot on the numero uno's tails are Bafflegab, home of the, frankly, incredible Scarifyer's and Vince Cosmos, and on the verge of its biggest year, release wise, I sat down to have a chat with founder and owner Simon Barnard about Bafflegab…

Interview by Tim Cundle

MM: Let's begin by going back to the origins with Cosmic Hobo. Why did you start Cosmic Hobo and was it named for/after the second Doctor?

Simon: Yes, it was named after the Second Doctor. The reason I started it, which was about 5 or 6 years ago was because I was working at Radio 1, and had been for about 10 years and I found that more and more drama was creeping into my documentary making – I was a documentary maker – so in the end I thought I might as well just make a drama. So I hired a studio and wrote a script, got some actors and that was that. I'd heard some of the Big Finish Doctor Who stuff and basically thought "I can do that"; because I'd worked in Radio such a long time I thought I could do something to a similar standard really. The Cosmic Hobo name was really just a blatant attempt to steal some of Big Finish's customers. Big Finish had created a market, so I got a couple of Doctor Who actors; I got Nicholas Courtney and Terry Malloy, called the company Cosmic Hobo and basically hoped we could get the Doctor Who fans to buy into it.

MM: You recently changed the company name from Cosmic Hobo to Bafflegab, why change the name?

Simon: The reason I changed the name is that this year, I've got lots of other stuff coming out that isn't related to Doctor Who at all. Plus, I don't really like the name Cosmic Hobo. I don't like the words Cosmic or Hobo and I always had to explain it to people on the phone. It's kind of embarrassing when you're talking to the BBC. So this year, instead of just The Scarifyers, I've got something called Vince Cosmos which is out in a few weeks, plus the biggest thing we're doing this year, which we record the first couple of episodes of tomorrow, but I'm not allowed to tell you what it is. So we've got a lot of stuff coming through this year and none of it is even remotely related to Doctor Who, so that's why I changed the name.

MM: Where did the idea for the Scarifyers come from and how difficult was it making that idea a reality?

Simon: It sort of came from an old script I wrote years ago – a film that we never got round to making. Basically I wanted to work with Nicholas Courtney, I'm a big fan and he's one of my favourite ever actors in Doctor Who, so it sort of came from wanting to write a character for him, then wanting to write a sort of M R James kind of character which became Professor Dunning. Also I wanted to write something Victorian, but as the first story for The Scarifyers involved Rasputin it needed to happen after Rasputin's time, and then we thought of the 1930s which we liked. So it ended up being this secret agency called MI13 which operated in the inter-war period. I wrote the first one, then my co-writer wrote the second then we kind of settled on a style after that. So it became a sort of comedy-horror thing but there was no grand plan in the beginning.

MM: You obviously had an idea about who you wanted to play each role...

Simon: It started with Nicholas Courtney as I said. He was the only person I really had in mind. Big Finish hadn't been using him very much at that time. They'd been making all these UNIT stories and had barely featured him which seemed like a waste. Then I heard Terry Malloy doing a DVD commentary and I thought what a lovely voice he had. Then David Benson – I was doing a documentary about the British Film industry and I got David Benson in to do the links for it in the style of Kenneth Williams (he does a stage show as Kenneth Williams) and we were talking afterwards and it turned out he'd done all these Big Finish things, so I asked him to be part of what we were doing.

MM: It's impossible to talk about the Scarifyers without mentioning Lionheart. With the tragic passing of Nick Courtney, how did it effect the series? Was there a time when you considered ending it?

Simon: We'd known that Nick was ill for a while. He had a stroke a year or two before he died so we had to delay recording the fifth one for quite a while. He woke me up one night actually, I remember him calling to tell me that he could read okay, and he could speak fine but he couldn't read and speak at the same time, so we waited for him to recover from that before recording the fifth one. Then after that, he got cancer and we were never able to record a sixth story. The sixth story was written – *The Horror of Loch Ness* was supposed to be Nick's story – and we all talked about what we would do. I was all for ending the series to be honest. Once Nick died it was clear that Lionheart needed an ending. So we wrote the *Magic Circle* pretty quickly and that sort of ended Lionheart's character. We still didn't know if we'd go on to make more stories, but in the end we just seemed to carry on...

MM: Was it difficult for David Warner to fall into the already established world of MI13 given the massive shoes he had to fill...?

Simon: Not really. David's just a hugely experienced actor who can do anything. It was a slightly odd recording that one, it was quite emotional. David, toward the end of the play when you find out the protagonist has been Lionheart the whole time, and you have that scene and then afterwards Lionheart's funeral; that stuff was really emotional. It mustn't have been strange for David Warner as everyone was so upset. It sent a shiver up your spine, and Terry was particularly upset. Apart from that, David's a complete professional and stepped right in without a hitch.

MM: What's the atmosphere like behind the scenes of the Scarifyers? The series is so much fun, it's hard to imagine that behind the scenes, it's anything other than everybody having a great time...

Simon: They are really, really hard work. There have been a couple, like the first one, where the time just crept up on us. These recordings are two hours long, and to record two hours of audio in just one day is quite a feat. In fact, when we moved studios, so that we were using the same studios as Big Finish; Toby, the engineer couldn't believe we were going to get through so much script in a single day. He said it was unheard of. Luckily we haven't failed so far. So, it's really hard work, but it's really good fun. All the actors love it.

MM: If you were forced to choose, which is your favourite Scarifyers story?

Simon: I'm really fond of *For King and Country* because I think we got the balance right in that one. It's got some fairly gruesome horror bits and it's also got some really funny bits, and it all builds up to a big climax in the end. So this is the one that I feel we should be striving to make more like, but my favourite for other reasons is the *Magic Circle*.

MM: How has the comic been received? How easy was it for you to transition from the audio to the four colour world?

Simon: The comic's been received very well. It's had nothing but good reviews. I actually found it really difficult to write. Far more difficult than I thought because it's sort of adapted from a script but there is lots taken out and there is lots of visual stuff in there – you have to make it interesting to look at. I just found it really difficult

MM: Is there going to be a second issue?

Simon: To be honest I haven't made any money out of it, so if I continue to do the comic in the same way, I won't be able to afford to do any audio, so we're trying to find a comic house to take it on.

MM: So, Vince Cosmos; did Paul Magrs approach you, or did you approach Paul?

Simon: It was sort of a combination of the two actually. When we did the Scarifyers, I got an email out of the blue from Paul Magrs saying how much he enjoyed it. Then, Halloween 2011, I ended up in Whitby for the Goth weekend, and Paul was there doing a reading in a bookshop, so I went to say hello. We ended up going out for fish and chips afterwards and hatched the plan there and then...

MM: Do you think there is an underlying appeal about the 1970's , like with Vince Cosmos, as they've almost become in vogue, a decade that people are finally starting to remember with affection...

Simon: I hope so, then we'll sell some more copies! Paul Magrs is slightly obsessed with the 1970s. I've no idea, but if people are fond of that era, they are going to love Vince Cosmos because it completely reeks of that time.

MM: You're also also about to release the second volume of Peter Cushing reading Sherlock Holmes...

Simon. Yes. It's been a long time coming. It's one of those things that hasn't sold that well. I don't know why. I thought that Sherlock Holmes is popular and Peter Cushing is popular, but it turns out that there is just a lot of Sherlock Holmes product out there so I've been trying to work out how to make that in smaller quantities. So I've worked that out and it comes out soon. I don't know if you've heard them, but they were recorded in 1971 when he was at the height of his powers, and he was a huge Sherlock Holmes fan, so he's doing all these voices, and it's absolutely brilliant.

MM: You said you had a busy year coming up so what are you releasing this year?

Simon: Vince Cosmos, then *Return of Sherlock Holmes Volume 2*. In April we start a new downloadable series, downloadable weekly, six episodes, which will then be release on CD afterwards. Then there is another project with Paul Magrs, the Bride series set in Whitby, where an older Bride of Frankenstein is running a B&B and it's a sort of supernatural comedy adventure as the Bride solves mysteries with her friend Effy. There've been six books, and Paul has finished the book series, but he's gone back to the beginning so there are some new stories and some prequel stories.

MM: You also mentioned you'd written something for Big Finish?

Simon: Yes, my Scarifyers co-writer, Paul and I. We wrote a Companion Chronicles story called *Council of War*. It has Sinead Keen in it from *Being Human*. Then we've written a Jago and Lightfoot which won't be out until 2014. It's a country house murder mystery with a twist…

Originally published in Mass Movement 35, May 2013

KEN CASEY
(DROPKICK MURPHY'S)

Mass Movement catches up with the affable Ken Casey from Boston Legends the Dropkick Murphys prior to the release of their new album *Signed and Sealed in Blood* and a packed out UK tour...

Interview by Ian Pickens

MM: What's the atmosphere like in the Dropkicks camp with the imminent release of the new album *Signed and Sealed in Blood*?

KC: Oh very enthusiastic, you know from the very start of writing the first song of an album to the release when the public gets to hear it, it's a long time coming; you truly are like a kid on Christmas morning, or rather more like a parent on Christmas morning, waiting for the kids to open a present; this is like waiting for the fans to open a present.

MM: You've been quoted as describing the last album *Going Out In Style* as intricate and difficult and this new album as catchy and fun; what's been the biggest difference in writing and recording the two? You certainly looked like you were having a lot of fun in the video of *Going Out In Style*..

KC: It's all relative I guess. I was talking more about the writing of it. With *Going Out In Style* all the songs had to connect the storyline of the character, which made it quite intricate; but it was still a fun album. It's always fun when it gets to the playing, but sometimes the writing is complicated, is what I meant. The fact that on *Signed and Sealed in Blood* we didn't have to adhere to a storyline... It was like someone took the leash off; we were able to let loose.

MM: From the first track on the new album. *The Boys Are Back* it's obvious you guys are having a lot of fun; is the title a nod to Thin Lizzy?

KC: (Laughs) I think the whole point of that song and that title is setting the tempo for the rest of the album. It's like 'We're Back'; it's a slap in the face right from the off you know?

MM: There's another song on this album about wakes (*Jimmy Collins' Wake*); what is it with you guys and funerals?

KC: (Laughs) Ah well, you know you're gonna have one eventually. That was basically the storyline of a guy where at his wake everyone came out of the woodwork. He was the first 'fan favourite' of Boston; he was a player, a coach; he was the first manager of the Boston Red Sox before they became the Red Sox; manager for the first World Series that we ever won; he was the original Fan's Favourite.

MM: You've come quite a long way from the early days of the band when you did split EP'ss with the Anti-Heroes and Al's old band the Bruisers; some would say the Murphy's have become part of the Boston establishment, yet you have retained your original fan base of punks and skins; is it a difficult balance to maintain; and how do you maintained that balance?

KC: I don't think it is difficult if you are legitimately putting your soul into something; doing something that you feel is right. The band has never tried to have success for the sake of success. We've always answered to ourselves, whether we are on our own label or on Epitaph Records, we've always done what we wanted to do; but the thing is if you're not growing and expanding your fan base, then you wither and die. If you stay where you are just to keep that core fan base happy, you're gonna lose that support eventually. You don't see the Anti-Heroes playing; the Bruisers very rarely play. It's hard to play in a band and not strive to better yourselves. We've grown at a slow, steady pace and I think the fans can handle that better than if one day you're playing your local pub and the next day you're playing to thousands.

MM: Do you think a lot of your fans have grown with you; from young punks to married middle aged people with kids?

KC: Well if you look at our shows, in whatever city it is, you find the people who maybe booked us the very first time we played that city, but 17 years later, like you say, they might have their kids with them; but yeah we stayed close to the original people who supported us

MM: On *Signed and Sealed in Blood* the band have taken on the tradition of writing a Christmas song; albeit in a non-traditional way; did you think the world needed a break from *The Fairytale of New York* ?

KC: *The Fairytale of New York* is one of my favorite Christmas songs of all time. When we were recording the album Tim came up with that riff on the accordion; we said 'that's a Christmas song right there'. We kinda just felt that the Dropkick Murphy's could take a tongue in cheek approach to a Christmas song. It's a fine line between cheesy and tongue in cheek. What I like is when people first hear that song, the intro sounds all sweet and nice, and it's like 'Oh my God are they going to write a cheesy Christmas song' and then BAM.

MM: **That was one of the strengths with *Fairytale of New York*, the juxtaposition between the music and the lyrics…**

KC: Exactly. When you put the words 'Scumbag' and 'Faggot' in a Christmas song, you know it's not going to be a cheesy Christmas song (laughs)

MM: For a lot of people their first exposure to the band would have been through Martin Scorsese's film, *The Departed* which featured the song *Shipping Up To Boston*; are you guys big fans of that film?

KC: Oh Yeah. To be given the opportunity to be involved in a Scorsese film about your city; it's a real gift for a band. The story of how it came about is kinda funny; a couple of our friends had small parts in that movie and they all claimed that they got us in that movie, but Scorsese claims it was Robbie Robinson the guy he goes to for all his music collaboration. It was just crazy to hear that the first people Scorsese thanked when he won the Oscar was us. It was just a real honour you know.

MM: And it got you onto the Simpsons as well...

KC: (Laughs) Yeah I guess if you make it onto one of the longest running TV shows in the US you're pretty legit right?

MM: Did you think *The Departed* gave an accurate portrayal of Boston?

KC: Yes and no. I laughed at a lot of it. Characters like Alec Baldwin's, and some of the lines he had, made me fall out of my chair laughing. I think parts of it are true but it's Hollywood so it's glamourized and dramatized. The Boston it portrayed was 20-30 years ago; it's a lot different now.

MM: Why do you think so many Americans of Irish descent have maintained such a strong link with their Celtic heritage and ancestry? It's not so common with Americans of Scottish or Welsh descent...

KC: Probably because in a place like Boston it was such a tightknit community, and maybe there wasn't such a massive migration of the Scots or Welsh to one particular location. I think it all gets watered down over time, but back then the patriarchs of the family, be they the fathers or the grandfathers from Ireland, obviously passed on the traditions accordingly. In a place like Boston it's really entwined within the fabric of the city whereas in other places it's just a case of 'my last names Irish; I'm gonna paint my face green' you know (laughs)I think here, it's a little bit more real you know?

MM: How's the tour going so far?

KC: We've just finished the tour in the US. We were playing six new songs each night. We opened with *The Boys Are Back* and people were singing along with the words already; it gives us a lot of encouragement.

MM: The number of UK dates is quite small compared to the tours you used to do back in the early 2000s' is that down to cost of touring in the UK...

KC: It's partly down to cost and scale, but we also like to leave a bit of room in case we want to come back and play some different cities like Cork or Edinburgh. When we did the big, big tours in the UK we used to just play the UK and Ireland; we didn't do mainland Europe; but because we're promoting a new record we wanna go everywhere; so we're doing UK, Ireland and Europe on this tour, and we still need to get home and tour the US after that, so you have to keep it moving, so to speak.

MM: What's next for Dropkick Murphys?

KC: The touring schedule is booked pretty heavily. After the European tour it's pretty much straight into the US, then it's Australia in April and then we go to Hawaii and then the West Coast, Coachella Festival, some TV shows... Conan O'Brian; we'll have a little break in May and then we'll be back in Europe in the summer doing the festivals; so it's a pretty heavy touring schedule but hey it's good to have places to go.

Originally published in Mass Movement #35, May 2013

THE GREEN HORNET
A DIFFERENT KIND OF SUPERHERO

There's an old adage that goes something like this: Some men accomplish great things, while others squander their existence. And still there are those who must follow a different path…a path that twists and turns its way towards a unique kind of truth –- Author Unknown.

We all have dreams, desires and things that we hope to accomplish during our lifetime. For some, it means a peaceful existence with a wife and family and that storied white, picket fence surrounding a beautiful garden. For other individuals, it means a more adventuresome life style, one filled with danger and excitement; something with a bit more of a challenge involved. Still, there are other individuals who fit in-between the two extremes and are happy just living life.

On a personal note, I have been a rather oddball of sorts. Neither wanting the picket fences or the daredevil life style, yet I desire more from life than just a mundane existence. So, where does that leave me? I guess you could call me a dreamer. I love the obscure eccentricities of life; the things that others consider weird. I love to watch horror films and those movies that most people think of as too bizarre for ordinary tastes. Above all, I love movie serials or chapter plays. I guess you could say that I live vicariously through the make believe world of film and its larger than life characters.

Many readers of this fine magazine may not realize that long before the modern day versions of Bat Man, Superman, and the countless other super heroes, many appeared on the silver screen as weekly chapter plays at the local movie theaters. They were also referred to as cliffhangers, because the hero/heroine would be left in a dangerous situation only to be resolved in the next episode.

Well, to make a long story short, I've decided to write a quarterly column featuring a specific superhero as my subject, to discuss their personalities as to what motivates them to do what they do for both themselves as well as for humanity. I've decided to begin my study with the Green Hornet. Don't ask me why I chose him to start this ambitious undertaking. I guess it's because I've just completed watching him recently, so why not start there.

It might be interesting to note that he started out as a weekly radio broadcast during the late 30's on station WXYZ out of Detroit. Because of his popularity, Universal Studios bought the rights to his character and made two movie serials: *The Green Hornet* in 1939 and *The Green Hornet Strikes Again* in 1940. The first entry starred Gordon Jones in the title role and Warren Hull in the second, but that's really not the importance of this article.

My goal, if possible, is to explore the actual psyche of the character himself, and to give the reader a glimpse as to what makes him and all of the other super heroes "tick" inside. Oh, by the way, *The Green Hornet* had a very short run as a television show during the mid 60's, which had nothing to do with the movie serial. It was also made into a movie in 2010, which, in my opinion, was absolutely terrible. What I am referring to in this article are the two chapter plays made in the late 30's and not the above-mentioned bombs.

The actual story of *The Green Hornet* involves Brit Reid; the Editor-in-Chief of a famous newspaper called The Sentinel. As an editor, Brit is alarmed by the many criminal activities in his city and feels somewhat helpless to do anything other than to report the stories as a matter of serving public interest. But wait just a minute. Suppose he could use his newspaper to sway public opinion. What better way could there be than to enter the criminal element at its lowest form as a masked man and become involved in nefarious activities, and then to report first hand on the events. Perhaps he could even prevent such unlawful practices in the process. The downside to this plan is that the police would consider him just another criminal, and the criminals themselves would consider him to be competition. What a dilemma.

Armed with only a gas-powered gun that temporarily immobilizes his victims and his faithful manservant Kato, *The Green Hornet* manages to work both sides of the law and uses his newspaper to influence public opinion. A very clever ploy.

From my prospective, *The Green Hornet* is a perfect example of how the power of the press, even today, has a definite influence on public opinion. But I think the thing that intrigues me the most about Brit Reid is his cleverness as both a newspaper reporter and editor of a large newspaper, to uncover criminal activities and expose the facts by way of the written word, but most of all, to let justice play itself out. His alter ego as *The Green Hornet* is merely a way to shelter his identity from the world. Since he is seen at the various crime scenes, he is a key suspect and is wanted by the police. On the other side of the law, criminals view him as someone who threatens as competition. Neither is the case. He is an ordinary citizen with no superpowers, only a desire to seek out the truth and use his disguise to intimidate lawbreakers. Along with his trusted bodyguard Kato, the two men do their best to maintain justice in their own inimitable fashion.

He is resourceful, intelligent, non-violent (even though he uses his gas-powered gun to temporarily immobilize his victims) and above all he is honest. The two serials are reminiscent of an early film noir adventure and this factor adds a unique ambience to the production. Unlike Republic and Columbia Studios, Universal's making of *The Green Hornet* is a perfect blend of action, but most of all good storytelling.

Reid's character is a well thought out creation of both bravado and subtleness, and he makes a very interesting character study. I find the dichotomy rather refreshing. Since he has no super powers, he must manage by his wits. In short, he is a man's man and nothing more. Interestingly, his alter ego is never revealed to anyone other than Kato, and to the rest of the world, *The Green Hornet* remains a phantom. As for Brit Reid, he continues his job as Editor-in-Chief of The Sentinel.

I feel that both of *The Green Hornet* serials are extremely well made and, therefore, are a pleasure to watch. I also feel that because they appear to be more character driven in content, they targeted a bit more of a mature audience than most chapter plays.

Doug Crill

Originally published in Mass Moveent #35, May 2013

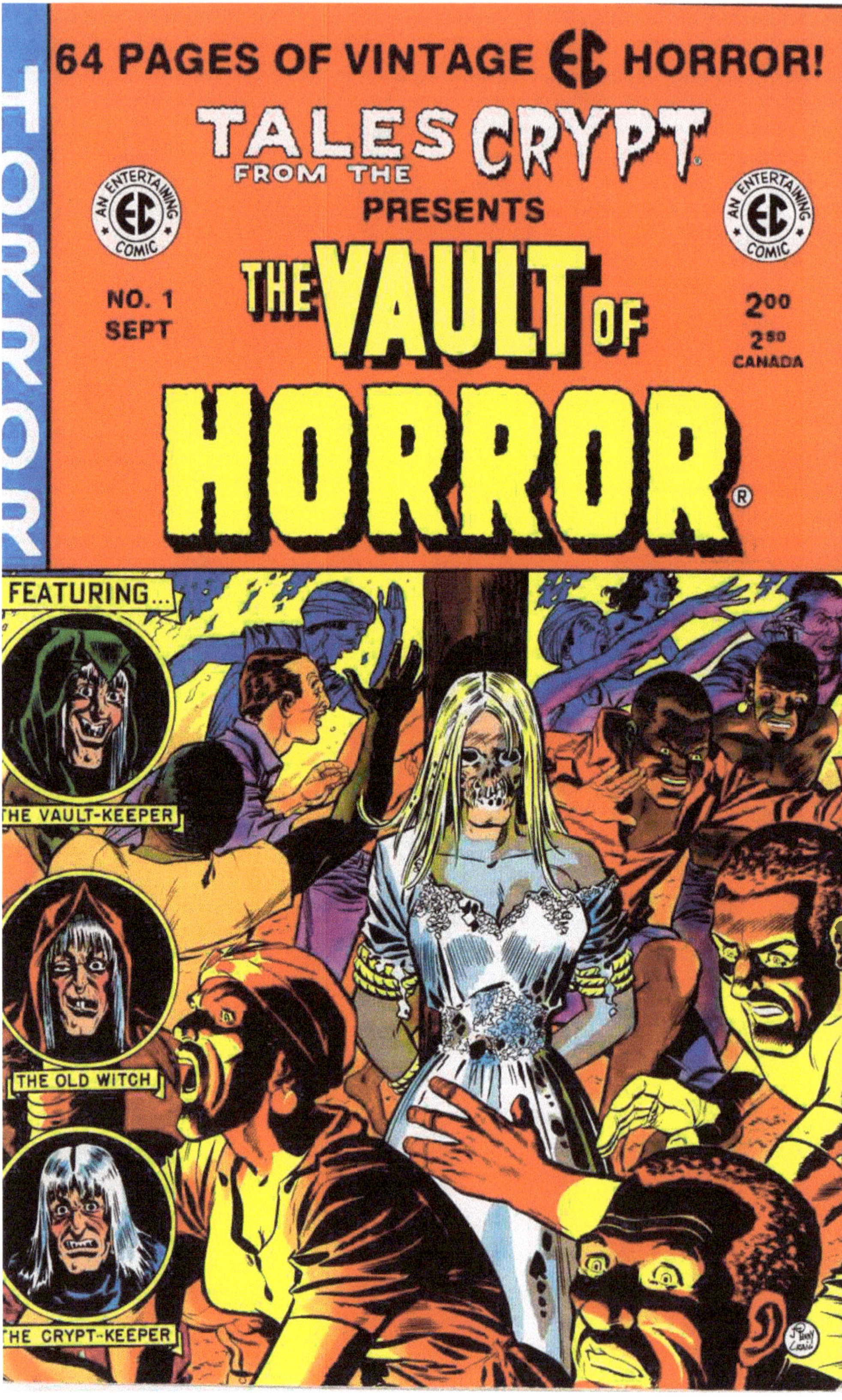

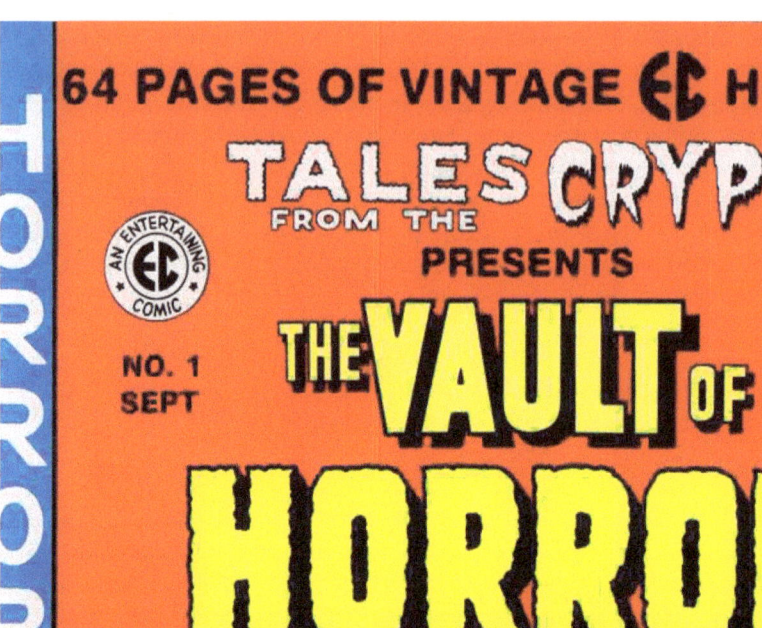

WHAT MAKES A COMIC SCARY?

Many people see comics as a bastard hybrid of films and prose, kind of like a movie on a page. While it's true that studying film and prose techniques will improve your ability to both write and draw comics, it's also fair to say that comics are a completely different medium, with a unique set of weaknesses, challenges and strengths. Nowhere is this more apparent than in Horror Comics.

One of the best ways to illustrate this is to look at the techniques that prose writers and film makers routinely use to scare their audience that comic creators just can't utilise. One of the major resources for a horror prose writer is the reader's visual imagination. No matter how graphic the writer is in their description of a beheading or a disemboweling, the reader will add more details in their minds eye and push themselves to the limits of their endurance.

On a comics page you have to show all those gory details without leaving the reader any room to add more. With a page of prose the reader is thinking 'OMG that severed head is spinning through the air and there's so much blood!' Whereas with a page of comics, where the action is actually depicted, they may be thinking 'hmm surely a head wouldn't spin like that and shouldn't there be more blood?' The visceral horror isn't limited by the reader's imagination, but by the ability of the artist to depict it.

One technique that film makers often use to scare their audience is to contrive tension and then release it with a shock appearance. You know the routine. The heroine has gone into the basement in search of her boyfriend who's just been murdered by the maniac. The maniac's hiding round the corner. The heroine's just about to turn the corner. The maniac's raising his axe. The heroine turns the corner. The maniac isn't there. No wait, he IS there! Boo! AAAH! It's a simple technique that's been used to excellent effect by many masters of the genre and no matter how aware we are of being manipulated, it gets us pretty much every time.

In comics this technique is completely redundant. You can't shock the reader with a surprise appearance because they only have to glance at the bottom of the page, or over to the next panel, for the whole shock to be blown. You can hide the reveal on the next page, but the reader might well have flicked through the comic on the way home to appreciate the art, or simply have turned too many pages at once and seen the image already. Either way it's a time honoured technique that we comics creators just can't use.

So comics are more limited in the techniques they can call on to scare the reader, and yet some of the scariest stories I've ever read have been comics. The question is how did they do it? How do you bring fear into the funny pages?

I think the best way to answer that question is to deconstruct two of the most frightening classic horror comics I've ever read and find out what makes their undead hearts beat.

I Balked With A Zombie

The first story I'm going to look at is *Till Death* written (most probably) by Al Feldstein and drawn by Johnny Craig. It tells the story of Steve, an American sugar plantation owner who brings Donna, his sweetheart, out to Haiti to marry her. Unfortunately Donna soon succumbs to jungle fever and dies. Overcome by grief Steve confides to his faithful manservant Jebco that he'd do anything to have her back, permanently by his side.

That night Jebco and his fellow natives resurrect Donna's corpse in a voodoo ceremony and bring her back to life as a zombie. At first Steve is overjoyed but as Donna's corpse begins to rot in the tropical heat he is increasingly repelled by the sight and smell of her permanently by his side. Steve tries to put an end to Donna's presence by shooting her, stabbing her, drowning her and even dropping her from a helicopter into the jungle. But all to no avail, she keeps coming back to his side, looking even more foul each time.

Finally, unable to stand it Steve takes poison and commits suicide, but still his horror doesn't end. He awakes from death as a zombie, resurrected by his faithful manservant and there, waiting for him, is his rotting zombie bride who will now be permanently by his side for all eternity ...

One of the first things that makes this story so effective is that it's told in the present tense and in the second person. All the way through the story the reader is addressed as 'you' forcing them to see everything from Steve's perspective. This is a technique that is really difficult to achieve in prose, because conventionally all fictional prose is told in the first or third person and in the past tense. If you break this convention you run the risk of alienating the reader and making the horror less real. In comics however, because the text is allied with the pictures it has the opposite effect and actually draws the reader in, letting them live through the story, as it happens, along with the protagonist, making the horror more immediate and real.

The other thing the story does, like all truly great horror, is to take a very real fear from everyday life and create a metaphor to explore and heighten that fear. In this case it's the fear of being trapped in a relationship with someone for whom all love has died and that you now find repellant and suffocating. In comics though, you can turn this metaphor into a potent visual image that really drives the point home. Craig's depiction of the way Donna's rotting corpse increasingly decays and how she submissively but steadfastly clings to Steve sums up the death of their relationship far better than any prose could. What's more the compressed timeline of comics means the story has far more impact than a film would, due to the time it would take to show Donna's corpse rotting away.

So despite the limitation of the medium, this story is far more scary *because* it is told in comic form.

Beneath The Streets ... The Horror!

The next story I'd like to look at is the *The Monster of Dread End* ... written by John Stanley and drawn by Ed Robbins,. The story starts with a brief history of Hawthorn Place a once thriving street in the middle of a bustling city, now merely a long row of deserted buildings. Hawthorn Place was the site of a series of child abductions and murders. The children were taken from their homes, often from rooms with locked doors and windows, and their corpses were unrecognizable when discovered. The police were at a loss to do anything and eventually all the residents packed up and moved out.

Seven years later Jimmy White, brother of the first victim, returns to the street determined to find the killer at all costs. He stakes out the street but by five in the morning he's seen nothing. As Jimmy decides to leave he sees a long reptilian arm, with a huge claw on the end, snake its way out of the sewer like a serpent. This is the monster that's been abducting the children. Jimmy tries to run but the arm pursues him chasing him through the back alleys. Then, just as the arm is about to strike it is mown down in a hail of gunfire.

The police have been staking out the street too, waiting for their opportunity to catch the monster. Thanks to Jimmy they have found it. A forensic scientist examines the giant claw and determines that the monster fed off the children by crushing their bodies then absorbing them through the huge pores in its palm. The monster's reign of terror is finally ended.

Once again the story creates a fantastic visual metaphor for a very basic primal fear. In this case it's the fear that beneath the everyday world of our streets and houses lies an ancient primal force that can pluck us out of our beds and take us when we are at our most vulnerable, and not even the comfort and security of our homes and our parent's care can protect us from it. Nothing can more perfectly embody this fear than a huge reptilian hand that rises from the sewers at night and reaches into the bedrooms of sleeping children.

What makes this story even scarier is the fact that we never actually see the full horror either of the monster or its victims. As I stated earlier, comics can't compete with the graphic descriptions of prose or the special effects budgets of film, so this story doesn't even try. The final gunfight is depicted only as a panel filled with sound effects. The monster itself is never fully seen, only it's hand and arm. Even the bodies of the monster's victims are not shown in the early part of the story. There is always an innocent bystander, or a crowd blocking our view. The captions refer to each body merely as a "balled up thing ... like an empty wrapper thrown carelessly aside". When later we learn that the monster crushed their bodies and fed off their bodily fluids the state of their corpses is almost too terrible to picture. All the horror takes place off the page where our imagination is every bit as vulnerable as those sleeping children.

The Horror Of It All

It would seem then, that there are a few key things that make a horror comic truly scary. One of the main things is a central visual metaphor that symbolises a very basic human fear and depicts it in a way that no other medium can. Another thing would be the ability to place the reader directly into the mind of the protagonist through the use of 'second person - present tense narrative'. In this way the horror becomes more immediate and far more personal than in any other medium.

Finally, even though horror comics are a graphic medium, what they don't show you is far more scary than what they do. The worst horrors of all lie just outside the panel borders, in a place so terrifying not even the most foolhardy would dare to explore.

Jasper Bark

Originally published in Mass Movement #35, May 2012

NEAL ADAMS

Whoever said "You should never meet your hero's" was wrong. Very, very wrong. About six weeks ago, I spoke to one of my hero's, Neal Adams, about...Well, about a load of different things, and he was one of the warmest, friendliest and funniest guys that it's been my honour to talk to. Ladies and gentlemen, boys and girls meet a living legend, meet Neal Adams...

Interview by Tim Cundle

MM: How did you get your first break in comics and do you think it's easier or tougher for people to break into the industry now than it was when you did it?

NA: It's a lot easier now, but when I broke into comics, everybody I spoke to within the industry was telling me that comic books would be out of business within a year. I went to Archie comics; there weren't many comic books out back then. There was basically DC, Mad Magazine and there was Harvey Comics, I had no idea who they were, so Archie Comics - I really didn't know where they were – they were in some hole in the wall at the beginning of Brooklyn. I went to DC and I couldn't even show my stuff, they would not look at it. There was this guy called Bill Perry, he came out and said "Do yourself a favour, get a job. Don't do this because it will be gone within a year". I don't know anybody who would tell you a story like that about their business, whether or not they give you a job, if they don't like your work it's a different thing; but they don't talk like that anymore.

Jack Kirby and Joe Simon you may know were at Archie Comics, doing *The Fly*, *The Shield* and a couple of other comic books. So I finally found out where Archie was and asked them if there was anyone who could talk to me and see my stuff. They said Jack Kirby and Joe Simon come in on Wednesday, otherwise they stay home. Why don't you come in on Wednesday to talk to them because your samples are pretty good. So I went in the next Wednesday with more samples and they weren't there. So I went in the next week on Wednesday and I had more samples and they weren't there. So finally I went in a third time (I would have kept going forever), and the guy said they're not here but why don't I get Joe Simon to phone you. So then there is Joe Simon on the phone and he says "Hey kid I saw your stuff it's pretty good but you know, I gotta tell you- I'm gonna do you the biggest favour I could possibly do you, and remember this because it doesn't sound good right now, but believe me this business is going to be out of business in a year and I'm doing you the biggest favour in the world. I'm turning you down despite the fact that your work is good, I'll be destroying your future and I don't want to do that. So I turned around and I must have looked like the Empire State building had fallen on me, and the Archie guy said "Maybe you wanna draw *Archie*?" I didn't want to draw Archie but that's what I did, I drew the Archie joke pages for $35.50 a page for writing, inking drawing and lettering, and that was my first comic book work.

MM: So let's talk about the new one, the First X-Men. What made you want to work on X-Men again?

NA: I spoke to the Marvel people and they were interested in having me do some stuff for them and they said "what are you interested in doing?" I had an idea for a story so I wrote it out and the idea was for a story about the X-Men before the X-Men. Because the first time you see the X-Men they are fully formed, with Professor X in his wheelchair, seven kids

139

standing around him in funny costumes and that's how X-Men started. But something must have happened before then.

Probably people thought they were aliens but eventually there were these people who were ultimately taken advantage of, they were captured and experimented on by the army and whatever. Why wouldn't someone round them up and try to help them out well before the X-Men ever happened? So I wondered who would be old enough to do that. And the oldest one around, pretty much is Wolverine- he's about 120 years old. So I proposed that we do it with the Wolverine being the guy that would round up these kids that were suffering the slings and arrows of outrageous fortune of the military industrial complex. Wouldn't he be the right guy to do it? Well the truth of the matter is that he probably was the right and the only guy.

Unfortunately Wolverine is kind of a mercenary and a warrior and what could he do for these people? He can train them to fight. But unfortunately what happens when you fight is that you die, which is not a good scenario. So I suggested this was actually a pretty good plot for a story and they agreed, so we're extending the legend of the X-Men back in time but it was a good series.

MM: Are you going to do another X-Men series?

NA: I don't know. I'm talking to them and settling some issues. I'm kind of talking to DC Comics as well. When I came back I did Batman, then I did X-Men, what do I do now? So I'm kinda talking to DC, I'm kinda talking to Marvel and we'll see. We also have our own characters which we stopped publishing when things got hard in the comic book business and 1500 stores went out of business because collectors had decided to get into the business and to buy comic books and put them away for five years, then one day they all woke up and realised that if they were all doing this how were they ever going to make money? Then they all stopped and then Bam! The industry crashed and 1500 comic book stores went out of business.

As a publisher I thought I'd rather not stay here so I closed up shop and we went back to doing a lot of advertising and things like that. I told people though that when things started to get a bit better I'd be back, because I'd started a project called *Rise of Magic* and it was a pretty good project, people kind of liked it, people were waiting for it, but with things so bad I put it aside. We continue to do some work on it from time to time and it's sitting on a shelf waiting to go, so we're considering whether to put it out ourselves or whether to go through someone like Dark Horse. Meanwhile as a separate artist thing, I'm looking for another project and you look at me and think "Well, he's done Batman, he's done X-Men what's he's going to do next?"

MM: It's got to be Green Lantern, with Jeff Johns leaving?

NA: If was right, and available I'd be on it...

MM: You've done Green Lantern before, and Green Arrow...

NA: I did, I did, and I'm not convinced I want to jump in to the many splendored, many coloured Green Lanterns – although it does seem interesting – I think it's kind of what took the Green Lantern movie down, didn't it? All that CGI, in terms of my personal interest. So I don't know that that's where it's where I want to go. Also there are a lot of good guys working on it? Where's the challenge? There are some things lying around, maybe Superman? What about a Superman that's kinda like what Frank Miller started? It kind of intrigues me... What do you do with Superman if you want to amp him up just a little bit?

Then there's the Avengers too... So we're talking and we'll see what comes up. Whatever I do it will be in a slightly different direction but not hurting anything. It will be a surprise. Right now I'm doing the *Cold Blood* for Dark Horse, I've just finished the last chapter of the first book. So to me, I'm kind of like a fan myself; I did a Batman Odyssey that provoked a lot of controversy with some people and had a tonne of fun doing it. I got a tonne of abuse about it on the internet even though I announced I was going to do a novel rather than a series of stories. People on the internet were saying "Oh I don't understand the first story" – It's not a first story, it's the first chapter of a novel!! It's a novel you're not going to understand what's going on until the last chapter!! What I did was, at the time, I didn't respond to it. People told me to just ignore it and pay no attention, but that doesn't even sound like Neal Adams! You don't have a go at Neal Adams and not expect him to come back at you. I don't do that. But I let it go, and DC comics didn't talk about it or promote it and I just let it happen, like a jerk and I could have just as easily come back to people and said, hang on, let's talk about it.

But I let it go, and now I have people come up to me and, leaning over, whisper to me "I loved Batman Odyssey" as if someone's going to come up from behind and say "What? You wrote Batman Odyssey what's wrong with you? I get these 13 year old fans contacting me and saying "people go on about these and how terrible they are but I just read them and I thought they were great, what' going on? What's it all about?" The poor kid is very confused about what's going on. My coming back was by doing what I considered to be the best stuff I'd ever done and people reacted in this weird way. So I moved forward in time by doing something that was terrific but I didn't move forward in time by not attacking back when they were attacking me. That's my mistake. That's not going to happen again. So what's happening now is that I have these people coming to me about Batman Odyssey, saying they like it because it's like a book and the last chapter blew them away. And guess what, do you think all this stuff is going to sit there and nobody's going to turn them into stories? The whole concept will be exploited, the underworld will be exploited, the whole thing. Someone's going to do it. It won't be me because I think I've done it? You've got loathsome trolls, you've got another Batman living under the earth, and it's all there. I'm thinking two movies from now I'm going to see that story. There's all kinds of stuff there and it has this underground fan following, which means people are already working with it. There are at least two radio shows that are effectively doing Batman Odyssey, it's crazy. I have to sit back like a fan and say Oh yeah , that sounds like Adams, in trouble again, better watch out!

MM: You're credited with having introduced realism into comics along with Denny O'Neil with your run on Batman in the 1970s and Green Lantern and Green Arrow..

NA: I'm not going to criticise Denny because he was a great partner when we worked on it, but I first developed this with Bob Haney. I changed Batman with Bob Haney. Then the editor of Batman was saying why is the only Batman we're doing is Brave and Bold? He came at me with a whole bunch of letters from fans talking about it and saying Batman should be more like Brave and Bold. So they put me on Batman and they told me they were going to pair me up with Denny who was a journalist. I agreed to give it a try and it went from there, so I had to leave Bob Haney behind over at Brave and Bold, but he was fine there and doing good work. Then Denny started working on my Batman and he turned out to be a pretty good writer and because he was a journalist, he wrote a more down to earth story, so we had a good time and started to crank out some good stories. But I never want to take any credit away from Bob Haney, we did seven books together. That really was the turn, Denny just jumped on and made in better.

MM: The Green Lantern/ Green Arrow run you did was maybe eleven issues? It's widely credited with bringing a sense of realism into a world of books that are anything but realistic...

NA: It almost happened by accident. Gil Kane had been working on Green Lantern and was doing a bang up job on it. He had an incredible way with anatomy and had the characters virtually flying off the pages. He was going to go on to do a thing called *Black Mark*, a graphic novel, and I saw they were hiring guys to do Green Lantern and each new guy would make it worse. Finally I went to the boss and said that I'd like to do Green Lantern some day, and he said to forget about it because it was going to be cancelled in a couple of days. I asked him to give me whatever it had left, even if it's only one or two issues, I'll do it because I think I can bring something to it. Maybe it won't go down the tubes. He said okay, what about if we use Denny on that too? It almost didn't matter to me because I wanted to do this.

People had been recognising that the stuff I'd been doing was more realistic, and Denny and I had an opportunity to create something. Denny had been going a little deeper into his newspaper background and he was really enjoying this because America was always involved in a lot of politics, a lot of liberal responses and Denny was there. Now I wasn't quite as crazed as Denny, but I was the Chairman of an organisation down in the Bronx and we used to get involved in politics there, so we started doing these books and college students were writing in, college professors; it was like the adult world had suddenly realised comic books existed. Carmine Infantino, who didn't quite know what we were doing, ended up doing a speaking tour across America about Green Lantern/ Green Arrow we had to fill him in . So we did about elven books. We kind of run out of steam at the end when Denny wrote a story about overpopulation – a liberal favourite at that time – I thought: we don't want to step into that whole overpopulation thing. If that's all we've got I think we've shot our load. It was hard to draw and hard to deal with.

Finally I did this cover and took it in, thinking we were winding down and it will never be used because it's against the comic's code, but it should be used. I took it to the boss and he kind of dropped it like a hot potato. So we took it to the executives, same reaction. So we said "Why don't you take it to the comics code see if they will accept it?" "They'll never accept it, what's wrong with you?" During this debate that was going on at DC, I was out of it because I'd clearly gone mad. Not only were they not going to pay me but they were actually going to suck money out of me for coming up with such a crazy idea. I go over to Marvel as a relief and speak to Johnny Romita, who is working on a book who, according to the story there is a character "Who is popping pills and jumps off a roof" I said "Gee, Johnny, I don't think Stan knows much about drug addiction, and if someone pops some pills and jumps off a roof I don't know if a drug addict would do that?" Johnny said "The thing is I think Stan's gonna run it. It got rejected by the comic's code" so I thought he's not going to do it, but Johnny said "He's going to put it out. He went to his uncle, the publisher and said he'd like to run it without the comic code seal." I said that was great, if he was really going to run it. And he was.

It was a Spiderman book. Two weeks later I go back and ask what happened. Johnny said "It went out, and nobody said a word. They didn't even perceive that the seal wasn't on it." So when I go back to DC there is a panic, the shit had hit the fan. They were going nuts, because they had this cover, they could have done the same thing but Stan had scooped them. The Comics Code had been put together by the publishers originally, so within a day or two they had called up a meeting of the Comics Code committee and within a week or so they rewrote the comics code. Then immediately it came back DC said "Okay, do that book!" so we got the book out. The Comics Code changed so much that it became a waste of time, and they essentially just forgot about it. I'd love to take credit but it just disappeared and no-one even noticed…

MM: With nearly five decades in the industry, are there any writers or artists you haven't worked with yet who you really want to work with?

NA: There are a whole bunch of guys. Back in the day, I worked with Roy Thomas at Marvel Comics who provided some of the best dialogue that I could possibly want. At DC I got to work with Bob Haney and then Denny O'Neil. So I essentially got to work with the best people at DC and Marvel. Then we have to jump forward in time. I was going to do the Batman with Frank Miller but I opted out of that because I was busy at the time, but now I have this whole roster of great writers that I could possibly work with. I could write it myself but the energy it takes to switch off is too much. So far the two stories I've done are my stories but there are a bunch of writers, all of whom would like to work with me, who I can choose, so I have the pick of the crop don't I?

Originally published in Mass Movement #35, May 2013

SCREEN DAMAGE
RIVERS OF BLOOD: GOING TO HELL IN A BABY CART

"When I was little, my father was famous. He was the greatest samurai in the empire, and he was the shogun's decapitator. He cut off the heads of 131 lords…"

Some cult films come from out of nowhere while others arise fully formed from well-established roots. For Japan's Lone Wolf and Cub, it's definitely a case of the latter – anyone who wonders why need only consider the love and care with which the source material has been lifted from the printed page and transferred onto screens around the world.

Starting out as a popular manga strip – its original run topped eight million sales in Japan alone – the comic adventures of Lone Wolf and Cub have gone on to become a celebrated series of theatrical films, a long-running television show, a miniseries, four separate plays, a cluster of television movies, a computer game and much more.

Cited on the album 'Liquid Swords' by GZA of the Wu Tang Clan, Lone Wolf and Cub have popped up in numerous other mediums, including several cameos in the *Samurai Jack* cartoons, a semi-official continuation of the original manga (this time with the Cub having grown up to become the Lone Wolf) and a futuristic (and badly received) post-apocalyptic reimagining.

Horror superstar John Carpenter has paid homage to the films, basing the look and style of the Three Storms in *Big Trouble In Little China* on villains from the manga, and even author Max Allan Collins confessed to the BBC that his graphic novel *Road To Perdition* is at heart "…an unabashed homage to Lone Wolf And Cub."

It's not hard to see why this 40-year-plus franchise has proven to be so popular. In the early 1980s, Roger Corman's New World Pictures recognised the money-spinning potential of the ace '70s film adaptations and hired Robert Houston (who played Bobby in Wes Craven's *The Hills Have Eyes*) to edit two of the films together with a newly dubbed audio track featuring early turns from the likes of Sandra Bernhardt.

With a superb new synth score by Mark Lindsay of Paul Revere and the Raiders fame, the resultant film was released as *Shogun Assassin* – a lightning-fast mash-up that was briefly banned in Britain as a video nasty and went on to feature prominently in 'Kill Bill II' as the bedtime viewing of choice for the Bride's young daughter.

There have been various abortive attempts to stage a modern Hollywood adaptation – it was a particular dream project for Darren *"The Matrix"* Aronofsky for many years – but it is now looking increasingly likely that hotshot director Justin Lin will be the man to finally succeed in bringing Lone Wolf and Cub to a modern wider audience. Once he has completed the latest entry in 'The Fast and the Furious' franchise, Lin has announced that he'll be taking on the property after Kamala Films acquired the rights and appointed David *Blade Runner, Twelve Monkeys* Peoples to write the script.

Peoples certainly won't be short of short of original source material. Under the title *Kozure Ôkami*, the manga ran to 28 volumes between 1970 and 1976. Part of the Chanbara genre, it was written by Kazuo "Crying Freeman" Koike, illustrated by Goseki Kojima and immediately recognised as an important and influential work.

The story tells the tale of Ogami Ittô, a master Suiô swordsman in 17th century Japan who serves as the Kogi Kaishakunin - the official executioner of the Tokugawa Shogunate. Ittô falls victim in a plot to discredit him by the Ura-Yagyû clan led by arch-enemy, Yagyû Retsudô. With his wife Azami dead at the hands of ninja assassins, Ittô is framed and made to appear as if he has been praying for the death of the shogun at his family shrine, and is subsequently ordered to commit seppuku – ritual suicide – along with his one year old son, Daigorô.

"They will pay... with rivers of blood!"

Faced with certain death either by his own hand or beneath the gathered swords of the Ura-Yagyû, Ittô surprises his enemies by choosing a third option – meifumadô, the road to hell. Offering Daigorô a choice of a ball or a sword, Ittô reveals that he is prepared to kill his son there and then, and send him into the afterlife to join his mother. But when the infant selects the sword, he seals his fate as a ronin – a masterless samurai - alongside his father.
As they are about to defy the will of the shogun, it looks likely that their new life will be short indeed. But when confronted by Retsudô and his men, Ittô displays his ruthless cunning by wearing robes bearing the official crest or 'mon' of the shogun. As it was considered sacrilegious to desecrate a mon or any other official shogunate document – point a sword at the crest and you may as well be pointing it at the ruler himself - the Ura-Yagyû reluctantly agree to allow Ittô and his son to pass through their wall of swords, furious that a noble samurai would even consider resorting to such a low trick. But as Ittô tells them, "We who walk the demon's path are no longer ordinary men. All Japan lives beneath this crest. The way of the warrior defers to this alone... it's time I got some use out of it!"

Determined not to allow his enemy to get away, Retsudô challenges Ittô to face his eldest son, Kurato, in a duel at dusk – the wily arch-manipulator knows that if the challenger stands with his back to the sunset, then its rays will blind Ittô, and give Kurato a deadly advantage in addition to the fact that Ittô has to fight while carrying his young son on his shoulders. But Ittô foresees the deception, and ties a small mirror to Daigorô's forehead which reflects the light back into his enemy's eyes.

A horrified Retsudô can only watch as the decapitator claims his latest head before escaping, and the sunset serves as an achingly beautiful backdrop while Kurato's body staggers on, fountains of arterial blood spurting high up into the early evening air.

"That was when my father left his samurai life, and become a demon."

From this launching point, father and son are transformed into the Lone Wolf and Cub – assassins for hire for whom no job is too difficult or shameful. Travelling around Japan's burgeoning system of roads and highways with a wooden perambulator that doubles as a pimped-out death machine (and which gives the franchise its alternative 'baby cart' moniker), Ittô and Daigorô quickly become legendary killers as they carry out hit after hit, always seeking vengeance on the Ura-Yagyû whom they aim to shame with each murder that they complete.

For their part, the Ura-Yagyû are constantly hunting the Lone Wolf and his cub, and spend the entire series plotting their downfall in a series of ambushes, battles and elaborate conspiracies.

Totalling almost 9,000 pages, the manga is both beautifully scripted and illustrated, and has become famous for establishing many comic 'firsts' – for example, the eventual duel between Ittô and Retsudô takes in 178 panels and is regarded as being one of the longest fight scenes ever published.

As well as its epic scope, one of the reasons why the manga series is so highly regarded lies is its attention to historic detail and accuracy. Lone Wolf and Cub takes place during the early Edo period (1603 – 1868), a 250 year span which saw the nation ruled by a succession of Tokugawa shoguns who maintained a distinct class system. The sword-carrying privileged samurai class accounted for about 10 per cent of the population and served military overlords called daimyos, who exercised the shogun's will. Both the Ogami and Yagyû clans were real – the Ogami disappeared entirely in 1655 and their former role as Kogi Kaishakunin was taken over by the Yagyû, who came to an end shortly after this in 1681.

The story that Koike fashioned using this historical fact may not actually be true, but there's no denying its effectiveness as a damn good yarn. In any event, it's certainly true that infighting, treachery and jostling for favour within the shogunate were commonplace throughout the period.

Below the samurai were the peasants, who lived only to provide for their samurai masters, and below them were commoner class outcasts such as prostitutes, beggars, actors and entertainers. The Lone Wolf and Cub adventures would feature all elements of this class system, and even the lowliest characters would regularly comment upon the scandalous life that Ittô and Daigorô were pursuing. By turning their back on humanity, father and son were freely choosing to adopt an evil existence based on the 'hell' or eternal anger state of Buddha's Six Modes of Existence.

Throughout the manga, Ittô steadily whittles down the sons and daughters of Retsudô until only the clan leader is left. The climactic end of the comic saga sees Retsudô slay Ittô after the decapitator's dôtanuki battle sword snaps in two – it transpires that, unable to defeat the Lone Wolf in a fair fight, Retsudô paid a sword polisher to secretly damage the blade. So, after a lifetime of fatigue and bloodshed, Ittô ends his path of meifumadô by failing to kill the enemy that he swore to destroy.

Ultimately, it is left to Daigorô to avenge both his fallen father and his slain mother. Retsudô does not resist – he spreads his arms wide and allows the boy to run him through with a spear, telling the child that he is the 'Grandson of my heart' as he dies, thus bringing the cycle of vengeance to an end in a suitably epic fashion.

As far as the Lone Wolf and Cub's various ventures onto both the cinema and television screens are concerned, the six films produced between 1972 and 1974 are considered to be the definitive productions, and take as much care to remain historically accurate as they do to remain faithful to the manga.

The first three in the series were directed by Kenji Misumi and produced by Shintaro Katsu, the star of the equally popular 26-part *Zatoichi* franchise. Portraying the role of Ogami Ittô was Katsu's brother, Tomisaburo Wakayama – an accomplished martial artist who was trained in disciplines such as Judo, Kenpo, Iaido, Kendo and Bojutsu. Stocky and powerful, Wakayama was nobody's idea of a traditional leading man, but his permanent scowl and understated performance is a major reason why the Lone Wolf films are so successful.
Also a busy actor in other areas, Wakayama made eight films alone in 1972 (three of them entries in the Baby Cart series). He stepped up to produce the next three instalments, which were directed by Buichi Saito, Kenji Misumi and Yoshiyuki Kuroda and released in 1972, 1973, and 1974 respectively.

In the first, *Sword of Vengeance*, Ittô and Daigorô set out on their quest for revenge after being framed and accept a commission from a local chamberlain to kill a rival and his hired soldiers. They find themselves in a remote mountain village which has been seized by Tobbicho - a gang of mercenary ronin who are also the targets of the Lone Wolf. The Tobbicho have taken over the village, raping and looting at will and routinely slaughtering anyone who dares stand up to them. Their leader suspects that he knows Ittô from somewhere, but the ronin tells him that he is mistaken.

Forcing Ittô to stay in a room with several other travellers, the bandits delight in calling him a coward when he refuses to react to their taunts, even threatening to kill a prostitute unless the pair make love while they watch. To everyone's surprise, Ittô agrees – the Tobbicho enjoy the spectacle way too much to wonder how a supposed coward who is afraid of death at their hands is able to bed the woman as if he doesn't have a care in the world. For her part, the prostitute marvels at the thought of a noble samurai who is willing to debase himself in order to save her life.

Come the morning, the Tobbicho announce that they are leaving the village, but before they go, they plan to slaughter Ittô and the other travellers to prevent them from spreading news of their crimes. The words of a sickly samurai and a monk at prayer help to unlock the memory of the leader of the Tobbicho, and the doomed man realises too late who Ittô is. The former high executioner emerges to face the gang, and a breathless finale ensues as Ittô reveals the many hidden secrets of the baby cart and proceeds to slice his way through each of the ronin in turn.

"Fear his wrath... the wrath of lone wolf and cub, assassin."

Next in the series was *Baby Cart At The River Styx* – or the river of Sanzu to be more exact (in Buddhist cosmology, the Sanzu performs a role similar to that of the Styx and is said to separate this world from the afterlife). With the origin story out of the way, the second entry runs at a breakneck pace and provided much of the action for the later *Shogun Assassin* mash-up.

A clan whose wealth depends on the production of their much-admired indigo dye hire Lone Wolf and Cub to kill a traitor who is being escorted to Edo where he plans to hand over industrial secrets that could put an end to the clan's monopoly. The shogun regards the traitor as being so important that he sends out his feared bodyguards, the Hidari brothers, to watch over him on his journey. Each brother wears a long cloak, a wide-brimmed straw hat and specialises in a different weapon – a studded club, spiked gloves and a huge pre-Freddy Krueger metal claw.

Meanwhile, the Ura-Yagyû instruct their allies, Kurokawa shinobi-class ninjas and the Akari Yagyû clan of female assassins, to track and kill the Lone Wolf and Cub. In a stand out scene, the lady killers first demonstrate that they are up to the job by taking on the Kurokawa's best man, whittling off body parts until the warrior is little more than a head and a torso.

Both ninja clans make various attempts to kill the Lone Wolf and Cub as the pair move to intercept the Hidari brothers, but all are defeated in some of the most breathtaking samurai action ever put on film. The final showdown with the Hidari brothers takes place amid a desolate plain of sand dunes. Ittô dispatches them with ease, leaving their leader to die from a fabled cut across the windpipe which creates an eerie wailing sound known in the manga as the *Flute of the Fallen Tiger*. With the traitor dead, Ittô and Daigorô walk off in search of their next adventure.

The third film in the series, *Baby Cart To Hades*, see the Yagyû ninjas still hot on the heels of the Lone Wolf and Cub, but all fall easily beneath his dôtanuki blade. While lodging at a guest house, Ittô meets a terrified teenage girl who has been sold by her poor parents to a yakuza pimp. Revealing that she killed the pimp when he tried to rape her, the girl begs Ittô for help. He duly faces off against her yakuza owners, who cannot let the girl go without losing face. Ittô earns their respect when he volunteers to undergo the girl's punishment on her behalf, and is tortured without mercy.

Once he recovers, the yakuza hire Ittô to kill a corrupt local official and his bodyguards, one of whom sports a pair of western pistols. Realising that he won't get close enough to draw his sword, Ittô uses his own son as bait, and as the six-shooter rides past a stretch of river, Daigorô pretends to drown. Diving in to rescue the struggling child, he first discards his guns, only realising his mistake as Ittô explodes out of the nearby reeds to strike him down. This makes the corrupt official realise what he is up against, and the climax sees an ambushed Lone Wolf fighting off a small army of warriors.

At this point, the baby cart is revealed to not only feature hidden knives, swords and spears, but a small battery of guns. It seems as if the former samurai will use anything and everything to vanquish his enemies, even surprising an opponent who has disarmed him by pulling out one of the pilfered pistols and shooting him dead. No act is too low or dishonourable for the disgraced ronin if it means getting the job done...

There is a coda of sorts when a proud ronin called Kanbei arrives as the battle ends to challenge Ittô to a formal duel. It only lasts a few seconds, and as Kanbei dies, he and Ittô discuss what it means to be a samurai. The way of the warrior, Ittô tells him, is not to simply live or die, but to live through death. As the Lone Wolf and Cub leave the battlefield, the awestruck young leader of the yakuza gang is restrained from following them by her own men, who tell her that Ittô Ogami is a monster made flesh.

In *Baby Cart In Peril*, Lone Wolf and Cub are hired to kill Oyuki, the renegade member of a daiymo's han. It seems that the daimyo has sent many of his men after Oyuki, but the swordmaiden has killed each and every one of them, cutting off their chonmage (a samurai's distinctive top-knot hairstyle) after death to add greater insult to her defiance.

Ittô discovers that while Oyuki is renowned for her great beauty, she has chosen to have a huge image of a kintaro demon tattooed on her body, its claws seemingly grasping at her left breast, while on her back is a grim depiction of a terrifying mountain witch from traditional noh plays called a yamauba.

It transpires that Oyuki has been killing the vassals and removing their hair to force the daimyo to send his best swordsman after her, an instructor who hypnotises his opponents with a burning sword trick. Oyuki reveals that it was the instructor who caused her to rebel against the clan, for after defeating her in a duel, he went on to humiliate and rape her.

Ittô locates Oyuki at the same time as the instructor, and duly steps back to allow her to confront her tormentor.

Mesmerising her with his flaming sword trick, the instructor steps in for the kill – just as Oyuki rips off her clothes to reveal her terrible demon tattoos, distracting him long enough for her to rush forward and penetrate his body with her knife. The look of satisfaction on her face as she twists the blade fades once her nemesis is dead; with no further reason to live, she agrees to duel Ittô. The Lone Wolf provides her with a splendid death, and dispatches her with dignity and respect.

Meanwhile, Retsudô has convinced Oyuki's former lord to arrest Ittô, but the Lone Wolf and Cub escape by taking the daimyo hostage. Deciding to kill the daimyo and blame his death on the Lone Wolf, Retsudô orders the Yagyû to attack en masse, and another huge fight provides the film with its climax. This time, Ittô succeeds in slicing his way to Retsudô, and the two battle it out with barely-restrained hatred etched across their faces. The fight ends as Retsudô impales Ittô on a sword, while for his part Ittô takes out one of Retsudô's eyes.

As Retsudô flees, Ittô falls to the floor, apparently dead. Daigorô emerges from hiding and calls for his father. Hearing his son brings the Lone Wolf back to the land of the living, and the films ends as Lone Wolf and Cub painfully leave the battlefield, wounded but still firmly set on the road of vengeance.

Father and son recover from their wounds in time for *Baby Cart In the Land Of Demons*, the penultimate film in the series. This time, Ittô is approached by a man who says that he is the first of five messengers, each of whom will test the Lone Wolf's skills by attempting to kill him. If he survives, he will learn a little more about his intended quarry. The messengers all employ different techniques to assassinate the Lone Wolf, including tricking him into drinking poison and duelling in a river where they fall for his famous 'wave-cutting' stroke.

After they survive the audition process, Ittô and Daigorô learn that a local daimyo has stepped down as leader of his clan in favour of his young son. However, the boy's mother is a concubine, and the true heir has been imprisoned. What's more, the changeling child is not really a boy, but a girl. If news of this scandal reaches the shogunate, the entire clan will be dissolved.

The loyal vassals want the Lone Wolf to murder the child imposter, their senile former leader and the concubine so they can avert disaster. At the same time, Ittô must kill a Buddhist priest that the clan entrusted with their secret, only to learn too late that the priest is really a Yagyû spymaster, and that he is now on his way to reveal the information to Retsudô himself.

In an inspired bit of cunning, the Lone Wolf assassinates the priest by swimming beneath his boat and using a special tool to cut through it, dropping the spy down into the river where he meets a bad end.

Taking the message cylinder which contains the clan's secret, Ittô flees for his life with the Yagyû in close pursuit. He barely makes it to the domain of the imposter lord, but succeeds in both delivering the cylinder and killing all three of his targets. If his willingness to murder a child seems shocking, it's worth pointing out that the young imposter also instructs the clan's samurai to kill Ittô and his son a split second after playing happily with Daigorô – and besides, what else would you expect from a couple of self-proclaimed demons?

The last of the '70s films based on the manga was *White Heaven In Hell*, and it's fair to say that the series went out with a bang. Retsudô's failure to bring the Lone Wolf and Cub to justice is forcing the shogun to consider declaring the pair national outlaws, and to order every daimyo in the land to hunt them down. Such a course of action would mean that the Yagyû would have to admit defeat, and lose the status that they have earned through years of treachery and subterfuge. Retsudô begs for one more chance – he will send his last surviving child, Kaori, after the Lone Wolf (Ittô and Daigorô having already slain all of her siblings).

With the future of the clan at stake, Retsudô sacrifices some of his best men in training Kaori, but it doesn't make any difference – when she duels the Lone Wolf with a trick which involves juggling several knives at once, he quickly deduces her ploy, and succeeds in dispatching her to join her dead brothers

Desperate, Retsudô turns to Hyouei, an illegitimate son whom he sired with a concubine and then abandoned, sending him to live with a fearsome mountain tribe of black magicians called the Tsuchigumo - literally, the 'Spider of the Ground' clan (loosely based on real-life ferocious, cave-dwelling natives that were said to exist in certain southern regions of Japan).

But Hyouei damns his father for abandoning him, and refuses to help. While a distraught Retsudô returns to Edo to try and think of another way to destroy his clan's nemesis, Hyouei decides to kill the Lone Wolf and his Cub in order to win favour with the shogunate, and to lead his adoptive clan out of the mountains to take over from the Yagyû.

This leads to a genuinely creepy initiation scene where the tribe dig up buried coffins containing three warriors and send the newly graduated killers to torment Ittô and Daigorô. The Lone Wolf can sense that he is being followed, but the only signs of this are the succession of people who are slaughtered immediately after approaching the pair – a pedlar selling sweet treats, a young woman who pauses to coo over Daigorô and more.

As Ittô and Daigorô stop at an inn for the night, a grubby hand emerges from the soil to clutch at the ankle of the innkeeper's daughter, and it is revealed that the three wild-looking killers can burrow through the earth like huge worms! The Lone Wolf quickly realises this after the entire inn is silently butchered, and a doom-laden voice whispers through the night to tell him that anyone who dares attempt to speak or approach either father or son will suffer immediate death. The voice warns that Ittô and Daigorô are to become outcasts, forever forced to shun the company of civilised folk, and as the pair head off towards the mountains, it appears that the tribe's supernatural powers may have defeated them after all.

But of course, it is all a ruse on the part of the Lone Wolf – travelling high above the snow-line, Ittô and Daigorô build an igloo, and settle down to wait for their persecutors to make their move. They know that the three killers will be unable to remain buried beneath the freezing snow, and will be forced to stage a more conventional assault, during which Ittô butchers them.

Following this failure, Hyouei attempts to deceive the Lone Wolf by imitating a potential customer, but he gives himself away when he dares to sit down on his sword – a true samurai would never do this, Ittô explains, because they consider their sword to be a part of their soul. His ruse uncovered, Hyouei resorts to a frontal assault which sees the Lone Wolf trapped in the mud of a fog-shrouded plain of reeds. Goading Hyouei into accepting a duel, he is able to finally escape the swords of the Tsuchigumo, and again heads up high above the snowline.

He has gathered together the 200 remaining members of his clan, and has abandoned the plotting and scheming of the earlier films in favour of all-out war. What follows is a fast and furious battle to the death as Ittô and Daigorô use everything in their arsenal of murder to wreak vengeance upon the Yagyû, and the snow runs red with spilled blood as the pair decimate what is left of the clan. Realising that all is lost, a loyal samurai forces Retsudô to escape on a sledge, and Ittô and Daigorô can only watch as their nemesis gets away yet again, vowing that one day, Retsudô's neck will fall beneath the sword of the Lone Wolf...

Except there never was a next time. The original '70s series of films ended here, but had the saga continued, the climactic battle between Ittô and Retsudô would have taken place outside the walls of Edo, and a huge crowd would have gathered to witness the legendary combat – peasant and samurai alike, all watching as the fabled Lone Wolf battles on with a broken sword, even appearing to get the upper hand at least twice before finally succumbing to his many, many wounds.

It would also have featured a pivotal scene from the manga where, sensing the end fast approaching, Ittô delivers a long, impassioned speech to Daigorô – one that the boy remembers as he finishes the job that his father started. As the youth kills Retsudô and brings the story to an end, the watching crowd are reduced to tears... truly a case of both living and dying by the sword.

"I don't remember most of this myself. I only remember the Shogun's ninja, hunting us wherever we go, and the bodies falling. And the blood..."

Goseki Kojima died in 2000, but in recent years that hasn't stopped Koike from writing an official sequel to his most famous creation, this time focusing on the adventures of the now grown cub. With Hideki Mori stepping in to provide the art, it seems likely that the rivers of blood will flow for some time yet...

Liam Ronan

Originally published in Mass Movement #35, May 2013

DUNCAN REDMONDS
(SNUFF / GUNS 'N' WANKERS)

I must admit I was more than a little excited to hear that Snuff were about to drop a new album. I've been listening to the band for a long, long time, right from their classic debut EP *Not Listening*, cranking up the wireless when the Peel Sessions were aired through to their later albums on labels like Fat Wreck and their very own Ten Past Twelve records. For me Snuff has always been a band than has transcended the petty subdivisions in punk rock and Hardcore and as a result pretty much everyone loves 'em! Punks, crusties, straight edgers, skinheads, Snuff seems to always find a place in people's hearts. The new album is a real return to form and picks up seamlessly from where they left off, and so of course I jumped at the chance of putting some questions to singer and drummer extraordinaire Duncan.

Interview by Tom Chapman.

MM: Although you've played gigs here and there this is your first studio album for a long time, what prompted the decision to become a recording band again?

Duncan: Borderline syndrome. Personally I never stopped recording with solo projects and with other bands but as snuff we started gigging again in 2008 then recording again early 2011. Japanese pop star Tamurapan recorded a track with us at the kinks studio in London that was a lovely moment. Then we started sofa bashes on a few new songs and decided to record a tour EP with 4 new tracks and 4 covers. Then went back to the studio in 2012 thinking to record an EP of the originals and it turned into an album. Really we did it for us and didn't think that in the present climate labels would be interested. There is little or no money in sales these days so it was a surprise that both Fat and CR Japan picked it up.

MM: Are you back as a full time band? Or taking things as they come?

Duncan: We can't be a full time band because of everyone's different schedules . So we're kind of an ongoing part time band. We can only do about 20-25 gigs a year so it keeps it as a fun thing with no strings attached. These days we probably wouldn't be able to do it full time even if everyone could. What made it possible in the past was royalties and tour support, but for better or worse the industry is dead and they are out of the equation, so we just do the fun ones we can, where we can. But it isn't all bad and it is an exciting time as long as you don't expect to make money, luckily for us that's where we started anyway so we'll still plod on regardless.

MM: Snuff for me has always had a unique place in the punk scene - you've been liked by everyone across the board - from the straight edgers, to pop punks, Hardcore kids, punks. I guess it is because your music can't be as easily pigeonholed as some other bands. Has your audience changed, or is it still the same mix of people?

Duncan: Our audience has definitely changed, now they are mainly old, bald, round, and standing at the back with their kids dancing and singing along in the "crèche pit" down the front. We always tried to mix up different influences, I think the more varied the influences the tastier the cake.

MM: You've always been incredibly prolific, does the song writing process come easily? Do you have songs floating round your head all the time or do they take a while to germinate?

Duncan: All depends. Sometimes a song just falls out, others it hangs about until a spark sets it off on a different direction, other times you can hammer out a song and in the end it's crap. There's always a pool of ideas floating about, some work but most come to nothing. With Snuff it's great to bounce ideas about and mix it all up.

Snuff seem to have a love affair with Japan, how did that come about?

Duncan: I fell in love with the country as soon as I got there in '91. The level of trust, the passion, the food, the treatment, the attitude. It was one of the bigger culture shocks I have ever had. Going from NW London to Tokyo was two completely different planets. Peer pressure is a strong force and if all around are honest and respectful then that starts to rub off, and the opposite is also true like Britain.

MM: What is touring in Japan like, is that any different to touring in Europe?

Duncan: Touring Europe overall is great and the venues are really well organised, but touring Japan is a step up. The fans are passionate and treatment is absolutely incredible, the pa's are normally top spec and they will go out of their way to be helpful and positive, this is a lovely culture shock compared to Britain. I wonder how many British people realise that many foreign bands avoid Britain because of the poor treatment? That said there are some great venues in the UK , we grew up with it so whether we like the treatment or not we're used to it.

MM: You've worked with many labels over the years, and are still working with US and Japanese labels at the moment. Did you not fancy releasing the new album yourselves on 10 by 12?

Duncan: Can't afford to lose money. We may do a run of vinyl. That's a small market but it's still there and growing, the cd has been a dead format for a few years now and mp3s don't sound that good plus everyone expects them for free anyway. I draw some schadenfreude from watching the start of the death of the mp3 as a format as people don't even bother clogging their machines up and go straight to YouTube and Spotify. At least with Spotify you get paid 0.000007 Pence so at the present rate we'll have enough for a cup of coffee in 2094, something to look forward to!

MM: Are you concerned about the changes facing the music industry?

Duncan: The music industry died a few years ago, and I mean the punk music industry which is a contradiction in itself? The music business, however, is doing fine but we we're never really a part of that. Downloading killed the cd and labels and bands made their money on that.

Most labels are gone or in trouble. Labels that only ever did vinyl survived but I would say at least two thirds of the people I know that worked in the punk music industry 10 years ago are now out of work or doing something else as there is no more work . This is good and bad. I think we were lucky to have been about at a time when the bands get paid so they can afford to carry on full time, I wouldn't want to be a band trying to get that going these days, it was hard enough when you did get paid royalties. For a few years it really irked me how many different justifications people would use for stealing your music and in the end it kind of gave me a different insight into how us humans will justify our actions to ourselves and change our morals at the drop of a hat to suit the situation., Whinge rant etc. But if I get on my soap box I'm a hypocrite as I used to tape stuff as a kid, trouble is now its global not local. Luckily Snuff never trusted anyone so although we may cry like pampered babies about lost livelihood it is no surprise to find out that most humans are inertly selfish self-justifying hypocrites, rant moan etc. But that said there is also literally a world of opportunity opened up and somehow the industry side of things will adapt and swing back in the bands favour. People are starting to realise that if they want their bands to gig and record they will have to make it happen, I think all that pledging stuff isn't the way to go for us, who wants to buy something before they've heard it? It should be the other way round, like it then buy it; it seems like begging to me?

MM: And it's not just the music industry, but society is moving on - are you "digital people"? Do the closures of household high street names affect you in any way? I remember buying Snuff records on the high street, and record shops were a meeting place for likeminded types, in fact I have become good friends with people you used to only meet in a record shop.

Duncan: We haven't completely kept up completely with digital stuff, it's off putting that 95 % of downloads are illegal or if its legal the slice the band actually gets is tiny. If it's on iTunes they take most of the money and don't put it back into the bands like a label would. It's a different planet these days, as a youth going to a record shop was the event of the week, or month. These days it happens in seconds. Labels and record shops would channel you towards the music that made sense to you, and it was a precious item, now there is a sea of bands to wade through at the touch of a button. In the end word of mouth is still the best promotion .

MM: Mass Movement has also made the transition from being a print fanzine to an online magazine. Do you follow much of the music press these days? How do you prefer to read up on things?

Duncan: Sorry but personally I stopped reading the music press decades ago. I'm wrapped up in my own world of music, the last think I want to do is read about someone else's. I don't mean to be rude it's just me.

MM: Apart from the high streets, have you seen much change in the venues you've played in over the years? do you have any favourite venues? Any you are sad to see no longer there? I used to love the punk and hardcore gigs at the Duchess Of York in Leeds for example.

Duncan: I've had a rant about treatment in UK venues already but I can say the promoters we have worked with in the past have generally been fine and for atmosphere and sound there are some great venues. The best venues seem to be run by ex-musicians, which is no surprise. Had some great gigs at the Duchess, I miss TJ's in Newport. There's a few venues I'd like to blow up as they have a meat head attitude from the top to the bottom but I am scared to start a slanging match as I'll probably end up playing them again sometime. I'm lucky enough to have travelled the world and seen the different national traits and can say it's a shame loads of British people have such a pointlessly negative attitude.

MM: The Snuff style seems so varied, with mod, oi!, hardcore, metal, punk, African beats and more all getting a look in. Do you listen to a lot of music? Do you listen to the new bands coming through?

Duncan: Because I am normally in a loud world of music I rarely listen to loud music through choice and if I do it will be short bursts of different styles, listening to the same thing over and over is so boring. I make a racket all day, so a racket isn't always such a relaxing alternative for me? I don't always keep up with new bands, takes a lot to get a jaded old hack like me going these days.

MM: Who were your contemporaries when you were getting started? Are you still in touch with the likes of Leatherface and co.?

Duncan: The Senseless Things, Sink, Mega City 4, The Abs, HDQ, Leatherface and tons of others. I'm still in touch with tons of the people from those days, we're the jaded lost it old men that sit around going on about how crap it is these days, he, he.

MM: The new album doesn't feature any of your trademark covers, is that firmly in your past? Also with the covers such as the selection on *Flibbidy*.... (Tom - 12" record which featured a couple of originals, covers of the likes of The Who, The Specials, GBH and a load of TV theme tunes and adverts) you often choose songs which are obviously geared towards a UK audience, has that limited your choice of songs to give the Snuff treatment to?

Duncan: There will be more covers; they just have to be right that's all. We have covered songs from around the world on various EP's and tour EP's but of course we understand the British psyche better coming from here.

MM: As well as cover songs you have always brought a bit of humour to the punk hardcore scene which can often be pretty straight laced, was this a conscious decision to be a bit different?

Duncan: We always wanted to try and make a party atmosphere if possible; people want release and fun away from their often boring or stressful lives not getting preached at and told what to do. However there is an argument for using anger as a force, but to be honest most musicians (us included) are so egocentric, snobby and up their own arses that they take themselves far too seriously and need a good metaphorical slap.

MM: And speaking of being different, pretty early on your line-up went beyond the standard guitar-bass-drums set-up, what inspired this?

Duncan: Ska soul and Mod music. Deep Purple had an effect on me as a youth with the drum style and the Hammond, the Small Faces, The Prisoners, the Skatalites and GBH had a massive effect on me. (Tom - all great bands you should definitely go and check out)

MM: How do you plan on following up the new album? I see that you have some touring in Japan on the cards, have you got much planned beyond that?

Duncan: There's no Japan tour on the cards as far as I know but I would go there at the drop of a hat. We have a few festivals planned in Europe and at some point will do more UK gigs. We will take it as it comes.

MM: As well as Snuff I know Duncan is active in other bands, in particular the Toy Dolls are busy at the moment. What other ongoing projects do you have?

Duncan: Acoustic, Duncan's Divas(a covers project covering woman's songs), Billy No Mates (originals collaborating with musicians around the world, Duncan's Geezers (covers of male songs), Bonzer noisy techno/guitar racket, and I play drums in Wonk Unit when I can.

MM: I think that's about it, thanks for taking the time to answer the questions!

Duncan: Bing bong all the best.

Originally published in Mass Movement #35, May 2013

JAMES TYNION IV

Ladies and gentlemen, boys and girls, meet James Tynion IV, the man charged with expanding not only the mythology of Batman, but also that of Gotham City with Talon, an assassin trained by The Court Of Owls, the secret society responsible for guiding and creating the secret, and not so secret, history of Gotham. And then there's Red Hood and the Outlaws, The Eighth Seal and…Wait, you know the rules about spoilers, all good things come to those who wait. So, are you ready? You are? Then we'll begin…

Interview by Tim Cundle

Images appear courtesy of DC Entertainment, DC Comics and James Tynion IV

MM: As with all things, it's generally best to start at the beginning, so with that in mind, would you like to introduce yourself and tell us a little bit about what makes James Tynion IV tick?

James: What makes me tick? Hmmm… Some weird combination of animated films, sappy teen dramas, and horror stories. Listed side by side, I definitely sound like some kind of weird serial killer. I'm not sure! I'm just a weird geeky kid from Milwaukee who managed to stumble into his dream career much, much earlier than expected, and now I'm just working my butt off to make sure I can stick around for decades to come. I think it was in Neil Gaiman's "Make Good Art" speech that he talked about the fraud police figuring out that he was writing for a living, and forcing him to get a real job. In his head, they came with clipboards; in mine it's definitely more of a torches and pitchforks situation. I'm doing my best to dig in and write the kinds of comic books that I would love reading. I want to write the comic book that would have been my favorite when I was hitting the stacks every week in High School and College.

MM: So, James, when did you first discover comics, what drew you to them and what is it about comics that's made you a, I'm assuming, life-long devotee of the medium?

James: I don't really remember a time where comics haven't been a major part of my life. One of my first memories is my father taking me to a comic book shop in New York City and seeing a huge cardboard cut-out of Spider-Man. That whole week I had nightmares about Spider-Man climbing down the drainpipe right outside my window and staring in at me. Just being a total creeper, staring in. Things that spook me tend to garner my interest pretty dang quick. When I was a kid in the early-mid nineties, I was a devotee of the Batman and X-Men animated series more than the comics themselves, but they slowly led me into the comic book world. It was mostly osmosis. Superheroes had been a part of my life since childhood, so I was always curious about reading more.

It was the alternate reality stories that I got my hands on later, *Kingdom Come* and *Age of Apocalypse*… Those captured my imagination in a way that none of the others had before. Those stories broke all the rules, and allowed you to build entire worlds that took these familiar characters, completely redefining them, while maintaining their core. Those stories fascinated me in a major way. The thought process stopped being, "This is so cool," and more "What would I do if I ever got the chance to write stories with these characters?" But what really broke me open was discovering Vertigo and less mainstream superhero comics in

High School. It was right around the time Brian K. Vaughan was at the top of the mountain with *Y: The Last Man*, *Ex Machina*, and *Runaways*... I was picking those books up on Wednesday, along with trades of *Sandman, Transmetropolitan, Planetary*... And then from those, more and more. I can viscerally remember my brain exploding with sheer joy when I read *Scott Pilgrim* for the first time. The possibilities of this medium are endless, and all the people in it seem to be weird geeky people who like all the same weird things I do. Folks ask me a lot whether comics are a stepping stone to another medium I'd like to work in, and that couldn't be further from the truth. I want to be writing comic's decades from now. This is my favorite medium. I want to stay in it forever.

MM: What made, and makes, you want to be a writer? Is it a lifelong calling, or was there a moment of clarity, an epiphany if you will, when you realised with all certainty that you wanted, and needed, to write?

James: I think it was the fact that everyone in my family is damn good at sitting down and telling a story, and I never have been. Not out loud, anyways. My mind is always racing in twenty different directions at once, and I when I'm talking I tend to get lost on a train going in one direction, then try to hop on a different one going somewhere else, and so on, until it's a whole big mess. But I knew I had stories in my head. Worlds that needed building, and exploring. So if I couldn't talk my way through them, I figured that I'd just write about them. Not in great big prose tomes, but in notebooks I would just list out the details of the different worlds I wanted to play with. Stories about Angels and Ghosts and Elves and Magic. And then eventually just stories about my life, the daily angst and turmoil of being a young teenager with lots of emotions but not a lot of outlets for them. I remember back in high school, when everyone hated writing essays, and I freaking loved them. I thought I had gamed the system somehow... I would write in this kind of direct, conversational tone and they would just flow out of me. I'd get some marks taken off for it, but that never bothered me. I was just playing with language, and I figured if they were asking me to write a report on Hemmingway, I was going to write it in the way that interested me the most. One of my teachers actually pushed me towards my first creative writing class. And that led to a summer writing program at a college. And that led to me realizing that I wanted to go to college to become a writer.

MM: Following on from the last question, do you think or writing as a calling or just a job? Does a writer NEED to write, or is that just something writers say? If it is a calling, why is it a calling, and if it isn't, why do writers say it is...?

James: I think the calling is more towards creation than just writing. I wish I could play an instrument. I wish I could sing better. And DAMN, I wish I could draw. I've never been good with coloring in between the lines. The sciences always frustrated me with their rigidity, and their need for me to memorize formulas and whatnot. I didn't want to learn the rules of this world; I wanted to write the rules for my own worlds. There is absolutely a drive in me to create SOMETHING. I worked in advertising for a little while in between college and breaking into the comics industry, and that was almost fulfilling, because it did scratch the itch of just sitting down and staring at a blank page and trying to come up with something brilliant nobody else has thought of before now. Mind you, typically the work was more of trying to figure out some basic site copy, but still, the big picture brainstorming was fun. But I was always aiming towards this. I want my job to be storytelling. I want the primary work that I put in, day-in and day-out, to be the act of creating something new and exciting. I can't imagine stepping away from it and doing something more typical. Mostly because I'd still be daydreaming and doodling in the margins, and I'd never really care about what I was doing.

The important thing is creation. Ideation. Late night conversations about Batman. Waking up excited from a nightmare because I've got some new story fodder. That kind of thing. That's what I want in life.

MM: Tying the writing and comics together... What made you want to write comics? What do you think, from a writer's point of view, writing comics, in terms of personal and professional satisfaction, gives you that other literary mediums can't? Why?

James: It's the collaborative nature of the medium. There is literally no better feeling in the world than seeing an artist bring your concept to life in a way that totally outstrips your every expectation. Seeing a thought be given weight and style and personality. I still get giddy when pages come in. Sure there's weird politics every now and then. Sure there's weird personalities floating out in this wacky industry. But I think that's true everywhere. But the key is, the collaborative nature of comics make you feel like you're a part of something... Some strange off-kilter vanguard of pop culture where imagination just bleeds onto the page. We're all members. Every writer, artist, colorist, letterer, inker, editor, and what-have-you. We're all in this together to create vibrant worlds to play in that outstrip every other medium that I can think of. Where else can you find this kind of diversity of content being produced week in and week out? Even prose, where you can do virtually anything, is becoming limited by what can sell in the contemporary market. But in comics, we have young adult coming of age stories, superhero action, graphic zombie horror, sci-fi westerns, hard-boiled noir, over the top silly kids' books... All coming out on the shelves next to each other week in and week out. The visual diversity that's out there, with all the different artistic styles that are being pushed forward in the contemporary comic market, and the diversity of the ideas at the heart of those stories, it's at a level I don't think we've ever seen before. It's better than TV. It's better than film. It's a whole insular medium that's just exploring the outer reaches of a bunch of geeky people's imaginations. What in the whole world could be better than that? Why would I ever want to leave?

MM: Let's talk DC... Being one of the big two, the four colour publishing giants, I kinda wondered how did you get your break in the big leagues? How did you wind up working for DC?

James: It was a weird and unexpected path, to be honest! I've been sending in unsolicited submissions to comic's publishers around the world since I was in high school, as well as drawing my own little crappy comics, and trying to find artists, and all that typical stuff. It was in college, when I met a young, like-minded professor, who happened to be talking to Marvel and Vertigo about doing some comics work. That was Scott Snyder. He sent me a very rough draft of the pitch that would become *American Vampire*, because we had hit it off talking about comics, and rather than just complement him on how awesome it was, I sent him back a ten page document with all of my thoughts, critiques, and ideas on how to make it better. Miraculously, that was not the end of the relationship. I spent a year working with him on a Young Adult novel that didn't end up happening, but did get us in the habit of brainstorming writing projects together. As I worked in journalism and advertising after college, I'd still spend hours in the evening, talking out ideas on his Detective Comics run, and ultimately Swamp Thing and Batman. It wasn't until the December after the launch of the New 52 happened that he called me in the middle of the work day, and asked if I would help him co-write the Back-Up stories in Batman. I, of course, practically fainted. A few months later, I got the gig co-writing *Batman Annual #1*, and that led directly to my pitching my first ongoing series, *Talon*.

MM: Writing Batman… How does it feel to be partially responsible, in that you're writing the back-up's, for the destiny of one of the most easily identifiable and recognized characters on the planet? How did you feel when you found out that you'd got the gig?

James: Terrified. Absolutely terrified. It felt like Batman was something that needed to be earned, and I didn't feel like I had earned him at all. I comforted myself at first with the back-ups, because it was all centered around Alfred and his father, and Bruce wasn't really around the main story at all. But then the annual came, and there was no escaping it. I had to sit down and put words in Batman's mouth. It was the most stressful writing experience of my life at that point. I needed to center myself, and find the Batman within, and let it pour out on the page. I had to remind myself that Batman's been living in my head since I was a little boy watching the animated series, and the way-too-scary-for-a-5-year-old *Batman Returns*.

MM: Is there a set of parameters, self- imposed or otherwise, that you try to adhere to when writing Batman? If so, what are they? Do you have a sense of where you're going to take the character and what you'd like to do with him, and likewise is there anything that you wouldn't do with the character?

James: Honestly, it's more freeform than that. I have two whole shelves in my room devoted to Batman comics, and there's something I've always understood, since I was a kid. There is a real Batman centered between all these interpretations. It's like imagine every interpretation of Batman. Every writer and artist on every take on the character in every medium. Imagine all of those interpretations laid out as a graph, plotting out where the personality of each Batman lies, weighting certain iconic takes heavier than others. If you balanced those on a pin, the center of that chart is the true Batman. The ideal, perfect concept of Batman. Everyone takes a different path towards the same center, but the center is true. When you write something that pulls you away from that center, you feel it. You know it's wrong. You balance every Batman story in your head, and you shoot for the iconic core of the character every time. Of course, you put your own take on it, every artist has an individual voice, so Batman changes in the hands of every person. Including me. But if you take that time to find Batman in your head, he's actually much easier to write than I ever would have guessed. Like I said, Batman's been living in my head since I was a boy. It's just all about the act of finding him.

MM: Tell us about Talon… How difficult was it developing a new mythology (the Owls and The Talons) that has to fit within the confines of an already established, even given the way that the New 52 is reshaping and has reshaped the DC Universe, mythology that is the world of Gotham and The Batman? The story is fairly brutal and uncompromising (and brilliant by the way), are you at all worried that the story might become too dark, and given the events of issue's seven and eight, that Calvin might tip too far toward, for want of a better term, 'the dark side'? Is there any way back for him after his fateful encounter with Bane? Or is Calvin destined to be a Talon and nothing else…?

James: Honestly, I'm thrilled about dragging the series into the darkness. The darkness is a fun place to write from. The whole Court of Owls concept I built this series out of is spawned from the dark. It's why the zero issue opens with a boy in a cage, desperately trying to break free. This isn't a happy-go-lucky world. This series is steeped in the dark and twisted history of Gotham and built to expand that history. As for Calvin Rose, I wouldn't give up all hope just yet… The core of his character is about escape, but his current predicament with The Court of Owls, and Bane in particular will be his greatest struggle yet. I'm not done putting him through the ringer, and I've been letting myself embrace the series' horror roots as I dig into the stories we're going to be telling later this Summer, into the Fall. I'm reaching the endgame of what I originally pitched for this series early last year. The pieces are all falling into place. I can't wait for everyone to see what we have in store.

MM: And, moving to on *Red Hood and The Outlaws*… Is it easier or more difficult writing for already established characters like Jason Todd than it is writing and developing your own, i.e. *Talon*? Why?

James: It can be both easy and difficult at different moments, especially in the New 52 environment where you're trying to balance the classic voice with the character with the newer personality that's been established over the last year and a half. Jason is different than Batman, because there are only a handful of examples of him being written in the modern era… So it's easier to stray off path from what Winnick, Morrison, Lobdell, and a small handful of others have built. With Batman, you can triangulate a center because there are SO many interpretations of his voice that when you read them all, it just becomes clear in your head. I have a lot of ideas about who Jason is at his core, but of course the current story strips that core away. When it's wrapped and we can dive back into who he really is, I'm incredibly excited to show exactly what I've had in mind all these months.

MM: What's the fan reaction to *Talon* been like so far and given that everyone is just a click away thanks to the internet, have you ever been tempted to interact more closely with fans, or have any fans got a little close, too close for comfort and closer than you'd like them to get via cyberspace…?

James: I used to be a comic book message board junkie, so I know what kind of visceral stuff can come out of those dark corners of the comics internet. Thankfully, I also know that most of that stuff pops up when you're in a bad mood and you decide to take it out on a comic that didn't really do it for you on that given day. I think, when I first started, I took reviews and comments and social media interaction a little too personally, and kind of boxed in my own weirdness and my own personality. I let my social media platforms transform into self-promotional mouthpieces rather than just extensions of myself and my weird interests and sense of humor. I think people kind of got sick of that, and I definitely got sick of that, so I started to let go and just let myself weird out all over the place. The nice thing is that the fans have been super into it. It's a nice affirmation that people still want to engage with me and talk to me, especially when it has nothing to do with my DC work. I've been good about not letting it get too close or too personal, and I definitely don't have any horror stories yet.

MM: Okay James, pretend we next to nothing about it (which we don't), and tell us all about *The Eighth Seal*…?

James: *The Eighth Seal* is a digital horror comic, available free to read on Thrillbent.com, and available for 0.99 on ComiXology with some fancy schmancy bonus features. I pitched the series last summer as "Rosemary's Baby meets The West Wing." It's the story about a woman involved in the highest rungs of politics in Washington DC, who believes she's going insane. She has visions of becoming this horrible monster and slaughtering everyone around her. But the truth is, there's an ancient, mysterious conspiracy that she's found herself at the heart of. We're really going all out in this story. The Thrillbent platform is unlike anything else in comics right now, in that it's built entirely for the web. My incredible artist, Jeremy Rock, and I don't have to worry about figuring out a way for this ever to make sense to print.

We're using this layering system of panels to change elements on the page mid-read. It's absolutely perfect for a horror story. Usually in comics, you only have one opportunity every two pages for a real, outright scare. It's on the page-turn. But digitally, especially the fact that we can twist and change elements as you're reading, every swipe forward is dangerous. It raises the tension something fierce. And it's all so new. Jeremy and I are constantly exploring how to make this as innovative and daring as we can. We try to come up with new storytelling tools in each and every issue, that really take the possibilities of digital only comics to their limits. Like I said, it's free to read, and Jeremy has brought some of my favorite nightmares to life in a brilliant way. Go over to Thrillbent.com now and check it out if you have a moment. There are three chapters up so far, and many more to come.

MM: What's next for you, and if there's anything that you'd like to add, now would be the time...?

James: Hooboy! Well, I wish I could talk about what's coming up in 2014, and even 2015. There are plans. Big plans. Both in terms of superhero comics, and in terms of my creator-owned work. I want to really start introducing people to the worlds that live in my head, and I have some fairly major stories that I've been laying out for months, and in some cases years, that have finally started to find homes. I want people to really see what my core is as a writer, and these are the projects I feel will be able to do that. I wish I could say more... But stay tuned. There is a lot of madness to come from this weird, geeky Milwaukeean. I can promise you that.

Originally published in Mass Movement #36, July 2013

THE MASKED MARVEL
THE KING OF COOL SUPERHEROES

The guy's the epitome of class. Complete with suit, tie, fedora and a mask, he's as neat as a pin. He has no extraordinary powers, just a desire to fight the enemies of WWII. I guess you could call him a true patriot. To be honest, he represents something special about being an American that has long since been replaced by dull, but, slick, Twenty-First Century superheroes who have nothing better to do than to look good in front of the camera and showcase a macho attitude. There's absolutely no substance to speak of when it comes to their character.

Of course, times have changed. America is no longer at war with the Nazis and the Japanese, although we have managed to do our best to fight other foes. But it's not quite the same. During WWII, there was a need for men like *The Masked Marvel*. He was a well-trained government agent who used both his skills as a fighter and a thinker to outwit the enemy, and he seemed to do it with ease. Originally, *The Masked Marvel* was a comic book hero that possessed extraordinary feats of strength and other superpowers, but as a radio character, he was merely a mortal man, and that's how Republic portrays him in the serial.

In the chapter play, his job is to uncover the whereabouts of a Japanese spy by the name of Mura Sakima, who is operating secretly in the states to undermine our defences. The plot is somewhat of a stretch since Sakima was once the former head of the Tokyo World Wide Insurance Company, but now he is the lead of a secret Japanese espionage service, as he collaborates with a crooked vice president of a legitimate insurance company. Sound too confusing for a ten-year-old kid to understand? Perhaps. But the action more than makes up for the rather convoluted plot.

Sakima sabotages certain government facilities, which are insured by the company, and then uses the money to advance his nefarious activities, and in the process, disrupts American war efforts against the Axis Powers. When Sakima gains knowledge that the honest president of the insurance company knows of his shady operations, he has the president murdered. Thus, enters *The Masked Marvel* to the rescue. He only reveals his identity to one person: the daughter of the murdered president. Meanwhile, Sakima and the crooked vice president, along with a band of criminals, continue their reign of terror on America's defence systems and collect insurance money for the damages.

What makes *The Masked Marvel* character uniquely different is that he works with three other government agents who all look very similar in appearance. When he goes into action, the Marvel slips on his famous mask to conceal his identity; however, the camera never shows the front of his face so the audience is unaware which of the four agents the real Masked Marvel is. To also keep the viewer guessing about his identity, the Marvel's voice is uniquely different from that of the other agents. This strategy of I.D. protection turns out to be a very clever writing ploy.

Like *The Green Hornet*, *The Masked Marvel* has no real superpowers, only a handgun and an ability to fight in a furious fashion. *The Masked Marvel* was a Republic Studio production, and they were known to produce more action in each chapter than the other studios. In fact, most film historians agree that Republic made the best action serials as compared to Columbia and Universal. The writers concentrated mostly on pure fists-a-flying rather than character development. And as far as their special effects department, it was second to none. It was the thirty-first chapter play of the sixty-six that Republic produced.

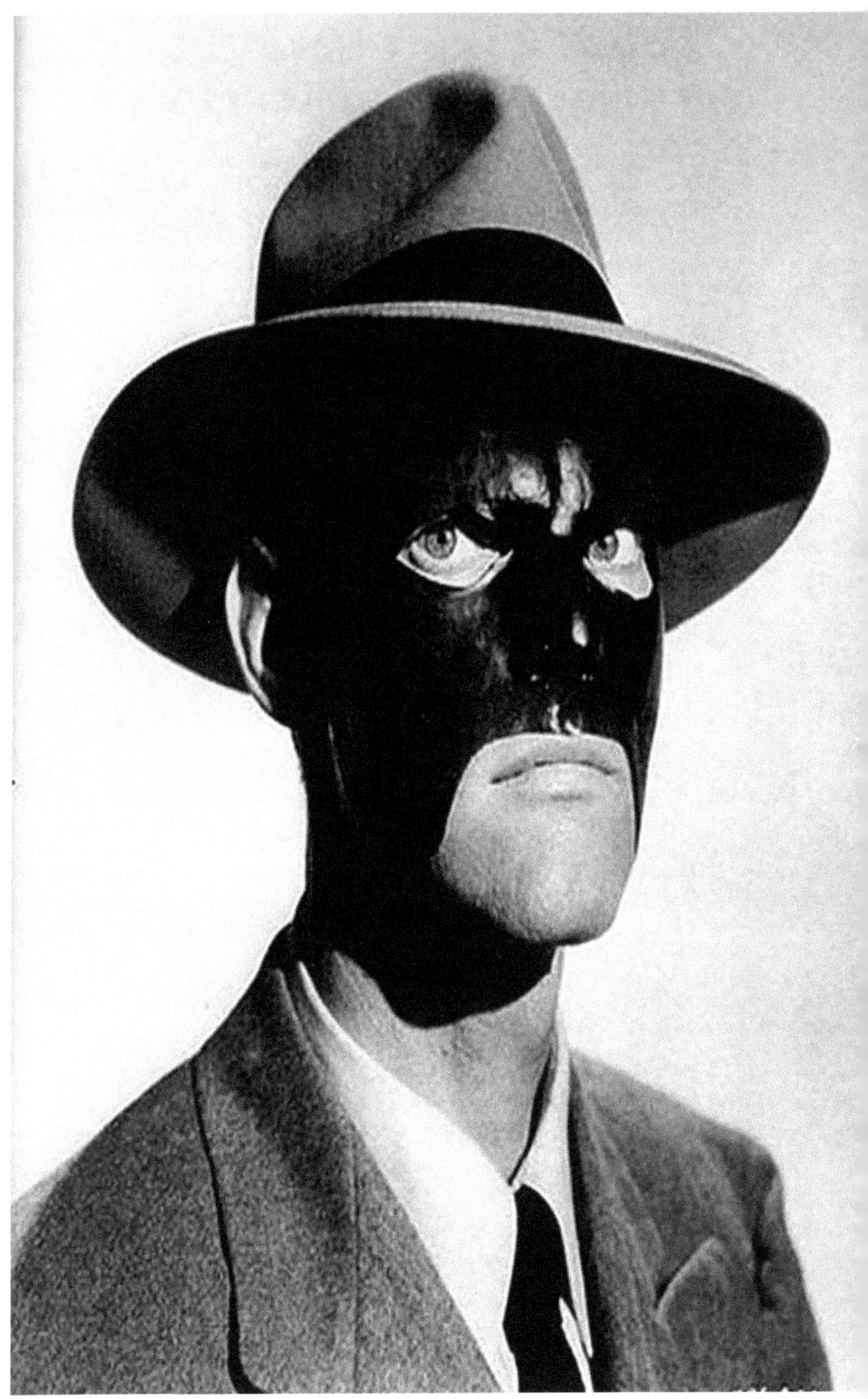

That doesn't mean that Republic totally neglected to develop their characters because most of the protagonist had certain traits that separated them from other heroes. Nevertheless, the emphasis was on pure action. Tom Steele, an extraordinary stuntman who was on contract with Republic at the time, played *The Masked Marvel*. Amazingly, he received no billing for his portrayal of the character, a major oversight by studio executives.

The idea of an enemy spy operating on American soil had been used many times during the war years, so the plot is somewhat redundant. As mentioned earlier, what makes *The Masked Marvel* an interesting character study is the fact that the audience never knew exactly who he was until the final chapter. It was a common device used when concealing the identity of the antagonist but seldom used to confuse the audience with the hero. Off hand, I can't recall another serial that was written as such (I confess my memory isn't what it used to be, so I may be mistaken).

Steele's performance of the lead is fairly straightforward, that is to say, he doesn't "ham it up," but plays the role in a relaxed manner and to the point. Even when he is called upon to "mix-it-up" with his fist, he is flawlessly accurate in landing punches. As the story progresses, *The Masked Marvel* uses his keen senses to expose the illegitimate vice president and several of the henchmen, and, in the final chapter, he manages to barely escape Sakima's hideout as a bomb explodes killing the famous, Japanese spy.

The Masked Marvel is one of my personal, favorite chapter plays, partly due to my admiration for Steele's portrayal of the famous character. He and stuntman David Sharpe were two of the best at their business, and they were able to gain steady employment throughout their careers. They both were students of the famous Yakima Canutt, who was considered to be a mentor to many apprentices in Hollywood. Canutt worked with legendary film director John Ford on several westerns, including John Wayne's famous film *Stagecoach*. While doubling for Wayne on a western chapter play, Yakima taught him how to correctly fall off of a horse during action sequences. Out of respect for Canutt, the two men became close friends.

Something that separates this serial from almost any chapter play ever made happened during the filming. Many of the stuntmen were injured because of the numerous fight scenes, and actor David Bacon, who played one of the agents, got the role because he was lucky enough to stay healthy. He jokingly commented that he would probably be injured driving home in his car. Tragically enough, he was found murdered in his car just two weeks after the serial had been completed. To this day, the crime remains unsolved.

The Masked Marvel is a good example of a wartime chapter play, and I highly recommend it as an action-packed, chorographical art form of fist-flying excitement. On a scale of one to ten, *The Masked Marvel* earns a solid nine.

Doug Crill

Originally published in Mass Movement #36, July 2013

JOE R. LANSDALE

Dean Koontz has likened him to "...a favourite uncle who just happens to be a fabulous storyteller." For Joe Hill, he is a "...true American original," while John Connolly maintains that his name "...deserves to be whispered with the greats." The New York Times Book Review has compared his work with no less a figure than Mark Twain. We're talking about champion mojo author Joe R Lansdale, a man with more than thirty novels to his name and too many short stories to count. Mass Movement sent Liam Ronan to talk to the man about drive-ins, dead folk and the Depression...

Interview by Liam Ronan

MM: Joe, thanks for taking the time to talk with Mass Movement Magazine. Your new novel, *The Thicket*, is out now from Mulholland Books. Can you tell us a little bit about it?

Joe: It takes place at the beginning of the twentieth century, deals with a kidnapping of a young man's sister, the murder of his grandfather, all of this on the heels of his parents' death by small pox. He gathers an unusual posse to help him, a dwarf bounty hunter and a black gravedigger, and a prostitute and a disfigured sheriff they meet along the way, as well as other characters who go after a wicked gang of murderers, thieves and kidnappers who are hiding out in the Big Thicket part of Texas, which was surely a thicket then. What happens to them along the way as they go about their search is just as important, and I think interesting and exciting, as the denouement.

MM: I know you're a big fan of Edgar Rice Burroughs. Do you credit any authors in particular for helping you set your sights on becoming a writer?

Joe: I wanted to be a writer because of comic books, and they led to me reading stories and novels, and when I discovered Edgar Rice Burroughs I went from wanting to be a writer to having to be one. I admired his stories a lot. They are dated now, racist and sexist and so on, but they were magical in their own way, and sometimes they were just the opposite of those 'isms'.

MM: I guess the social conventions may be at odds now, but they still don't get in the way of his stories.

Joe: Burroughs conflicted with his own views of the time frequently, and those may well have been his actual views. But his magic was in archetypical storytelling, and its appeal was primarily to young boys and young men. I read everything I could get my hands on. So, he's my sentimental favourite, though many other authors have replaced him as far as style, character, motivation and so on go. But I still think his forward, hard-driving narrative remains a part of my writing. Later, I discovered so many other authors.

MM: Like who?

Joe: Richard Matheson, Ray Bradbury, William F. Nolan, Charles Beaumont, then Mark Twain, Jack London, Kipling, Hemingway, Fitzgerald, Steinbeck, Flannery O'Conner, Harper Lee, Carson McCullers, Elmore Leonard, Raymond Chandler, Dashiell Hammett, James Cain,

Philip Jose Farmer, Cyril Kornbluth, Henry Kuttner, Pete Hamill, Faulkner, Fred Brown, Chester Himes and Ralph Dennis, who was a big influence for the Hap and Leonard novels, as was Himes. Arthur Conan Doyle, Jules Verne, H.G. Wells... Man, it's a long list of writers who influenced me.

MM: How about contemporary authors?

Joe: I read a lot of new writers, but the influence period seems to have been those writers, and a few I just can't think of at the moment and don't have room for. Many writers taught me many different things.

MM: When your work first started to get noticed, you were tagged as being part of the splatterpunk scene. Did you make a conscious effort to try and distance yourself from this?

Joe: I've always tried to distance myself from labels. You may fit one to some degree in one story or novel, but I didn't want a label to define all my work. I wanted only one label, the Lansdale Genre, to be my listing. I've tried to stick to that, no matter what others say. Horror writer. Crime writer. Western writer. Weird writer. Cult writer. Literary writer... I've had all the labels at one time or another, and I don't embrace any of them, other than the one I mentioned - Lansdale.

MM: Is it true that you were working as a janitor when your debut novel *Act Of Love* was published?

Joe: That is true. I got word at work. I think my wife came and told me or brought me the letter. I don't remember. But I gave my notice and I was out of there. That was in 1981. I had a tough time the first five or six years, but then things really started to click, and I've been going strong ever since, which is not to say there haven't been slumps here and there.

MM: It sounds like you're in a good place right now, though...

Joe: I love my career and my life. My family is wonderful, so is my work, and I still practice martial arts, teach part time at Stephen F. Austin University (I was a janitor in buildings where I now teach, though that was not the janitor job I had when I quit and became a writer). I travel a lot, read constantly, fiction, non-fiction, watch movies and so on. It's a full existence.

MM: In many ways, *Act Of Love* is very different to a lot of your subsequent work. Do you look back on it fondly?

Joe: I don't hate any of the novels or short stories that bear my name. But *Act Of Love*, though unusual for its time in the way in blended a lot of genres, is more conventional in other ways. Some suggest that it was the forerunner to things like Thomas Harris' *Silence Of The Lambs* or *Red Dragon*, and it just might be, though he did it much better later. But it's a sophomore novel, and I know it. But, it has its fans.

MM: A lot of your stories – *Edge of Dark Water*, *The Bottoms*, *All The Earth, Thrown To The Sky* **- have been set during the Depression. Why do you keep revisiting this particular era in your work?**

Joe: My parents became adults during that period. They were older when I was born, and I grew up on their stories and the stories of my uncles. My dad was born in 1909, my mother 1914, I believe, and I've used many of their stories to make my fiction. My entire family, aunts, uncles, used to sit out under a tree in my grandmother's yard at night and talk about the old days, their experiences here, and my Uncle John and Uncle Jim talked about World War II some. I also grew up with people who knew a lot of stories that had been passed on from their relatives in the Civil War and so on. Reading and imagination filled in the rest.

MM: You've also used the Old West as a setting for the likes of *The Magic Wagon*, *Dead In The West* **and the** *Ned The Seal* **trilogy, and you wrote a straight cowboy novel with** *Texas Night Riders*…

Joe: I've incorporated both The Great Depression and the Old West into my stories. My grandmother was nearly a hundred when she died, and stories she told about seeing Buffalo Bill's Wild West Show, seeing Indian camps and so on, coming to Texas in a covered wagon, also added to my other interest. She also told me a few Scotch-Irish ghost stories when I was a kid, as well as just tales of the Ozarks.

MM: In your introduction to the first *Preacher* **collection, you memorably described Texas as being "…the Mount Olympus of hard-boiled stories with Western grit"…**

Joe: Texas has a colourful history, warts and all, so I use it. Warts and all.

MM: Pardon me for saying so, Joe, but you're a collector's nightmare when it comes to picking up your work – I've yet to find a copy of your erotic novel *Molly's Sexual Follies* **(although my local library does feature Batman: Captured By the Engines in their children's section). What appeals to you about working across so many different genres?**

Joe: I like to try different things. Things like the Stone novels and *Molly's Sexual Follies* are among the few things I wrote for money to stay in the game early on. Molly was rewritten so much that even if you find it, there's little of me left in it. Brad Foster took some elements of my story and re-wrote it. It gave him a framework. That's about all that remains of it.

MM: And the *Stone: MIA Hunter* **titles?**

Joe: The Stone novels were written to general outlines and revised by Stephen Mertz, who created the series, but a lot of me remains in them. I think Steve didn't care for them much when I wrote them, but time has made him feel a little different, as they are the ones that people tend to remember for their quirks, and I had a few. I also wrote a chapter of one of the *Cody's Army* that Stephen invented. Just one chapter, a quirky, parody/pastiche of the South.

MM: Your work has been recognized with the likes of eight Bram Stoker Awards, the American Mystery Award, the British Fantasy Award and the Grinzane Cavour Prize for Literature. Has there been any single accolade that you are particularly proud of above?

Joe: Nine Bram Stokers - they count the Lifetime Achievement award, but hey, who's counting? The Edgar, Herodotus, Sugar Pulp and many others. I got an award from the Edgar Rice Burroughs Bibliophiles for my work on *Tarzan: The Lost Adventure*. That was so full-circle, it means a lot to me.

MM: Yeah, I can see why it would be special...

Joe: Actually, a little piece of paper from my martial arts students and a belt they got me with my name on it and the Grandmaster recognition are among the most important to me.

MM: Is *Edge Of Dark Water* still your personal favourite title among your own work?

Joe: It is, though sometimes I waver and *The Bottoms* resurfaces. My earliest favourite was *The Magic Wagon* and then *Mucho Mojo*, and then *The Bottoms*, and then *A Fine Dark Line*, and then *Edge Of Dark Water*. I think it's my favourite, but I must admit, I'm fond of the new one, *The Thicket*. I think I'm going through a growth period in my work, which is what you want to do. Not become hidebound. The novel I'm working on now, which I can't talk about, I'm pretty excited to write.

MM: You're one of the few authors who have really embraced the idea of using social media such as Facebook as a way of interacting directly with your readers, but it seems as if this has also put you in the firing line for a lot of criticism, too. Is it worth the flak?

Joe: Actually, I've had hardly any criticism. I just find sometimes someone wants to know why I promote my own stuff, and because you have to, and it's because my page is a fan page and that's what it's for. I also promote others I want to promote, and I never say my shit don't stink. I just say this is what I have to offer, it's for sale, here's what some reviewers have said, and maybe it will appeal.

MM: You're particularly generous in offering advice to would-be writers...

Joe: Sometimes, giving writing advice you have someone, usually someone unpublished or marginally published, who wants to argue with something you state very clearly is your own opinion. I just say this is what I think. It's not the law. It's a way of helping other writers. I learned it mostly on my own from reading and writing. It's minor, but I just don't suffer fools well. I like people and enjoy them, but someone who wants to split hairs over something that is obviously an opinion is just a bore. If you don't like my site, don't come to it. End of story.

MM: Yet this doesn't seem to sink in with everyone...

Joe: I have political opinions and other ideas about this or that that people disagree with, and that's okay. Comes with the territory. But discuss it intelligently. I'm not patient enough to deal with assholes or people who want to tell me the joys of what Jesus has done with their lives, or call themselves professional writers because they self-published a fucking poem about a tree. Good for you. But it doesn't make you a pro who makes their living at it. But since this is so rare and I'm not bashful, it's all good.

MM: I'm paraphrasing here, but you once summed up the rules for writing as being 'Buy typewriter, plant ass in front of typewriter, insert paper, type.' Do you have a particular approach or ritual to how you go about writing?

Joe: Sometimes it varies due to circumstances, but mostly I get up, have a coffee and granola bar or some equivalent, and write. I usually write about three hours, or three to five pages, though I don't hesitate to keep after it if it's rolling. But that's it, Monday through Sunday, with some exceptions for travel, or if an idea is so strong it hits again during the day or night. I do this regularly and it makes me seem prolific. I'm steady. Earlier I wrote more hours - five, eight - but I find this is the best program for me, again with those now-and-again exceptions.

MM: How about music? Do you find it helps to have something on in the background to set the appropriate mood?

Joe: I love music, but not when I work. I find it too distracting. I wrote one novel to music, *Captured By The Engines*. I'll never do it again. It helped with that one for some reason, but I have never wanted to make that effort again. And mostly I listened for a while, and when I got into the work, I cut it off.

MM: What kind of music do you enjoy? I have an image of you sipping whiskey while listening to country and western…

Joe: I don't drink alcohol, but I love country music, but not much of the modern stuff. I really love rockabilly, blues, Motown, soul music of the sixties and odds and ends of all manner of music. Me and what has been called modern jazz for a long time do not get along.

MM: While we're on the subject, your daughter Kasey has a lovely, smoky quality to her voice. Has she sought your advice at all in composing her songs?

Joe: No. She has on fiction, which she is now writing, but she doesn't need my advice on songs. She knows more about it than I do. She is good, and sounds a little like she smokes and drinks whisky, but she does neither. She sounded like a grown woman singing when she was a child.

MM: You've been published by the small press as well as some of the bigger companies, which is not something you see very often with established writers. Has there been a particular reason for why you've done this?

Joe: Because it keeps me in the game and keeps me in touch with the raw base of fiction, which is the small press. They also allow me to do some kinds of things I couldn't get a New York publisher to do, like say *The Ape Man's Brother* that Subterranean recently published.

MM: Some of your most popular books feature Hap and Leonard, two very ordinary guys who keep stumbling into the most violent and extraordinary adventures. Why do you think they've struck such a chord with your readers?

Joe: I think because they have a lot of the same everyday problems everyone else does, think like a lot of people out there without the filters. I love them and keep coming back to them. Hap is based on me, especially a younger me.

MM: The next Hap and Leonard book is called *Blue To The Bone*, isn't it? When do you expect it to be out?

Joe: I don't know when I'll finish *Blue To The Bone*. I think I'm closing in on it. It may turn out to be a novella.

MM: What's the status on the long-rumoured television show?

Joe: It is currently looking interesting, but that's all I can say. It could go either way.

MM: Your work has been adapted for both the big and small screen. Perhaps the most well-known of these are *Bubba Ho Tep* and *Incident On An Off A Mountain Road* which were both helmed by Don Coscarelli. Were you happy with the results?

Joe: Very happy with both. I would love to work with Don again, or Bruce Campbell. Good guys, and very talented.

MM: And of course, your son Keith adapted *Christmas with the Dead* on which you acted as an executive producer. This presumably helped you maintain artistic control over the material – did you enjoy the experience?

Joe: Yes and no. There were a lot of things that came along unexpectedly, the usual snafus, and some of them seemed unnecessary to me, but on the whole I had a good time and a good experience. I'm considering directing a film that Keith and I will write.

MM: Incidentally, did Keith inspire your children's novel, *In Waders From Mars* which you co-wrote alongside your wife, Karen? (shame on you for that pun, by the way).

Joe: Keith came up with the story. All I did was type it up, clean it up a little, and Karen gave it an ending. She's good at stuff like that. But it's Keith's tall tale he told me.

MM: Is it true that you are acting as co-producer on several projects based on your work? I've heard that you're trying to line Bill Paxton up for the film of *The Bottoms* while SFX supremo Greg Nicotero wants to do *The Drive-In*...

Joe: This is true. I think *The Drive-In* film has gone south, but *The Bottoms* still has some life to it.

MM: I've also heard whispers that you've been thinking about putting together an anthology film. Are there any specific short stories that you'd like to see on the screen? The likes of *Pilots*, *On The Far Side Of The Cadillac Desert With Dead Folks* or *By Bizarre Hands* would surely all be strong contenders.

Joe: This is true, but that's all I've done - think about it.

MM: How did you enjoy acting in the 2001 film *Dead Flesh*? Are you keen to act more?

Joe: Oh, that wasn't acting, that was filling in for friends. Kasey was also in it. Do I have plans to act? No. Would I? Maybe, some small piece. For fun.

MM: Tell us more about this directing role you're thinking about...

Joe: I've never had a burning desire, but in the early eighties I began to think about it because of so many independent films, and the fact I might get something of mine to direct. It's not as passionate an interest as writing, and if I do it, it may be something I do once. I wrote a screenplay of *Dead In The West* with the intention of directing it, and it was optioned many times but never made. A French film company bought the film rights to the book, and never filmed it. That killed that one. Too bad. Ridley Scott did the same thing with *The Big Blow*, though there's some chance it might be filmed.

MM: News broke recently that the *Cold in July* movie has been given a green light at last, and that Jim Mickle and Nick Damici of *Stakeland* and *We Are What We Are* fame will be bringing it to the screen. They seem like the perfect pair to adapt your work – in fact, I can easily imagine Damici portraying vengeful ex-con Ben Russell.

Joe: *Cold In July* is supposed to film this late summer or fall. Damici is way too young, or looks too young. The character is in his sixties at least. But Nick would be good at anything, a very underrated actor. I'd like to use him in a film I'm planning. *(note: 'Dexter' star Michael C. Hall has since signed up to star in the film as Richard Dane. There's no word on who will portray Ben Russell at the time of writing).*

MM: You've written the likes of *Jonah Hex*, *The Lone Ranger*, *Conan*, *Fantastic Four*, *The Spirit*, scripts for the animated *Batman* TV show and an updated adaptation of Robert E. Howard's eerie *Pigeons From Hell*. Would it be fair to assume that you're a comics fan?

Joe: I am a comics fan. I don't read new ones much anymore, but now and then... I read a lot of old archives and oddball comics that pop up.

MM: Your own work has been adapted into comic form with the likes of the *By Bizarre Hands* anthology and *The Drive-In*. Did you get a kick out of these?

Joe: I did. I enjoyed them very much.

MM: What would an all-new super-hero comic character created by Joe Lansdale be called, and what would their superpowers be?

Joe: I actually have one I'm working on, and may finish one day, but I'll not talk about it just yet..

MM: Your work has covered horror, thrillers, westerns, hard-boiled noir, post-apocalyptic adventure, rural whodunits, erotica, theatre, steampunk, two-fisted pulp action, children's fiction, comics, screenplays... it's as if you're on a one-man mission to write in every genre and medium possible! Is there anything you haven't done yet that you'd like to try – a radio play, maybe?

Joe: I actually have been asked to do a radio play, and it could happen. I have had my work adapted to that form.

Originally published in Mass Movement #36, July 2013

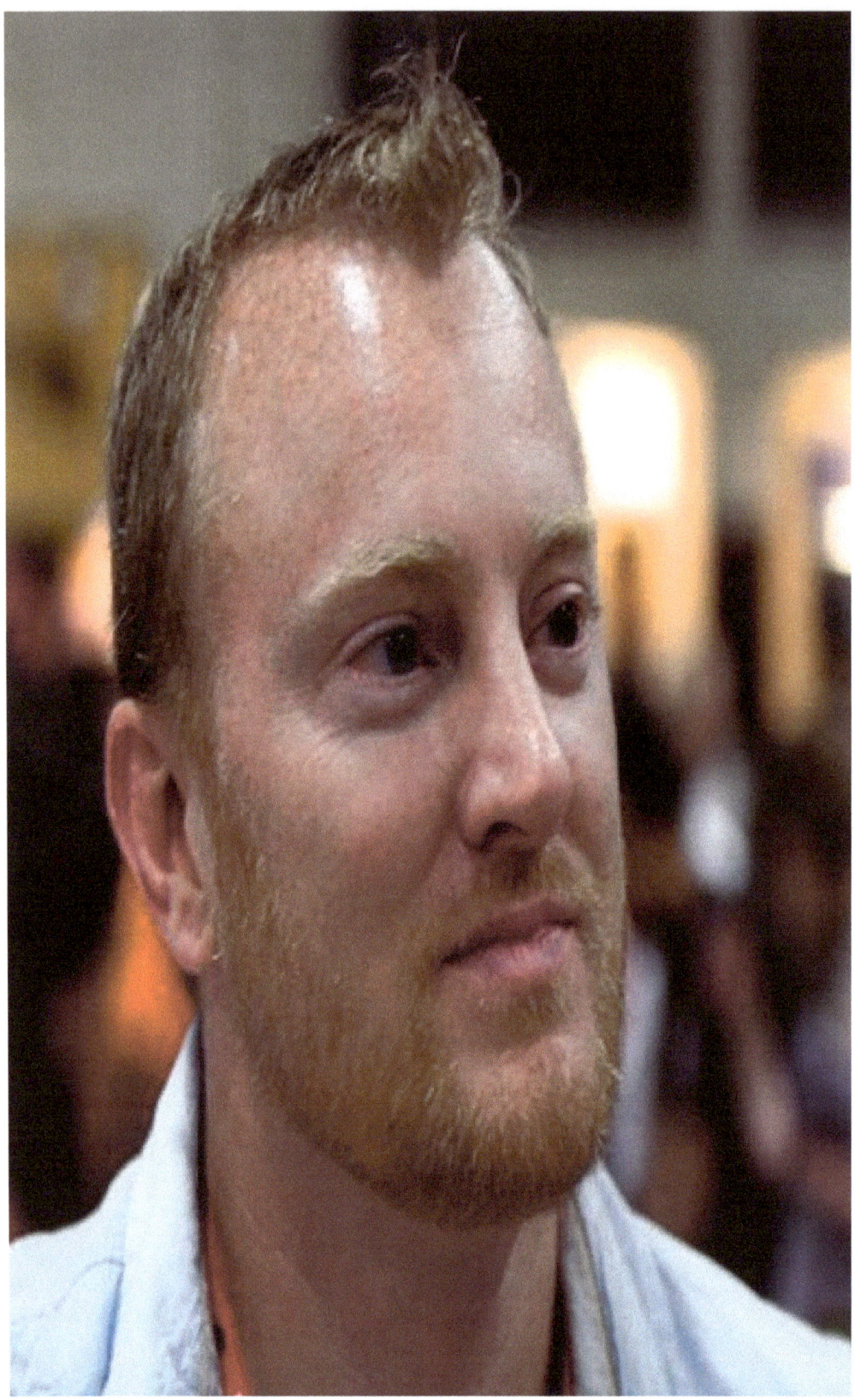

MICHAEL ALAN NELSON

So, who can tell me what links Great Cthulhu and Kara Zor-El? Actually folks, it's a trick question, as it's not a what, it's a who, and the who in question is Michael Alan Nelson. Not long after his debut issue of *Supergirl* hit the shelves of comic book stores everywhere, I caught up with Michael to talk about monsters, elder gods and superhero's, and here's what he had to say...

Interview by Tim Cundle

Images appear courtesy of DC Entertainment, DC Comics & Boom! Studios

MM: As ever, the best place to start is at the beginning, so would you like to introduce, and tell us a little about, yourself?

MAN: Well, I'm a pretty average guy from the American Mid-West. I grew up in rural farm-land surrounded by cornfields then went off to school where I received a degree in English Education from a quiet State University. After teaching for a year and discovering that it was not for me, I moved to Los Angeles around the turn of the century where I was immediately besieged by culture shock. Yet throughout all of this, I've been writing. I started scribbling stories in crayon when I was six and have been writing ever since (though not quite as much with crayon any more—editors seem to frown on that for some reason).

MM: So, where did it all start for you Michael? What was it about the medium that initially made you fall in love with comic books, and have your feelings about, and toward the medium changed as you've grown older?

MAN: As I mentioned, I grew up in farm country and we didn't have much in the way of comic shops or newsstands. But what I did have was a Power Records LP featuring *Spider-Man and the Mark of the Man-Wolf* on one side and *Spider-Man and the Invasion of the Dragon Men* on the other. I would listen to them all the time, but interestingly, I never identified with Spider-Man in those stories. I always wanted to be Draco the fire-breathing dragon. Not sure what that says about me, but there it is. Other than that, there wasn't much else. All we had was a tiny public library that carried a couple issues of *Elf Quest* and the Goodwin and Simonson graphic adaptation of the movie *Alien*. I LOVED the *Alien* graphic novel. The art was incredible and, again, I found myself wanting to be the monster and not the heroes. Plus, it was the first time I ever read four-letter words in print and felt like I was getting away with something under the nose of my parents.

But that was the last proper comic I read until I was almost out of college. I just didn't have access to them. By the time I was near any place that carried comics, I was already big into speculative prose and not much else. It wasn't until my brother started colouring comics that I became interested in them again. Unfortunately, I had missed so many incredible stories, but the nice thing was that I was able to plough through a wealth of amazing work without having to wait for the monthlies. And there was so much, from Moore to Gaiman to Morrison, that I came out of that secondary exposure completely enamoured with the medium. It was fantastic and the story-telling so completely different from the epic Fantasy and Science Fiction I had been reading for fifteen years prior. It was a much needed breath of fresh air.

MM: What, or who, made you want to write? A wise man once said that we're all composed of the sum of our influences, created by the world around us and the things that inspire us, and that being so (or not, depending on which side you take in the whole nature versus nurture argument), who and what influenced you in the beginning, and have your influences changed over time? How, if at all do you think your influences manifest themselves in your writing style?

MAN: I can tell you exactly when I knew I wanted to be a professional writer. Like I mentioned before, I've always been writing, but it was always one of many childhood creative outlets. But I was eleven years old when it finally >clicked< for me. Our tiny library actually had a decent selection of fantasy and science fiction, so I checked out a book called *The First Book of Swords* by Fred Saberhagen. It was the first in a trilogy of novels, a trilogy that I blazed through. And when I finished the final book, it hit me like an angry god. You see, the first sentence of the first book and the last sentence of the last book were exactly the same. But because of the story that happened between them made the meaning of that sentence completely different. It is, to this day, one of the most profound moments of my life. As soon as I read that final sentence, I thought to myself, "THIS is what I want to do!" I want to tell stories that affect readers like this story affected me. Seriously, I still get goosebumps thinking about it, it was that powerful of a moment for me.

As for my influences, I don't know if they've changed so much as I've just added to the list over the years. And it would certainly take too long to list them here. But I just love talented writing and I always find that inspiring. And though I've worked hard to develop my own voice and style, I can definitely see the influence of my favourite writers in there. From the wonderful chapter outs of Fred Saberhagen, the brilliant characterization of Joss Whedon, to the heartbreakingly gorgeous wordsmithing of Catherynne M. Valente, great writing is always an influence and I strive to write stories that affect readers in at least a fraction of the way that the works of these great talents affect me.

MM: How did you get your break as a comic book writer?

MAN: I like to joke and say I did it the easy way. I wrote a novel and published it online for free. I was proud of it and just wanted people to see what I was capable of doing. Fortunately, the founder of BOOM! Studios, Ross Richie, had read it and loved it. He contacted me and told me he was starting a new comic book company and asked if I had I ever thought about writing a comic before. I had and saw it as a great opportunity. So I wrote a little 8 page zombie tale and, lucky for me, he liked what I wrote, published it, and has been asking me to write for him ever since.

MM: Boom! Made me do it… Or at least, it's thanks to them that I became aware of you, via *Fall Of Cthulhu*, which being a huge Lovecraft fan, I don't mind admitting, I became slightly obsessed with… So, where did the idea for the book come from? I'm assuming that you're a Lovecraft fan, so what do you think it was, and is, about HP and the pantheon that he brought into being that has stood the test of time and led to him being regarded as one of the founding fathers of the horror genre? How do you, with the gift of hindsight, feel about the book and is there anything that you'd do differently if you were writing it now? I'm honestly not brown nosing, but I think it's perfect as is, but hey, don't let that sway you…

MAN: Thanks, I'm really glad you dig it. I'm actually quite proud of *FoC* and think it's one of the best things I've done. It was the series that really put me on the map as a comics creator so it has a very special place in my heart. The idea for the series came out of the success of the *Cthulhu Tales* books BOOM! was publishing at the time. They liked the idea of a Lovecraftian ongoing series, so they approached me and asked what I would do if I were writing it. They liked my pitch and that's the series you have today. Though I feel, like I'm sure most writers feel, there are certain things I would go back and tweak.

A line of dialog here, a panel adjustment there, but nothing major. It really is something I look back on and can say, "Yeah, that isn't too bad."

MM: Between *Fall Of Cthulhu* and *28 Days Later*, I always sort of thought of you as being a Horror writer, so was if difficult making the transition from writing Horror to writing for and about superhero's? Are the "rules" different, and if so, what are the major differences from a writer's point of view?

MAN: It always fascinates me that people think of me primarily as a horror writer. Of course it makes sense since my most popular books have been horror, but I've never seen myself as a strictly horror guy. I mean, one of my personal favourite stories was a romance I wrote for *Pirate Tales*. Though I certainly must admit that I lean toward darker stories, I also see my books *Hexed* and *Dingo* as more truly representative of who I am as a writer. They have dark moments, but they're mixed with humour and pathos, all entwined with a weird sense of the mystical and, at times, the absurd. I'm not one of those guys who focuses on one genre and thinks that it's the be-all end-all of entertainment. I love smaller romances like *Beautiful Ruins* just as much as I love epic fantasies like *Game of Thrones*. Good writing is good writing, good stories are good stories. And no matter what genre I'm writing in, I try to tell the best story that I can. I've written revenge westerns, period Japanese fiction, post-apocalyptic, romance, sci-fi, sword and sorcery, urban fantasy, and several different shades of horror. I just love telling stories, regardless of the genre.

When it comes to superheroes, my approach is the same. I want to tell a character-focused story that makes the reader feel as if they've gotten their $2.99 worth. I want them to enjoy what I do and hopefully come back for more. Writing superheroes isn't inherently any more difficult to write than any other genre. Yes, there are some hiccups when writing superheroes because they are often plagued by decades of mind-numbing continuity issues, but beyond that, it's still all about telling a compelling story. I want the reader to care about the characters. It doesn't matter what genre the story is in. And the rules for superheroes aren't any different than any other speculative genre. Whether its alien technology, magic, or super-powered beings, you just have to make sure that the rules are established and then don't break them. Otherwise it feels like you're cheating.

MM: I'm sort of curious, how and why did you make the transition from one genre (horror) to another (capes)? Was it something that you wanted to do, or something that you stumbled into….?

MAN: I've certainly always wanted to write superheroes, but it took a while for me to finally get in that position. I've been writing comics professionally since 2005, but it wasn't until just before the launch of the New 52 that DC began courting me. I had worked with them trying to develop several ideas for a number of titles, but nothing quite gelled properly until they tapped me for *Ravagers*. From there, I went to *Supergirl*. And I absolutely LOVE telling her story. Kara Zor-El is just one of those rich and amazing characters who is so much fun to write. What's great about writing her is that I get to scratch a lot of my creative itches. Great character interactions, super-powers, crazy locales, I mean there's just a whole host of fun to be had with this title.

MM: I wanted to ask you about *The Ravagers*, as you've been the lead writer for the last five issues… They're not exactly what you'd refer to as a "run of the mill" hero team, and as such, how would you describe the book to someone who isn't familiar with it? What attracted you to the title, and did you immediately know what you wanted to do with the book and how you were going to give it your own spin, and make it a Michael Alan Nelson book?

MAN: The way I saw *Ravagers* was a sort of a group of runaways all suffering from PTSD. They were kids who knew nothing but pain and torment and war, yet they longed to find a place to belong, to have some semblance of a family. And for me, that's what the story was about. Their struggle to not just survive, but to find a reason to survive. As for my own spin, I try to do that with every story I write. Be it a line of dialog or a crafty page-turn, I'm always trying to find something interesting to do. If I'm excited about a scene within a story, then the chances are greater that the reader will be too.

MM: And, then there's *Supergirl*. Saying that all hell breaks loose in your debut issue would be an understatement, as you put Kara through the ringer and then some... Is that indicative of what's to come, or will you be taking Kara in a completely different direction, and what you can you tell us about you have in store for Kara?

MAN: I'm not going to be easy on *Supergirl*, that's for sure. I do know where I would like to take her and the kind of stories I would like to tell. And though I really do want to inject a sense of fun and humour into the title, it won't all be puppies and rainbows. There's a lot going on in the DCU and the Super books in particular, so getting her to a place where she begins to build her life on Earth may take some time. Kara has some emotionally difficult situations in her future and it's my hope that she comes out of those struggles a stronger, wiser person.

MM: Did you feel a sense of trepidation, or where you at all nervous when you found out that you going to be writing *Supergirl*? How did you prepare for the take-over, and how do you feel about Kara now that you're in charge of shaping her destiny ...?

MAN: There's always a sense of trepidation and nervousness when writing a character like *Supergirl*. So even though my first thought was, "I'm writing *Supergirl*!" it slowly evolved into, "Oh... I'm writing *Supergirl*." She has legions of fans, many of whom have been reading her for decades. There's some pressure there. But after a day or two I stopped worrying about it. The only thing I can do, the only thing I WANT to do, is tell a good story. That's it. Not everyone will like what I do and that's okay. My kind of story-telling isn't for everyone and I get that. My vision of who *Supergirl* is as a character, what her goals are, what her needs are may be different from how others see her, but I believe that if I'm true to her character and tell good stories that stem from that characterization, people will want to come along with me and share in Kara's journey.

MM: I've always wondered...How does a writer get assigned to a book? Is it something that you actively campaign for or something that you're asked to do out of the blue? Or a little of both? How did you find out that you going to be writing *The Ravagers* and *Supergirl*?

MAN: That's a question that the folks at DC would best be able to answer. But I think what did it was that they liked the way I wrote female characters. They liked what I did with Rose Wilson on the *Ravagers*, not to mention that two of my strongest titles, *28 Days Later* and *Hexed*, had female protagonists. So I believe that was the genesis for putting me on *Supergirl*. And like I said before, I had been talking with DC for a while about possibly working with them so things must have finally clicked for everyone when it came to *Supergirl*.

MM: What's your dream writing job? If there was one book that you'd love to write, and one character that you'd love to write for, more than any other, what and who would you choose and why?

MAN: That's a tough question to answer. It's either going to be Dingo or *Lucifer from Hexed*. It just depends on the day of the week which character I'm more in love with. Oh wait, maybe it's the Harlot (Hexed). It's so hard to choose. I mean, they're all mine, my own creations in my own universe and there's something special about them. I have so much more story to tell with each of them and I would give almost anything for the chance to write about those characters again.

MM: What's next for you Michael? If there's anything that you'd like to add, now would probably be a good time …

MAN: Quite a bit actually. I have a new series from BOOM! called the *Day Men* that I'm co-writing with Matt Gagnon and Brian Stelfreeze on art that I'm really excited about. I also have a couple of Young Adult novels that I'm developing along with another original comics series. Lots of stuff coming down the pike, so if you like what I do, stay tuned.

Originally published in Mass Movement #36, July 2013

SPY SMASHER
THE SLICK MOTORCYCLE RIDING CRUSADER

During WWII, it was common for many businesses, industries and governmental agencies to promote a message of patriotism to all of America and to keep the spirit of freedom alive and well in the minds of its citizens. It was a very powerful use of dissemination that America was indeed winning the war.

Everyone was well aware as to the dangers that could befall the free world should the Axis Powers prevail. Unlike today, the public during that era knew the importance of a united effort, and they were eager to meet the various wartime needs of the nation. Many factories converted their normal operations to create weaponry, aircrafts and specialized vehicles to support the war effort. It truly was a different time to be alive.

Hollywood was no exception in supporting this very important cause. Countless films were made, from an American perspective, about how our armed forces were winning the war and liberating those oppressed nations that were once occupied by the enemy. The studios such as: Republic, Columbia and Universal were at the forefront of producing chapter plays about our war efforts, and one of the most popular superheroes to emerge from the pages of a pulp comic book to the silver screen was *Spy Smasher* (1942). He wore a cape, a leather riding helmet, a pair of goggles, and he rode a hot motorcycle. In short, he was as cool as they come, and he never walked away from a fight. Since he was a product of Republic Studios, action was in his blood.

As mentioned earlier, my goal is to examine what makes these specific superheroes so unique as compared to those who have real superpowers. I refer to all of them as superheroes event though they don't have the capability of personal flight or remarkable, physical strength. I purposely focus my efforts on ordinary men with exceptional moxie and an unusual propensity for doing the right thing. Honour and glory for a worthwhile cause is their battle cry. They truly are men among men. Rah, rah, rah for the good guys.

Spy Smasher, whose real name is Alan, is a perfect example of true patriotism. What makes his story an interesting character study is that he has a twin brother (Jack), and the writers do a masterful job of using this fact to advance the storyline. Originally, *Spy Smasher's* assignment was to disrupt German operations in Europe, but, in the process, he was captured by the Gestapo and sent before a firing squad. However, due to a very slick manoeuvre, a French solider named Captain Durand saves him from certain death, and he returns to America as *Spy Smasher*.

Back home, Alan is reunited with his twin brother, who was under the assumption that Alan had been killed in Europe. Alan informs Jack about his close scrape with death and explains his new assignment of exposing enemy forces in the homeland. Interestingly, he still wears the same outfit as he did in Europe, which would certainly draw attention to his alter-ego as *Spy Smasher* After all, the guy does have a cool looking outfit, so why not capitalize on his image, right? Another interesting addition to the storyline is that Jack is engaged to the daughter of a high-ranking Admiral (Corby), and there are times when she thinks that Alan is really her fiancé. Hum…wonder what today's writers would do with that scenario?

The main antagonist is a German officer who works aboard a U-Boat off the coast of America, and he uses a television screen to deliver various assignments of destruction to his underlings.

While on television, he conceals his identity by wearing a crude, cloth mask; hence, he is referred to as "The Mask" (so much for creativity). His intentions are to counterfeit America's currency, which would have a devastating effect on a wartime economy. A shrewd plan if it works.

Fortunately, Admiral Corby and *Spy Smasher* are able to destroy the phony money as well as the presses used to print the currency. Of course, that doesn't stop "The Mask" in his efforts to wreak havoc on America, as he attempts to destroy airplanes, oil and munitions headed for England, but his plans are thwarted by our hero.

As the story continues, the action accelerates to a climatic ending, when Alan kills "The Mask" in a furious fight aboard the U-Boat, only to narrowly escape death himself in a sea of flaming oil. Unfortunately, the Nazis kill his brother Jack earlier in the chapter.

As expected from Republic chapter plays, *Spy Smasher* is full of action and suspense, and the special effects are top-notch. In particular, there is an unbelievable flying object that resembles a cross between a wing and a flying saucer. The Lydecker brothers were experts at creating large models of airplanes and other devices and filming them in natural light. This process gives the illusion that a real airplane is flying instead of a much, smaller model.

Many critics consider *Spy Smasher* to be one of the best serials ever made, and while it certainly has all the hallmarks of a first-rate chapter play, it's very similar to many, other wartime serials. The villain is probably the weakest link in the storyline: you simply don't love to hate him. He isn't necessarily unique either. The idea of wearing a white cloth to conceal one's identity and calling it a mask is ridiculous. I don't care if it did have two openings for the eyes, it's hardly a mask. I realize that's how it was written, but the fact remains, he still lacks a certain malevolent presence that is needed to portray a memorable villain. Nevertheless, that takes nothing away from Kane Richmond's portrayal of the lead. With his rugged good looks and manly stature, he is a perfect choice for the role.

I'm surprised that Kane's career wasn't as successful as it might have been had he worked for a larger studio. Maybe he wasn't unique enough to be more of a leading man type. At any rate, he made several chapter plays, including *The Lost City* (1935), which was banned for several years because of its portrayal of black actors as mindless, slave-like zombies and nothing more. But that having been stated, *The Lost City* is still a very enjoyable serial to watch as well.

If you're looking for a fast-paced, adventure-filled cliff-hanger, *Spy Smasher* is one that you don't want to miss. As one of many wartime serials, it served a purpose to convey a message of patriotism. For that fact alone, I give it an eight on a scale of ten.

Doug Crill

Originally published in Mass Movement #36, July 2013

JEFF "SWAMPY" MARSH

I love cartoons, always have and always will, so when Jeff 'Swampy' Marsh, the man responsible (along with Dan Povenmire) for two of my favourite shows, *Rocko's Modern Life* and *Phineas And Ferb* rolled into town to talk about *Mission Marvel*, come hell or high water, I had to talk to him about his shows and life in animation. Oh, and just for the record, Jeff is one of the nicest, most open, pleasant and funny individuals that I've had the honour of crossing paths with..

Interview by Tim Cundle

Images courtesy of Jeff 'Swampy' Marsh and Disney XD.

MM: So, Jeff, what are you going to do today?

Swampy: Ha, ha, ha, I think I'm going to do be doing interviews today...

MM: *With Phineas and Ferb*, where did the original concept come from and how much of that made it to the finished show?

Swampy: The original show all started with just Dan and I wanting to continue working together. That was the idea. The only idea we really had when we sat down to write the series was "Quick, let's create something so we can continue doing this". That took thirteen years. The idea that we latched onto for the show itself was to liberate old man rants about how kids today didn't go out and do things anymore; they just sat around playing video games and watching DVD's. We remembered – we both had fairly similar upbringings – our parents encouraged us to get out and do all crazy things.

We put plays on in our back yard, made movies and built tree houses, made go-carts out of spare parts, all kinds of whacky stuff. I used to spend hours modifying my bicycle in the garage and that's just what we remembered as being great about our childhoods. We just wanted these little characters we had created to celebrate that. That was the genesis of *Phineas and Ferb*. The pilot that we first wrote and all of the original drawings – if you see the proposal that we came up with back in 1993 – it's virtually indistinguishable from what went on the air. A little group of characters was lost; the character of Isabella we kind of made bigger but really other than that, it's hard to tell the difference between that and what's on the air.

MM: If we're going to talk about *Phineas and Ferb*, we have to talk about the songs. Was it always your plan to include a song in each episode?

Swampy: Oh yes. When Dan and I first started writing together, we put in a song in each episode and song writing is such a wonderfully joyous process, we could write a song about just about anything, in practically any style in about an hour. So from the very beginning we wanted to write songs for the show. We wrote the theme song and then another one of the episodes needed a song in it so we sat down and wrote that pretty quickly; and thank gosh the network liked the song so much they said "That's a great song, who wrote that?" and we said "Well, we did", "Great", they said "Could we get one of those in every episode?"

Absolutely you can, because even if you hadn't asked for it we'd have given you one. We've now written – we calculated it recently – well over 300 songs since we started doing this, and at one point we had at least three different albums that they've released and have charted.

MM: So why, out of all the animals that walk on the Earth, choose a semi aquatic egg laying mammal to fight crime and, ultimately, Doofenshmirtz?

Swampy: Well it just seemed like a natural choice. If you were going to go out and pick a crime fighting animal you couldn't do better than a platypus. We just assumed that all platypuses fight evil in their spare time. There were a bunch of different reasons that went into it. One was that we could make up what we wanted to about platypuses and very few people would know if we were making it up or not. The description of them alone is fantastic: beaver tailed, duck billed, semi aquatic poisonous, egg-laying... They're fantastic.

The fact that nobody had used them before astonished us. The other premise was there was all this controversy all the time when an animal, a type of dog or something, would be in a film or a television series and a bunch of kids run out and buy one then later they get discarded. So we thought "This is definitely not going to happen with platypuses". People wouldn't be running out and buying a platypus for their home. All of those reasons made the platypus perfect.

MM: Let's talk about the next chapter in the ever evolving story of *Phineas and Ferb: Mission Marvel*. How and when was this cross-over event born in your mind?

Swampy: As soon as Disney and Marvel got together and the two companies became part of the same family, we thought it would be a fun thing to do. Then Disney came to us and said "Hey, do you guys think you might be interested in doing a Mar...." and before they got the rest of the sentence out we were like "Oh yeah". Having said that it was a very, very intimidating prospect. Marvel fans really know what they like and they want you to be careful with those characters; and all of us on our show we have a huge contingent of rabid Marvel fans, and they'll tell you that.

We didn't want to do anything that was disrespectful to the brand or characters, but we wanted to be able to derive humour – our kind of humour – and we knew that would take extra resources and extra time. We had Marvel guys come down and help us navigate the characters the way they are now, currently. Then there are the legal aspects and the rights issues and everything, because we really wanted to be able to push the envelope, but do it right. Both Disney and Marvel and the executives and everything were really good about pushing the boundaries and giving us the resources that we needed to get it right. To end up with something that we were both equally happy with, we were overjoyed with. In the end when we saw the final product we were pleased beyond our wildest expectations and so were Marvel and the channel. For a labour of love like that we couldn't have had it come out any better.

MM: What can you tell us about it?

Swampy: Well... Phineas and Ferb inadvertently create a device that, because of a mix up with a device that Doofenshmirtz makes, accidentally drains the power from four of the Marvel superheroes: Iron Man, Thor, the Hulk and Spiderman. They are able to trace the beam back to Danville and Phineas and Ferb's house. In the meantime, four of the super villains:

Red Skull, MODOK, Whiplash and Venom are also able to track the beam back to Danville and they go and find Doofenshmirtz. They think he's some kind of super genius who has managed to create a device to drain the powers of superheroes. They meet him and find out he's actually just an idiot, then they use him to recreate that device.

In the meantime, Phineas and Ferb have to help the Marvel superheroes restore their powers. Along the way Tony Stark offers Phineas and Ferb a summer internship because he sees how clever they are. We actually get a little bit of crime fighting from Perry and a cameo from the one and only Stan Lee.

MM: This is going to be good. It's going to be so good...

Swampy: We're very, very proud of it.

MM: Is it going to be a one off event or do you see any potential sequels or spin-offs? If you were given an opportunity to create a spin off, what would you like to focus on?

Swampy: I don't know about a spin-off, but I know we had so much fun doing this format and it was received so well that I certainly hope we get the opportunity to do more stuff like this. I'd happily do a Marvel 2 and I've love to see other areas where we could do crossovers and more extended specials of *Phineas and Ferb*. I think that would be my biggest joy; getting the chance to do a *Marvel Phineas and Ferb Crossover 2*. Maybe play with some different characters.

MM: *Phineas and Ferb* is now the longest running show on Disney isn't it? Does that kind of success ever translate into pressure for you to keep coming up with original ideas and to keep it fresh?

Swampy: Oh absolutely. And a lot of that pressure is still internal. We want to make sure that we are doing stuff that is pushing the envelope with the characters and format and don't get stuck in a rut. You want to make sure you're aware and honest with yourself. If you think you've gone too far, if you have run out of ideas you want to put your hand up and say so. So yeah it's a tricky process. Disney, though has really been very supportive of us. The pressure is truly pressure that we put on ourselves. Sometimes the desire in our marketing department for bigger and better episodes as far as promotions go, does challenge us a bit. But I can honestly say that most of the pressure for that is internal and comes from us.

MM: What's next for *Phineas and Ferb* after *Mission Marvel*?

Swampy: One of our favourite things that we have coming up next year is that we managed to get all the guys from *Top Gear* to come over and do a voice on the show. I'm such a massive fan and earlier this week I got to go down and watch them do a taping of the show and Richard Hammond agreed to do the *Phineas and Ferb Take Two Talk Show* and I couldn't be happier as the episode turned out incredibly well. It's one of my favourites...

Originally published in Mass Movement #36, July 2013

PAUL MAGRS

It isn't often that you get the chance to interview one of your favourite authors. In fact, if I'm honest, this is the first time that it's happened, and when Simon Barnard from Bafflegab Productions mentioned that Paul Magrs had written one of the stories for *Hammer Chillers*, the brand new and rather excellent series that's loosely based on the anthology series (*Hammer House Of Horror*) that the studio that dripped blood produced over three decades ago, I jumped at the chance to interview him about his career, Doctor Who, Brenda & Effie and of course, *Spanish Ladies*, his contribution to the latest offering to proudly bear the Hammer name. So, without further ado, it's time to meet Paul…

Interview by Tim Cundle

MM: For the benefit of those who came in late, would you like to both introduce, and tell us a little about, yourself?

Paul: I'm a writer from the North East of England, born at the end of the Sixties, and now settled in Manchester with my partner Jeremy and our cat Bernard Socks. My first novels were published by Chatto and Windus at the end of the 90s and they were Magical Realism set on a council estate in Country Durham. Since then I've written Spooky Mysteries, science fiction, black comedy, short stories, radio plays, Doctor Who … everything!

MM: When and where did your love of literature begin Paul? When did you fall for the written word, which tome seduced you and how and why did it entangle you?

Paul: The first books that made me want to write were read to us at school: the Narnia books by C.S Lewis, the Borrowers books by Mary Norton, and *The Secret Garden* by Frances Hodgson Burnett. Lots of time spent with really wonderful kids' books at school was extremely important.

MM: Writers and authors always say that they need to write, that it isn't a job, it's a calling… Do you think that's true? And if so, when were you called, or summoned, and what made you want to follow that voice and become a writer?

Paul: It's a job. It's a vocation, too. But it's a job. Writers need to be paid properly. And, on the whole, they aren't!

MM: I think it's time to talk about Doctor Who… When and how did your path cross with that of The Doctor, and what appealed, and still appeals, you about Who? Have your feelings about, and toward, the show changed over time, and if so, has that affected your perception of, and the way you view, Doctor Who?

Paul: I've always been in love with The Show, since the first episode I saw – which was part six of *Planet of the Spiders*. We've had many ups and downs since then. My favourite moments are stories that would be seen by most as the quirkier ones: *The Web Planet, The Mind Robber, Carnival of Monsters, Warriors' Gate, City of the Damned, the Tides of Time, The Five Doctors, Timelash, Voyager, Happiness Patrol, Lungbarrow, the Crystal Bucephalus, The Dying Days, Devil Goblins from Neptune, Love and Monsters…*

I think that, throughout fifty years, it's still basically the same show – and it's always recycled itself and imagery from popular narrative and mythology. I must say, I like it most when it's being clever rather than clever-clever.

MM: Sort of following on from the above... Having written multiple Who stories (more on that later), I wondered if, now that you've added to, and become part of, the mythology of the Doctor's Universe, whether you still thought of yourself as "fan" of the show, or if the responsibility and challenge of adding to the canonicity of the Whoniverse somehow blurs and negates the ability to just be a "fan"...?

Paul: Nope – still a fan. I'd hate to become cynical about it.

MM: Which sort of brings us around to *The Diary Of A Doctor Who Addict*. Even though it's a work of fiction, was writing it a cathartic experience and release for you, and did the line between fiction and reality ever disappear while you were writing it?

Paul: It doesn't really work like that! These things aren't in the slightest bit cathartic. It's work!

MM: Traveling back to the Whoniverse... Where did the character of Iris Wildthyme come from? A gift of Universal inspiration, an epiphany or did she just pop, fully formed into your subconscious? What is it that you like about the character, and what do you think her lasting appeal with fans is? What, if anything, would you like to have Iris do that she hasn't already, and what lies in store for her?

Paul: Gawd knows where she came from. She's every tipsy aunty who says inappropriate stuff at family gatherings. She's every one of those aunties but one who's been given the keys to all of space and time and the cocktail cabinet. Her career has been ad hoc, and I'm startled to see her still pootling along. I don't know what she'll do next. I'd love her to have some more Doctor Who adventures at some point – perhaps with the Fourth Doctor.

MM: More Who I'm afraid... How did you feel when you were asked to write *Hornet's Nest*, knowing that Tom Baker was returning to his most famous role and its success or failure would be largely dependent on you? I'm guessing that there was a little self-inflicted pressure? Were you involved in the recording process at all, and if so, how was it?

Paul: I was very involved in the whole process, and there for as many of the recordings as I could get to. Very exciting, creative days – with lots of brilliant actors clustered around the microphones, rather like in the old days of radio drama. A lot of experimentation with technique and layers of narration and always pushing in different directions with the shape that Doctor Who stories can take. I was conscious of taking the Gothic motifs of classic Fourth Doctor stories and making them even more grotesque and macabre. When Tom was the Doctor every season was different. Everything evolved as his years went on. I wanted to keep pushing those changes forward and see where it could go. Audio drama has endless potential.

MM: Talking about recording… How different is writing for radio / audio compared to writing prose? Are they very similar mediums, or are they vastly different, and if so, how do they differ and did, and do, you have to adjust your writing style when creating audio drama?

Paul: Both are more similar to each other than writing for a visual medium. TV and film are more literal. 'Here is what is happening right now' the visuals mostly tell us. I'm a very wordy person, so as I see it, audio stuff and prose are happening inside the language, inside your head and they need decoding constantly, at every level as they unspool. For me, they require more attention than just looking.

MM: Focusing on the audio side of your career for a while… It's Vince Cosmos time. As with Iris, where did the idea for Vince come from? I mean, an alien Glam Rocker preventing a Martian Invasion in seventies London, it's not exactly a run of the mill tale… How has the series been received, and will Vince return in another set of adventures?

Paul: Hopefully it'll return. There are a lot more stories to tell. The underlying tale of serial Martian invasions of Earth is something that runs through everything I write – and so all these things are really a part of the same overall story.

MM: I think it's time that we talked about Hammer Chillers… How did you become involved with the series, and would you like to tell us a little about your tale, *Spanish Ladies*? What do you think the enduring appeal of Hammer is? Why Hammer? What did, and do, they do that no other studio could?

Paul: Simon Barnard asked me to pitch when he got the rights. He knows I'm a big horror movie fan – Hammer in particular. I always loved the extravagance and the theatricality of what they did – and the fact that, having grown up with 70s Doctor Who, one of the things you realise it's doing is echoing 50s and 60s Hammer. It's part of the same lurid and literate continuum. My story is an homage to the 'crazy ladies' strand of Hammer movies – the ones in which Bette Davis or Tallulah Bankhead went bananas and started killing folk. (*Die, Die My Darling* has one of the most startling casts in movie history – with Tallulah, Yootha Joyce and Donald Sutherland being, essentially, the Texas Chainsaw Family in the Home Counties, and holding Mrs Hart from *Hart to Hart* prisoner against her will.) *Spanish Ladies* also has a flavour of the 1980s *Hammer House of Horror* TV series – in which the plot hooks had less to do with the supernatural than they did with nastiness and revenge… and no one ever came to a good end…

MM: And of course, it wouldn't be right to not mention Brenda and Effie… Where did the idea for them come from? Why Whitby (as wonderful as it is), and, I hate to ask you this and put you on the spot Paul, which if their adventures has been your favourite so far, and why? What does the future hold for them Paul, or is that a secret…?

Paul: My favourite Brenda and Effie story so far… It's very hard to say. But actually, these new stories for Bafflegab are currently my favourites.

MM: Is there any truth to the rumour that Brenda and Effie will soon be appearing in their own audio series, and if so, what can you tell us about it?

Paul: Yes – and it's soon to go into production. There are four new stories – all set at the time of Brenda and Effie's first meeting. So the audience doesn't need to know anything about the series or characters at all. It all starts from scratch again – with new stories – right here! You'll meet Egyptian Mummies, the Elephant Man, the monster hunters known as the Smudgelings, Tolstoy the Long Eared Bat, Mrs Claus at the Christmas Hotel and the Demon King himself.

MM: What's next for you Paul?

Paul: I've a new series – with Audiogo, premiering in the autumn – and that'll be appearing in a new, interesting format. I can't say anything else about that just now, because it hasn't been announced. And I've got my first ever play in the Radio 4 Afternoon Drama slot coming up quite soon, too. There's another lifelong ambition sorted out!

Originally published in Mass Movement #36, July 2013

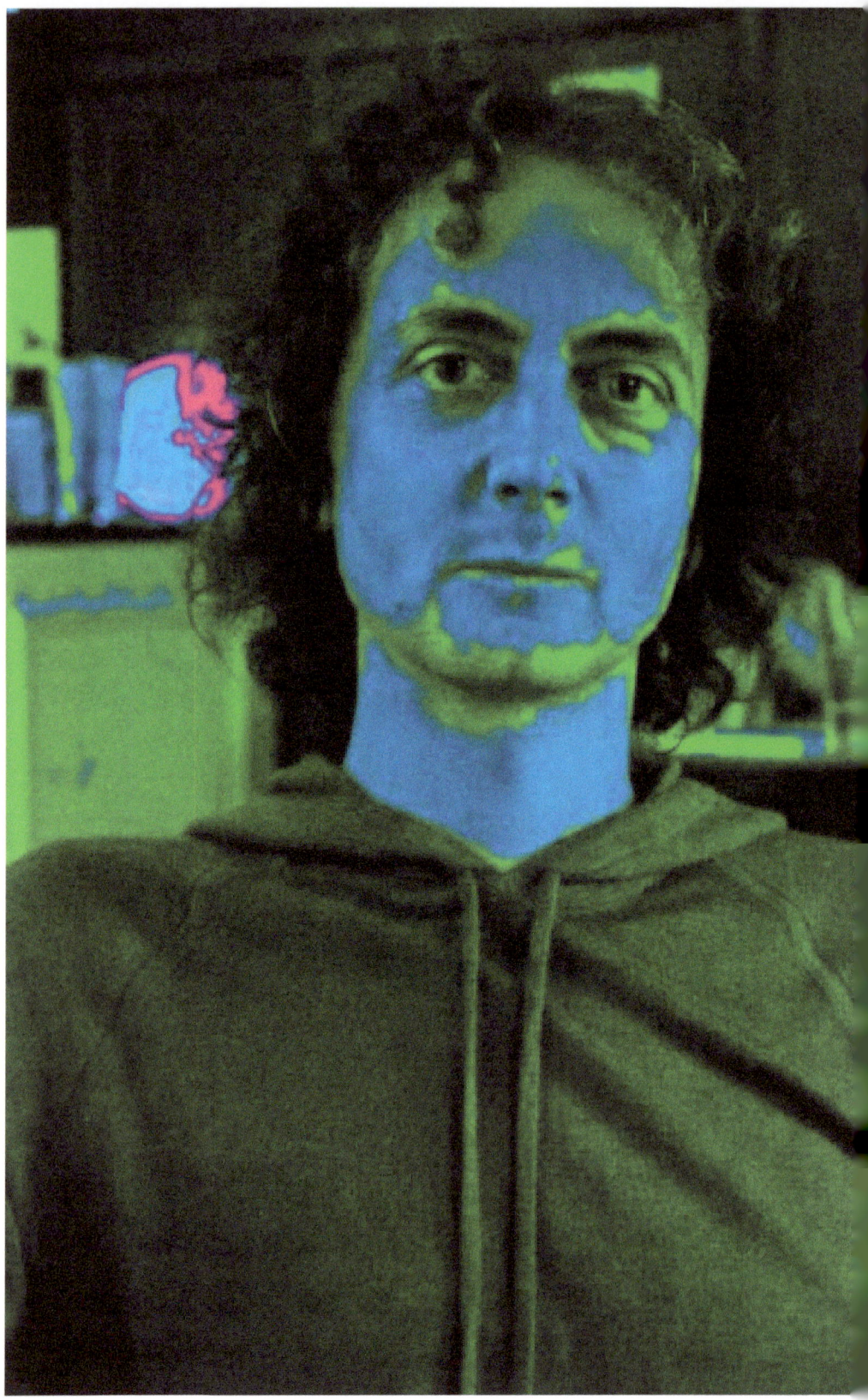

PIMP MY WRITE

LOL is the nervous laugh of internet interaction. I doubt anyone is actually laughing out loud as they type it. If they were, given how most people use it, they're either mentally deranged or a cackling comic book villain. "Bank's just foreclosed on the mortgage, could lose the house - LOL!"
"LOL, just found I've got a brain tumour."

LOL rarely has anything to do with real laughter or humour. LOL is the nervous way the neighbour laughs when they ask to borrow your hedge trimmers, or the apprehensive giggle you have in your voice as you phone up a casual lover to let them know you've got chlamydia. "So you should really get checked out yourself -LOL."

It is also the inane grin on the face of a door to door salesperson. Especially if a writer or artist uses it. Especially if that writer or artist has a fracking novel/graphic novel out. "LOL just thought you'd all like to know that my latest book 'Please Help Me Quit The Day Job' has 50% off on Amazon all this week'. LOL is the new spam siren, a red flag that one of your creative chums is about to infest every page and forum you visit with their desperate pleas for love, money and artistic vindication.

When I was in my twenties, one of my flat-mates got involved in a pyramid selling scheme. He was encouraged to keep a list of the birthdays of all his friends, family and acquaintances so he could phone them up a week beforehand and sell their partners his dodgy wares as a 'great present'. Every traveling salesman who came to our door found themselves the target of an aggressive counter sales pitch. The postman started leaving our post with a neighbour and we all hid in our rooms for fear he'd beg us to buy another dodgy bottle of perfume that smelled just like a name brand. The rise of Internet 2.0 has turned every writer and artist into an army of just these sort of Amway style sales drones. Instead of inviting you to Tupperware parties we invite you to like the page dedicated to our latest work. Rather than hammer on your door when you're home from work we post on your Facebook page. Rather than cold calling we tweet endlessly about whatever we're currently hoping will bother the best sellers chart. The things is though, we'd never dream of selling our wares door to door. So how did we all end up as the Jehovah's Witnesses of the world wide web?

Well for a start, the brave new world of web piracy has had such an impact on sales that few publishers can afford to invest in marketing for all but their big name writers and artists. This means the rest of us have to fall back on guerilla marketing techniques if we want anyone to read our works. We take a look at the thousand plus people we've befriended on Facebook and the hundreds of followers we have on Twitter and think 'wow if everyone on this list bought just two of my books and encouraged their friends to do the same then I'd be a best seller in less than a month!'

Sadly all our colleagues, most of whom are our Facebook friends, have had the same thought and are in direct competition with us, diminishing our pool of potential buyers/victims. Then our quarterly royalties statement arrives, in my case usually on the same day that my mortgage statement turns up. One of these documents contains a sum so paltry that the accounting department have had to use a dead currency to accurately reflect its value. The other is my mortgage. So naturally I turn to guerilla marketing with a renewed vigour. Only now I post pictures of my children weeping with packed suitcases and beg you not to see them out on the street, after all there's 20% off all my works on Amazon for the next four days. Eventually you leave every Facebook group and any forum of which I'm also a member. This is the point at which good writers go bad and cross over into the posting equivalent of a sex pest,

or a lap dog that's gotten too friendly with your leg.

I like to think that I've yet to cross that line myself, but I'm betting that every person reading this knows someone who has. One writer I know posted from the hospital that his wife had just given birth to their first son. He'd just cut the umbilical cord. He was holding his child for the first time with one hand and posting on his smart phone with the other. Having held my own child for the first time I know the sort of awe and affection it inspires in you. Not ten minutes later, seeing the hundreds of people who were congratulating him he couldn't help posting: 'Thanks for all the well wishes LOL. Don't forget my latest novel '******* Wars' is still available on Amazon, LOL". His son was still sticky with amniotic fluid, his wife was being stitched back together and he was busy pimping his wares on Facebook.

Another writer I know posts thinly veiled suicide notes to entice people to buy his books. "I don't want to drag you all down or anything - LOL, but I'm feeling kinda fragile and it would really help if just one person could check out my latest deal on Amazon". Trying to get us all to make the purchasing equivalent of a sympathy f*ck.

Of course the main thing that annoys group members and forum users is the writer who's a fair weather friend. Who only posts or interacts with other members when they have something to sell. Then as soon as they've plugged their books they're nowhere to be seen. So it always pays to remain a fairly active member of any group or forum in which you post. Not only as it's the best way to sell your books and comics but because you can have a lot of fun and learn something too.

However, you do want to avoid turning into a troll. There's another graphic novelist I know who has some really interesting ideas about online marketing and who is an active member of practically every comic book group or forum on the net. When he puts his mind to it he can drive a lot of traffic to his various web comics, but unfortunately he just can't keep his mouth shut or his reactionary views to himself. As a result he's hated by just about every member of the international comics community and all his promotional efforts inevitably backfire on him.

Online marketing is an amazing resource for professional creatives, no matter what level they're at. It not only puts you in touch with like minds and potential customers, it also gives you an unprecedented level of feedback, not only on your work itself, but the effectiveness of your marketing campaign. However if you get it wrong it can bring out the worst human traits, both in yourself and the people with whom you're trying to connect.

Now, the more observant readers of this column might have noted that it's supposed to be about horror comics and I've hardly mentioned either horror or comics. To be honest, that's quite a niche market and this week is royalty statement week (sigh). So I figured I'd write something that applied to the world of horror comics and a much larger potential readership as well. Because, as the really observant among you might notice there is a link at the bottom where you can buy my books on Amazon and I do have two kids and a very hungry overdraft to feed.

I'm just saying.

LOL

Jasper Bark

Orginally published in Mass Movement #36, July 2013

STERLING GATES

I don't believe in astrology, fortune-telling, predestination or any other semi-mystical hocus pocus that tries to convince you, me and everyone else that the future is written in stone, that our destinies are planned and plotted and that the road that we travel down in life exists for no other reason than to ensure we arrive where we're supposed to and do what we're supposed to do. Or at least I didn't believe in any of it until I met Sterling Gates. He was born to write comics, and life has made sure that he's followed that path, and having written for *Tales Of The Sinestro Corps* and been the lead writer on *Supergirl* for nearly two and half years, he's now guiding Vibe through the DCU. This is Sterling Gates, and this is his story so far...

Interview by Tim Cundle

Images appear courtesy of DC Entertainment & DC Comics.

MM: Let's start at the beginning shall we... Would you like to both introduce, and tell us a little about yourself?

Sterling: My name is Sterling Gates, I'm a comic book writer from Los Angeles, California. I grew up in Tulsa, Oklahoma. I'm an Eagle Scout, and I earned a degree in Art: Film and Media Arts from the University of Oklahoma.

MM: I guess that it was inevitable that you'd end up working in the comics industry.... What was it like growing up in a comics book store, and being surrounded by books all the time? What was the first comic that made you think, "You know what, this is what I want to do for a living, I want to write comics..", and why did that book have kind of impact on you?

Sterling: It was one of the most amazing ways to grow up. My parents owned a small comic book store in Tulsa, so almost every shelf in our home and garage was covered in back stock. I would go out into the garage for hours, just digging through long boxes of comics and pulling out whole runs of, like, *Power Man & Iron Fist* and reading through them in a day. Superheroes became a big part of my life and helped me to process going through middle school. I was a terribly awkward 11-year old, but knowing that Superman was just as awkward in his day-to-day life — that he was secretly the most powerful man in the world, it's just that no one knew — helped me through a hard adolescence. As I got older, though, I got more and more interested in guitars and girls. Superhero books sort of fell to the wayside.

I honestly never thought I would be writing comics for a living. I made comics through college, writing and drawing these slice-of-life stories that had more in common with James Kolchaka's daily diary strips or Adriane Tomine's work than Superman and Batman.

The turning point, the thing that brought me back to superhero comics, was the death of my father. He passed away in 1998, and one of the first decisions the family made was to shut down our comic store. That store was my father's passion, the thing he loved most in the world outside of our family, and it was just too painful for us to keep up with it. My mother said, "If there's anything you want out of the store, take it now." So, I started digging around in long boxes like I used to when I was a kid.

And that's how I found Mark Waid's *Flash* run.

It was galvanizing. Here was a superhero – Wally West — trying to deal with the death of his father figure and mentor, all the while trying to carry on the mantle. Wally was one of the first superheroes to actually graduate from being the sidekick and putting on the costume of his mentor. I identified with every page, and I became a Wally West collector. That lead me to Grant's *JLA* run, which lead me to James Robinson's *Starman*, which lead me to a ton of comics that I'd missed in the 1990s because I'd been away from mainstream superhero comics. I distinctly remember buying my first issue of *Starman* at a small comic convention in a hotel ballroom. I picked it up because Wally West was in it, and I was fascinated by the ideas of legacy and family that James was writing about. I gave that issue of *Starman* to my brother, and he and I used that series to help us process what the landscape of our family looked like without our father.

MM: Is it true that you tried to relate all of your academic career, or at least the parts of it that you enjoyed, to comic books? Do you think the same rule can also be applied to everyday life, and if so, how would you apply the rule to say, an average day in the life of Sterling Gates...

Sterling: OU's School of Art is an extremely creative place within a very rigid academic structure. The first few years are very, very broad artistic training. Once you pass your Foundations classes, you choose your artistic discipline and everything you do, every class you take for the next three years is designed to train you and focus your work to elevate it to a professional level. I choose the film department because I wanted to make linear, story/character-driven films. Some students wanted to make experimental films and videos, or focus on video installations, but I wanted to tell stories.

I studied screenwriting and film editing and illustration, all while doing my own comic work on the side. I loved shooting films and directing actors, but for my Senior thesis, I wanted to do something comic-related. My advisor – a wonderful instructor named Heidi Mau — gave me permission to write and draw a 20-page comic book instead of shoot a final film.

The catch, however, was that I had to write a massive paper detailing how the juxtaposition of panels in comic books was similar to the juxtaposition of images in film. Scott McCloud's *Understanding Comics* saved my life that semester, because I cited something from almost every page in that paper (laughs)

MM: So, let's talk about the formative years of your writing career.... What were your first forays into writing the four colour world, and how, if at all, did your early experiences of writing prepare you for working in the major leagues?

Sterling: I moved to Los Angeles because I wanted to write for television. The comics I'd written and drawn were just things I was doing for fun at that point, nothing I ever want anyone to see. I would often trade a black-and-white four-panel comic with my friends for stuff like a home-cooked meal or help with my laundry...or a little drawing for a ride to campus. Stuff like that. Those same friends now threaten to publish those strips online from time to time. Thanks, TKA. You jerks. (Laughs)

MM: Again, this is another of those this is true questions... So, Sterling is it true that you bumped into Geoff Johns at a diner, and that it was that fateful meeting that really started the ball rolling for you? If it is true (and I really want it to be, because it's the sort of moment that keeps hope alive), do you want to briefly tell us all about it?

Sterling: The short version is: my friend drunkenly accosted Geoff Johns in a convention hotel lobby in San Francisco. I pulled him away and we went out into the streets of San Francisco to look for food to sober him up. We found a Mel's Diner around the corner, and we walked in and Geoff and his editor Steve Wacker were inside waiting for a table. Awkward city. We exchanged some small talk and then said our courtesy goodbyes and they got seated. And then my friend and I get seated at the table directly next to them. AWK. WARD.

All four of us ate our food, doing our best not to look at the other table. When our bill comes, I quietly asked the waitress for Geoff and Wacker's check. I came back and told them I covered their dinner and apologized again for my drunk friend, and Geoff asked me if I want a job. I'd been in LA a month and hadn't had any luck finding employment yet, so of course I said yes.

Geoff forwarded my resume to a television show he was working on called *Blade: The Series* and I became the writer's room production assistant. I made coffee, drove scripts to people's houses, that kind of thing. I worked on that show for six months, and then Geoff called me on a Sunday and said we were canceled. He asked if I wanted to be his personal assistant, he had a number of projects coming up including a movie he was writing and directing.

I said yes to that, too.

MM: And, then it was DC time... You made your DC on one the flagship titles, or at least on a book tied in with one of the flagship (Green Lantern) titles, *Tales Of The Sinestro Corps*... That's one heck of a stage to make your debut on, so how did you feel in the run-up to the story being published, and how did you feel once it was out there in the big, bad world? Are you a GL fan, and if so, did being a fan make it easier or more difficult to write the initial story and slide into the world of the Corps?

Sterling: I'm a huge Green Lantern fan, so I was extremely happy to work on that project. Geoff and I had already started work on *Green Lantern/Sinestro Corps: Secret Files* by the time that story hit, so I was deep into the Green Lantern trenches at that point. (I spent six months of my life researching every Green Lantern that had ever been in a DC comic for that book! I'm still pretty sure I missed a couple...)

For me, the most exciting part about writing *Fear is a Baby's Cry* was finding out that Jerry Ordway was going to draw that story. I think Jerry is one of the modern masters of American comic books, so cracking open that Fed-Ex package and seeing photocopies of his pages was one of the most exciting moments of my life.

MMM: Then came your near two-and-half run on *Supergirl*. What made you want to leave the book? What do you think your defining, and what's your favourite moment is from the time you spent writing *Supergirl*?

Sterling: Well, I *never* wanted to leave that book; it was the sales that did me in! I was very sad to exit Kara Zor-El's life, but the sales on *Supergirl* took a severe tumble after the New Krypton mega-arc ended, so issue #59 ended up being my last. I loved working with all the

phenomenal artists we had on that book, everyone from Jamal Igle to Matt Camp to Fernando Dagnino to cover artists Josh Middleton and Amy Reeder. Editors Matt Idelson and Wil Moss gave me some of the best collaborators in the business for that run, and I'll always be thankful to Matt and Wil for all they did for us on that book.

I think Jamal Igle and I had a couple different defining moments in our run. It was important to me when I came on that title to refine her origins. That book had six different creative teams in three years, and each of them had put their own spin on Kara's origins. I wanted to address those issues – as well as the DCU public's perception of *Supergirl* – in the first two issues, which is why Cat Grant wrote her story called *Why the World Doesn't Need Supergirl* and why Zor-El recognized Kryptonite Poisoning within his daughter. With those elements in play, we had a lot of great new story opportunities with Kara. We took those and ran with them, as well as dealing with the New Krypton angle that Geoff and James Robinson had come up with.

The other thing that was important to me was having an almost entirely female cast in that book. If you read my 28 issues of *Supergirl*, the main players are Kara, Lana Lang, Cat Grant, Lois Lane, Lucy Lane, and Alura Zor-El. I wanted to do for the Superman universe what *Birds of Prey* had done for the Batman universe. The Superman universe has some dynamite female characters, so why not have all of them interacting in a big way in one book? I felt that Supergirl was the place to do that. We didn't announce it or talk about it in interviews or anything, we just let it be what it was.

I have a bunch of favorite story moments from our run, probably too many to list, but here's a few:

Supergirl fighting Reactron using the Kryptonian martial art of klurkor ("Just because I can't use my heat vision doesn't mean I'm helpless")

Supergirl's silent reaction to Cat Grant's article and the card she leaves on Cat's desk

Introducing Linda Lang (no one had ever done that before)

Supergirl hanging out with the Legion of Super-Heroes and finding Excalibur (thus putting a lot of those Silver Age stories in Kara's timeline)

Supergirl asking Lana why couldn't her mother have died instead of her dad (SUCH an emotionally-charged scene)

Kara and her best friend Thara's childhood adventures on Krypton (co-written with Greg Rucka, one of my favorite writers)

Supergirl and Batgirl (Stephanie Brown) teaming up in World's Finest.

"I'm Kara Zor-El of Kandor, Queen. I'm a superhero. I don't scare easily." (A reference to SUPERGIRL THE MOVIE

Supergirl finding a mourning Bizarrogirl in a cave on Bizarro World (Bizarrogirl learned an emotion, making her different from the other Bizarros)

The moment Cat Grant realizes that calling Supergirl is her only way out of danger

My favorite real life moments on that book were:

Getting the text at San Diego Comic-Con that Helen Slater – the actress who played Supergirl in SUPERGIRL THE MOVIE – was going to write the introduction to our first trade paperback, "Who is Superwoman?"

Dan Didio offering his personal Michael Turner Supergirl sketch to us to be the cover to Supergirl #50. I was moved to tears by that. Mike Turner co-created this version of Supergirl with Jeph Loeb in Superman/Batman before he passed away, and it meant a lot to me that Dan volunteered a piece of art out of his own collection to help us acknowledge Mike's contribution to the Girl of Steel and celebrate such a landmark issue.

MM: So, The New 52… What was your initial reaction when you found out about the reboot? I'm guessing that, from a writers point of view, it must have been incredibly exciting, with a Universe of possibility opening up, and now that its established, I wondered if there were any books or characters that you'd like to work on that you haven't yet? If so, who and what would you like to get your hands on and why?

Sterling: Well, I'd love to do more with Kid Flash or Superman. They're my two favorite DC characters, so I try to take any opportunity that I get to work with them.

My first response to the reboot was trepidation, because we fear what we don't understand. As I wrapped my head around the idea, though, I began to see the possibilities and opportunities that came out of such a massive change.

MM: Which sort of brings us to Vibe… What initially appealed to you about the character, and how would you describe the book to anyone not familiar with it? It feels like it's going to be a multi-thread story, with everything being connected to the fact that he's a guy who just wants to do the right thing, who's caught in the middle of something much bigger than himself and as such is torn between doing what he feels and knows is right and, for want of a better phrase, 'obeying orders', so how big is Vibe's story going to get, do you have it all planned out (in your head) and what can you tell us about what's in store for him…?

Sterling: That is a very long question! [laughs] What I like most about Cisco is his optimism. He still believes in the good in people, and his time with ARGUS is going to shake that belief to its core. Which is good. You want to challenge your characters and their beliefs. Challenge the things that make them the people they are, and then see if they change or bounce back from those challenges. Cisco wants to do the right thing, which makes him dangerous to his superiors. He's not someone you can predict, either, because you never know what the "right thing" is to him. His reactions always seem fresh and interesting to me, which is why it's so fun to write him.

As for plans for Vibe, we're going to send him through the wringer in issues 6 and 7 as the interdimensional breachers that ARGUS has imprisoned break free, then we're sending Vibe to another dimension in issues 8 and 9. It might not be the most fun trip for him to take, and he comes back from that experience a changed young man.

I don't want to spoil where he goes after that, but I guarantee you won't be able to predict it.

MM: The five book question... What are your five favourite comic books and why are they special to you? What makes each of them great?

Sterling: I'm gonna list my Top Five Trade Paperbacks, because there's no way on Earth I could possibly pick my Top Five Single Issues. It would take me weeks to whittle that list down! [laughs]

- *Batman: The Long Halloween*: I give this book to anyone and everyone who expresses an interest in reading comic books. It's a great Batman story featuring all of his rogues and spotlighting the friendship he had with Commissioner Gordon all those years ago. Jeph Loeb writes a great mystery with some fantastic Tim Sale artwork to boot. One of the modern classics of comics, and I think it's a great hook to get new readers interested in comics.

- *Green Lantern: The Sinestro Corps War*: Geoff Johns, Dave Gibbons, Pete Tomasi, Ethan Van Sciver, Ivan Reis, and Patrick Gleason all contribute their talents to expand the Green Lantern universe in a such a simple-yet-massive way. I find it interesting in that it's a story where the villain actually wins...though it's not the victory that anyone expected (including Sinestro!). Huge in scope, the story never loses sight of Hal Jordan's heart. For me, this story is the template for doing "big" DCU stories.

- *Longshot*: Ann Nocenti and Arthur Adams introduce us to the lucky freedom fighter from the Mojoverse. This was the first comic series I was really obsessed with collecting when I was a kid. I put the first trade paperback on layaway for almost an entire summer to get it, but it was worth every allowance I spent on it. Still have that trade, too, it's a prized possession.

- *The Greatest Flash Stories Ever Told*: I received this for my eleventh birthday. This collection of Flash stories by John Broome, Gardner Fox, and Carmine Infantino showed me the scope of the DC Universe.

- *Blankets*: Craig Thompson's masterpiece inspired a lot of the comics I wrote and drew in college. Just a beautiful, beautiful book. Thompson followed it up with the even greater CARNET DE VOYAGE. That man is an incredibly talented storyteller, and a master of the brush pen.

MM: If you could write for any character from the four colour universe, who would it be and why do you want to forge their destiny?

Sterling: Superman. Because there are an infinite number of stories to tell with the Man of Steel, and it's up to us to craft stories that say something about humanity with this incredible alien. Which is also why I'd like to write some Doctor Who stories someday, too.

MM: What's next for you Sterling? If there's anything that you'd like to add, now's the time to do so...

Sterling: I just wrote a web-series that's in postproduction called *The Posthuman Project*. It's about five teenagers who are in a massive accident and gain superpowers. The trailer is up at Posthumanmovie.com if you'd like to check it out. I'm developing some other things that I unfortunately can't talk about just yet. Stay tuned. Oh, and I'm also working on a novel when I have free time...which isn't that often anymore! (laughs)

Originally published in Mass Movement #36, July 2013

LECKY VOORHEES
(VOORHEES / WALK THE PLANK)

It was just a couple of months ago that I jumped in a van and drove down to Bradford through knee deep snow for a visit to the 1 in 12 Club and Voorhees' *20 Years Of Violence* gig. After a day that showcased some great bands from the UK, Ireland and the mainland, Voorhees hit the stage and destroyed everything.

I remember seeing some of their first ever gigs and as I watched them over the years, they never failed to impress me and they went on to record plenty of records and gig and tour with some of the biggest names in the scene from across the globe. Although they broke up a few years ago there has been the occasional reunion gig but this time it seems there are more plans afoot... I'm very pleased to have had the chance to catch up with vocalist Lecky from UK Hardcore institution Voorhees and get the lowdown on what's happening.

Interview by Tom Chapman

MM: You've done the occasional reunion over the past years, but this one seems a bit more permanent, is that right?

Lecky: Yeah, Break It Up and Walk The Plank played the Morrowfest gig last year so I got up and sang a few Voorhees songs with the Break It Up guys then after that a lot of people started asking us to play shows so we decided to do it.

MM: This time around it's quite a strange line up with people from various periods of the band, how did you get this line-up together. Has the band gelled well?

Lecky: I think it's a really strong line up, everyone gets on well, and some of us were already doing bands together anyway so it was a natural choice me (vocals) and Sean (guitar) were there from the start, Atko (guitar) and Dave (drums) originally joined before the *13* LP and Sam (bass) stood in for the 2010 reunion shows at the last minute when Paul and Graeme got stuck in the U.S. due to the Icelandic volcano ash cloud, but like I said we were already doing stuff together - me, Sam and Atko are all in Rot In Hell, Dave and Sam are in Torn Apart so it was easy to get together and rehearse.

MM: Let's look back to the early days of the band when you were emerging from a couple of Durham bands - it feels to me that you were one of the leading bands of a newer generation that brought the UK hardcore scene into the modern era, do you have many memories of those early days, any highlights?

Lecky: There seemed to be a lot of new bands all at once in the early 90's, especially in the north, Kito, Dead Wrong, Kickback, Nailbomb, Submission, Ironside, Health Hazard, Suffer, Bob Tilton, etc. basically the whole roster of Armed With Anger Records, Flat Earth Records and Subjugation records which made up the entire scene, then later on came Stalingrad, Hard To Swallow, Kitchener, Baby Harp Seal, Underclass, Vengeance Of Gaia and Withdrawn who I ended up joining, and more labels like Days Of Fury and Sure Hand....it was just really good timing, I think we were lucky, that all-dayer at Leeds Uni was the kick start and it drew me away from Durham towards West Yorkshire as there was more going on. Our first few gigs in Durham were great though, we had a good local following for our previous bands Steadfast and False Face so when we started as Voorhees we had an instant crowd of kids wanting to see us and they just went crazy, we played in a nightclub a couple to about 150 people, 50 of them were there to see us and the rest had no idea what Hardcore was, so we were getting heckled and Sean put his guitar down and went into the crowd and kicked the shit out of someone and we played Agnostic Front's *Victim In Pain* straight after, the bouncers just picked the guy up off the floor and carried him out while we played. I used to get pig-piled a lot in those days too, not even by people trying to sing along, it was just kids trying to crush me for fun and the other bands didn't know what the fuck was going on, they just looked concerned for their equipment when kids were jumping off tables and the mixing desk was getting kicked (they should have moved it to a safer place when we told them to) ha, ha.

MM: Was your early sound directly influenced by just the Boston bands or was there more in the mix? And how would you say the sound evolved?

Lecky: Initially it was just Boston Hardcore circa 1982, then a bit of Negative Approach started creeping in followed by DRI, Infest, Discharge etc. but after Sean left and Arms joined it took a very different direction, he said he wanted us to sound like a cross between Spazz and Black Sabbath?!?!?! But after the *13* LP came out (which I hate) we changed direction back to a more traditional Hardcore sound.

MM: You then became one of the more prolific bands from UK and Europe with a lot of touring, how did the US touring come about?

Lecky: A U.S. band (I've forgotten who it was) were playing at the 1 in 12 Club in Bradford and Neil Robinson from Tribal War Records was with them and I knew he lived in New York and had booked a Varukers tour for them, so I asked him if he could book a tour for Voorhees, he seemed interested and we exchanged phone numbers. A month or so later he got in touch and we figured it all out. He was looking for a support band who could lend us equipment in New York but everyone was unable to do it, then out of the blue he got a call from Jamey from Hatebreed saying he had heard we were touring and could they play with us, he had the *Spilling Blood* LP and thought it was an awesome record, they had just put out their first tape when we toured with them, we had no idea they would become so huge! When we booked the 2nd tour we did it with Ben from Drop Dead, he had put out the *What You See Is What You Get* 7" just in time for the tour but the covers hadn't come back from the printers so we had to make 200 different ones just for the tour. After that Will from Chainsaw Safety booked the tours, he made a lot of dumb mistakes the first time which ended up costing us a lot of money but Arms insisted we go through him again as they were friends but it was the same story the second time, I haven't spoken to the guy since.

MM: You also played with tons of bands over the years, who were some of the standouts?

Lecky: Sick Of It All at the 1 in 12 Club, Drop Dead at ABC No Rio, Kill Your Idols, Stalingrad, Health Hazard, Charles Bronson, Los Crudos, Agnostic Front, Hard To Swallow, Nerve Agents, F-Minus, Out Cold, 25 Ta Life, Born Against, that's all I can think of right now.

MM: I remember when the UK scene was absolutely tiny but pretty tightly knit - even bands like Rorschach would only play to forty or so people - do you think you guys are more popular now than you were back in the day?

Lecky: Definitely, but there's all the old crowd and all the new crowd too, but a lot of its nostalgia, the more often we play the less of that there'll be.

MM: When Voorhees broke up, what bands and projects were you guys involved in?

Lecky: I did Walk The Plank, Meatlocker, Cockfight and SickFuckinO. Sean did The Haters and Break It Up. Atko and Dave did The Horror and Sex Maniacs. Sam was in Closure, Cockfight and SickFuckinO.

MM: And what bands are the current line up doing?

Lecky: Me, Sam and Atko are in Rot In Hell, Dave and Sam are in Torn Apart, Sean is in The Orphans and Mid Life Crisis. Atko is also in Gentlemans Pistols and Dave has a few other projects going too - including a wedding band.

MM: The twenty year anniversary was quite an event with a ton of the new breed of hardcore bands playing and quite a few sounding like they have been influenced by Voorhees in much the same way that you were inspired by the greats from the 80's how was the gig for you?

Lecky: It was great fun to play at the 1 in 12 Club again, the line-up was really good, some of the best bands in the UK right now played it.

MM: What do you think of the state of Hardcore in 2013, are you still actively involved?

Lecky: I'm involved in as much as I am playing in bands, I don't buy many records these days, I usually only pick up stuff by bands who impress me live. I run rehearsal rooms in Leeds and we've just started doing shows there so I'll probably get to see more of what's going on in the future. I think UK Hardcore hit a bit of a low point a couple of years ago but it seems to be getting better now, there's a lot of new bands who are really good, as for the rest of the world I'm too out of touch to comment much, but there seems to be a lot of older bands reforming and playing shows again, so there must still be a healthy scene.

MM: I hear you have been working on some new material, is that right? Any plans to record?

Lecky: Sean has written some music and I've written lyrics but we haven't done anything else yet, no rehearsals, nothing. I'm not sure what we're going to do, I'm in two minds about it, I would like to make new music, but I'm not sure anyone who comes to see us will be interested in anything but the old stuff.

.

Originally published in Mass Movement #36, July 2013

DEAN BEDDIS
(BAD SAM / LAS VEGAS ELVIS /COWBOY KILLERS)

Back at the tail-end of the eighties, I stumbled across a split seven inch featuring a criminally underrated band called The Cowboy Killers. They were a scruffy bunch of punk rockers who proved that the UK could easily stand shoulder to shoulder with the best that the US and European HC scenes had to offer. I immediately declared them (in my, ahem, humble opinion of course) to be the best UKHC band ever, and in the last twenty six years, no-one has ever managed to topple them from that position. Hell, they even played my wedding, and for longer than I care to remember, I've also been fortunate enough to be able to call their singer Dean, my friend.

But like all good things, The Cowboy Killers came to an end and Dean and the rest of the band moved on Now fronting Bad Sam who are about to release their new record, *Working Class Holocaust*, I figured it was time to catch up with Dean, shoot the shit about the old days, the state of the union, punk rock and of course, Bad Sam…

Interview by Tim Cundle

MM: Introduce yourself then Sunshine….Tell us about the man known simply as Beddis…

DB: I was in the Cowboy Killers from beginning to end, all four albums worth of fun, then I was in a band called the Ginger Arsonists for a bit; I was an Elvis impersonator – still am sometimes - and I've been with Bad Sam for about 3 years. We've just recorded a new record.

MM: I'd got the impression after the Cowboy Killers and Las Vegas Elvis that you wouldn't want to be in bands any more…

DB: I said I wouldn't again because it had become too stressful. But then I went to prison and came out, and wanted to try the old screamer out, find some drum sounds and put something together again. This was the Ginger Arsonists. We played a few gigs but after a while Dave didn't want to do it anymore. It was a bit more experimental that was, a bit different. It had some strange visuals and was a bit arty farty in some strange psychotic way…

MM: It's more metal, the Bad Sam record, than anything you've done before…

DB: It all comes down in the end to the tunes as they appear in my head and what the other guys want to do with them. For a long time Ritchie was playing guitar- now he's back on bass – but he was listing to AC/DC and whatever. I don't mind you know? As long as there's not too much guitar wankery I'm okay with that. As long as it's not too long as well, that's important. I like System Of A Down, stuff like that; it has social and political comment.

On the new record there's a theme of everything being dumbed down over and over again to stop you thinking. It's like this American trend obsession. People talk about how drugs and gang culture have come over here and now its obesity. When I was in school there wasn't a fat kid there but now obesity is exploding and diabetes is on the rise.

People draw the comparison with America and say it's part of a trend, but really it's just people living to their means. Sure they could cook and eat properly, but there is an epidemic of ignorance in this country since the Thatcher years that has meant that when combined with the poverty which has also proliferated, you end up with no money, no idea, let's go to McDonalds. Over and over again. You can tell there is a problem with the education system as people don't know how to ask questions. They don't think to ask where the food comes from or anything else – it's just ignorance. It's not copying America.

MM: So you don't think it's inevitable that we've become a carbon copy of America?

DB: I used to with most things, whether it's foreign policy or whatever, we follow America in most things. Just look at Afghanistan, Iraq and now Syria, Yemen and the rest of it. We follow America in many ways but it's always the negative things. If you like punk rock, hardcore and that then we import some of the good stuff as well.

MM: And now you're on the telly, well YouTube anyways, with the videos for *Black John Wayne* and *Bastard Son of A Teddy Boy*. Were the two videos filmed close together?

DB: Ish – six months apart. We did *Black John Wayne* and other songs about Obama and because he's black people think he's going to be cool and left-wing and want to change everything. But this guy was all the time supporting the Republicans and all the right wing policies over Afghanistan etc. In some ways it's a parallel with Obama; because he was black and was voted in, everyone thought it would mean change, but it's just more of the same. But there's also a sense of humour running through the lyrics and especially through certain songs.

MM: Speaking of sense of humour, have you been down to the Elvis festival in Porthcawl?

DB: Yes I have. There are basically three types of Elvis there: those just out to get pissed, those, like myself, who are out to have a bit of a laugh; then you get the people who actually think they are Elvis and are mentally ill. Which is quite a lot of them.

I went on the piss there once and there was me and nine Elvi in the loos which was fun. Then there was this committed Elvis who was sitting there with this woman who called herself Queen Priscilla. She was a very large lady with a pink ribbon in her hair and the pair of them looked psychotic. Don't get me wrong. There are a lot of people who like Elvis who happen to have a mental illness – and so what? But there are some people who like Elvis and they like nothing else.

MM: When was the last time you did the Las Vegas Elvis thing?

DB: I like doing that. I think the last time was last year. We did some really crazy gigs, we had about 400 people turning up. But although it's good to have the anonymity, you can't do it forever, or all the time. I like the fact that nobody knows it's you. It gives you a freedom you just don't get otherwise. From a creative point of view though, doing cover versions all the time and not writing your own music or lyrics. They've got no social comment in them either, things like Heartbreak Hotel

MM: On a more sombre note. It was the end of an era when John died, leading to the closure of the legendary TJs in Newport...

DB: You know, in some ways John's death just underlined the fact that that era was over. People often ask why Simon stopped doing Cheap Sweaty Fun at TJ's, and the answer was simple: the whole way that bands dealt with venues changed. Back in the old days when he used to deal with Green Day or NOFX, he may have to deal with a band's manager, but mostly the band itself. Therapy? Just phoned him up and asked him for a gig. Now it's all about the agents and the booking companies, and it's had an effect on the costs. Bands that used to cost £300-£400, now cost £2000 or £3000. So Simon used to organise the gigs, but it was always John who greeted you and fed you and made you feel welcome. He sat at the bar during the gig and held court. He didn't like the music but he liked the scene. People had a lot of respect for him. He was a shit businessman, and the place never stayed the same.

You would go in there from one week to the next and never know where the stage was going to be or what was going to be what. The roof leaked and it was a shithole, but it was a lot of fun. He's sadly missed by a lot of people, and so many people played there from Kurt Cobain, to Oasis. A wonderful twenty years. He was a really nice guy, always gave you food and a bed, and woul buy you a drink if you needed it...

MM: And now you're running Kriminal Records...

DB: Yeah. Simon started it up years ago (as Rockaway Records) as a sort of HQ for Cheap Sweaty Fun and all the people who went through there. I worked there for years away and then took it over about three years ago, and the rest is history. The great thing about a place like this is that it's the centre of life. People come here and they talk about their life and spill their souls and you do the same. They buy a couple of records and feel part of something, getting together for a chat about all kinds of stuff. It's what life's about.

MM: Why do you think harder music is coming back again?

DB: It's all to do with the atmosphere. It feels like the late 70s early 80s again. So much misery and poverty and people losing their jobs, it brings back the popularity of music which was underground then but has since come into the mainstream. After all, when times are good and everything's great, there's no music in that is there? Plus the airwaves are filled with X-Factor and all that crap, people are looking for something more.

I think John Peel's death had an effect too. It exposed a lot of what used to be underground and brought it to a new audience. It's important because if you're accessing music through X-Factor or MTV, you're never going to discover local bands, or touring bands as they won't get that kind of exposure. John Peel used to play all that stuff and discover new sounds and new ideas and make them accessible. Nobody's doing that now, so it's hard for bands to make an impact. People just don't have access to them. They get stuck with the kind of stuff they sell in Tesco and Sainsbury's. It's all the same, designed to get stuck in your head whether you like the tune or not, it just gets stuck there like Bob the Builder. I go to the gym and they are playing these songs and even though I hate them, they get stuck in my head. A lot has changed over the years, some for the better, some for the worse.

Originally published in Mass Movement #37, November 2013

BL'AST!

Well here's a BL'AST from the past (sorry couldn't resist). Santa Cruz' resident skate-punk Hardcore/metal crossover pioneers return with a bang in the form of an alternate recording session of their classic *It's In My Blood* album featuring current Alice in Chains vocalist William DuVall on guitar and engineered by long time BL'AST fan Dave Grohl. MM gets the skinny from vocalist Clifford Dinsmore (CD) and guitarist Mike Neider (MN).

Interview by Ian Pickens and Tim Cundle

MM: Did you think you would be participating in a BL'AST interview in 2013?

MN: Yes, well not with you in particular but sure.

CD: Not really, but I'm always up for some Bl'ast! action! It was awesome music, and I'm always into playing those songs live

MM: BL'AST were often unfairly, but some would say accurately, labelled as Black Flag sound-alikes; did that ever bother the band?

MN: We had a member, when the band first began, that was very short lived, that wrote some tunes, and his approach to writing music was to listen to *My War* and rip it off to write *Fucking With My Head* then would listen *Thirsty and Miserable* and write *Break It Down*' - you get the picture?

This same person had a run in with Rollins after trying to write down Ginn's guitar settings and Rollins confronted him. So Rollins wrote about us because of this, I guess. So this baggage was cut off really quick into the bands existence to eliminate that. We grew up with BF and became friends and were even signed to their record label. Comparisons are limitless in any band situation.

CD: The people that would say "accurately" are brain dead, mentally retarded, bandwagon jumping sheep that never really listened to what we were trying to convey. By the time *It's In My Blood* rolled around, that comparison was dead and buried. I think that misconception did, however, push us to strive harder to make truly original music. So thanks to the clueless herd of mongoloids that came up with all that! We couldn't have done it without you!

MM: To me you were always a four piece. But there was more than one occasion when you had two guitar players, it seems. Could you give me a little more information?

CD: Steve played guitar on the first record and decided shortly after that he was leaving the band. He had received a letter from William DuVall, saying that if we ever needed a guitar player, that he would be into it. He ended up coming out to California during a very productive time period and many of our best shows were played with him.

MM: Were you ever a straight edge band? There's the line: "And I don't need drugs", but not much more. On the other end there is this heavy stoner vibe in the Spaceboy stuff.

CD: Steve wrote that song and may have claimed straight edge for a short period of time, but I will never understand the motive behind that song as none of us were straight edge.

MM: The band are often credited with helping to create the hardcore/metal crossover sound that culminated in bands like Annihilation Time; is that accurate? What were the bands main influences back in the day?

MN: Not sure, but we took Black Sabbath and Flag`s approach to having a band and then dwarfed it into our own aggression and beliefs. Anti-Conformity. It would be cool if it were true.

CD: That is accurate. When we formed we were seeing all the punk bands like Black Flag, SSD, Minor Threat, etc. but were more directly influenced by Sabbath , Maiden, and Trouble, and just applied those influences to the form of music we were participating in, which was Hardcore

MM: BL'AST were always intrinsically linked to the Skate Punk scene and had quite a tight relationship with Santa Cruz boards; do any of the band still skate these days?

MN: In 82` I moved to Santa Cruz to start Bl'ast! and lived with Rob Roskopp(pro skater) as a roommate. I got a job at Santa Cruz skateboard right away and our apt. was about 50ft from work. Our pad was the place for pro`s and such to stay at during their time in town. I ended up working there for around 18yrs or so. The owner Novak was really cool with Bl'ast! and let me tour etc. As long as I listened to his story about being the only person in history to pull out a band he managed from playing Woodstock.

CD: I surf every day there's waves, but don't really skate that much. I've always been more into surfing

MM: You guys only released three albums and had quite a short time together, and yet are one of the most well-known bands from that mid 80s era of Hardcore; why do you think that is? Was it something to do with Corrosion of Conformity being such big fans?

MN: California had a great scene and it was very interactive with skateboarding. We were hugely into what we were into because of skateboarding. We have literally probably watched Black Flag for example 25+ times through their career, and when that happens you become friends with these people. Bl'ast! being signed by Black Flag and their record label SST was amazing for us. Didn't get better than that. So that and Skateboarding along with all the rad friends like COC helped.

CD: We were playing music that was really new and different for that time period...even in the beginning, when there was still the SSD, Flag influence, it was still delving into areas that most Hardcore bands couldn't even comprehend at that point, and that's where we found a common bond with C.O.C. The second show we played under the name Bl'ast! was with Black Flag, Saccharin Trust, and C.O.C. We were both unknown bands that had an immediate impact on the stagnant Hardcore scene, and have been good friends ever since. God bless those loveable Motherfuckers!

MM: Back in the day you guys played with a lot of the most popular Hardcore and underground metal bands around; do you have a favourite show from that time; any bands you would have loved to have played with but didn't get the chance?

MN: Many great shows to speak of. SST had a lot of BBQ's with great bands and we hosted Fenders ball room quite a bit which is a story of its own, along with the bands we played with on tour. There are some bands that didn't exist back then that we would like to play with now. I think Minutemen, Germs, Devo are about the bands that we never had the chance to play with off the top of my head.

CD: The ones that got away. We almost got to play with Motorhead, and we almost got to play with Celtic Frost... Fuck!!! Still pissed off!!

MM: Obviously there's a lot of attention on the band again due to the release of *'Blood'*; the story behind the release is quite an intriguing one - could you flesh out the details for us?

CD: Some "lost, unearthed" tapes turned up and the rest is history. Very, very recent history!

MN: Lost tapes were found, Southern Lord was told. Dave Grohl was told, they jumped on this rare opportunity as cool bros they are. Cliff and I were stoked and it turned out amazing!

MM: The release is significant due to the presence of current Alice in Chains singer William Duvall on guitar, and Dave Grohl's engineering of the album; were there any concerns in the BL'AST camp that you could be seen as 'trading on their names'?

MN: (Laughs) Seriously?

CD: It definitely adds to the mystique. Both those dudes have backgrounds in hardcore and will never forget their roots. There is a common pride amongst people from that era that we all share. It's sort of a "gotta stick together like glue" kind of thing.

MM: Whose idea was it to call Dave Grohl?

CD: It was Greg's idea, but we all assumed he would be way too busy to do it. We were very surprised and stoked when he found a window in his schedule to make it happen.

MM: These sessions were the only ones recorded with DuVall and his tenure in the band was pretty short; why didn't things work out?

MN: I think times were tight and it was hard to be in a band that didn't make money and live far away from your surroundings. It just dissolved.

CD: William moved to SC from Atlanta to join Bla'st! What dedication and sacrifice that took at such a young age. At this point, all I've got to say is thank you!!! That took a lot of balls!!

MM: The songs are alternate versions of what went on to become your second album *It's In My Blood*; some people are saying this version is even better than that release; do you agree? Are you all pleased with way it's turned out?

CD: Fuck yeah!

MN: Well I hope technology and experience has taken control of *Blood* to do so. It turned out really fuckin' good.

MM: You might share the impression that *It's In My Blood* and *'Take The Manic Ride* were suffering on the sound side compared at least to *Power Of Expression*; what went wrong?

CD: Basically, back then no one knew what to do with music like that, in terms of trying to record. So, it was basically the luck of the draw. Depending on what engineer you got at the studio you were recording at. For the most part it was just dumb luck that the *Power of Expression* turned out the way it did. It's a shame we don't have the tapes to *Take The Manic Ride* because that was the album that we had pushed ourselves the hardest musically. But the recording quality is so poor that it is hard for the listener to get the gist of what we were doing. If we could remix it, people would really be able to understand what a truly ground breaking record that really was.

MM: Can we hope for a "corrected" version?

CD: We have got some great people trying to re-master it. However, we are limited in what we can do with it without the master tapes.

MM: So maybe you could help us out with what happened after the records, and what your plans are. Touring? European tour? There was a tour planned for Europe as I was told. But you had to cancel it. Why?

CD: Limited U.S. engagements, some regional and some festival dates in Europe. We were supposed to come to Europe in 1988, but were forced to cancel because some members in the band were unable to go.

MM: Do you feel the band is now getting some of the wider attention it deserved back in the 80s?

CD: This kind of attention didn't exist in the 80s - - it was a different world back then without all this Internet shit

MN: Whatever. Dig it or don`t. It is great to hear it like it like it is now. To have some of these folks show us that they truly dug it is really cool. I really had no idea. It has been treated with respect and that's huge.

MM: Your early releases were on SST and *Blood* has been released by Southern Lord; it must be pretty gratifying to have your albums released by two of the biggest names in underground metal/Hardcore?

MN: Ya , stoked!!! Met some amazing folks. Great labels. It just makes sense. Appreciative. Lucky.

CD: It's nice to keep it in the family. Southern Lord is a great label, and Greg A. is a long-time friend

MM: Will this release trigger a reformed BL'AST?

CD: I can't really disclose that information, but maybe we can talk more about that in person this spring (hint, hint).

MN: Ya, We are working on that now. We look forward to creating and raging soon. But ya never know with this blast!.

MM: How did Nick Oliveri come into the picture? It seemed a bit strange to hear about that first. And unfortunately I found out a little too late, otherwise I would have asked him when he was in town, doing his solo stuff...

CD: Mondo Generator was playing at the Catalyst and we were all hanging out. Nick asked about Bl'ast! and I mentioned that Southern Lord was releasing the record and there might be some live shows in the works. When he asked who was playing bass, I kind of jokingly said," YOU!" To my surprise, He said, "Fuck YEAH! I'll play that shit!"! And then came the question of who would play drums? Then I saw Hoss play and the rest is soon to be history.

MM: Are you still involved in playing Doom Metal? Since probably you're not necessarily full-time musicians these days – what are you occupied with?

CD: I play in a band called Dusted Angel and I work at a concert venue called the Catalyst in Santa Cruz, Ca.

MN: Always. Some kind of doom (laughs)

MM: What's next for BL'AST? Are there any other long lost recordings to surface?

MN: Live action, recording new and possibly old. Rage! Rock Roll Shred.......

CD: Come to think of it… You never know what's gonna turn up - the ghost of some weird forgotten archive might come creeping to the surface to freak a few people out!

Originally published in Mass Movement #37, November 2013

CAPTAIN MIDNIGHT
THE MANIC ACE OF THE AIRWAYS

This guy was a very popular character, indeed. He was a comic book hero, a radio and television personality as well as a chapter play star. Although that's a lot of ground to cover, I think that I'll just focus my attention on his character in this fun-filled cliffhanger. Produced by Columbia Studios, *Captain Midnight* (1942), played by David O'Brien, is a fast-talking, fist-flying, energetic character in pursuit of a villain known as Ivan Shark. He wears a leather flight suit, headgear and goggles on most occasions. After all, he's an old-time aviator. On a side note, probably one of O'Brien's most recognizable roles was that of a drug crazed character in the infamous public service film *Reefer Madness* (1936). Who could ever forget his maniacal laughter as he puffs away on a "joint" while spouting the command for the pianist to "play faster, faster?" I can remember seeing *Reefer Madness* as a young hippy and laughing hysterically over that scene in particular. So, I guess he is a perfect choice to play a rather nervous, manic-type character in this chapter play. O'Brien did have a very successful career as a "B" movie star, mostly in westerns and low budget horror films. Later on, he became a rather prolific comedy writer of several television shows, most notably, *The Red Skelton Show*.

The daring Captain, whose character's name is Captain Albright, is an ace pilot capable of flying blindly through a thick fog, parachuting from a flaming airplane just moments before it crashes, running his car off of a cliff and leaving the wreckage without even a scratch and on and on. He's an indestructible force without the superpowers — your average guy with a lot of luck on his side. His prowess as a fighter is second to none. In fact, he would never avoid a conflict of any nature, no matter how improbable the odds against him. In a nutshell, the guy is on a certain drug free "high" that makes him seem nearly physically impenetrable. Along with his two, bumbling sidekicks, he manages to find a way to outwit his nemesis and escape death, albeit, only by the skin of his teeth. His identity to the lawless is known only as *Captain Midnight* As for the villain, James Craven plays the character of Ivan Shark. His portrayal of the evil antagonist is, at times, so "over-the-top" that it's downright insanely hilarious. So, you have both the hero and villain on equal terms of insanity. Maybe that's too much of a stretch. Let's just say that they both could use some drug therapy to calm their manic ways. Shark barks out his commands to his henchmen like an Army drill sergeant, and they obey his orders without question. However, should they fail in their given assignments; there would be hell to pay. Shark's daughter (Fury) is also involved in his plots, which works out well for a few laughs as she goes "head to head" with Midnight's friend Joyce.

Director James Horne, known for directing Laurel and Hardy films and other comedies, made this chapter play laughable at times. But that's part of the charm of a chapter play. Not all of them were polished productions ready for an Oscar. All of them, however, were meant to entertain, primarily a younger audience. The script is nothing out of the ordinary. Basically, it's a routine example of the villain wanting to dominate the world with a secret invention that he plans to steal from a well-known inventor (John Edwards). Back then, it seemed to be a rather popular theme that chapter play writers used as your basic storyline.
Shark's ambition is to acquire, by any means necessary, the model of a range finder that can destroy aircraft and naval vessels from anywhere in the world. He orders his henchmen to steal both the model as well as its blueprints at Edwards' home. However, just prior to their arrival, Edwards instructs his daughter, Joyce, to mail the model to *Captain Midnight's* headquarters as a matter of safekeeping. When the henchman break into Edward's house to steal

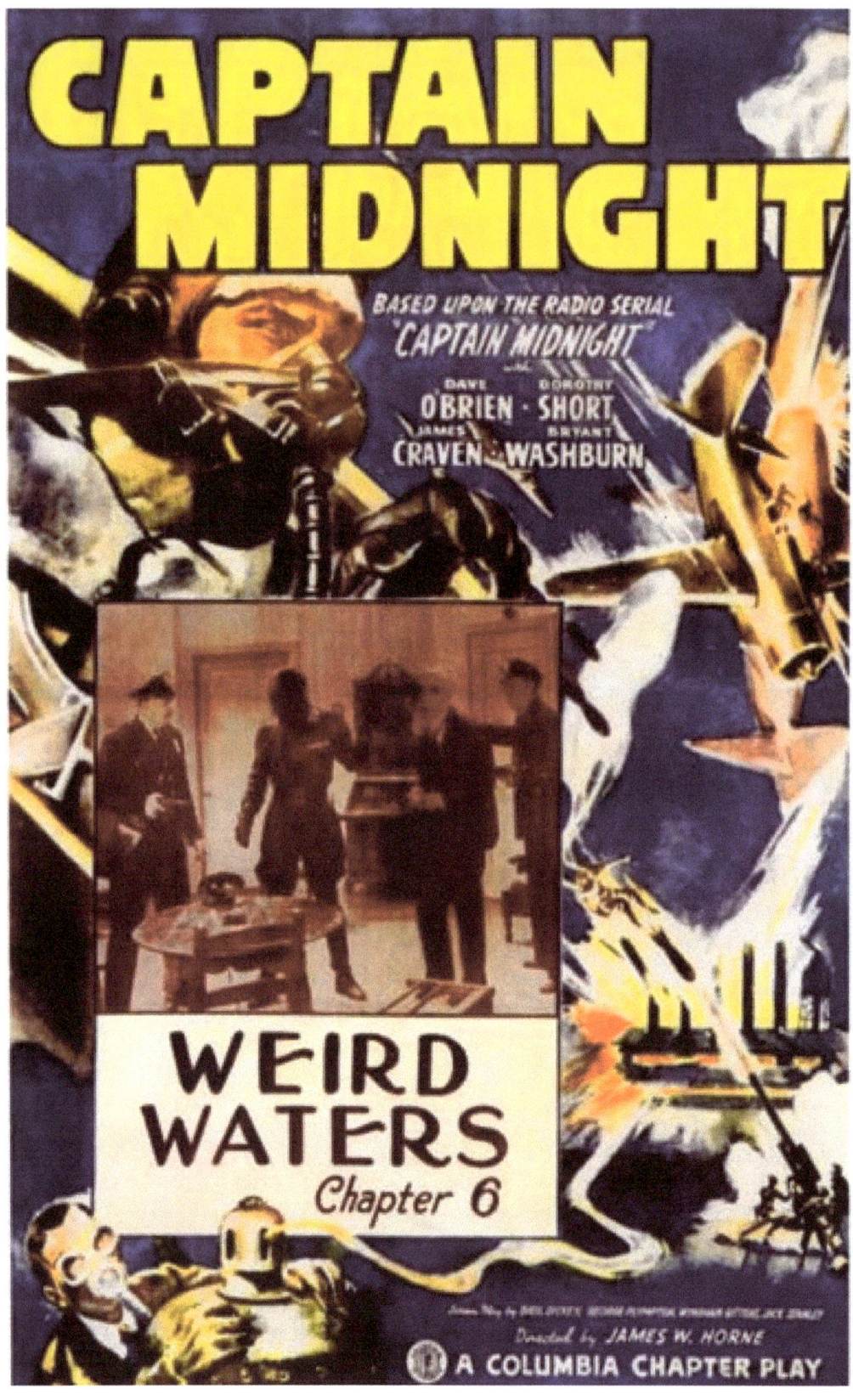

his model, they discover that they are too late to retrieve the goods, so instead, they kidnap Edwards as well as the blueprints, and they take him to Shark's secret hideaway. Strange, that he wouldn't send the blueprints along with the model.

The trick is that the inventor's blueprints are in code, and he refuses to comply in deciphering it for Shark, that is, until Edwards is threatened with his life. What follows next is another clever device from the minds of the writing staff: it's the old telephone dial routine. Edwards secretly bumps the telephone receiver just enough so that he can dial his daughter for help, and then begins (as he dials) to explain to Shark that his code is somehow based by the numbers on the phone. When his daughter answers at her end, Edwards cleverly mentions where he is being held prisoner, but Shark soon catches on to the ruse, and he abruptly stops the inventor from completing his message. In the meantime, Shark learns that Edwards had the model shipped to Albright's headquarters, and he sends his men to recover it. When they fail to find the model, Shark decides to pressure Edwards by threatening his daughter's safety. By the way, I forgot to mention the fact that Shark is also a master of disguise and voice impersonations, and he uses his talents to deceive Joyce in order to capture her as a hostage. It's just another clever method that was used quite frequently in several chapter plays to help confuse the opposition

As the story progresses, *Captain Midnight* is at the mercy of Shark's ingenious means for disposing of him, but he always manages to escape, as do all heroes, from certain death. One device in particular that Shark uses is a giant spinning wheel that forces a person to fall into a fiery pit below as the wheel increases its rpm's. Chapter after chapter involves numerous situations of incredible circumstances that can only be appreciated by fans of the genre.

Unfortunately, most of today's moviegoers would consider such a chapter play as *Captain Midnight* to be silly and much too unsophisticated to enjoy. Of course, that's merely my own opinion, and hopefully by my exposing some younger readers to these dated gems, they will understand the significance of the genre. Don't forget that famous directors such as Steven Spielberg and George Lucas have tipped their hats to the chapter plays in the making of many of their blockbuster mega-hits. *Star Wars* and *Raiders of the Lost Arc* are just two examples that owe much of their success to cliffhangers. It was the spirit and action of the era that inspired studios such as: Republic, Columbia and Universal, as well as a few independents, to make over three hundred chapter plays, from the silent days of movies until television took over as a major source of entertainment. As with all serials, with one exception, the villain is brought to justice. In the final chapter, Shark is accidentally electrocuted (but only unconscious) by one of his own devices as he battles the good Captain.

I chose this chapter play primarily for the emotional similarities of both the hero and villain. The only difference being, that one is on the side of justice, and the other is on the opposite end of the spectrum. It truly is a fast-paced serial and, by all means, extremely hilarious at times. In short, it's a heck of a lot of fun to watch, and I highly recommend it to anyone for a good laugh. But most of all, it's a visual time-capsule that reflects our nation's history, when life seemed to be a little less complicated, and chapter plays were a great source of entertainment. On a scale of one to ten, I give this one an eight, mostly for the laughs.

Doug Crill

Originally published in Mass Movement #37, November 2013

GREGG HURWITZ

Every now and again, you stumble across a writer whose work subtly alters the way you perceive the genre they dwell within, almost as if you walked through a doorway you hadn't noticed before, a door that leads to new horizons and new vistas. Gregg Hurwitz is one of those writers, a best-selling author and Sci-Fi TV writer and the man responsible for shaping the destiny and life of The Dark Knight. Folks, say hello to the literary polymath, Gregg Hurwitz...

Interview by Tim Cundle

Images appear courtesy of Gregg Hurwitz and DC Entertainment

MM: Let's start at the beginning... Would you like to both introduce yourself and tell all the boys and girls something strange about Gregg Hurwitz, something that hardly anyone knows...

Gregg: When I was a kid, I used to go to bed with a dictionary instead of a teddy bear...

MM: So, when did the literary bug bite you? When did you know you wanted to be a writer, and what came first for you, as fan and reader, comics or books? Which of literary mediums drew you in and refused to you go...

Gregg: As long as I can remember. I have mystery "books" I wrote and illustrated with crayons from third grade on (though the crayons got wearisome in college). I started my first novel when I was 19 and never looked back. Then I added screenplays, and later TV and comics.

MM: You started writing as you were finishing college / university didn't you? Was that when you knew your path was set, that what you were doing was going to be what you'd always do? How long did it take you to break through and become successful as a novelist...? Was it an over-night thing, or is the story a little more complicated...

Gregg: I was pretty fortunate. I was young and dumb enough to think that if you wrote a halfway decent book, it would get published, and my first book indeed got bought right after I'd finished school. So I never had to have a real job.

MM: How did you break into comics? You started work at Marvel didn't you? How different was, and is, it writing for comics, compared to writing novels and writing for TV (more of which later)...? Is it harder, easier, or so completely different that you can't really compare the mediums? If so, why?

Gregg: Axel Alonso, one of my favourite folks in comics (or anywhere) called me and offered me a few characters from the Marvel vault to build a miniseries around. I was obsessed with Ennis's Punisher and so I chose The Foolkiller and wrote a hard R MAX series. Then Ennis decided to end his epic run with Frank Castle and Axel offered me the next arc after that.

MM: We have, as I'm a BIG fan, to talk Moon Knight… How did you end up forging Marc Spector's (or more accurately. Jake Lockley's) destiny? What drew you to the character, and what do you think his (lasting) appeal is? Did you achieve everything you wanted to do during your run on the book, or was there anything that you wished you had done, but didn't, and looking back, anything you might have done differently?

Gregg: I was drawn to Lockley's craziness! I love that he had all these different personalities within himself and that his struggle was primarily an internal one. I'm pretty proud of how I (and my artists) built up Moon Knight.

MM: And then (well not immediately after, but you know, a while after) you moved to DC, and started to write Batman… But before, we move on the Dark Knight completely, having written both Moon Knight and Batman, what do you think about, and of, the comparisons that inevitably crop up between the two, especially that refer to the former as an ersatz version of the later? What, from your perspective and in your opinion, separates and differentiates the characters?

Greggg: Yep - a lotta similarities. But some key differences too. Moon Knight is crazy, and much of his efforts are spent in holding himself together. Bruce is sane and able to devote more time to his relentless discipline.

MM: It's Batman time… How did you feel when you found out that you were going to be writing for one of the most iconic characters in comics? Was it difficult to separate the legend from the character that you wanted to write for? What do you think, and what do you know that, you've added to the character with your run?

Gregg: When I first went to DC, I asked to write a Penguin miniseries. I loved *The Killing Joke* and the more recent Joker OGN and wanted to do give a similar in-depth analysis of our boy Oswald. So the first time I wrote Batman, he appears from the Penguin's perspective — as a villain! Then I was offered The Dark Knight with Finch drawing and that's not an offer any sane man would turn down.

It is hard to take on a character who is in the public trust like Batman. We all have such a rich history with him. I'd like to think I've added a bit to the legend — not just by adding more depth to some of the rogues, but by also drawing out Bruce's psychology and showing why intimacy interferes with his quest for perfection.

MM: Is there a particular period of Batman's history or a story arc that you've drawn inspiration from for your Dark Knight? If so, what part of the characters history influenced your vision of Bruce Wayne? Why?

Gregg: My vision of Bruce Wayne stems from Miller, of course, but also there is a heavy influence from the Goyer/Nolan work.

MM: Is there anything that you'd like to do with the character that you feel you can't because of already established canonicity and mythology, and is there anywhere that you'd like to take the character but are a little bit wary of doing so for the same reasons? Do you think that the characters long history is a boon or bane (yeah, I went there) from a writers point of view? Does it, the history that is, hinder or help the creative process? Why?

Gregg: I want to put Batman in a musical. Kidding! No, I don't feel particularly constrained because I arrived at Batman with a pretty good concept of who he is and the world he lives in. The history is both boon and bane — so much to draw upon, but one does have to stretch to find something new.

MM: What's been the stand-out moment on the book (Batman The Dark Knight) for you so far? What's coming next and, for us fanboys, what can you tell us about the "Wow!" moments and surprises (without giving anything away of course) that you've got lined up and ready to go….

Gregg: For me, the stand-out moment is when the Mad Hatter gets hold of Natalya. I'd imagined her as a very different type of girlfriend for Bruce. Smart, witty, talented, no nonsense, from a tough background, and unwilling to put up with his nonsense. She represents the ultimate opportunity for him to find intimacy. So when the Hatter gets her, you can imagine Batman would go Bat*** crazy!

MM: Tell us about *Tell No Lies* …

Greggg: It started with a simple idea: What if you started receiving death threats — accidentally? Threats intended for others with concrete life-or-death deadlines? My hero, Daniel Brasher, finds himself inadvertently in the middle of a killer's vendetta. And this story is played out on the labyrinthine streets of the city of my birth, San Francisco. Like many of my recent thrillers, it has a Hitchcockian "everyman" hero who is pulled in over his head and has to rise to the occasion. I suppose in certain regards, it's my homage to "Vertigo," where the winding and complex alleys and hills represent the increasing dark psychological stakes — it's almost as dark and fog-drenched as Gotham!

MM: It's *V* time… How did you end up writing for and working on the re-imagined *V*? What was the experience like, and what did you think, overall, of the series? Was it tough to shake off the memories of the original series and fans expectations of the new series?

Gregg: I don't usually staff on shows (I do more pilots) but my buddy was the showrunner who pulled me. I wound up doing a lot of writing and producing — it was an absolute blast. We did have to pay our respects to the old show while finding something new. In that regard, it was a bit like writing Batman; whenever I face the blank page with Bruce, I find myself walking that same tightrope.

MMM: What was tougher, being on a demolition range with SEAL's or infiltrating a cult, and why and how did you come to do both of things?

Gregg: Both were a blast. Going undercover into mind control cults was more incredible though. I'd never have believed some of that stuff if I didn't experience it first-hand. That's why it's important to me to do so much research for my thrillers. My job is to give the reader a front-row seat to watch the action and if I haven't done something myself, I can't paint it as effectively.

MMM: What's next for you Gregg? If there's anything that you'd like to add, now would be the time...

Gregg: A great new rogue will be clawing his way into the pages of TDK. And I also am doing an experimental story arc — can't wait to see how it turns out. I'm just finishing my tour for *Tell No Lies*, which has been a lot of fun and took me all over the US and across the Atlantic. And am working on some TV and film stuff which should be ready to announce soon.

Originally published in Mass Movement #37, November 2013

INJURED EYEBALLS

Writers, gentle reader, are SO full of shit it beggars belief!

Considering I'm a writer myself, and knowing the silo loads of shit with which I'm stuffed, it shouldn't really beggar *my* belief. But let's just say, for the benefit of this column, that it does. Let me give you an example of this outrageous and completely unqualified claim.

If, like me, you're in contact with a lot of writers through twitter and facebook (and if you're reading this I'm presuming you are, unless you've just stopped by because you heard this column contains celebrity fisting anecdotes) then I'm sure you've read a tweet or status update like this one:

"Just written 4,000 words of my latest novel before breakfast and done 50 laps of my Olympic size swimming pool. Now I'm off to make love to my super model partner - WOOT!"

What the writer might not realise, as they type those words, is that the word "CUNT!" springs involuntarily to the lips of every other writer who reads them. Not because we're eaten up with bitterness and jealousy (which we are), but because the claim they make is so intrinsically opposed to the actual experience of writing professionally. A more honest post would read something like:

"Just stared desperately at my laptop screen until I wept tears of pure blood, then beat my forehead against my desk for over an hour. Now I'm off to inject smack into my eyeball and lie on the piles of unpaid bills that clog my hallway."

Maybe it's because this so much the norm for our careers that, on those rare days when do manage to be positively productive, we want to share the joy with our writer brothers and sisters. Or maybe it's because, as stated previously, writers are FULL of shit.

Still not convinced? Hmm, you're a tough crowd. Okay well here's another bug bear of mine. Quite frequently I'll read in the trade and fan media that a colleague of mine in the comics industry has been commissioned to write a regular comics series. When asked for a quote the writer will often say something non-committal along the lines of: "Just started work on the first couple of story arcs and I'm having SO much fun writing it!"

Let's just look at those last five words again: "SO much fun writing it". If you honestly believe that the words 'fun' and 'writing' belong together in a *book* that describes the profession, let alone a *sentence*, then you're either heading for a universe of disillusion, or you're a writer, and therefore -full of SHIT.

Unless of course, your idea of fun is an experience akin to tearing out one of your innards and tying it round the throat of an epileptic Doberman. Then kicking the unfortunate creature over the side of a cliff in mid seizure. Because that's what it really feels like to tear concepts, plots, characters and dialogue out of yourself, to meet an unrelenting deadline, on a daily basis. Don't get me wrong, there are occasional moments of unparalleled elation when everything comes together, but these moments usually result in the sort of manic episodes that have me writing letters of apology to all the neighbours and promising never to go near root vegetables or KY jelly ever again.

All of which brings me to the point of this column. *You mean*, I hear you ask gentle reader. *That there IS actually a point to this column?* Well no, but let's pretend that, even though I'm

a writer, I'm not actually full of shit, and I'm not just changing the subject because I'm getting bored now. As the point I'm making *does* start with another example of writers and the shit of which they're full.

Whenever a writer reminisces about public appearances, they always claim the one question they're asked most is "where do you get your ideas from?" Strangely I've never been asked that question. Even more strangely I've never once heard anyone ever ask that question at all the hundreds of signings, readings and conventions to which I've been. I don't know if this is because everyone now knows this is the most asked question and doesn't dare ask it anymore for fear of being derided by their favourite author. Or if this is a collective hallucination that all authors share and no-one ever bothered to slip the right drugs in my drink (probably because they thought I was on enough already).

Or maybe it's because writers are actually the ones obsessed with where their ideas come from. So whenever they're asked to write a quick article for someone they trot out the standard line about "whenever I make a public appearance, someone always asks me ...". Whatever the case, it isn't the most asked question in my experience.

The most asked question that I've ever heard (and I DO hear this at just about every public appearance) is: "do you just sit around and wait for the mood to strike you?" I think they picture me lying around on some chez lounge, surrounded by naked dwarves with a feather quill in my hand, awaiting the arrival of the muse (or my dealer). I've always thought this a pretty strange question seeing as this is what I do to pay the bills and, seeing as all the fluffing work dried up when I hit 40, it's *all* I do to pay the bills.

No-one ever imagines other professions sitting about and waiting till they're hit by inspiration. Have you ever heard of a tradesman suffering from 'plumber's block'? As I write this, we're currently having a kitchen fitted. While I admit that every time I walk into the gaping hole that used to be my kitchen, the builders do seem to be standing around either scratching their stubbly chins or waving a coffee cup hopefully at me, but I'm pretty sure they're not waiting for 'the mood to strike them'. They want to get the job done as quickly possible so they can move on to the next. Just like I do now - writing this column, even if I never seem to get to the point.

Some years ago, when I was still a music journalist, I interviewed Brian Eno (and no, if you've been hanging on for that celebrity fisting story for last 1,500 words, I'm afraid this isn't it). We spoke about his working methods and he told me how he wrote his latest album by walking into the studio each day, grabbing hold of the first idea he could think of, and working on it until he had a finished track at the end of the day. He seemed to think this was a pretty novel way to work, but I remember thinking it was pretty much business as usual for most professional creators toiling away to meet a deadline.

This is the truth about where our ideas come from. We torture our imaginations with pressing deadlines and financial imperatives until they rupture and bleed. Then we catch those precious few drops in a story or a script that we've hastily cobbled together to keep an editor and/or a mortgage provider off our backs. It's not always 'fun' and we rarely do it in 4,000 word blocks between bouts of healthy exercise, but it is usually the very best we could do given the circumstances and the short amount of time we were allotted. This is what Wilde really meant when he said "art is never finished, only abandoned."

Anyone who tells you different is either full of shit, or a writer which, as I'm sure we've now established, amounts to the same thing.

On a completely different note, I'd like welcome Simon Bestwick, fellow TIH columnist and acclaimed author of *Tide of Souls* and *The Faceless* to the column. Simon and I both have stories in a new anthology called and in a desperate attempt to boost sales and our royalties, we've decided to interview one another about our respective contributions to the book.

Simon, thank you very much for hitching a ride on my column.

I want to start with the genesis of the idea behind Lex Draconis. Was it something you'd been toying with before you were asked to contribute, or did you develop it especially for the anthology?

It came from the premise of the anthology. Adele Wearing said there had to be either a nun, a dragon, or both, so I went for the 'both' option. The Catholic Church is not one of my favourite institutions for a number of reasons, not least its attitude towards women and its related loathing of natural sexuality, so that was always going to be an element, and I wanted to do something other than make the dragon an evil monster. I may also have used the phrase 'hot nun on dragon action' at some point and found it stuck in my head.

Did it take a bit of work to put the whole plot together or was it one of those wonderful gift-stories that come as one almost fully formed package? The sort that impels you to just sit down and start writing it?

The elements I'd mentioned above were bubbling in my head, and then one day- while I was on a bus to Bolton Market, if I remember aright (you know how inspiration can strike at the oddest, most random times) the idea of Sister Leonora's mission came to me and the basic plot clicked together around that. I always tend to outline story plots these days- I have to slot them in between bigger projects, so it's handy if I know roughly where I'm going and can get straight to work- but it slotted together pretty easily.

Without letting any spoiler slip, I'd like to explore a little more of the back story of Sister Leonora, the central protagonist. Prior to the events of the story Sister Leonora has had a serious relationship with a young man called Neil. It's apparent that the relationship ended, and most probably so badly that it caused her to take the veil. Could you let us know a little more about the circumstances surrounding the break up and how much of this is pertinent to her state of mind at the beginning of the story?

The way I saw Sister Leonora was as a woman in whom a deeply and prescriptively religious upbringing is at war with a passionate and sensual nature. She's been brought up to regard sex as wicked and herself as lesser and sinful, because she's a woman. Neil I visualized as a fairly straightforward person- someone intelligent, caring but predominantly secular, who questioned the values she's been brought up with, and more importantly led her to question them too. Ultimately she was torn between what she wanted and what she'd been brought up to believe was right, and her religion won, leading to the break-up of the relationship and her decision to take the veil- something she regrets but feels guilty about regretting. In her heart she's discontented and yearns for the forbidden. The events of the story don't transform her into a different person so much as reawaken what's already there.

Finally, without giving too much away again, do you think the events of the story have ensured that dragons won't be extinct for a little while yet?

In the broad scheme of things, things won't change much, but the dragons will endure, as they always have. It's what they do.

Thanks once again for hitching a lift with me Simon. I'll drop you off at the next paragraph, but before I do you can probably tell by that hand on your knee and the devilish glint in my eye that there's no such thing as a 'free ride'. What do you say to a quick game of Fallen Nuns and Dragons hmm, big boy ...

I knew when you talked about me 'riding your column' that this wasn't going to end well...

Jasper Bark

Originally published in Mass Movement #37, November 2013

OUT COLD

When Out Cold Vocalist/Guitarist Mark Sheehan sadly passed away in 2010 it also signalled the end for one of the most intense and respected Hardcore bands of the 90s. Little did we know that in 2013 we would be talking to OC drummer and founder member John Evicci about a new album of material partially recorded before Mark's death.

Interview by Ian Pickens

MM: I'd usually start the interview by asking the band to introduce themselves but I'm guessing that most, if not all MM's readers will be familiar with Out Cold, so instead why don't you tell us who played what on the new album?

JE: Hi Ian! This album has Mark Sheehan and Deuce on guitars, Kevin Mertens on vocals, Mikey Flynn on bass, and myself on drums.

MM: The new album *A Heated Display* is the first release following Mark Sheehan's tragic death in 2010; it must have been pretty emotional putting this together? I'm guessing you didn't think that you would be doing another OC interview at this point in time?

JE: Extremely emotional. I can't even begin to describe all the twists and turns and ups and downs that have led to this point. All I can say is that I'm extremely happy to see it finally out. If you had told me I'd be first interviewed about this material in 2013 when we were writing it back in 2005, I'd have not believed you.

MM: Mark had laid down the basic guitar tracks for the songs but no vocals, so original OC singer Kevin Mertens, stepped up; how did it feel be working with Kevin again? To be fair he's probably one of the only people who could have delivered the songs in the same spirit as Mark.

JE: First and foremost I was very glad Kevin was willing and able to step in to fill the void. You're exactly right: he was the only person who could do this given the circumstances. It's weird enough as it is, but to bring a completely new person in to do vocals on this stuff would have just not been acceptable. We could have maybe done that and called it something else, just to salvage the material, but it wouldn't be Out Cold.

MM: Was it logistically difficult to get the final product together? You guys are all spread out geographically now right?

JE: Yes it was difficult, but that was more due to the equipment we're using rather than our disparate locations. All of the existing overdubs that were done in the intervening years were recorded on this recording device that is not very common and working with it proved to be a real pain in the ass. Fortunately, we managed, but it added a lot of time and expense.

MM: Am I correct in thinking that the original recording you had for this album got lost until a friend found a copy on their hard disk?

JE: This is just one of many strange twists and turns to this whole saga. Mark and I recorded the original drum and guitar tracks onto 2-inch tape with the intention of using this during the final mix and blending in the overdubs. Simply as a backup, the engineer dumped it all into Pro Tools and gave it to us on an external hard drive. Mark had possession of both the tape and the hard drive. In the nightmarish aftermath of his death, neither could be found. All the other masters he had were located, but for some unfathomable reason, not this stuff. I was devastated, thinking these recordings would be lost forever. After a short time, though, I got an email from some guy who I had never met before, saying that he had a hard drive with some Out Cold recordings, which turned out to be the ProTools backup of these sessions. Relief! At this point the hard drive was over 5 years old, though, and when I tried to access it, it wouldn't work at first. Thankfully, though, a techie friend of mine managed to extract the data from it in the end. The 2-inch master tape still has never surfaced to this day and remains a befuddling mystery.

MM: How has the response been to *A Heated Display*; it had a universal thumbs up from the MM team. Are you happy with it?

JE: I'm never 100% happy with any of our recordings. There's always some aspect to it that I think can be better, and this one is no different, but overall I am very happy with it. I think Mark would be as well. Kevin really came through and delivered on this stuff and I give him a lot of credit for his contribution, which as I said before, was crucial. The response so far has been very minimal, but positive, which I am very happy about.

MM: Does this album put Out Cold to rest now, or would you consider carrying on, either playing live or making further recordings?

JE: We have no intention of carrying on or playing live, but as for recordings, this material is only half of what Mark and I recorded back in 2005. There are still another 14 songs from that session that we intend to put vocals to and release posthumously in much the same way as this record. That will officially put Out Cold to rest.

MM: You and Mark also worked with CJ Ramone in Bad Chopper; are there any 'lost' recordings from those sessions that will see the light of day?

JE: Not that I know of.

MM: You've eased off on releasing records through Acme over the past few years; is the label on temporary hiatus or permanently put to bed?

JE: It's been euthanized, put out of its misery. It took me over a decade and a lot of my personal finances to realize that I just don't have what it takes to run a successful label. I had the passion but not the business acumen. I keep the website up at this point just in the hopes of trying to chip away some of the mountain of back stock that I have collecting dust in my basement.

MM: Have you burnt out on Hardcore or is it simply other things in life are taking priority now?

JE: I wouldn't say I'm burnt out on it, but maybe, to a degree, saturated. I'm definitely not up on the latest crop of bands from the past ten years or so. I find myself these days delving into other genres of music more. I've always done that, though, and I still love Hardcore, so nothing's really changed.

MM: You seem to have quite an affinity with Iceland; what is it about that country that appeals to you so much? Would you ever consider relocating there from Boston?

JE: Funny you ask that as I just got back from my twelfth visit there just 5 days ago. I love everything about Iceland except the weather and the prices, and even those are tolerable for the most part. I love the landscape, the people, the culture, the language, the music scene, just everything. It completely captivated me since the moment I first visited in 2001. I feel a profound connection with the place that I've never experienced anywhere else, not even close. I would love to move there and have long dreamed of it. I don't pursue that due to various practical considerations in my life right now, but my heart has definitely been pulling me there hard for years.

MM: Are you currently working on any music projects?

JE: Yes. I have a new band called Oblivionation. More raw, fast, loud Hardcore type stuff. We're a bit slow going because we all have a lot of other shit going on in our lives, but we're just now finishing up our first real recordings which are due to be released on LP, hopefully soon, on Rock N Roll Disgrace Records right here in Massachusetts. I also did some home recordings with Kevin Mertens last summer which is somewhat similar, but maybe a hair more "proggy", for lack of a better term. We're talking about getting together again soon to do some more, but not sure what will become of this.

MM: What's next for John Evicci?

JE: Not sure exactly. I'm hoping we can finish up those final Out Cold recordings with a lot less pain and consternation than the first batch. Other than that, just the usual musical and traveling endeavours, I guess. I'd be happy with that.

Originally published in Mass Movement #37, November 2013

ROBERT VENDITTI

When I was offered the chance to talk to new Green Lantern writer Robert Venditti, I grabbed it with both hands as I've been a fan of Rob's work since his time at Top Shelf and *The Surrogates*, and I'm a huge Green Lantern mark. Put those factors together, and it was a no brainer that I'd want to talk to Rob and find out everything I could about what was happening in the Universal domain of the Green Lantern Corps. In brightest day…

Interview by Tim Cundle

Photographs appear courtesy of Robert Venditti and DC Entertainment

MM: So Rob, how did you come to make the move to DC?

RV: Writing work for hire comics us something that I've just always wanted to do y'know as it offers balance to working on creator owned as it's your creation, it's wide open and you can do what you want. That's one sort of creativity, and the other is to be given a pre-existing continuity and pre-existing characters and work within the confines of that, which means that you get to exercise a different set of creative muscles, so it was a challenge that I've been looking to do for quite some time. Of course, I did it with *X-O Manowar* over at Valiant and I had a friendly relationship with Matt Idelson, I'd been in contact with him over the years and when the Green Lantern job came up, I made the pitch for it as it seemed like too good a challenge to pass up y'know?

MM: How do you approach writing a title like Green Lantern, one of DC's flagships titles when you're following in Geoff Johns wake…?

RV: Yeah, Geoff leaves behind huge shoes to fill and in a lot of ways those shoes can't be filled, I mean he wrote the book on these characters, developing the mythology over the course of his very long and very well regarded run, and I try not to think about in those kind of terms and just sort of think about telling the kind of stories that I like to tell, in the way I like to tell them and just hope that the readers like it. Ultimately, all you can do as a writer, or as any kind of artist, is embrace the things that make you different from everybody else because if try to imitate what other people have done, then you're going to end up reading like that, as a copy of what's been done before…

MM: Where you a Lantern fan before you took over the reins of the book…

RV: You know, I didn't start reading comics until I was in my late twenties and all that I knew about established characters was the same as everybody else knew from the Christopher Reeve *Superman* movies, *The Incredible Hulk* television show and things like that, so I didn't dislike Green Lantern, but I wouldn't say that I was a reader of the series and I still haven't seen the movie. Until they called and offered me it, I'd never read a Green Lantern comic in my life, but what I did know about the character from general pop culture immersion was very interesting to me, but it's not like I was a life-long fan or anything like that, and the same (for me) is true of any super-hero really…

MM: Given the sheer scale and scope of Green Lantern, and given that you've now got the whole Universe in which to play as a writer, does knowing that put more pressure on you or is it strangely liberating?

RV: A little of both. I mean, there's a lot of pressure in that it's a very popular series coming off a long, popular run and Green Lantern is an integral part of the DC Universe so it's not like a creator owned book such as *The Surrogates* where I know the whole thing in and out, this is a much larger tapestry. It's also very rewarding as a writer to be able to work on concepts and have them become a part of that tapestry, looking at a character like Relic, the primary villain of this *Lights Out* crossover that we're doing right now which is a villain that we've created and being able to create an entire Universe and destroy it in twenty panels, things like that are tremendous fun and extremely rewarding.

MM: What can we expect as regards the characters evolution is concerned, and how will he, they and the book itself differ from previous incarnations?

RV: There's a few things that we're doing differently, but a lot of it is just picking up the threads that were left hanging at the end of Geoff's run and introducing new threads. Between *Rise Of The Third Army* and *Wrath Of The First Lantern*, the Corps was really in a lot of disarray, and had been through a lot of really tough times, so one of things that we're doing is shifting around the roles of some of the characters. For example, Hal has now become leader of the Corps because the ranks have become so decimated and the Guardians are gone and they've been replaced by a newer team of inexperienced Guardians, and so we're looking at how Hal's new role rubs up against his inherent nature of being the going it alone flyboy.

We're also introducing a lot of new Lanterns, both new recruits and veterans that we just haven't seen before and exploring different parts of the wider Universe that we haven't seen before, while looking at the emotional spectrum and exploring the greater mythology that Geoff laid down over the course of his run. So we're taking it in some now and unexpected directions that I hope readers will be surprised by in a good way, and as we come out of *Lights Out* which will conclude in October with *Green Lantern Annual #2*, I think we'll see a radically different status quo for each of the four books involved in the event, *Green Lantern*, *Green Lantern Corps*, *New Guardians* and *Red Lanterns*, and we've worked hard to give each of the main characters in those titles a very significant role in the event to make sure that the event, and its aftermath, had a legacy that was going to run through each of them.

MM: Given that you're also writing *Green Lantern Corps*, is there one character who stands out for you, one Lantern in particular that you enjoy writing for?

RV: I Like John, I think he's great as a polar opposite to Hal and we're going to see a lot of, and learn a lot about, him in *Green Lantern Corps #25*. Its sort like his zero issue, the zero issue he didn't get to have the last time around as that zero issue focussed on Guy Gardner. I like Kilowog as well, I think he's just an amazing character and Billy (Tan) does an amazing job of drawing him so I'm finding new and enjoyable ways to feature him in the series...

MM: What do you think Green Lantern's lasting appeal is? Why do you think this particular character has managed to weather the storm when so many others have fallen by the wayside?

RV: I think it's a great high concept, particularly with the American audience as police shows, law enforcement shows on television and in film and books as well, are very popular and Green Lantern takes that structure and applies in on a very cosmic scale and in a galactic setting. I think that's a great mix, and it's a great hook that a lot of people can grab onto easily.

MM: Okay Rob, hypothetical question time. If you were handed the keys to the DC Universe and could write any story you wanted featuring any character or characters that you wanted to use, what would it be and who be leading the charge...?

RV: See, as I didn't grow up reading comics and don't have any allegiance to any particular characters, I don' really have any stories that I've been dying to get out since I was a kid. For me, what I really enjoy is having someone call me up and say "We've got this character, we'd really like you to take a look at them", and then have to start from zero, read up on that character, learn about them and come up with stories for them, which will hopefully be different to something that a lifelong reader of comics would come up with. I've always seen that as a greater challenge and a lot more off the wall...

MM: What's next for Hal Jordan and Rob Venditti?

RV: Coming out of *Lights Out*, we're going to have some radical changes across the Green Lantern books, we're planning out our next storylines which should take us all the way through 2014 and we have a lot of things coming up. New characters, new challenges, new settings, some characters who people haven't seen in a long time coming back, so there's a lot of stuff to be excited about...

Originally published in Mass Movement #37, November 2013

SHAI HULUD

Reach Beyond The Sun is quite a different album for Shai Hulud. It's breathing less desperation and some sort of notion the world isn't, always, the horrible place you feel it to be. Playing in Shai Hulud, and sharing stages all over the world is amazing. What's also quite different to *Reach Beyond The Sun* is all former singers are having their say, or scream if you like. We caught up with guitar player Matt Fox for some insight in the band's most recent album...

Interview by Martijn Welzen

MM: How have you managed to maintain a more or less steady Shai Hulud vibe / sound over the years, when so many musicians have been in the band, some for only very short time...

Matt: I've been in the band since the beginning, write a good amount of our material both musically and lyrically, and everything we have released, even if it was written by another member of the band, goes through the "Shai Hulud filter" - a long established filter understood and perpetuated by every member of the band, seasoned or new. In addition, newer members we've had who were inclined to create with us joined because they loved what the band was doing and wanted to help further that sound that made them want to join in the first place. Having people join that feel an attachment to what is we do helps both maintain our sound and keep it fresh.

Shai Hulud's sound and style is noted so even when transient members offer their creative input, it always either fits right into the mold, or helps us effectively broaden our parameters. I truly enjoy having other ideas outside of my own. Yes, too many cooks in the kitchen may spoil the food, but two heads are mostly always better than one. I welcome the brainstorm.

MM: Is it difficult playing Shai Hulud songs with a different line up time after time, or does this add some flavour to the songs?

Matt: It can definitely have its hiccups. We never want to change members, but life happens in band life just as it does in real life. You adapt and overcome as best as you can; cherish the moments when it clicks easily, and work hard to smooth things out when it's not as conveniently immediate.

Every new person brings something new to live show. Similar to what I mentioned above, all those who ever joined the band never expect to change who it is we are, but new and different people, similarly, are who they are, and they bring with them different and unique characteristics; new flavors for sure. Just like every new James Bond, every new Batman, and every new Doctor Who...

When forced to take in new band members, we make sure we find as right a person as possible, and we understand that everyone will bring with them their own personality that will obviously bleed into the songs to some degree. We welcome that. We've been fortunate in continuously finding people that work very well within the Hulud framework. The new characteristics always seem to serve the songs well, and often the new flavours do keep things fresh and stimulating.

MM: Do you like how other guitar players or singers interpret your older songs? Have you ever been surprised by how your songs came out when different musicians played / sang them?

Matt: I truly love new members' interpretations and ideas. We've never had someone join, on any instrument, where we hated what it is they brought to the table. Then again, that's what jamming and preliminary conversations are for. I'm pretty sure we would know after a first meeting or two if someone was just too far out of step with who we are and how we play.

When we do confirm a new member, invariably they always bring a new twist and interpretation that's both effective and exciting. Our songs have been given many little makeovers over the years; that really does keep them fun to continue playing. I think even with a stable line-up for a decade I would still want to make slight changes to the songs. Re-interpretations keep older songs from growing stale.

MM: For the new album, you have invited all old singers for a (guest) performance. Would you say that all former members of Shai Hulud are part of the extended family?

Matt: Absolutely. It is very safe to say we are on incredible terms with 99% of the people have who have spent time in Shai Hulud then moved on. It is definitely an extended family. And I love that. Again, life happens. When people leave a unit, it doesn't have to be the end of a friendship. Sometimes things just can't continue the way they are, and as always, we adapt. We overcome. And that's never to say anyone who has left the unit will be forever abandoned to the cold. That's childish, and not how I want to live my life.

One of my favourite aspects of the new album is that all the former singers came together to sing on *Medicine To The Dead*. It makes me happy. Gives me a warm feeling. Our love and respect to Damien Moyal, Chad Gilbert, Geert Van der Velde, and Matt Mazzali. Hugs and hi-fives all around.

MM: How did you decide which song would fit what vocalist best? Did the singers also have a say in this? And was Chad the obvious choice being the main singer of *Reach Beyond The Sun*?

Matt: Funny you should ask... We had the plan to have all the former singers appear on this album for years now; all said alum were contacted, and they all agreed to take part. We simply needed to make the decision of where to put who. We had ideas though noting was set in concrete other than the fact they all would appear somewhere; where exactly would be up to us. They would receive the lyrics, be given a place and cadence within any song, and set free to have at it.

As it happened, the song *Medicine to the Dead* was the last song to be written lyrically. By the end of the scheduled studio time the lyrics still had not been finished, and Chad was leaving for tour. This wasn't to be a problem as he was on Warped Tour where apparently there was a studio truck; he said he should be able to finish the vocals there once I sent him the lyrics. Regardless, I always knew we would give former singer Geert a guest spot on this particular song because it was most reminiscent of the music on our second record, *That Within Blood Ill-Tempered*, the album he sang on. Having him appear here made perfect sense, and we thought it would stir up a warm sense of familiarity.

The lyrics trickled out slowly. By the time I had everything finished, the option for Chad to record on the road was slim, why, I can't exactly recall - I think he may have gotten sick on tour. Whatever the case was, it looked like we were going to end up with a song where Chad's voice only took up a fraction. Even after we added Geert's vocals, more vocals were needed, and the irony of this situation was *Medicine To The Dead* was and is the most vocally dense song on the album. Just our luck.

With all the former singers ready to record their respective vocal spots, *Medicine* having plenty of empty space, and Chad not being able to get back into a studio until after our completion date, as you can guess, the decision to have everyone now appear in the same song was a no-brainer. Though not at all the original plan, this happy accident made for one of my favourite, and more charming aspects of the album.

Chad was certainly the obvious choice to be the main singer on *Reach Beyond The Sun*. He was confirmed to produce, even when we had another singer in the band planning to sing on the album. When we parted ways with that singer - believe me, the fact that our producer had a great voice and also happened to be our former singer was extremely convenient! We put a lot of hard work and heart into *Reach Beyond The Sun*, additionally, it was also the recipient of a lot of stray pieces falling into very fortunate places.

MM: Is the title, of the new album, in any way linked to the idea one should already reach for the stars in life? Never to give up, and keep reaching for your dreams….

Matt: That certainly could apply - as with anything, any individual can take these lyrics and relate them to their own particular circumstance, but the original intention was indeed the most fundamental of the "never give up" notion: to move forward, move through depression / lethargy, or any debilitating, immobilizing situation. Truly, more often than not, "Our days are as bleak as we permit." The first step is critical, and often the most difficult... Extend. Outreach.

MM: What can you tell us about the general feeling of the album. I personally think this one has more of a positive vibe, where you seem to be breathing more hope. Yes, still very much angry, but with less desperation. Does that maybe also link in with the title of the album?

Matt: I think you are very correct regarding the link between the album's overall feel and its title. It immediately comes off as more hopeful because *Reach Beyond the Sun*, no matter how you read it, is a very encouraging phrase, likewise, the song is also inspiriting. Most every song on the album does offer some varying degree of hope, with maybe exceptions for *Medicine to the Dead, Monumental Graves*, and *A Human Failing* - all of which are more unrelenting in their despair.

This record was intended to be somewhat of juxtaposition to *Misanthropy Pure*; we meant for Ms. Pure to offer a minimal amount of positivity, and a maximum of anger, sadness, and aggression. This is why *If A Mountain Be My Obstacle* was excluded. It was just far too optimistic. Lyrically, it has a more fitting home on *Reach Beyond The Sun*.

MM: The titles of the songs sometimes seem to suggest otherwise. Like *A Human Failing* or *Monumental Graves*. Is contradiction in words and music deliberate?

Matt: I always mean for our song titles to be intriguing and pique interest. This is why I shy away from overly simplistic titles; personally, they do nothing for me, whereas if I, myself, saw a song titled *Man Into Demon: And Their Faces Are Twisted With The Pain Of Living*, I would very extremely excited to hear it. Our titles absolutely aim to pull people in to pay attention the song, read the lyrics and see what he song is about. Again, regarding simpler titles for songs, movies, books, and even band names, when they are bland or seemingly meaningless, it takes more autonomous energy for me to look deeper. I prefer a title to be striking, provoking, and arouse curiosity upon first glance.

Additionally, creating contradictions in music, musically or lyrically is always fun and interesting - whether it's the title to the lyrics, the lyrics to the song, or any other combination to stimulate thought and emotion.

MM: There also seems to be more of a Hardcore feeling to the album. Is that Chad's influence on the songs?

Matt: At our core (no pun intended) we are rooted in Hardcore / Punk, that's where the band started, no question, the scene from which we spawned. Further beyond that, all the key creative players who have ever been involved in Shai Hulud are lifelong metal-heads, and lovers of progression in all music. We are truly an amalgamation of all the aforementioned; no doubt that will always be evidenced on every album.

With *Reach Beyond The Sun*, one of our first focuses was to not over-think, overwrite, or overproduce the individual songs or the album overall - Matt Fletcher, long-time bassist, was a huge proponent of this as he felt *Misanthropy Pure* was far too guilty of said overages. Intentionally keeping things more on the organic side - song-writing, production, overall tracking - *Reach Beyond The Sun* allowed not only more emotion to flow, but also our true sound to shine through. I can't say there was a different approach to song-writing on *Reach* other than simply not to overcomplicate anything just for the sake of doing so. Admittedly, though I do love the album, *Misanthropy Pure* did exactly that. *Reach Beyond The Sun* is Shai Hulud raw, with all our varied loves and influences very much intact.

I think if the songs were overwritten or any less organic when we showed Chad the original *Reach* demos, he may have declined to work on the album with us. The approach we were taking was the approach Chad also had in mind which is partly what helped make things work so well. Granted, there was a bit of a tug-of-war between he and I. My nature is to pull to more of the progressive side, his nature to keep the songs more accessible. Maintaining that balance is essential.

MM: In between every album there's five or six years, quite a long time in Hardcore and even metal. Would you say you need a couple of years to make sure you're in a different mindset when writing a new record?

Matt: The gap between albums is more a result of refusing to force creativity. So much space between records may work against us career-wise, but when all is said and done, we will be able to look back and smile on the fact that everything we released was sincere. I like that. That said, recently I have made an effort to fiddle with my guitar more often; I would love to not wait another half a decade to release the next album if at possible. We'll see what happens.

We never need to be in a different mind-set - in fact, I'd rather not be. I prefer to simply be honest with the music. Honesty and ideas defines what we are. On every album we release you will find the consistent thread that is Shai Hulud - it's weaved in everything we have ever released; that will always be prevalent, though it's unlikely there will ever be two Hulud albums that sound the same.

I wouldn't say we have ever had the goal of re-inventing ourselves, we like what we are, but keeping fresh is very important, and hopefully it isn't delusional to state that we have managed to accomplish that. We are always intent on pushing forth new ideas - ideas new to Shai Hulud. When we weave our 'signature' thread within new ideas a fresh yet familiar sound be the result. In theory.

MM: Is that also the reason why you wanted to shed the label 'metal-core' fairly early in your career? How would you like us to remember Shai Hulud?

Matt: The term "Metalcore" these days can be poison (laughs) Then again, so can almost any genre label. If we ever started steering clear of that term it was simply because we are not what it is. If we were, we might be a much more popular band!

I'm not sure there is any specific genre label we'd like to be remembered as; so many labels could really apply. We've tossed around a little catch phrase for a few years, and I think that phrase would be an agreeable way to be remembered: Shai Hulud, A vehicle for thought and emotion.

MM: Is Chad now also going to be part of the band for the upcoming tour? Is he going to continue with the band for the foreseeable future?

Matt: There has been no discussion of Chad doing any tours with Shai Hulud, though he is part of the extended family and always welcome to join us in whatever we do. Truthfully, I wouldn't expect to see him live with us any time soon. He surely has his hands full, involved in a number of projects that consume his time.

We plan on doing some recording in the near future with our current line-up, and we will certainly invite Chad to be a part of it. While it's safe to say Chad is not an active member of Shai Hulud, you can count on him being involved with the band in some capacity for as long as we exist.

Thank you kindly for reaching out to us. Onwards and upwards!

Originally published in Mass Movement #37, November 2013

THE SPIDER'S WEB
THE RUTHLESS TWO-GUN SUPERHERO

He's known to the general public and the police as Richard Wentworth, a famous criminologist devoting his efforts to combat the forces of evil and eradicate crime. However, in some ways, he is not at all unlike *The Green Hornet*; that is, he works both sides of the law to fight those who oppose it.

His main alter ego is known only to his servants and fiancée (Ninta Van Sloan) as The Spider. Although on the side of justice, The Spider has at times been made to appear guilty of the very crimes he is trying to prevent. As a result, he is accused by the law to be a dangerous criminal and sought after by police officials.

The idea for The Spider started out as a pulp magazine in the 1930's and soon became a popular seller. Columbia Studios bought the rights to make a chapter play starring Warren Hull as the lead. Hull plays Wentworth and The Spider as well as a shady character known as Blinky McQuade. With makeup to disguise himself as a shabby tramp, Wentworth uses the character of McQuade to obtain valuable information from the criminal underworld, since he appears to be on the wrong end of the law himself.

The Spider's manic side is somewhat of a mystery to understand. Once he dons his caped costume, he becomes a ruthless killer of anyone that he even remotely considers a threat. Armed with only a pair of twin pistols, he very effectively guns down the bad guys with reckless abandon. One movie reviewer remarked that The Spider killed more criminals per chapter with his pistols than any other serial character on film. There's no mistake about it, The Spider makes short work of the opposition. Wentworth, nonetheless, "appears" as a mild-mannered crime investigator eager to solve his next assignment and to work "hand-in-glove" with police authorities. Although in one chapter, he guns down two household intruders by shooting them in the back and then, in a very relaxed manner, he phones the police and jokingly informs them to send the "meat wagon" to retrieve the bodies.

It's difficult to establish a dividing line that separates Wentworth's true identity from that of his alter egos as The Spider and Blinky McQuade. I guess that's what makes him such an interesting character study. Like *The Green Hornet*, The Spider has no real superpowers, so he must rely on pure wit and the force of his trusted weapons. For his protection, he entrusts his servants and fiancée to guard his true identity from both law enforcement and the public.

In his first serial, *The Spider's Web* (1938), the enemy is a mysterious masked man that goes by the name of the Octopus, who is hell-bent on destroying the cities' transportation systems in order to cripple all operations and seize control of the city itself. To stop the Octopus' maniacal plot, Wentworth uses his detective skills to outwit his opponent. Of course, as in any serial, Wentworth/The Spider is faced with certain death at the end of each chapter, but somehow he manages to escape the inevitable outcome.

The Octopus is ruthless in his own right as innocent citizens are killed in order to accomplish his insane plans. He is a true terrorist in every sense of the word. This type of villainous activity is standard fare for most serials: it's your basic case of a megalomaniac who desires world domination.

In essence, the Octopus is fighting two enemies at the same time, since he doesn't realize that Wentworth and The Spider are one in the same person. It's a clever device for a plot and a great character strategy. For all intents and purposes, the storyline is about an "anti- hero" that leads a double life and an evil, masked villain, both of whose identities are unknown to the public, and both of whom have violent tendencies. Which force will win out? The fact is that in all of movie serial history, there has been only one villain that escapes justice, and we'll save that story for another day.

On a side note, I refer to The Spider as an anti-hero because of his violent approach to crime solving. Technically, an anti-hero is a protagonist who displays no morals, courage or virtues, thus, making the line between hero and villain a little less definable. The historical documentation of the term can be traced back as far as 1605, with the story of Don Quixote. Some literary critics even site Shakespeare's character of Sir John Falstaff as being an anti-hero. It all depends on how society views the concept of the traditional hero at any given point in history.

The Spider's Web is a gun-blazing adventure that is entertaining, although rather conventional. What makes it better than the average run-of-the-mill serial is the complexities of both the hero as well as the villain. It's not rocket science, but it is a lot of fun. As with most serials, the villain is equally as important to the storyline as the leading man. In fact, at times, he is even more of a character study than the protagonist. A good example of this would be Republic's four-part serial of the famous detective Dick Tracy, played by Ralph Byrd. Byrd more or less plays the role straight and lets the villain steal the spotlight. At least it made the writer's job a bit less complicated. It is your basic storyline of good versus evil. *The Spider's Web*, on the other hand, requires a more complex examination of the principals. Both the villain and protagonist are somewhat "cut from the same cloth" when it comes to their methods of operation. It's a simple case of violence against violence, leaving in its wake, destruction and mayhem as a byproduct.

After having watched as many movie serials over the years as I have, I try to find an interesting character aspect that separates one protagonist from another or, for that matter, one villain from the next. Most, if not all, chapter plays are based on proven formulas since the purpose was meant to entertain a younger audience with plenty of action rather than to bore them with character driven storylines. It is my attempt to explore some of the character traits that separate these very colorful creations of yesteryear from the average flatfoot detective types. The Spider is certainly a violent protagonist. He is a perfect example of a cold, calculated crime fighter. Although not quite as overt in his approach to solving crime, Wentworth's temperament is often times unpredictable, which makes the entire experience enjoyable to watch. In this particular serial, I would have to say that both the hero and villain are on equal terms when it comes to their methods of operation.

Recently, Moonstone Publications released a series of nineteen original Spider stories entitled, *The Spider Chronicles*. Although I haven't had a chance to read all nineteen stories, those that I have read are of great interest. They seem to capture the same raw grittiness of the original 1930's chapter play. So, like *The Green Hornet,* The Spider uses both sides of the law to accomplish his objectives. Fortunately, they both remain unscathed by their actions. To them, the ends do justify the means. On a scale of one to ten, I give *The Spider's Web* a solid eight.

Doug Crill

Originally published in Mass Movement #37, November 2013

TOBY HADOKE

One of the biggest surprises of the last five years, for me, was stumbling across *Moths Ate My Doctor Who Scarf*, a hilariously funny, deeply moving, Whovian rites of passage one man show by stand-up comedian and actor, Toby Hadoke; a man whose life-long love of Doctor Who was now the focus of his professional life. Whether he's on stage making audiences laugh and reflect on their lives as he shares the Doctor's impact on his own, creating a multitude of characters for Big Finish reuniting legendary seventies Doctor Who stunt team Havoc, presenting *Who's Round* or hosting Who DVD commentaries, Toby Hadoke has become a one man Whovian force of nature, and as I'm also a life-long fan of the Doctor, I set out on a mission to talk to him about all things Who…

Interview by Tim Cundle

Photographs courtesy of Toby Hadoke

MM: Let's talk about the Doctor. When did you first stumble across Dr Who?

TH: In my living room at home when there was a repeat of *The Invisible Enemy*. I know it was a repeat because my brothers, who I remember watching it with, knew what was going to happen, and lo and behold, they were right so it must have been a repeat of one they had seen before. And with that Doctor Who hit.

MM: So it's been a lifelong obsession with you?

TH: Definitely yes. My two older brothers had Target books and things like that and when Doctor Who wasn't on I used to get out these things and flip through them even before I was really old enough to read; I used to like the illustrations. It was a natural childhood interest that I just took to another level.

MM: Do you think your younger self's obsession with Doctor Who effected your later career choice?

TH: Yes absolutely. I wanted to be an actor because I wanted to be in Doctor Who. I wanted to do directing too, and when I did that I knew it was the actor's life that I was really interested in. So I went to see plays that had Doctor Who actors in, which gave me a Shakespearian education. And because I had that Doctor Who fan gene, if I like something I just like it. So I pawed over each Shakespeare play through the summer holidays. I practiced them through the summer holidays. So it began an interest, not just in Doctor Who and science fiction but in classical theatre, British film and all those sorts of things so I had to give it a shot.

MM: With *Moths Ate My Doctor Who Scarf*, where you initially surprised by how well it was received when you started performing it?

TH: Yes. It was a big deal. A lot of comics go to Edinburgh. I thought I might do well in terms of seats, because Doctor Who might give you that extra 5 or 6 seats, but I got slightly more than that… The title; I remember there was a buzz about the title of the show and I guess I didn't know how many people knew who I was in terms of the industry. I was fairly well known on the Manchester circuit but I'd pretty much stayed in the North West.

Being known, though meant that critics who might have stayed away for another first time show, came to see me and gave me good reviews. Instead of waiting for audiences to build up and coming and seeing it at the end of the run, they were asking me if they could come over that first weekend. So I was lucky and they were good. Then when they talked about doing it in a larger venue, I thought it was going to be an anti-climax, but they moved it to a bigger venue and it sold pretty well. We sold out on the last night, the Saturday, I think, which is what we really wanted to do, to go down well in a big venue. Then a guy came in a couple of nights before and asked how long we were going to tour it. We were thinking: well there's tonight and tomorrow…. But he got us on a West end run and a proper national tour. It just kept on going to my continued surprise yes.

MM: It seemed to take on a life of its own…

TH: Yeah. I guess it made my name as a Doctor Who fan. Which wasn't my bright idea, if it was a bright idea at all. When I played my home town of Ludlow, people were bemused. Someone told me that the show was all about me, and it was all the Doctor Who stuff that was the proper, interesting stuff. It's hard to hear though as when you're a comic, you write about what you know, which for me is the kids and stuff. So making it all about Doctor Who and being a Doctor Who fan wasn't the grand plan. We went through the stuff working out the best stuff, and it was a dialogue between me and my Doctor Who fan self. But because it wasn't just for Doctor Who fans, and there will be people there who will go just for that, it needed to be such that you could say "Oh but it's not really about that, it's about how this happens to him and how he copes with that". Of course I talk about things that happen and the basic human emotions that are common to all of us. I think that's what it was really, what made it work for the audience as well as the Doctor Who fans

MM: You're part of Doctor Who cannon now having been cast in a number of Big Finish audio dramas, how does it feel?

TH: Some people don't think Big Finish is Cannon, so I'm glad to hear you say that. It's incredible. What I love about them is that they don't necessarily cast to type. When I played an Australian for them, they didn't ask if I could do an Australian accent, I've got a voice reel knocking about somewhere, and I do a lot of voiceovers and I've worked a lot for Radio 4. I also played a highly strung man under pressure in the Sylvester McCoy one I did, *Robophobia*.

They didn't offer me any funny parts which I would expect them to, and they didn't ask me to read for anything, unlike television where you are so often cast according to type. It's like the last battleground for the character actor. Every time I did one, I thought: "Ooh that's a good one, that's probably me done with Big Finish for a while" and then they turned round and offered me four stores with Tom Baker and David Warner. I'm well aware that's it's a job of work and I'd love to say that I worked in and my ten year old self sort of floated through, but you have to be grown up and responsible about it while also enjoying it. But it was Tom Baker and David Warner and I was thinking "Say something interesting, say something interesting, otherwise they will think you're an imbecile".

But they didn't because they are very nice people. I remember when I did *Cyberman 2* which was the first one I did, which, isn't Doctor Who, I did a scene where Nick Briggs did the *Tenth Planet* Cyberman voice and I wasn't expecting it because I thought they'd do it in post later. Then suddenly there's this Cyberman voice and that was a real hairs standing on the back of the neck moment. That voice, it was terrific. I had a line in one of the Tom Baker Dalek ones which was something like: "The Dalek ship has docked" – it was a very sci-fi line – and I did a sort of Lenny Henry-esque emphasis on the word Dalek at the end and Nick saw it, and even though I couldn't see him, I could imagine him sort of peering over his glasses as he was saying (adopts world weary tone) "Yes, Toby, very fine sci-fi acting"; when I was thinking "Well, it worked fine in my bedroom". At the same time, Tom Baker's over there, and David Warner's over there – Cor, that was exciting!

MM: So what's happened to *Volumes 2* and *3* of *Running through Corridors*?

TH: Well it's supposed to be *Volumes 2, 3 & 4*. The first volume was written in a splurge, and the problem with writing something in a splurge is that there is no time to fine tune it. There is editing involved, but that's the sort of duller process, and we (*Running Through Corridors* was co-written with Rob Shearman) need to find time to get together and edit it, because we wanted to do it ourselves. *Volume One* was edited while I was in Edinburgh and I only had a chance of a quick perusal, and so this time we wanted a little bit more editorial input both from me and him who meant we had to be available at the same time.

The problem with that is that he got really busy, and then I got really busy so it hasn't really worked out. But the short answer is: I am done. I have finished my stuff for *Volume Two* and I'm supposed to be meeting Rob to work on it next week. We've both been so busy.... So apologies to anyone who may have been waiting, it is coming.

MM: So what was it like getting Havoc back together, and have you ever thought of pursuing your burgeoning career as a stunt man?

TH: (Laughs)... I'm never going to jump off anything ever again. It was really good and I'm really pleased with the warmth that comes out of that documentary. I think I've found my niche which is being so very interested in other people. When I was a kid I used to read through cast lists to try to find out who these people were, and I've always thought that you can benefit from the stories and experiences of other people. I'd sort of decided not to do any more DVD documentaries because I didn't want to end up being so ubiquitous that they would get somebody else to host the DVD commentary which is the bit I enjoy doing the most.

Then Chris suggested the idea and I thought (adopts really excited tone of voice) "Ooh stuntmen with stories" and they are really lovely people. Derek Ware was one of the first Dr Who people I met because my brother's only brush with professional theatre was when he was with Richard III as a schoolboy and Derek Ware was also in it. As he was one of the first Doctor Who people I met, it was nice to be there for the last hoorah for the Havoc boys. It was his idea that I jump off the platform which I didn't really enjoy. I'm not a total wimp, I've done sword fighting and stuff like that, but it's the height thing I don't like. Even though most of the reviews were very very nice, there was one review online that really got to me as they said "The fun of this is watching a middle aged man getting scared by jumping off something that's not that high". And I thought "How dare you – I'm not a trained stuntman. If you think it's not so high why don't you jump off it yourself?" I think they really missed the point; which was just that it was a bit of fun. And Derek Martin is one of the nicest men I've ever met, who most people probably know from EastEnders. He had such a positive attitude. I remember him saying to me in one of the breaks "Toby, don't waste a minute mate. Even it's just about reading a book, don't waste a minute because it goes by so fast."

It's such a great attitude to have.

And when we picked him up he started moving the camera tripods and we said to him "Derek you don't have to do that" to which he replied "Yes I do lads, we're all in this together". What a top fella. I think Chris makes very good looking films and I'd do whatever he wanted which is why you have shots of me striding towards camera looking a bit of a Charley, but if he thinks it'll make the film look good I'll do it. It's a great looking film, it's got heart and it's got me landing between the mattresses (which wasn't supposed to happen but it's an interesting moment) and a good ending.

MM: So tell us about Toby Hadoke's *Who's Round*...

TH: Ahh, this came about because I wasn't enjoying Christmas as I wasn't very well and somebody on twitter said: "My wish for Doctor Who's 50th anniversary is for Toby Hadoke to interview everybody involved in Doctor Who." And I can't remember what possessed me to think that was a good idea, but I sort of moulded that and it became into getting an anecdote from every story which is a much more containable question. There is a beginning and end and it's not so random.

I know Anneka Wills, Frazier Hines and Louise Jameson so I thought it would be a doddle. This was all being done on Twitter, so I asked Nick Briggs if Big Finish would be interested and he said "Sure, send us the tapes and we'll put it on the Big Finish website. So I started getting in touch with people I knew, and people I didn't know, and people started coming out of the woodwork which I thought was rather nice. I started to get some people slightly off the beaten track. So one night I just asked (on Twitter) if anybody knew Kevin McNally, having seen him in *The Twin Dilemma* and within half an hour I had a contact for him, and within a week I had an invitation to his house. The conversation sort of drifted away from Dr Who onto other stuff, and when I tried to edit it down I thought "There's too much good stuff here so let's keep it as a career tour from Kevin Macnally".

This made me think "Let's get people who haven't really spoken in public before, and some who have, and talk to them about their lives outside of Doctor Who and just use Doctor Who as a leaping off point. Suddenly I started getting contact from PA's, with people wanting to get involved and I started, myself, getting more fired up as I sort of liked the detective work; tracking people down through Skype because I sort of knew who they were and where they lived. The whole process was quite exciting and gave me something to do when I wasn't doing anything else. When you're an actor and a comedian you'll find endless ways to waste your time when you should be doing something. Take today, I'm still in my pyjamas and was watching a second *Tales of the Unexpected* just before the interview began. I've got loads of things I'm supposed to be doing but I just thought I'd do that instead. I'm nearly there. I've done 128 interviews and as the anniversary year approaches its end I know I'm not going to do it again, but I'm so close to getting an anecdote from every story. And looking back now I know I must have been ill at Christmas because if I hadn't been there is no way I'd have started this.

But it just goes to show that even if you're useless at doing something – I'm terrified of talking to people on the telephone on a one to one basis and call someone out of the blue – I really have to build myself up to make an unsolicited phone call because I'm frightened that they will hang up or won't give me their time. It's easier by email because if they don't answer they don't answer.

This was so not the ideal project for someone as cowardly as me to do. I've done something that is always going to be there. It again comes back to people and the stories they have to tell which is something I've always been interested in. Good old Doctor Who was the keystone to hearing all these great stories from people who worked in TV in the sixties, seventies and eighties.

MM: The new show *My Stepson Stole my Sonic Screwdriver*.....

TH: I decided to do another Doctor Who show with some encouragement from the guy who toured with me for the first one. So about seven months before Edinburgh I stopped drinking so that I could get up early and write after the show, because it's easy getting into the pattern of having a few drinks after a gig and getting up late. So I stopped that and tried to stay focussed and professional, and write a show that would appeal to the same audience the other show did, but be a continuation of the story and not a carbon copy.

So I nailed myself to the keyboard and out of all the stream of consciousness stuff I poured in, I pulled the best stuff out and creating an hour wasn't' really the problem, because when you get up to do it, it's actually an hour and three quarters. It was (designed) to tell the story of what happened after the first Doctor Who show as five or sx years had elapsed and a lot had changed, Doctor Who had changed, and to carry on some of the themes but in a different way as there are no teenage diaries or music in this one. And to tell a story about my stepson who is deaf.

It becomes a story of communication, and as Doctor Who is a universal language to a certain sort of person, communication and forging a story with someone with whom I couldn't talk as I'm not good at sign language and he uses his hands to talk; and he hadn't seen Doctor Who until I came into his life. So it's a different story told in a different way. I think it's a better show for it. It's a stronger show... There are elements of *Moths* when I look back at it, that are incredibly angry as I had that hangover of people who mocked Doctor Who and now I just think "It's your loss". It's less of an angry show, a bit more grown up, about some harder realities, but told in a more accepting way.

MM: Toby, to finish off; time to put you on the spot. Who is your favourite Doctor?

TH: Patrick Troughton...

MM: Good man. Why?

TH: Because he was the best at straddling the humorous and the dramatic, and he's also a very naughty and inventive actor. You can't stop looking at him. He never mugs, he's never over the top, and he always delivered an energised performance, and a gravitas coupled with a pixie like sense of fun and huge intelligence. I think that combines the two things that Doctor Who does so well. I think he's marvellous.

Originally published in Mass Movement #37, November 2013

C.J. RAMONE

I was 14 years old when I entered the hallowed halls of high school in 1989. I was one of the smart, weird kids and immediately fell in with a group who wore black t-shirts, Converse All Stars and ripped jeans. There, through divine intervention, I was introduced to an album entitled *Mania* by a group of four leather jacket wearing punks from Queens, New York. The songs were short. The lyrics were about sniffing glue, beating on brats with baseball bats, getting sedated, shock treatment, wart hogs and a lot of other goofy/great things. The friend who had this tape (Jason Cornelius) dubbed a copy for me and now, 24 years later, I'm still completely in love with the Ramones. I own every studio album, the Acid Eaters EP, two of the three live albums (I lost my copy of *We're Outta Here* somehow), the Ramones Raw, End of the Century: the Story of the Ramones and Rock N Roll High School DVDs and even saw them live in 1995 when they were on their 'Adios Amigos!' Tour.

During their career the Ramones had three drummers and two bass players. That's not bad for a band that had a twenty two year track record. Even though three of the founding members have gone on to that hall of fame in the sky (RIP Joey, Dee Dee and Johnny, you will forever be missed) their legacy will endure until the end of time. They have touched countless lives with their anthems of escape, love and a dubious enjoyment of chemicals. They earned their place in the pantheon of rock gods and should any throw stones at their images they shall certainly be cast down. Without the Ramones my life would be much poorer than it is today. Now, thanks to my job writing for Mass Movement I have had the great, glorious honor of interviewing CJ Ramone, the man who saw my beloved Ramones through the last seven years of their career. During our conversation we talked about many things including his time in the band, why he turned down one of the biggest bands in the world after the Ramones' retirement and his kids, one of whom, his four year old daughter, could be heard in the background eating lunch and pulling the stuffing out of whatever she could get her hands on. That forty minute phone call definitely counts as one of the best times in my life and I can't express how I felt, sitting in my living room, talking to CJ Ramone. I can't possibly thank him enough. Take it CJ!

Interview by Jim Dodge

MM: When you joined the band you took over Dee Dee's vocal duties as well as his bass playing spot. Were you ever intimidated by the idea that you were replacing one of punk rock's most beloved icons?

CJ Ramone: I couldn't think of it as replacing Dee Dee. Dee Dee was the original, he was the guy who invented punk rock bass playing pretty much. He's the guy who invented the whole look. The way I approached it was a lot more pragmatically. I just looked at it as I was hired to do a job. That's how I went at it. Of course there are things that I do when people said I ripped that off from Dee Dee but it wasn't that I was trying to be Dee Dee or that I was trying to rip him off, it's just Dee Dee was a big influence so a lot of the things I did, while they came very natural to me, of course, were influenced by Dee Dee. It would be absolutely too intimidating…I don't compare myself to Dee Dee. It's a pointless comparison. He's the original, he's the master.

MM: Was there ever any hazing from the other guys in the group after you joined?

CJ: Not what I would call hazing but definitely a period in the beginning where Johnny was very critical of everything I did and trying to make sure that the quality of the shows and stuff didn't go down with me in the band. He was hard on me in the beginning. I had just come out of the Marine Corps and I was used to that type of thing and I had no problem dealing with it. It actually made me feel comfortable that he was hard on me and critical and stuff because it's what I was used to for a while there.

MM: What was the best moment you ever had during your time with the Ramones?

CJ: That's a tough one. The obvious is the first show. Very few people can trace back in their life to a moment in their life that they were never the same after. I can go to that moment and say I was never the same. There's a couple big ones in there. Playing on stage with Lemmy at the last show; standing next to Lemmy and playing the song and singing harmonies together. Outside of being in the Ramones I'd be hard pressed to come up with another way to top that. I got to get up on stage and do a song with Soundgarden on Lollapalooza. Some real big moments there.

MM: I can imagine knowing that Lemmy accepted you as a Ramone probably helped out a lot with the people who were critical of you coming into that spot after Dee Dee left.

CJ: Even to this day the hair on my neck stands up just thinking about when I heard that he wrote a song (note: *R.A.M.O.N.E.S* from Motorhead's 1991 album *1916*) a song about the Ramones I was like, wow that's so cool and then listening down to it and hearing when he mentions "CJ now, hit the gas," I was like, oh my god! Between that and Joey singing "all is very well, CJ is here..." (note: *It's Gonna Be Alright* from The Ramones' album *Mondo Bizarro* released in 1992) It's really hard to get comfortable in the situation that I was in. Those two things probably made me feel more comfortable and accepted than just about anything else.

MM: Do you have a favorite Ramones song?

CJ: That's a near impossible one. I mean I have songs that are my favorites, you know, *Endless Vacation, Wart Hog, Sitting in my Room*... There's so many great ones. I struggle now when I'm putting together a set when I go out and play live, it's difficult for me to put a set together. There are so many favorites. I'm really like, how do I make the set better? In all seriousness I could probably do a different set every night for a month and never play the same songs.

MM: With any band you like there's bound to be song you don't like and the only one by the Ramones that I never cared for was *Every Time I Eat Vegetables*. That's an awful lot of albums to like that many songs but Wart Hog was always one of my favorites. Probably because I share that same metal background that you do and to me that was the closest to probably a metal song that the Ramones ever did. When you sang *Wart Hog*, did you have a lyric sheet or did you just make a guess and roll with it?

CJ: I had to do my best to learn the lyrics and just go with it. I'm sure most people have heard the story but, coming right out of the Marine Corps...I literally came out of the Marine Corps and five weeks later was doing my first show with the Ramones. I had to learn forty songs in five weeks. We did thirty five live. There were always alternate songs and what not that I had to know also. It was not easy but *Wart Hog* was one of the more challenging things, just learning the lyrics because nobody ever knew them. They were never written down anywhere.

MM: And the one album sleeve where it mentioned it, it had the lyrics to the other songs on the album and then *Wart Hog* and it just had like a row of question marks.

CJ: Right, yep. That was definitely a challenge.

MM: I don't know where you stopped to take a breath during that one either. We tried playing around with it a couple times and it was just like, nah, we'll do a different Ramones song because we like to breathe.

CJ: (chuckles) Yeah, that's one of the challenges of doing that song. You really have to plan ahead of time where you're gonna take a breath.

MM: Whose decision was it for the band to retire?

CJ: Johnny's pretty much. It was time. Everybody knew it and accepted it. Joey had been sick since '94. For the last two years he absolutely struggled to keep up and it was obvious live. He did a lot less singing and a lot more improvising. He was just struggling and I think the general consensus was we couldn't really keep going and doing it the way we were.

MM: It was better to go out on a high note...

CJ: Right. That was always Johnny's thing. He said they should have forced retirement in music kind of like they do in sports, where they just kind of force you to retire. If you're not the absolute best you can be you don't prolong after that. He was the first one to vocalize it and everybody else agreed pretty much.

MM: Did you stay in touch with the rest of the band after that?

CJ: Not all that much and not because we didn't like each other, blah blah blah or anything like that. Mostly because right after the band retired I went out with Los Gusanos and started touring my band and then I started a family almost immediately. The Ramones retired in '96 and in '97 my son was born. I started a family and then once my son was diagnosed with autism I kind of dropped out of the world pretty much for a while, while I got used to what that was gonna be like, just trying to keep the family together. It wasn't like I stopped talking to them altogether and that was it. We still talked every once in a while. Johnny called me up to tell me about the Metallica audition. We were still friendly, still in touch but just not on an every-day basis.

MM: CJ Ramone in Metallica? That sounds like a weird combination but I would pay to see that.

CJ: Not coming from my background. Back in the day I was a very technical style of bass player. I was definitely, like I said, more like a metal guy. When Johnny called me up to audition for Metallica I could totally see it. I was like, I could bring them back to how they were before but there was just no way I could do it. My boy was diagnosed with autism and I even spoke to his doctor and his doctor said he's gotta wake up in the same place every day, go to school at the same time and eat the same things and have his mom and dad around...so I had to turn it down. Johnny called me back a couple weeks later and said, listen you know they still have not found anybody, it's not even an audition, they really want you... I said, okay I appreciate that and tell them I have nothing but respect for them, I love the band, I appreciate the opportunity but there's just no way I could do it.

MM: What do you think your life would have been like if it hadn't been for your time with the Ramones?

CJ: I probably would have stayed in the military. I probably would have stayed in for as long as I could have and come out and maybe become a cop or something like that. To tell you the truth I went into the military because back in the early to mid '80's the economy on Long Island where I lived at was a mess. There were no jobs. There was not much going on. That's why I went into the military. That was my plan. I figured I'd go into the military, get out, get a job on a police force and retire from there. As best I can figure, that's probably how I would have ended up although after everything that's happened in the time since that with all the jobs with contractors, who knows? That was my plan anyway.

MM: It seems kind of wrong for a guy with a punk rock and metal background to be working for The Man one way or another.

CJ: (laughs) I know a lot of people said that but when I was young I was just completely undisciplined, no direction, totally just not...I didn't have anything going on. I wasn't good in school. I wasn't doing much except partying and pretending that someday I'd be a rock star. Going into the military was the first time I felt like I ever had control over my life. I could see something happening and I liked it. I totally fell right into it. It was exactly I needed and what I was looking for. In fact, had I never been in the Marine Corps I would have never lasted in the Ramones. I would have got there, I would have started partying like mad and acting stupid and doing stupid things and Johnny would have booted me out real quick.

MM: I can imagine the rigid touring schedule you guys seemed to keep would have been hard to keep up with too if you weren't taking care of yourself.

CJ: Yeah. The fact of the matter is, is that Johnny went to military school. He went to military school as a kid. That's one of the main reasons I got into the band. He saw me as somebody that understood what it's like and he'd be able to get me to do what needed to be done a lot easier than hiring some young punk rock kid who just thinks that it's all about partying and what not. I'm not saying that the military's for everybody or anything like that but for me, chances are I wouldn't have even been alive had I not gone in 'cause I was just on a bad path. I was just doing a lot of stupid things. I really had no discipline, no responsibility for anything or anybody, I just couldn't stay in a job...

MM: That's punk rock...

CJ: The beautiful thing about it is, is that it really enabled me to be able to maintain my position in the Ramones and that's, for me, for my life, I'll never do anything that tops that. I could stay in music for the rest of my life, record a million albums and nothing will ever top that. That's an achievement beyond anything I would have been capable of on my own I think. I can honestly say I owe all that to being in the Marine Corps. That's an absolute fact.

MM: Do you ever catch flak for continuing to use the Ramones name even though the band no longer exists?

CJ: Not to my face. I've never seen it in writing but I've heard that people have said something about it. I really tried with Los Gusanos and again with Bad Chopper to not use the name but what I found was that I was alienating people that wanted to hear my music. I wasn't including all of these people that wanted to hear what I was doing and because I do everything grassroots, I don't have a record company, I don't have a publicist, I don't have a lot of things that other bands have. I do everything myself. When I say myself, I mean myself. When you see something on the internet, like my Facebook page, I'm closing in on 50,000 likes and the reason why it's like that is because I answer every message to me myself. I go on every morning and play music and have my coffee and trade messages with the fans, going back and forth. That's how I've always done it. For me to use 'CJ Ramone,' first off, I have the right to, I earned the name. It ain't like I was in the band for two years at the tail end of their career. I was in the band seven years. I sang like five, six songs a set, I sang at least two songs on every record I ever played on... I feel like I earned it. And not only do I feel that way but Johnny, Joey and Dee Dee, they all told me what my contribution was and what I meant to the band and the fans tell me. There's haters, you got people out there that have something to say about it. That's fine, I'm totally comfortable with it at this point.

MM: It seemed like the closer to retirement you got, the more you were singing on the albums. Was that due to Joey's illness?

CJ: That was one of the beautifully cool things about Joey and this says a lot about his ego and the type of guy he was. Generally the way we did records was I would get all the demo tapes. I would figure out all the songs and then go to rehearsal. I would teach them to Johnny. After rehearsals I would have to sing all of the songs 'cause Joey didn't come to rehearsals. Later on when Joey would come to the rehearsals, when we got closer to the recording time, he would hear the songs that I was singing and hear the way I was singing the songs and if there were songs that he felt like I sang better he would pass them on to me. There was never any arguing or fighting about it. That's how cool he was. That's how comfortable he was with who he was. It really takes a very specific type of personality to handle that because, you know, he's Joey Ramone. He's one of the greatest rock and roll singers, in my opinion, of all time and here he was kicking down songs to me like, I like the way you sing this one. I was definitely singing more towards the end of the band and for no other reason than Joey was totally comfortable with himself and he was worried more about us having a good record than him singing every song on it.

MM: You've mentioned your son. How many little CJs are running around out there these days?

CJ: I have three. I've got two girls and a boy. Sixteen, thirteen and four.

MM: My son's eleven years old and he's actually named after a metal singer from a band called Acid Bath. That's my metal background showing and that was actually my wife's idea so that was even cooler.

CJ: Yeah, my wife's a total punk rocker.

MM: Oh yeah, everybody in my family, we all like the Misfits, the Ramones and Bad Religion so we've got what I consider the big three covered and my son's favorite band is Rage Against the Machine.

CJ: That's cool!

MM: I just got the new solo album from Doyle, from the Misfits and I can't put that album down. I listen to it like three or four times every day...

CJ: That's cool. I haven't heard it.

MM) It is like all the best things from Danzig and Pantera put together.

CJ: Oh, that's neat.

MM: It's badass. I got it as a review copy and, man, that's the best metal album I've heard all year.

CJ: Cool, who else plays on it with him?

JD: He's got the Abominable Dr. Chud on drums, and then the singer is Alex Story from a band called Cancerslug. I mean it's just the best, ass-kicking, evil metal album. It's everything metal should be; it's the best one I've heard in a long time in the metal genre.

CJ: Wow, that's cool.

MM: I didn't mean to sidetrack us like that but I'm just so stuck on that damn album it's not even funny.

CJ: Yeah, that's cool. I actually just had a conversation with a kid. I posted a video by H2O and I said thank God for these guys. There isn't all that much going on in New York any more. He immediately posted me back. He was like, hey, if you don't see anything happening you ain't looking. He private messaged me and had a conversation. I said, if you know any good bands brother point me in the right direction because I'm an old guy. I don't get to go out to shows and stuff anymore. I said I appreciate any help with pointing out some stuff. I'm always on the prowl for checking stuff out. I totally dropped out of doing that back when, like, emo took over everything. That lasted so long it just kind of wore me out and I just stopped looking around I was so disgusted.

MM: Yeah, I hate emo...

CJ: You know now, like I said, I put out a public appeal. If you hear anything good do me a favor and kick it down. I'd love to hear something new that's halfway decent.

MM: There's a band in New York, I actually got to interview the main guy that writes all the songs called The Bunny The Bear that you might want to check out. They're not really metal but they're very unique. It's got two vocalists going at the same time and they've got three albums out through Victory Records and then one did before that and I like them quite a bit myself.

CJ: Okay. (mumbles The Bunny The Bear as if he's writing it down) Cool. That sounds good. I appreciate that.

MM: So other than your role as a father what do you do to pass the time these days?

CJ: I'm really into motorcycles. I've been into motorcycles for years. I try to get out and do a trip a year, get out for a couple weeks and just go ride around a little bit, see some sights and do a little bit of hunting, do a little bit of fishing, spend most of my time with my kids... Now I'm working on a new record, gonna record a new one in March. The last one I put out, Reconquista, I did through Pledge Music and we really had a good response so I wanna get another record out real quick and make that happen. My life now, pretty much though is my kids, driving them around here and there, going to all their school stuff and their music lessons and what not. That's really how I spend most of my time but, when I can get away this time of year I'm usually hunting or fishing. Then jumping on my bike, going for a nice long ride, that's pretty much what I do for fun.

Originally published in Mass Movement #38, December 2013

HOPS & BARLEY
WENSLEYDALE BREWERY

One of the key factors that attracted me to underground music, whether punk, hardcore or metal, is the DIY ethic. Barriers between bands and fans are broken down. At most gigs I go to you'll see the band hanging out with the audience before and after the gig - there is no them and us. Record labels are similarly approachable, as are the distributors, the venues, the merch companies and the zines, with people working together to make this lifestyle work.

Another industry with a real DIY tradition is the brewing industry. I'm not talking your Carlsberg's or Guinness's or other commercial giants, but the real ale industry. Real ale has seen a real turnaround in recent years and is now enjoying huge and well-deserved popularity. The industry has a long tradition, and the real ale festivals that take place up and down the UK are testament to the passion and enthusiasm that these beers inspire.

I love the fact that all over the country you can find microbreweries that are not only producing some high quality beers, but show imagination and great taste in the variety of beers they brew and a creativity in the packaging and labels that makes some bottles almost as collectable as a rare record.

As dedicated fans of the hops and barley we thought it would be great to give some real ale producers exposure here in Mass Movement - from one thriving creative scene to another.

Here to get the ball rolling I am proud to introduce you to the Wensleydale Brewery and their fine ales, born and brewed in the heart of the Yorkshire Dales...

Interview by Tom Chapman

MM: Can you give us a little history of the brewery? What motivated you to start brewing?

WB: Well I started washing up in the pub, The Foresters Arms in Carlton, where the Brewery first started in 2003, and when I needed a part time job I pestered the owner to take me on, which he did. Then when I left school I did the same again about a full time role, and he with a bit more persuading he did! Then my friend Carl left school, and luckily another position came up, and that's how the Brewery worked for a few years. Then earlier this year one of the owners decided he wanted to pursue a different career and the Brewery's future looked uncertain, so after some careful consideration, Carl and I decided to take over. At 23 and 24 respectively, its made us one, if not the, Youngest Brewery Owners in the UK, and its been a good year to start, so we look forward to what comes next.

MM: How is the atmosphere in the industry? Is there a friendly camra-derie (sorry I couldn't resist!) between breweries or is it cut throat?

WB: Great pun there! Any industry is competitive, and there is so many Micro Breweries producing good beer out there, so it has every reason to be very cut throat, but from our experience it's a brilliant trade to be a part of. Everyone seems to be out to help each other, we have 2 other Micros in our area, who are exactly the same size as us and we're mostly going for the same trade, but we all know we can thrive without hindering each other so we order materials together, deliver each other's beer, pick up empties and recommend to other people. And the bigger breweries open their doors to let you have a look round their plant and give advice if needed, there isn't many industries where that sort of thing goes on. Then there's the outlets that sell your beer, most are very passionate about what they do, and look to push your products to customers new and old, with people like that you barely need a massive marketing plan!

MM: What is your target market, are you trying to get your beer into more pubs locally, nationally? Or are you more keen on the bottled market?

WB: We do both cask and bottled beer, but cask makes up most of our sales. Like most micros our local trade is our busiest, people want to buy things sourced locally as possible, but we do deliver to pubs and independent bottle retailers all over Yorkshire. With Yorkshire been the size it is, there is plenty of trade to go at before worrying about anything National anytime soon!

MM: What factors do you think are responsible for the slow demise of the local pub? Is there any way of halting the process?

WB: I think it's a hard one to pin point really, even aged 24 the pub trade seems worlds away from when I first starting going out. I think a combination of things like economic issues, people been convinced their skint and why would you pay three pound for a pint of lager when you can buy a tin for less than a pound in the shop and sit at home? Socially its more of a culture to "pre-drink" now and although I support the smoking ban I do think smokers don't like going out to stand outside. But I do think some of this is key to why real ale has become popular, if people are going out and buying a pint they want something artisan and different that they can't pluck off a shelf for less than half the price, and it does seem that pubs promoting real ale now are those that are surviving.

MM: Do you know of any pubs that are a success story, that have bucked the trend or fought against the odds to make it work?

WB: We're quite lucky up here in that we have quite a few good pubs that continue to thrive, but it is a rural area and trade is seasonal so it can be difficult for some pubs. But one of a few success stories is the pub where Wensleydale Brewery first started, The Foresters Arms in Carlton. Carlton is pretty bloody rural and the pub isn't really in walking distance for many, but for years it's been a social hub for the many hamlets in Coverdale.

A few owners down the line from those who owned it/started the Brewery there, the landlord fell out of favour with many and following a period of slow trade, they pushed to try and split it up into houses. The local residents began campaigning to raise funds for a Community buy out, the second of its nature locally, and were successful. In the couple of years since then and it's the busiest it has been in living memory, a combination of good food and ale been key to its popularity.

MM: Which beers are your most popular? And what are the specialities that you enjoy brewing? Have you brewed anything crazy?!

WB: Our pale ale, Semer Water is by far our most popular, it started out as a Summer Special many years ago and became that in demand it had to stay on permanently. But our range consists of copper coloured best bitters, dark milds, IPA's, Stouts, Porters and anything else we fancy brewing! That's one of the great things about been a Micro, you can do small batches of lots of beers. Whatever beer style we do there is always a following somewhere for them, so their all popular in their own right and we like to cater for all tastes. I'd say the craziest beer we did was a 8.5% Winter Ale, a couple of those by the open fire kept you warm!

MM: Is the industry changing? For the better or worse?

WB: Again we've only been in the trade about 6 years but from what I can see its changing for the better, the swing definitely is towards real ales at the moment with pubs/outlets that never traditionally served it wanting a piece of the action, and even pub cos having to change their thinking to accommodate this change in trend.

MM: Real ale is considered by many as being a success industry right now. Can you see this lasting, with competitors such as the fruit ciders becoming ever more prevalent?

WB: As you can probably gather from what I've said previously it is a fantastic time for Real Ale, and it is a massive change in trend, but it is just a trend? There is always some new trend round the corner! And there is so many breweries at the minute, with new ones opening up every week, so im sure it will get to a stage where there is more beer than there is demand, and like every boom it may run into difficulty, but who can say, I haven't got my crystal ball handy so we'll just have to enjoy it for as long as we can and adjust as the market does!

MM: I enjoy music festivals, and often there is a tie-in with breweries and other drinks companies. I actually prefer the smaller events, and at some of these (Cock Rock in Cockermouth, Nice N Sleazy in Morecambe) it has been the independent brewers that get a look in rather than the corporates. Is the events side of the business something that interests you?

WB: Both Carl and I are massive music fans, and most importantly live music, so we have thought about approaching a couple of our favourite bands to do a collab with. We've had our beer on the bar at a couple of small festivals, Galtres Festival, for example, but would love to do more. For our launch party we organized a night at Bolton Castle, featuring a few of our favourite local bands and a bar with all of our beer range on, so we totally understand the importance of decent live music and proper beer!

MM: For many you have a dream job - is it all fun?

WB: Every job has its downsides, be it digging out the mash, jumping in the boiling hot copper to get the hops out, cask cleaning, early mornings brewing and late night deliveries, and the extreme cold of working in a barn the dead of winter but to name a few! But at the end of the day, I make beer with my best mate in the heart of the Yorkshire Dales, so its not all bad I suppose...

Originally published in Mass Movement #38, December 2013

VINNIE FIORELLO (LESS THAN JAKE)

Following the release of *See the Light*, their latest incredible album on Fat Wreck Chords, and on the verge of their forthcoming UK tour, MM caught up with Less Than Jake drummer Vinnie Fiorello for a chat about punk rock, Florida and all things LTJ...

Interview by Tim Cundle

MM: Okay, so would you like to bring us up to speed with what's been happening in the LTJ camp between the release of *Greetings And Salutations*... and *See The Light*?

Vinnie: The usual. Touring, writing our new record, working on future touring, and having a personal life. There's this saying "If you don't constantly work on the things you love, someday they'll not be around when you start to pay attention..." I believe that and take apply it on a daily basis.

MM: Before we talk about the new record a little more, I was kinda curious about why you made return to Fat instead of carrying on with your own label? You're re-releasing all of your previous records through Sleep It Off, or are planning to right? Do you want tell us a little about it...

Vinnie: When we originally started our own label there had been large chunks of free time to cover all the bases to release new music but current and future touring didn't really give us time to properly self-release. Time and timing plays a big factor in self releasing and for "See" we needed a partner to cover the bases while we carry the torch.

MM: Sorry, one more before the new record. From your point of view, what are the advantages and disadvantages of releasing through your own label as opposed to signing with someone else, and vice versa... That is, what are the advantages and disadvantages of releasing records through a label, like No Idea or Fat?

Vinnie: Like I said time and timing are the main stumbling blocks on any given release, generally speaking most labels on our genre have the same scope and reach marketing and distribution wise. I'm not saying all labels are created equal but I am saying that marketing and distribution of music these days is much more within the grasp of everyone these days. Bottom line happens to be the passion you have for the projects you do, and giving yourself time to work through any issues that come along.

MM: Alright, let's talk about *See The Light*... From a band insiders point of view and in your opinion, how does *See*... differ from your previous albums? *See*... is an incredibly immediate, hook laden, energetic album, and as the kids would say "It's all killer and no filler", so what you learned about song writing and recording throughout your career, and how have you incorporated what you've learned on *See The Light*?

Vinnie: First, thanks for the kind words about the record. That's a hard question to get specific answers in a few lines. *See* was a very organic record that we worked collectively on. I guess the answer is more individual than band related.

Each one of us brings personal lessons learned into the writing and recording process. We have always been "the sum of its parts" type of band and with this record it really shows how well the machine is working.

When you start to write and record new music, it becomes a snapshot of who the band is at that time and this record shows is at our best, relaxed and focused.

MM: So, what kind of lyrical themes and subjects have you explored on *See The Light*? Could you run through the ideas, what they're about, behind the songs on the new record for us? Go on, pretty please…

Vinnie: The record constantly asks the listener about faith. Not always in a religious sense but more so in the question "Do you have faith that things will be okay in the future". We wanted a record that talked about seeing the light at the end of the tunnel. These are trying times and we wanted the lyrics to challenge the listener to weather the storms.

MM: More importantly, are you pleased with the way the record's been received so far? What's the overall reaction to it been like? Do reviews matter, on both a personal and professional level, to you chaps? Why? Or indeed, why not?

Vinnie: Overall, reviews don't matter. It's one person's opinion who happens to be in the position of some power. Occasionally that person wields that power like a complete ass. You can't try to make someone understand all genres of music and the scope of media is so cut up and specific these days that it's almost impossible to "Win them all". For this record the reviews have been great, even the cop out reviews of "It sounds like Less Than Jake " are ok by us.

MM: There was a time when the world went distinctly ska-core shaped, but that's all changed… You guys, The Bosstones, and to a much lesser extent The Mad Caddies, seem to be the only bands who have truly weathered the storm and survived when many others fell by the wayside. So, what do you attribute the bands longevity to? Tenacity, beer and (like Popeye) spinach, or something else entirely?

Vinnie: We are passionate about what we do, have fun while doing it, and are surrounded by friends and family. It creates this chemical reaction that gets sparked from the fans and keeps the flames burning. There's a lot of credit that goes out to the constant support of friends, fans, and family.

MM: I have to know… As you guys are from there, what makes Gainesville the centre of the punk rock Universe, the Hardcore Mecca, and what's the town like during Fest compared to what it's like the rest of the year?

Vinnie: Fest is both magical and a curse. It's a fantastic weekend filled with great bands and unforgettable hangs but it's a fantasy to believe that it's always like that all year round. People show up after Fest and can't understand why 10 people are at the show and PBR tall cans are more expensive. Gainesville has always had a great driving force in punk rock and it continues steady all year round without the stupid flipped up "wasted" hat or ironic t-shirts.

MM: Do you still think of yourselves as a punk rock band? Why, or again, why not? What do punk rock, and the term "punk" mean to you personally and as individuals?

Vinnie: We do what we want and when we want and that's what punk rock always meant to me.

MM; I now music and genres are, by their very nature, cyclical, but do you think we've already seen the "Golden Age" of punk rock and Hardcore, and if so, in your opinion, when was it and which bands best embodied everything punk was, is and could be? Or has the "Golden Age" not happened yet...?

Vinnie: Music continues to collide with itself leaving these wild blends of music. I think we already have see the golden age of punk as we know it but are headed for a golden age of new sounds honed from the rough edges of all these musical collisions that have been happening.

MM: Does touring get harder or easier with age and experience? Why? Do you enjoy more than you used to, or isn't it as much fun as it used to be...

Vinnie: Touring is a blast, you see the world, you meet new people and do all of that while doing something you love. It's gets harder when you become a dad and a husband, part of you wants to be home always.

MM: You're all pretty busy outside of the band, so would you like to tell all of the folks out there what you all get up to when you're not hitting stages as LTJ?

Vinnie: Roger records bands at his studio The Moathouse, I run a toy company and record label called Paper + Plastick, Buddy plays on Coffee Project, Chris and Jr. Have a show coming on the Food Network, so yeah we all are fairly busy.

MM: What's next for LTJ?

Vinnie: The UK and Australia are right around the bend and then more touring and always more music to be written.

MM: If there's anything that you'd like to add, speak now or forever hold your peace...

Vinnie: Thanks to everyone that continually supports LTJ. I owe you a beer sometime...

Originally published in Mass Movement #38, December 2013

MATT FITTON

Ladies and gentlemen, boys and girls, meet Mr. Matt Fitton, Doctor Who writer extraordinaire and having cemented his place in the Whoniverse with his tales of The Doctor and Counter Measures, he's now got his sights set firmly on Survivors and... Tell you what, why don't I let Matt tell you what he's up to? Mr. Fitton, the floor is yours...

Interview by Tim Cundle

MM: As ever, the best place to start is at the beginning, so would you like to both introduce, and tell us a little about yourself Matt?

Matt: Hello. I'm Matt Fitton. I am a human male from Bradford, now living in Oxford with a wife and small child.

MM: When and where did you first cross paths with the Doctor, what was your initial reaction to Who and do you still feel the same about Doctor Who now as you did when you initially became a fan, or have your feelings toward, and about, Who changed over time? If so, in what way have they changed?

Matt: I was born during *The Ambassadors of Death* (not actually while it was on TV, but somewhere between episodes three and four). My mum always watched **Doctor Who** anyway, so I'm sure I have audio memories from within the womb, but the first visceral visual image I can recall is Sarah Jane Smith with a giant spider on her back, and Jon Pertwee collapsing on the floor. As such, Tom Baker is my Doctor, and I watched all the way to the end of the Eighties run, missing only one single episode (*Horns of Nimon* part four, due to a family party, during which I sulked under a table). I managed to keep up with McCoy as I started university, then the powers-that-be very kindly put the whole thing on hold to allow me to find a job, a wife and have a family. I discovered the books and Big Finish after the TV Movie reignited my love for **Who** (and restarted my *Doctor Who Magazine* subscription). And I remember the thrill when McGann joined the audio adventures and it felt like the series was fully alive again. So both the Eighth and the Fourth Doctors hold a special place in my heart. Then, of course, the TV revival came in 2005, when I'd conveniently had a child in whom I could instil the love. We just attended the 50th Celebration event at the ExCel together and it was one of the most thrilling and happiest days of both our lives!

MM: When and how did you find yourself writing for the Doctor? How does it feel knowing that you're now a part of the mythology of the show, or rather knowing that stories you've created and drama you've written is now part of the Whoniverse and that you're, at least partly, responsible for dictating the direction of The Doctor's life?

Matt: Of course, I first started writing for the Doctor when I was aged about 11. Don't know why I left it that long. I think I probably believed all Tom Baker's adventures were actually true rather than works of fiction that someone had written down. But I've some (very badly drawn) comic strips of Peter Davison meeting Yeti, Colin Baker meeting Sontarans, and exercise books full of stories. In particular *The Six Doctors*, which I never actually finished, but must dust off and show to Nick Briggs one day (not really). I came into Big Finish via the writers' opportunity held a few years ago as one of the also-rans, picked out by Alan Barnes as having potential. My story, *A Most Excellent Match* – with the Sixth Doctor and Peri trapped in a Jane Austen simulation – eventually appeared on the *Recorded Time* anthology. And I haven't stopped writing since! It is quite the most exciting thing to be part of the mythology, and I keep having to pinch myself to make sure I really am doing the thing I always wanted to do: not just writing, but writing **Doctor Who**.

MM: Let's talk about *Afterlife*, the latest Who drama that you've shaped. Do you want to tell us about it? Given the subject matter, and the central core of the story (the aftermath of Hex's 'death' and all that it entails), did *Afterlife* provide a unique, or different, set of challenges to you a writer, and if so, what were they?

Matt: As soon as I heard what was going to happen at the end of *Gods and Monsters*, and that Alan Barnes was going to use the single release to follow up on it, I begged to write the first episode, thinking then that it would be another anthology. I know how good Sophie and Sylvester are, and so I just wanted to do something focused on them and the emotional fall-out. It's essentially a two-hander, that first part. I wanted to make the emotions as raw and real as I could, even within the context of a time traveller and his companions battling extra-dimensional gods! Of course, Alan had ideas where it should go next, and so *Afterlife* became this single, four-part adventure which deals with the memory of Hex and what he's left behind... The challenges this story offers are exactly the things I like to do: to make the characters behave in a realistic, consistent and believable way, but in extraordinary circumstances which really let me push them to the limit. Normally the Doctor never changes, never 'learns', so it was good to be able to do something along those lines here.

MM: *Afterlife* follows the path of the Seventh Doctor, and as you've also written adventures involving the Sixth and First Doctors, I was wondering which of the Doctors you've written for (so far) is your favourite? Why? Is there a Doctor that you'd love to write for but haven't yet, and if so, which one? Again, why?

Matt: Actually (if you include Companion Chronicles and Destiny of the Doctor!), I've written stories with the First, Fourth, Sixth, Seventh, Eighth and Eleventh, which have either been released or announced so far. And there are more to come – I'm definitely checking them off on my list! I know all the voices so well in my head, and there are such different things you can do with all of them: having two Colins in *The Wrong Doctors* was a treat, and all the puppet-master Seventh Doctor stuff is great to plot out, and his enigmatic dialogue lovely to write. I never imagined I'd one day be writing dialogue for Hartnell's Doctor, so that too is a particular privilege, and bringing us right up to date, giving lines to the current incarnation for the final Destiny story was just as much fun as you'd think. But there's something hugely exciting about the Eighth Doctor, that open-ended era of his (well, not so open-ended now...) that made me particularly excited to take on *Dark Eyes 2*. A Doctor I'd love to write for? Well, the Fourth was my Doctor growing up, so although I've a Companion Chronicle coming up, there'd be something magical about Tom himself speaking my words one day.

MM: You've also written a new Companion Chronicle, *Luna Romana*. What can you tell us about it? How does writing a Companion Chronicle (apart from the characters involved, of course) differ from writing a Who drama? Is it more difficult writing for the Doctor or for his companions? One more time, why?

Matt: *Luna Romana* is the finale to the 'Stoyn trilogy', the Companion Chronicles' own celebration of the 50th anniversary. This Time Lord engineer has had his life turned completely topsy-turvy by the Doctor's involvement and he's found himself out in the universe, unable to cope, and pretty much doing the opposite to the Doctor – hitting out, instead of embracing the cosmos.

The interesting challenge with Companion Chronicles is the limited cast, and of course the additional narration to help steer the listener through the story with fewer characters being voiced. I think it helps to write scenes as immediately as possible, to bring out the drama. Of course, it helps when you have a cast as good as this. Like the Doctors, I've had the companion voices living in my head for practically my whole life, so to be honest they come just as easily as the Doctors. Although I consider Romana pretty much on a level with the Doctor anyway (as I'm sure she considers herself), I'm always keen to give the actors something interesting to do, and so it's good that she doesn't require much 'What's going on, Doctor?' dialogue. I think maybe some of the companions from earlier eras would be a challenge for me as I'm just not quite so familiar with their voices. But it's a challenge I'd love to take on.

MM: Which of the Who adventures that you've written so far is your personal favourite? I know it's a difficult one to answer, but you have to have a favourite and there has to be a reason why it's your favourite….

Matt: I do have favourites, but they change all the time. I remember hearing *The Wrong Doctors* and just being blown away at how good Colin and Bonnie were, how the whole insane epic actually worked pretty much as I'd imagined in my head. Then there's *Return of the Rocket Men*, where Peter Purves and Tim Treloar's performances came together with Howard Carter's score to deliver something far beyond my wildest hopes. But at the moment I'm very excited about *Afterlife*. Jonny Morris script-edited and was hugely helpful and encouraging, and I'm really pleased I managed to do everything I wanted with it, and I think it's one I'll be proud of. I just need to hear it…

MM: So, having written for both series (so far) Matt, tell us about Counter-Measures and how you became involved with the series. Do you think the team changed, or evolved, between the first and second series and if so, how do you think they changed, and how do you think that the ongoing evolution will affect the dynamic of the team and the series itself as it approaches and enters the third series?

Matt: David Richardson approached me with the idea of writing for something code-named The Jensen Project back at the recording of *A Most Excellent Match*, my very first script. The development of the first series was fascinating, and was very much a collaborative process with him and script editor John Dorney. Discovering this world. Inventing it. Working out the limits of what we wanted to be able to do. As always, I'm keen to give actors exciting things to do, and one interesting thing about that first series is how much the writers all developed Allison's character. The big unknown was the new Counter-Measures overseer, Sir Toby Kinsella, but again, all our ideas seemed to chime together and he became absolutely key to the whole thing. We were all that much more confident in the world for the second series. It certainly helped me hearing the end result – with the music and the soundscapes so evocative of that 1960s setting. We think series two really builds on what we established in the first. Of course, those who've heard it will know some of the ongoing arcs and developments, and I imagine we'd very much want to follow up on those in any future series…

MM: And then there's Survivors… Again, do you want to tell us all about it, how you became involved in writing the new series and how long did you have to keep your involvement in the project a secret? Will the series follow a similar path to the original Seventies show or the short-lived reimagining, or are you taking the series down a completely different path?

Matt: David Richardson approached me once again – I always like getting those mysterious emails from him! – and asked if I knew the original Terry Nation series at all. I remember some of the later episodes fairly vaguely, but do vividly recall those terrifying opening titles. Things were still at the planning stage, so yes, I had to keep quiet for a while, but I immediately got hold of the DVD box set. I'd watched the recent revival, and while there were some good things going for it, it wasn't really recognisable as the same show as the 1970s incarnation. Those series one episodes hold up incredibly well today, and that's what we're going back to with this audio series: Terry Nation's original vision of the effect of a global pandemic and the sudden destruction of society as we know it. The bleak, desperate drama of ordinary people in terrifying circumstances. So, we open in parallel with that very first episode of TV Survivors and tell the story of the outbreak through a set of new characters. Then we join some of the TV regulars during their journey through series one. It was fantastic to have Ian McCulloch and Lucy Fleming on board with our own original creations, along with Carolyn Seymour, and we are now planning out what happens next for them all…

MM: And then there's *The White Witch of Devil's End*… So Matt, what can you tell us about the forthcoming DVD?

Matt: By the time I came to it, lots of the hard work had already been done. *White Witch* is the life story of Olive Hawthorne, told by the lady herself. We visit various points in her history through first-person narrative, and there are some fantastic, scary tales from Sam Stone, Suzanne Barbieri, Debbie Bennett, Jan Edwards, David J Howe and Raven Dane, telling of Miss Hawthorne's steadfast defence of Devil's End against attack by supernatural forces. Keith Barnfather asked me to come on board for a final eye over the whole script, but really the ingredients were already there, bubbling away. Filming with Damaris Hayman was completed earlier this year, and I can't wait to see the final result.

MM: Everyone has a favourite Doctor, so which Doctor is your Doctor and why is that particular incarnation your Doctor, Matt? And, as it's the fiftieth anniversary of Doctor Who this year, in your opinion, what's the secret of Doctor Who's longevity and continued success?

Matt: As I've said before, for me, Tom Baker is the Doctor I grew up with. He just inhabited the role and made the unbelievable believable for my young self. There have been many great actors in the part, but I think it helps to have some innate eccentricity thrown into the mix, and of the modern Doctors, Matt Smith has had that in spades. I'd also give a special mention to Paul McGann, the most effortlessly charismatic leading man to play the role. The Eighth Doctor's adventures alongside Charley, Lucie, and now Molly, are a huge part of my love of audio, and the revival of my enthusiasm for all things Who. There is something to adore about every one of the brilliant actors we've been blessed with over the last fifty years, but you made me choose, so I've chosen three! As for the show's longevity, another thing I've said before is that quite simply, Doctor Who is the best sci-fi-fantasy-tragi-comedy-(pseudo)historical-(melo)dramatical-farcical-serio-family-kids programme there has ever been or ever will be. And it thrives on change, which means it will be around in some form or other much longer than any of us. It's a legend that's been formed in modern times, something new that will last forever – which is a very rare thing indeed.

MM: What's next for you, Matt? What else do you have planned? If there's anything that you'd like to add, now would be the time…

Matt: Uppermost in my mind today, as we've just finished recording, is the Charley Pollard series. Yes, she's back at last! And Jonathan Barnes, Nick Briggs and I have had a whale of a time creating new stories to tell what happens next to the Edwardian Adventuress, after *Blue Forgotten Planet*. I'm delighted I finally got to work with India Fisher, who is just as wonderful as you'd imagine. And what an amazing guest cast we've assembled to accompany her on all-new travels – no doubt more will be announced soon.

MM: Other than that, there'll be more Counter-Measures, more Survivors, more... other secret things.

Matt: And, of course, more Doctor Who. I've contributed to *Dark Eyes 2*, the next set of adventures for the Eighth Doctor, coming out early next year, and we are already planning the series beyond that. I'd like to tick a few more Doctors off my list too, so watch this space...

Orignally published in Mass Movement #38, December 2013

THE MYSTERIOUS DOCTOR SATAN
A MAD SCIENTIST READY FOR WORLD DOMINATION

Okay, here's where the fun begins. This is where the bad guy is more of an interesting character study than the hero. In my past article of *The Spider's Web*, it was a close match as to which character made a better study – the protagonist or the antagonist. And in the case of *Captain Midnight* as well as *The Batmen,* both heroes and the respective nemeses are "dead even" when comparing their importance to the storyline. Not anymore. Now it's time for the villain to take center stage, and the hero to take a back seat. So, meet Doctor Satan. He's a mad scientist who has his sights set on world domination with an army of robots. There's only one problem; he currently has only one, and it (the robot) is in need of some repair.

Edward Ciannelli, mostly known for playing many gangsters and bad guy roles, is outstanding as the "good doctor," but we'll save the details after we discuss the basic storyline.

A series of crimes have swept the area, and the governor of the state is aware that it all boils down to *The Mysterious Doctor Satan*. Because of his knowledge, the governor is murdered by one of the doctor's henchmen. Shortly before his demise, he explains to his adopted son, Bob Wayne, about the identity of his natural father: an outlaw vigilante who wore a copper mask and was referred to as "The Copperhead." The governor entrusts the mask to his stepson and continues to explain that The Copperhead was really not a criminal, but, instead, he worked incognito to eliminate the real outlaws. He simply wore the mask to protect his identity from both law officials and members of the criminal element. Reluctantly, Wayne accepts the mask and vows to continue his real father's work as The Copperhead; his first assignment is to bring Doctor Satan to justice.

What Doctor Satan needs are the plans for a remote control device that will allow him to activate his robot over long distances, thus, enabling him to seek unlimited power and wealth (another example of a madman who wants to dominate the world). Presently, his mechanical friend can only be controlled at a very limited distance, and the control device that he so desperately needs is the property of Thomas Scott, the inventor.

Doctor Satan attempts to kidnaps Scott and his plans aboard a train, but our protagonist, the newly appointed Copperhead, thwarts his efforts. Of course, that doesn't stop Doctor Satan from gaining access to the goods. He continues every effort that he can think of to steal the remote control unit for the completion of a fully-operating robot. Eventually, he is able to kidnap the inventor under duress, as he threatens the safety of Scott's daughter, Lois.

I should mention that Satan's robot does play an important role in the storyline, especially in the final chapter. But we'll save the best for last.

In each chapter, Doctor Satan's plans are stalled by interference from the Copperhead. The elaborate means by which Satan uses in an attempt to eliminate his opponent are at times ludicrous, but that's preciously why chapter plays make for such great entertainment and laughs.

For example, at the end of chapter six, Doctor Satan ingeniously secures Lois to a chair with poisonous gas pellets below and "hot wires" the door as to electrocute The Copperhead should he try and save her. To outsmart Satan's plan, The Copperhead enters the room via the fire escape and saves the damsel in distress from certain death. Ah, foiled again.

After a lengthy process, Scott has finally completed one remote controlled device and installs it in Satan's robot, allowing it to be operated from a longer distance. To test out for any" bugs" there may be, the robot is driven to a nearby bank, where it uses a torch-like device to rob one hundred grand from the vault. In the process, the robot disables the night-time guard just long enough to escape in the get-away car. Not a bad haul for one night's work, huh?

Now that the robot is working up to speed, Scott needs more tungite, a chemical element that is required to complete many more control units for Satan's army of robots. Ah, yes, tungite. Just another one of the many made up chemicals/elements created from the minds of the writing staff. Many chapter plays had similar such made up nonsense as being actual substances. I guess to a ten-year-old kid it was believable.

Controlled from Satan's headquarters, the robot is shipped in a crate, to the warehouse where the tungite is kept. There, the metal monster is activated to free itself from the wooden crate and dispose of the guard, while the henchmen search for the tungite. Somehow, The Copperhead also discovers the location of the tungite and prevents the thieves from stealing it. After a furious fist-fight with the henchmen, he disables the robot by throwing a bottle of acid directly at its metal exterior. The robot falters and knocks over a shelf of various chemicals, trapping our hero beneath the weight of the shelf and a fog of vapours. Does The Copperhead escape certain death? Of course he does, in chapter eight. As for the robot, the damages are only superficial and it, too, survives to fight another day.

Chapter after chapter, Doctor Satan's plans are somehow foiled even though his robot is able to eliminate a few individuals along the way. As I mentioned earlier, I saved the best for last. In final chapter, The Copperhead manages to breach the inside of Satan's headquarters and knocks "the good doctor "unconscious. Cleverly, he then slips the copper mask over the head of Doctor Satan, which in turn, confuses the robot into grabbing its master, and the two fall from the top floor of the building to their demise below. Scott is freed from his bonds, his daughter is unharmed, and the world is safe from total domination, all because of The Copperhead's timely arrival.

Republic Studio tried to acquire the rights to make *Superman* into a serial but failed to secure the property. As a result, the studio writers created the character of The Copperhead, but in my opinion, he lacks the special image needed to be a unique superhero. To put it another way, his copper mask is the only means used to disguise himself from being recognized, and when he speaks, it's obvious the voice is that of Bob Wayne. Unlike *The Masked Marvel*, who only wore a simple mask, the audience never knew his true identity because they never saw him without his disguise until the final chapter. Also, if you'll recall, *The Masked Marvel's* voice was somewhat different while in character but changed when his identity was revealed. Perhaps, for these reasons, the protagonist is really not the focal point.

As written, he merely plays "second fiddle" to the bad guy. Robert Wilcox, who plays Bob Wayne, A.K.A.: The Copperhead, does a credible job of acting, but I believe the script was ostensibly designed as a vehicle to showcase Ciannelli's character.

Born on an island in the Gulf of Naples, Ciannelli was the son of a doctor and, oddly enough, became a doctor himself as a surgeon. But his real interest centred on acting, where he began onstage shortly after WWI in a number of Broadway productions before turning his attention to Hollywood. It is estimated that he appeared in over 150 films during his career, not including his appearances on television. The bulk of his work was usually devoted to playing the role of the "heavy," mostly some type of master criminal or gangster character.

As Doctor Satan, Ciannelli demonstrates his ability to portray the character of a deranged but ingenious mad scientist with his various mannerisms. It's the way his eyes seem to flit from side to side, or the nervous action of his hands wringing together as the wheels in his diabolical mind spin out of control that makes him a perfect choice for the role. He cleverly installs a belt-like device that straps around all of his henchmen and renders them at his mercy by electrocution, should they decide to leave his services. His every facial movement is a precise, cold and calculated expression of pure treachery. No situation, no matter how improbable it may seem, is beyond his domination, at least from his perspective. Even his robot is an extension of his twisted and distorted mind. Speaking of which, the robot's performance is a close second to steal the spotlight away from its master.

The whole production is simply a joy to watch. The action is top-notch and the villain is definitely worth the price of admission. *The Mysterious Doctor Satan* is one of my all-time favourite serials, and perhaps this article will entice others to enjoy it as well. On a scale of one to ten, I give this one a nine.

Doug Crill

Originally published in Mass Movement #38, December 2013

THE WEIRD WORLD OF BILL ALEXANDER

There is a lot of talk amongst the Horrorati at the moment about Quiet Horror. A sub-genre that seems to mainly concern itself with timid vampires and shy werewolves whose worst crimes would appear to be dropping a thigh bone in the school library or letting one rip during the two minute silence on Remembrance Day. However, the subject of this month's column is an exponent of anything but Quiet Horror. The work of cover artist, cartoonist and illustrator Bill Alexander is best described as Gibbering, Screaming, In-Your-Face Horror of the highest calibre.

Unless you're a fan of the now obscure publications put out in the seventies and early eighties by Myron Fass, or a collector of less than salubrious paperbacks from the fifties and sixties, chances are you've never heard of Bill Alexander. So, just in case you didn't know, to my mind, Bill Alexander is the greatest horror-comic cover artist to have ever put blood soaked brush to gore-stained canvas, even though he has some stiff competition in Lee Elias, Bernard Bailey, L B Cole, Don Heck and Jack Cole.

Alexander's main claim to this fame comes from the covers he did for a group of titles known as Eerie Publications. These were put out by the aforementioned Myron Fass, a former horror comic artist who became the king of pulp-exploitation quickies and fly-by-night publications. With titles like *Weird*, *Terror Tales*, *Tales from the Tomb* and *Witches Tales*, Eerie Publications magazine were the horror comics equivalent of the gore ridden grindhouse movies they used to play between porn movies in the seventies.

Eerie Publications began by printing black and white versions of the precode horror comics from the fifties that were out of print and therefore in the public domain. They would slap a new cover on the comic and touch up the old artwork to make it more gory. This worked quite well for a time, as they were sold as magazines and not comics, so weren't subject to the same censorship that had killed horror comics fifteen years before. After a while though, Fass began to run out of old horror comics to pilfer and the fifties fashions and styles looked a little dated by the dawn of the groovy seventies. Undaunted, Fass simply hired a bunch of cheap and hungry (but exceptionally talented) artists from South America to redraw the same stories with seventies hair cuts and a gallon or two more gore. Sometimes the same story would be redrawn up to three times by different artists to varying effect.

While there is still a lot of debate among horror comic aficionados as to whether Eerie publications are simply cheap knock offs or have a twisted merit all of their own, one thing is certain, the cover was usually the best thing about the whole magazine. In fact, it's arguable that without the covers Eerie Publications would be all but forgotten today. While many fine artists turned in their share of stomach churning Eerie Pubs covers, (Chick Stone and Fernando Fernandez chief among them) Bill Alexander is without doubt the king of crepuscular covers.

Bill Alexander's career began in the forties supplying cartoon art to the independent record label Miltone. Following that he teamed with his friend Gene Bilbrew to create what was arguably the first black superhero strip *The Bronze Bomber* for the weekly African American newspaper the *Los Angeles Sentinel*. Given his obvious talent, it's interesting to speculate how much of an impact being African American had on Alexander's employment prospect in comics in the late forties and nineteen fifties. There were notable black artist working at this

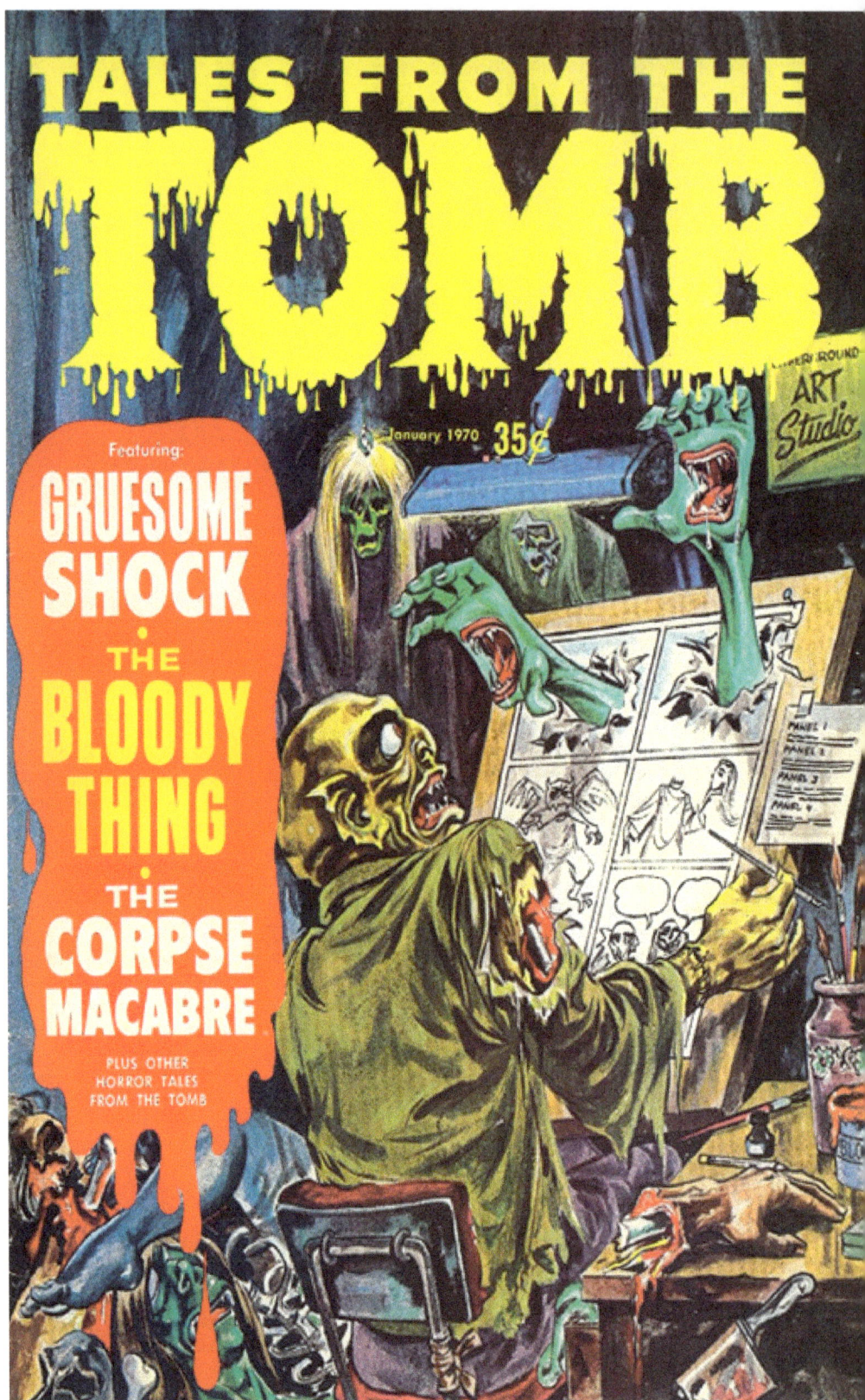

time such as Matt Baker, A. C. Hollingsworth and E. C. Stoner, but many of these artists were known to have lost jobs to white artists returning from the war in the mid to late forties.

Whatever the case Alexander never drew another regular superhero strip after the *Bronze Bomber*. Instead he built a still dedicated following among collectors of fetish art. In the early fifties he began providing comics and illustrations to Irving Klaw, the man who would introduce the world to fetish art star Eric Stanton and go on to make a household name out of Betty Page. In the early sixties Alexander started to produce book covers, providing hundreds of titillating covers to soft core paperbacks in the After Hours line, which were put together in an editorial office above a New York Strip Joint.

At the end of the decade Alexander came to the attention of Myron Fass. In addition to the amazing covers he painted for Fass, Alexander also drew black and white illustrations for a variety of publications and ongoing strips for Fass's Playboy knock offs - *Jaguar* and *Buccaneer*. These strips were saucy and satirical in the same vein as Kurtzman and Elder's *Little Annie Fannie*. The reading tastes of the general public had changed as the seventies dawned and Alexander's work began to reflect that. Not only in the unbelievably over the top horror covers, but also in the hardcore work he did for mob run porn publishers Star Distributions. Alexander provided covers for the Harding Files series that catered to every sexual kink imaginable (and more than a few that defy imagination).

In 1974 Alexander did his last horror cover for Myron Fass. In 1978 he stopped working for Star Distributors and moved to California to work for London Enterprises where he became the art director for their slick line of bondage periodicals. He continued in this role until at least the mid-eighties and little or nothing is known of what he did or where he went after this point.

While Alexander's many paperback covers have a lot of charm and are eagerly sought out by collectors, it's for the horror comic covers that he'll be best remembered. It's not just the vivid covers and the subject matter that made them jump off the spinner racks and the newsstands. It's also the sheer WTF nature of the subject matter. You quite honestly have never seen anything like most of them. One of my favourite covers is from *Tales from the Tomb, Volume 2, Number 1*. It shows a demonic gargoyle, who looks as though he has just been brought back from the grave due to his decaying body, sitting at a drawing board sketching out a comics page surrounded by decomposing and dismembered bodies under the watchful eye of an obviously undead editorial board. As if this wasn't weird enough, the comic on the drawing board appears to have come to life and two green skinned arms are bursting out of the top panels on the page. In the centre of the palms of the grasping green skinned hands on the end of these arms, we can see see two blood thirsty mouths filled with sharpened fangs, which are greatly distressing our recently reanimated gargoyle artist.

For me, more than anything, what distinguishes Alexander's work is the sheer brio and gusto with which he paints. There is a great sense of vivacity about his work and a respect for the subject matter. He worked on topics and depicted subject matter that were shunned by both mainstream artists and publishers, but there is never a sense with Alexander's work that he would rather be doing something else more befitting a man of his talents. He embraced the subjects and reveled in them and in doing so I believe he created art. Given the nature of his work you would think that the sadism more than anything else would shine through in his painting. However what I gain from it is a sense of empathy and humanity. I actually find it quite life affirming.

But then again, I am a seriously disturbed individual. Maybe what I get from Alexander's work is a sense that I'm not alone after all.

Speaking of seriously disturbed individuals I'd like to welcome Mike Howlett to the column. Mike is a comics historian, musician and the author of The Weird World of Eerie Publications which has to be one of the single best books of horror comics history I've ever read. I'd go so far as to say it's a text book study in how to write a history of a comic book publisher. I have Mike to thank for most of the information about Bill Alexander, so I thought it only fair to get him in to say a few words about the great man.

Mike thanks for agreeing to join me in this month's Injured Eyeballs. *To begin with, I'd be interested to find out when you first became aware that Bill Alexander was the artist behind all those amazing Eerie covers and how you found this out?*

When I was researching the Eerie book, I was paying a lot of attention to the other magazines published by Countrywide (Eerie's umbrella company) and saw examples of artwork that was similar to "that Eerie guy"s style. Among those examples were the covers to their crime comic mags (MURDER TALES and TALES OF KILLERS) which, to my delight, gave cover art credit to one Bill Alexander. His style is pretty distinct, so I was able to identify dozens and dozens of Eerie Pubs covers and, subsequently, hundreds of comic strips, book covers, and illustrations over the years.

Alexander, like Carl Barks and many talented comics artists, worked in relative anonymity for a series of niche publications, but there is never a sense in his work that he is just grinding it out. Do you think that he took a pride in his work and conceived of it as more than just a job?

It depends. Many of his horror comic covers look like he put a lot of effort into them, planning his layouts and colors meticulously, I would guess. His charcoal illustrations for the Countrywide girlie magazines are among his finest published pieces (in my humble opinion); obvious care was taken. On the other hand, he did hundreds of illustrated covers for hardcore smut publisher Star Distributors and some of that looks like he knocked it out pretty quickly. He must have been doing a cover a day and some of it shows. Still, his talent was great enough that the artwork still shows signs of quality.

Researching a marginalized figure like Alexander can't be too easy, I wonder if you could tell us how you go about undertaking a project like that?

Alexander proved (and still proves) to be a tough nut to crack. The common name doesn't help! Most of the research that has actually turned up any kind of information has been his artwork. You can follow his trail a bit by seeing where he worked at what time. From Miltone Records to Irving Claw to Myron Fass... I haven't had any luck (yet) finding any family members or friends, but it will be something I will work on until I am satisfied! Until then, I have to let his art speak for him!

In your book you say that you lose track of Bill after he goes to work for London Enterprises in the early 80s. Have you learned any more about his final days since the publication of the book?

Other than finding new artwork (I found three new Star Dist covers today!), no. I still have feelers out and might have a new lead right now, but nothing to report yet. Since the Eerie book was finished, I started planning a possible Alexander art book and I have been trying to compile a checklist of all of his published work (a daunting task indeed!) and I will, of course, try to find out anything I can about the man. A few projects have sidelined this research for the past year or so, but I look forward to getting back to it.

What, for you, are the qualities that make Bill Alexander stand out as an illustrator and cover artist?

Alexander's Eerie Publications covers appeal to me for a number of reasons. First and foremost, the colors; he had an amazing palette! I'm sure he was being instructed to make them colorful, but he really produced some eye-catching paintings! His monsters are colorful, their clothing is colorful and the backgrounds are as well. I also really appreciate his sense of humor. Even on the notorious "meat-grinder" cover, he has a funny sign on the wall (Werewolf Meal, Inc. "All Meal No Filler")! His lurid, grimacing monsters are all cartoonish and fun. They really represent the Eerie Pubs look for me... colorful, fun, multi-monster-mayhem! (Having a fetish-art background didn't hurt with the requisite damsel-in-distress images, either!)

It is a shame that his work was often relegated to the bargain bin publishers. Let's face it, I love the Eerie Pubs, but Fass was a bottom feeder and Alexander was just one of his pawns! If he had the chance to do some "serious" art instead of cranking out the covers for Star Distributors' porno books, who knows where he might have ended up. As it stands, we have an immense body of work to explore and learn more about and perhaps in time, Bill Alexander will get his due.

Thanks once again Mike, I couldn't agree more.

If I've whetted your rather dubious appetites with this article and you'd like to learn more about Bill Alexander and Eerie Publications grab yourself a copy of Mike's book

Trust your Uncle Jasp on this. You know it makes sense.

Jasper Bark

Originally published in Mass Movement #39, April 2014

THE CRIMSON GHOST
THE NEATEST COSTUME IN SERIAL HISTORY

The Misfits seem to like this character because they his image for their logo. That proves that they have good taste, right? I just so happen to agree with their selection but for different reasons. In my opinion, he has the best costume of all chapters play villains, with a close second going to "The Lightning." So, who is "The Lightning," you ask? You'll read about him in the next serial. But for right now, just take my word.

The Crimson Ghost (1946) wares a skeleton mask with matching gloves and completes his attire with a crimson-colored frock, something on the order of a Halloween- type costume. His true identity is that of a professor at a local university, alongside of five other board member scientists, a fact that the Ghost explains to his henchmen in the first chapter. However, since he always appears in costume, his identity remains a mystery until the final episode.

The group's purpose is to test a device called the cyclotrode (here we go again with another crazy invention) that can stop any electrically, controlled mechanism as well as lightning. Good luck with that idea. It is intended as a means to repel an atomic attack by a foreign enemy but, in the wrong hands, it has the unlimited power to paralyze entire cities and beyond.

Presently, there is only one working model of this device (or so the writers lead us to believe), and it has too small of a range to inflict massive damages or prevent any real attacks. If the test is successful, then a larger version of the device can be made. The lead on this project is Professor Chambers, who works in concert with his colleague, the criminologist and outstanding physicist, Professor Duncan Richards, our protagonist.

However, should *The Crimson Ghost* gain access to the cyclotrode, then he could control the city's transportation and electrical systems, paralyzing the activities of the police and creating panic and terror among the citizens. This scenario would open the city up for unlimited extortion and blackmail, just another example of a villain's delusional scheme of world domination. It seems to be the favourite goal of almost every chapter play villain, and *The Crimson Ghost* is no exception. He is a mastermind of the thirty-second degree, one degree shy of reaching the highest level of a Free Mason. Just kidding. He is, however, a very formidable foe who wants to rule the world, and he will stop at nothing to achieve his fiendish objective.

The first order of business is to steal the working model of the cyclotrode, so he sends two henchmen to heist it, but Richards and Chambers interfere, leaving the room in disarray and the cyclotrode smashed. Actually, in order to prevent the men from stealing the device, Chambers purposely smashes it against the wall with the knowledge that he has another model safely hidden in a secret location. How convenient. Even though Chambers informs the group that a second cyclotrode exists, the only other person that knows of its location is Duncan Richards. At this point in the story, it is obvious that neither Chambers nor Richards is the Ghost, since both men have proven their innocence by fighting off the henchmen. Oh, and another thing. During the fight, one of the two henchmen manages to escape, leaving behind his partner, who has been knocked unconscious on the floor.

As the dust settles, the other board members enter the room and discover that the man is wearing a collar device around his neck. Hum…Wonder what that's all about? As you may have already guessed, it's intended as a means of controlling the villain's henchmen, but upon its removal, this henchman will die. And die he does, as one of the scientists accidentally rips the device from the man's neck, resulting in instant electrocution. Now, the board members have no way of obtaining information about who ordered the botched attempt at stealing the cyclotrode.

In the next scene, the shadowy figure of a man (*The Crimson Ghost* out of costume) phones his henchmen, ordering them to kidnap Chambers and take him to a secret laboratory, where he will be forced to disclose the location of the second cyclotrode. When Chambers refuses to talk, *The Crimson Ghost* places a collar, similar to the one worn by the unfortunate henchman who was electrocuted earlier, around Chambers' neck, and injects him with a drug that will help to loosen his tongue about where the second cyclotrode is hidden. With this information, the henchmen and the powerless Chambers arrive at a warehouse where the model is kept, and they manage to steal it, despite Duncan Richards' interference.

When the men arrive back at the secret laboratory, the Ghost safely removes the collar device from around Chambers' neck so that the good professor has a clear mind to finish the cyclotrode project. After testing out the second model, our villain decides that Chambers needs to build a larger, more powerful version and forces him to comply. All that Chambers needs is an X-7 tube to complete the project and that is kept in a vault at the university. Little does the Ghost realize, that Chambers lied about the tube and, instead, it is really a deadly radium device which he plans to use on the Ghost and his henchmen.

Once again, the henchmen are successful in their attempt to steal what they believe is the X-7 tube, despite further obstruction from Duncan Richards. Since the stolen device is made with radium, Richards is able to use a Geiger counter to find both the location of the cyclotrode and Professor Chambers. In the meantime, Chambers has successfully installed the radium device into another strange looking instrument, and he aims it at the laboratory door. Unfortunately for Chambers, he is the victim of his own device when he tries to prevent Richards from walking through the door.

As far as chapter plays go, *The Crimson Ghost* follows the same, basic formula that most serials do, with plenty of action and interesting devices. Along the way, two of the professors have been murdered, leaving two remaining as suspects. In the end, the identity of the Ghost is revealed to be Professor Parker, who is brought to justice by Richards. But really, there's nothing special about the storyline; it's the characterization of the villain that makes this serial special.

I must admit that my interest in choosing *The Crimson Ghost* as a character study is based more on his outward appearance than for any other reason. Sure, he meets the standard criterion of most chapter play antagonists: he desires to control others and destroy any opposition for the sake of global domination as his goal. But that alone is not enough of a reason to choose his character.

One look at him and you know that he means business, more so than other disguised villains. Maybe, it's the fact that the man behind the garb chose to be a skeletal figure instead of choosing an elaborate or, for that matter, a common outfit such as what "The Mask" wore in the *Spy Smasher* serial. Remember him; the German U-boat commander that concealed his face with a plain, white cloth when giving orders over the television screen? How impressive is that?

Think about it, if you're going to conceal your identity as a villain, what better choice could there be than to represent death itself? That says it all. In a way, *The Crimson Ghost* reminds me a little bit of "The Grim Reaper." No words are necessary to convey his message. When the Ghost does speak, he is absolute in his intentions. There is no room for any interpretation. He speaks – you listen.

As for the leading man, well, all I can say is that he lacks the lustre necessary to be considered as a first-rate hero. Yes, he can fight with the best of them, that is, his stunt double can. But as it is written, he simply is a plain and ordinary character that thwarts any advances made by the villain. The actor who plays the role is Charles Quigly, who starred in a number of chapter plays and low budget films. He was a lesser-known leading man that could deliver standard lines and not much else. He had the looks, but lacked the charisma.

It might be of some interest to note that the main henchman, whose character's name is Ash, is none other than Clayton Moore, better known as "The Lone Ranger" in both television and the movies. Moore's version is not to be confused with the chapter play that starred Lee Powell as the famous masked man.

One a scale of one to ten, I give *The Crimson Ghost* a ten for his costume and a solid eight for the serial.

Doug Crill

Originally published in Mass Movement #39, April 2014

CRUMBSUCKERS

For me, Crumbsuckers were the band that changed everything. At the tail end of 1986 (the exact date is a little hazy), Mark 'Warmer' Williams and yours truly bought twelve cans of beer and two copies of an album called *Life Of Dreams* after the guy who owned the local record store had sold it to us saying, 'It's fast and loud, you pair of idiots will probably love it". And we did. We drank our beer and we were blown away by this hitherto unknown, to us anyway, NYC band.

Fusing the tight, technical musicianship of thrash metal with the raw energy, fury, speed and emotion of HC, *Life Of Dreams* instantly became one of my favourite records, and I'm pretty darn sure that in the last twenty eight years, I've played it at least once a week. I've worn out four vinyl and three CD copies of the record, and it still sounds as fresh and exciting now as it did when I first heard it way back when. Crumbsuckers and Warmer may be long gone, both having departed for the ever after, but that record and it's follow up, *B.O.M.B* still burn brightly and defiantly. And more than twenty years after the band initially broke up, occasionally getting back together for the odd reunion show here and there, MM caught up with bass-player and founding member Gary Meskil to chat about the band that changed everything...

Interview by Tim Cundle, Mark Freebase, Ian Pickens & Tom Chapman

MM: When, where, why and how did the band originally get together? Did the band's name really come from something that happened in your High School cafeteria, and if so, can (and will) you share the story behind the band's moniker with us? What was it about the name that appealed to you and made you want to choose, and use, it for the band?

Gary - I began forming the band in the summer of 1981. I was looking for something to do during my High School summer vacation, and so I thought "Why not start a band?" At the time, I was a self-taught bassist and self-proclaimed punk rock / Hardcore enthusiast. As a result, I called a guitar player classmate of mine named Frank (Franco) Cupelli and asked him if he was interested is starting a band. He said "Yeah, what should we call it?". I enthusiastically said, "Crumbsuckers!". The name stems from a moniker we had given to a former classmate who had a strange yet funny habit of inhaling every last crumb from his cafeteria lunch plate. We found this character to not only be hilarious, but to be worthy of broader attention. The next recruit into the band was 12 year old drummer Jason Bolognini, followed by another classmate of ours named Chris "Hendo" Anderson. Our 1st rehearsal room was called Crumbsucker Cave (in Baldwin NY), and our 1st set list consisted of cover songs from bands like UK Subs, Misfits, The Clash, Stray Cats, and others from that era. After somewhat mastering our craft, we then began writing original songs, and the rest is Hardcore history.

MM: You guys are commonly referred to as being an NYHC, and later crossover, band, but you always sounded different from the other bands in the NYC scene who were around at the same time as you. Did coming from Long Island have any influence on way you wrote music and your overall sound, and if so, how did it influence of affect the band? Did the fact that you were from outside the city, and away from any scene politics and / or expectation, also have any bearing on the band as a whole?

Gary - In the early 80's there weren't many kids from Long Island who shared my enthusiasm for Punk and Hardcore. The scene was already blossoming in NYC, but Long Island was a bit of a late bloomer with regard to those aforementioned styles of music. So, my Hardcore / Punk tinged writing style became infused with the musical influences of the other members, and their influences were generally quite different from mine. So, that's where the "crossover" thing came from, at least as far as Crumbsuckers are concerned. In my opinion, Crossover was a natural evolution of Hardcore / Punk, so although we had a lot to do with that evolution, we do not solely take credit for it, as there were other "crossover" bands coming out of different cities around the same time as Crumbsuckers (i.e. C.O.C., DRI., etc.).

MM: Let's talk music... Looking back, how do you feel about both *Life Of Dreams* and *B.O.M.B* now? Which record do you, personally, think of as being the definitive Crumbsuckers record? Which record defines the band for you? Why?

Gary - For me personally, *Life Of Dreams* is the definitive Crumbsuckers album. The bands roots are firmly planted in that recording, and all of the members and ex-members from 1981 - 1986 contributed greatly to the potential that became fully realized on *LOD*. It was sort of a "greatest hits collection" of our earliest works. *B.O.M.B* is a different animal, in my opinion. After becoming a bit disappointed with the NYHC scene, we were then striving to achieve something new, something challenging, and something which leaned more toward the metal side of our musical spectrum. In the end, we made 2 very different albums. Considering that we unfortunately only made 2 albums, I can definitely appreciate such a contrast.

MM: As NYHC became a marketable musical force, did you get "head-hunted" by many labels before signing with Combat/ Rough Justice?

Gary - Yes, we did. I remember there being somewhat of an indie label feeding frenzy back then. Having said that, I suppose the last thing on our minds was the notion that somehow the band would get signed to a record label, especially with a name like "Crumbsuckers". However, as a result of an action packed gig at CBGS's one Sunday afternoon, we found ourselves being "courted" by at least 4 different labels. We eventually signed with Combat Records, and our debut album *Life Of Dreams* soon followed.

MM: Why has such an influential band stayed quiet for so long? There is a massive cult appreciation for the album *Life Of Dreams*; and *Beast On My Back* started to make good headway into the metal market...

Gary - After disbanding sometime in 1989, we decided to go our separate ways. I think we're all aware of what the band means to "x amount" of people and that there's somewhat of a demand for us to return in some way, shape, or form. The most recent reunion was in 2006, and it was great fun playing those old songs again with the guys. It was definitely something special, and I think the fans would agree. Will we do it again sometime? Who knows? I hope so.

MM: Why did the reformation and tour with The Accused fall apart? What really went down?

Gary - The Booking Agency (Metallysee) went "belly up" and the tour was abruptly cancelled. It took a lot of planning for us to be able to play a select number of dates, so it became next to impossible for us to re-group after that. We were very disappointed, as were the fans.

MM: What are your memories of the tour with UK thrashers Onslaught...

Gary - Great memories. Onslaught were more than kind to us, and they were spectacular on-stage every night of the tour. Great to see that they're still kickin' ass in 2014!

MM: The Crumbsuckers always had one foot in both the Hardcore and metal camps but aren't name checked as often as bands like Suicidal Tendencies, DRI, COC and Broken Bones etc. in terms of the development of Crossover; do you feel the band got it's dues?

Gary - Well, we never set out to change the world or to leave some sort of legacy behind. We were very passionate about our music, and we had quite a bit of integrity with regard to how we presented it to our fans. In the end, I'm not quite sure where we fit into the big picture or just how much Hardcore / crossover real estate we command. I think I can speak for all of us by saying that we're very proud of our accomplishments as a band, and that we're thrilled that people have such fond memories of us.

MM: What was the bands greatest achievement in your opinion?

Gary - In my opinion, our greatest achievement was our successful reunion concert at BB Kings NYC in 2006. After so many years apart, we sounded as if we were playing a Sunday Matinee at CBGB's back in 1986. Complete with guest appearances by Dave Brady and Dave Wynn! Magic!

MM: Has it surprised you that people around the world are still interested in the band after all these years?

Gary- Yes and no. I'm surprised sometimes because the band began with such humble aspirations, and so we never expected it to amount to anything more than killing time via having fun. Then, we eventually (and unfortunately) found ourselves going through some of the same trials and tribulations that most young signed artists go through, and suddenly the fun was gone. In retrospect, what we were able to achieve during our time together was achieved with honesty, creativity, and integrity (all of which have legs).

MM: Were you happy with the recent *Turn Back Time – The Early Years* release on FOAD records? How did that come about? Did it feel strange working with Dave Brady again after all these years?

Gary - I'm actually thrilled with it, and I think it's a very important addition to the bands catalogue (from an historical standpoint). Until this release, many Crumbsuckers fans were completely unaware that the band had a rich history within the NYHC scene years before *Life Of Dreams* was conceived. There were many pre-*LOD* songs which were quite celebrated in the scene but never had the benefit of making their way onto vinyl. *Turn Back Time / The Early Years* preserves our earliest works in one "Class A" package, thanks to Dave Brady and FOAD Records.

MM: Do you feel the band had more to give than just the two albums you released? Are there any 'lost' Crumbsuckers' recordings lurking in the background?

Gary - In retrospect, after *B.O.M.B.*, I think we had exhausted our resources as a unit. It seemed as if the band had split into opposing factions. We found ourselves arguing just for

the sake of the argument and no longer functioning as the band which fans got to know and appreciate. Hence, our time was simply up. As for "lost" recordings, unfortunately our creative cupboards are bare. .

MM: What are the ex-members all up to these days? Are any of you involved in any current bands?

Gary - I know that Chuck is still active in playing music to some degree. He plays in a band called Glitter Guns, as well as a couple of tribute bands (NIN, Bowie, etc.). Danny owns a transportation company in South Florida. Chris (from what I understand) is in the textile business and resides somewhere out on Long Island. I live in Sarasota Florida, and currently play in Pro-Pain, Darkhaus, and Salvation. As for the rest, I'm not quite sure exactly what they're up to these days, but I hope they're all doing fine.

MM: How did the band balance seemingly contradictory views such as those expressed on *The Longest War* and *Brainwashed*?

Gary - Different songwriters with somewhat different ideologies.

MM: *Hubrun* was originally titled *Jailbait* – is that the reason you didn't print the lyrics to them – replacing them with the word 'Irrelevant'?

Gary - From what I recall, Chris was fairly adamant about not wanting to sing *Hubrun* "as is" due to the lyrical content. It's a song about going on a journey to score weed. Simple enough, but Chris didn't want the song to represent him or his ideology at the time. The original title was indeed *Jailbait*, but that was well before LOD.

MM: Hardcore, metal, punk... where did the true sounds of the Crumbsuckers lay? Was it the cross-pollination that caused the band to split?

Gary - Hardcore, metal, punk, classic rock, jazz fusion, etc. We were all of those things in a blender, but we found it difficult to maintain. By the mid-late 80's, thrash became very popular (and tough to resist). It had the power to make followers out of once strong leaders.

MM: Are there any bands that were around 'back in the day' that have now really hung onto the roots whilst keeping going? And were any bands that should have carried on that didn't really off the starting line?

Gary - Agnostic Front and Sick Of It All are two fine examples of bands from "back in the day" that are still keeping it true. As for bands which should have stuck around longer: The Abused, Void, Negative Approach, Minor Threat, etc. All have gotten more popular in time, and two have had reunions in recent years (The Abused, NA).

MM: What are your favourite memories of being a part of Crumbsuckers?

Gary - All great memories: The house parties, gigs at CBGB's, A7, Right Track Inn, 1/2 Crown Pub, the US and Euro Tours, and the fans who made it all possible!

MM: Will there ever be another Crumbsuckers gig? Maybe even a tour? Or a record...?

Gary - We get asked those questions a lot, and we've had some pretty solid offers for gigs since the last reunion. At this time, I can't say with any confidence that the band will return, but it's certainly a nice thought!

Originally published in the Mass Movement Crossover Special, July 2014

ENGLISH DOGS

Remember I was telling you about that whole Crossover thing, and from what I was saying it would be all too easy to assume that it was a US based and centered movement. But, there were bands forging their own path, and finding their own way in the original Crossover movement, and right at the forefront were English Dogs, a band who I only discovered, and lost my teenage thrash mind to, after they'd crossed over. And now they're back with an incredible new record, *The Thing With Two Heads*, an album that once again reinvents and revitalizes Crossover. Ladies and gentlemen, boys and girls, it's time to meet the thrash powerhouse and crossover pioneers, it's time to meet the English Dogs...

Interview by Tim Cundle

Photographs – Trip / Punk Ass Photo's, Rosa Parabicoli

English Dogs are ; Adie Bailey – Vocals , Gizz Butt – Lead guitar , Ryan Christy – Rhythm guitar , Craig Christy – Bass guitar , Pinch – Drums

MM: Let's get the "burning issues" out of the way shall we? Why did the English Dogs split in the first place? What happened during the mid-nineties when you started playing and recording again? Why did you guys split again? And now the band is back together again, and ready to thrash with a new record… So what made you, Ade and Pinch realise that thrashing is what you guys do best, and finally get back together and start making music once more?

Gizz: In '86 there was a tense moment when things started to look shaky . We'd recently released *Metalmorphosis* and toured the USA to an amazing reaction . We returned home very positive with a plan to record a new album (*Where Legend Began*) when Jon Murray left the fold. It must have shaken Pinch as Jon was his closest ally. We came together as tightly knit as possible and rehearsed and wrote *Where Legend Began* like crazy. The studio experience wasn't inspiring though as we didn't have a producer or mentor as such so the results sonically were very weak and we felt we'd failed. The huge power in rehearsals had been reduced to a whimper. Dismayed and soon to be a father, Pinch left the band and the remaining 3 of us soldiered on with another drummer (Spike) but in Summer of '87 Adie left the band and things quite rightly came to a halt.

Me and Pinch and even Wattie did hook up a few times but it was in '89 or '90 that we seriously started to hang out together again. Then a surreal thing happened - Pinch moved to my hometown Peterborough with the full intention of starting a new band with me. Our friend Morat from the London punk scene encouraged us to reform the Dogs so we went for it, reaching out to Wattie, Jon and Wakey. One by one, those three dropped off and left us to find solutions eventually streamlining the band to a 3 piece (with me on vocals!!!!- check the album *All The World's A Rage*) when I got asked to join The Prodigy and the Dogs were once more put on hold. Pinch and myself (and bassist Shop) morphed into Janus Stark but as I toured the world with The Prodigy, mine and Pinch's relationship suffered (he even formed a band with Ross and Jock (From GBH) and Wakey with the intention of calling it English Dogs but settling on The Werent) when the whole picture came crashing down in late 99 with me and Pinch parting ways and The Prodigy handing me my P45 as well.

Pinch joined The Damned and I formed The More I See. In 2003 I was asked to regroup the

Dogs for a USA tour but seeing the impossibility of this I called together Spike, Shop and rhythm guitarist friend Gavin King (at that point he was in The More I See) and formed a group AtWar to play those shows playing *Forward Into Battle* material. A few weeks later Pinch toured the USA with The Weren't line up as The English Dogs!!!! In 2007 an avalanche of offers came in .The Fields of the Nephilim asked me to join, Steve Ignorant asked me to join him and Wakey called and asked me to reform the English Dogs with him!!!! This reunion request was sent out to all of us. I didn't know at that time what Pinch thought of the idea but after I emailed Jon Murray with the suggestion that we put together a "set to represent all eras" the reply was "We're not going to play any of the metal stuff so you're not needed"! How charming!

Two years later Wattie called me up. He was then the only original in a band of totally new guys (everyone else had left including Wakey) and asking me to join them. I was still interested in reforming the *Forward into Battle* line up and had an American agent interested if I could get it together and had reached out to Adie on Facebook. Wakey called me and announced that he had left the English Dogs and was "handing the baton to me" !!!! I wasn't sure how I was going to make this happen but I thought I'd try and organize some rehearsals with Adie , Wattie and a new guy he had playing with him called Nick (that Wattie insisted had to take Jon's place if he was to be involved). Me and Nick jammed together a few times but there was no hope in organizing Wattie. Wakey phoned me at this time and asked me to once again form an English Dogs line up with him and once again I told him I was only interested in a *Forward into Battle* line up! What do you know but a couple of weeks went by and I get a call from Nick saying that Wakey has called him and they will be forming a band together and calling it English Dogs! By this time the Steve Ignorant Last Supper tour was in full swing and I was busy but I warned Wakey that I had every intention of one day making the *Forward into Battle* tour a reality. Wakey warned "as long as you don't use the name English Dogs..." but I'd had enough of him and the people around him by this time. As far as I was concerned he didn't care about discrediting the name of the band obviously as he was running a band with only him in and a bunch of totally new outsiders. The time came around sure enough when me and Pinch were able to meet and discuss the concept in detail and that I had a USA agent interested . He thought about it for a couple of months and was up for the idea and had found two guys to take over Jon and Wattie (Jon was now suffering from health issues , sold his gear and pulled out of music altogether) and they were Ryan and Craig . Adie was already on board and we all started to get the songs together. Pinch began rehearsing with the twins in San Diego and Me and Adie rehearsed over in my studio and we would send the files back and forth and construct rehearsal tapes that way. When the tour came around we flew out early to rehearse in San Diego and the magic happened. That incredible moment when we struck into the opening album track. Sheer magic!!!!

Adie: I don't think it was ever a proper split it just seemed to be a gradual whittling away of the band. Jon left for personal reasons and I think things changed from then on and after that Pinch decided he had had enough. After that there seemed to be a lot of violence occurring at gigs and it became unbearable for me so I decided I was out too. It was nothing to do with any of the other guys, it was just a bad scene to be in at the time and I hated it. So off I went. I should let Gizz explain the mid-nineties stuff. I seem to remember the decision to record again, came one hazy night on the *Forward Into Battle US Tour* when we realised that people gave a fuck about us and when we returned home from that tour there were riffs and lyrics coming from both sides of the Atlantic and we realised we really had something, the result being *The Thing With Two Heads*.

MM: The other, uh, awkward question. Are there still two English Dogs line-up's? Wakey's lot and you chaps? If so, how does the whole thing work and how do you feel about the other line-up being out there?

Gizz: Look, our lineup has three original members from a successful English Dogs era that we are representing .We have 2/3 of the songwriting team and the chief lyricist. FACT: Pinch formed, named the band and played on every release, I played on every release except for two then the original lead singer forms a band with three totally new, unknown guys and calls it English Dogs. I would personally say that we have more right to the name. Even more so when you consider that we have legally registered it! For a while Wakey kept sending me hate text messages, beginning with threats and moving onto tales of my wife having an affair. It was a sad situation that clouded what was genuinely important that was going on at the time. Wakey texting me nonsense as my eldest brother was trying to reach out to me. My brother took his own life due to depression. And still the text messages came!!! None us need to take band wars as far as that. It's desperate.

Adie: It doesn't really matter to me. The two versions are a million miles apart musically they do what they do and we do what we do. We do not lie and we do not threaten. Make of that what you will.

MM: Let's talk about the new record, *The Thing With Two Heads*…. How do you get in the right frame of mind to write and record something that precise, musically versatile and aggressive? Was it difficult getting back into the English Dogs way of doing things, finding that sound again and writing the new songs given that you've all been playing in other bands and doing things, musically anyway, differently to how you used to in the 'Dogs? How did you get your 'bite' (groan, sorry, terrible pun) back?

Gizz: Well Pinch hasn't lost it has he because he's been keeping it up with The Damned. The album was beginning to get written when we were on the *FITB* tour .We talked about what we demanded of ourselves in between the gigs and started working on riffs there and then. I played a reunion show with my old punk metal band The Desecrators prior to the *FITB* tour and the rehearsing and preparation for that was great for getting back in the mode. I don't think Adie ever lost it one bit. He came to mine for rehearsals and belted out the loudest voice I'd ever heard. Who needs a PA? Even for Glastonbury!!!! Actually I think he's excelled himself on this new album.

MM: Do you want to run us through the songs, thematically, on the new record? What kind of subject matter have you pursued with each of the songs?

Gizz: *Turn Away From The Light*- Life is full of external influence. The only one that matters is inside yourself. Don't be led, be the leader.

Adie: *Turn Away From The Light* is kind of an anti-suicide song, the anguish and pain and contemplation.

Gizz: *Freak Boy*- Some people are only happy when they are in pain. Who are we to argue?

Adie: *Freak Boy* is about a person who is never happy unless he is unhappy and has to cut a smile into his face

Gizz: *Gorgonized* - Men and Women are different species. How else do you explain the effect they have on each other? *Hate Song* - You can only let someone abuse your friendship so many times before you have to cut them out of your life.

Adie: *Hate Song* speaks for itself and could be about anyone you like.

Gizz; *Ghost Note* - In a dog eat dog world, you have to be the one who bites first, but make sure you cover your tracks.
The Thing Will Arise - A story of evil conjoined twins taking different paths in life, but never able to escape each other. Or a story of a band with two careers that mirrors the twins.
Planet Of The Living Dead - Technology was supposed to free us, instead we are more isolated than ever. There will be a generation only communicating through technology, and it will happen in our lifetime.
Royal Flying Corpse is based on a saying "You die twice – once when you physically die and twice when your name is spoken for the final time" It goes out to the nameless soldiers and pilots of WW1 especially the ones who got killed first , with no glory not a single reward whatever that may be.
Rectify is based on Ouroboros and the eternal cycle and was dedicated to a dying cancer sufferer and the message was to give them hope that they are part of the eternal cycle and will not be forgotten.
Down With The Underdogs - The futility of achieving leadership over a broken people. Humans will only bend so far before they snap.

MM: You guys were there when the whole crossover "legend began' (I know, I know, another bloody awful pun. I should be shot...), so what were the early days of the whole crossover movement like? When did you first become aware that it was happening, that punk and hardcore bands were adopting a more technical and "musical" approach and metal bands were becoming more aggressive, faster and more socially and ethically conscious and aware? Did you have any idea that the scene you found yourselves in was going to change the face of aggressive music forever?

Gizz: There was a hell of a lot of punk bands in every town that were playing to a formula. Four chord riff sequences played four times in a verse, chorus, verse, chorus template. The same old chorus chants of anti this and that, four minute warnings and chaos. What I was doing was hardly any different but I was trying to squeeze licks and solos in every space I could! The heavy metal kids were never too far away and they dug what I was trying to do and I think that was going on in little pockets here and there. The Ruts notched everything up as they were much more progressive and talented than all the other Punk bands. They had complex arrangements and wild drum fills. The Damned released *Machine Gun Etiquette* and Motorhead exploded onto the scene and it seemed like the banks of a dam were breaking. I just did my thing. I wanted to play like Van Halen and Hendrix and I just made it work in the Punk format. Crass had the greatest, most vivid lyrics of everyone and even they showed a progressive side to their musicality with *Bloody Revolutions* and the entire mix just made perfect sense to me. When The Destructors split up I hooked up with a couple of other local guys Mark Massey and Tim Head that were digging their metal and called the band The Desecrators , but when metal drummer Scott White came into the mix we arranged and wrote everything so we had a full Punk Metal crossover set. This was early 1984 and when The English Dogs asked me to join them it must have been July or August so when I jammed with them for the first time I knew something was catching on.

Adie: Personally for me it just seemed to happen, we were listening to Discharge, GBH, Chaos UK etc. and we started hearing this new breed of band coming out of the States. We managed to get our hands on the *No Life Till Leather* demo by some up and coming band call Metallica. What was this? Was it a punk band playing metal riffs and solos or was it a metal band with a punk singer? Whatever it was, it definitely influenced us heavily and then along came Slayer, Exodus etc. and we loved it so I don't think we ever crossed over intentionally I think it just evolved in our music. It was refreshing and *To The Ends Of The Earth* was a great crossover record and that changed our direction.

MM: What's your favourite memory from the early days of crossover? What's the one story that whenever you think about it, always makes you smile, or even laugh?

Gizz: The 1985 USA tour was pure magic. One night at Fenders Ballroom in Longbeach it seemed like we were only down the road from where we had played at the Olympic auditorium like a week before and here we were again in front of 2000 people and it was nuts. D.I., who I was listening to at the time, were really kind and lent us all their gear as I believe this gig was a recent addition to the tour as no equipment had been arranged. Anyway, after all these great bands, we hit the stage to a hot bed from hell. The crowd were frenzied like nothing I'd ever before or since witnessed. Pinch was gasping for breath, and vomited over his drum kit. I jumped on and played *Free To Kill* which was insane because I'd only played drums when jamming with Scott in The Desecrators. The police came in afterwards to check if we were drinking because we were all underage and a lot of weed was going on but they didn't care about that. The people were really warm and kind to us. They looked after us. It was different because we weren't hanging out in bars but it felt good to be English and young and in America.

Adie: Ha, ha, when we were playing gigs and there seemed to be a lot more hair and denim appearing alongside the studs and Mohicans. Which was never a problem for us.

MM: When you guys started "crossing over", how did the UK punk scene originally react to what you were doing and the bands "new" musical direction? Some of those mid-eighties punk and HC shows were a little, uh," rough" for, and on, us young metal-heads...

Gizz: Conflict wrote a song about us *Metal Mania* which some punks used as a way of creating a divide. We didn't feel like we strayed too far off the path with *Forward into Battle*. I don't think anyone else did either really at first. The gigs were a perfect mix of Punks and Metallers with London, Leeds and Birmingham being the peak cities where it was going down the best. Then the violence came. We noticed it in Nottingham, Leicester and Pinch's home of Grantham. Even Adie was attacked when we played one of our usual slots at the 100 club. Maybe it was a one off, but it was ruining the punk scene. Metal gigs didn't have any of that shit going on.

Adie: It changed, I remember doing my first shows with the band just after the release of *To The Ends Of The Earth* and it was still a totally punk audience and they got very chaotic, a lot of stage diving and it was great. After *Forward Into Battle*, especially after the US tour, it became a more metal crowd and mosh pits were appearing. I really don't think the English punk crowd received it very well.

MM: What's changed? What, in your opinion, are the major differences between the modern crossover scene and the original eighties movement? Have things changed for the better or worse? Why?

Gizz: There was an underlying current of violence in the UK scene in the 80's which I feel isn't the same anymore. That's not to say it doesn't happen ever but back then it was bloody ridiculous. I've been to lots of UK shows such as Toxic Holocaust and Havok both at the Camden Underworld and going by that and our FITB tour I would say the violent element has calmed down. Good riddance!

Adie: It is a lot better these days. I think more people are open minded about it. A lot more people embrace the fact that really, HC, Punk and Thrash metal are not that far apart and you can see that in the audiences these days.

MM: After more than a quarter of a century, how do you feel about *To The Ends.., Forward.., Where Legend...* and *Metalmorphosis* now? How do you think they've stood, and stand, the test of time?

Gizz: Through the 90's period English Dogs period I couldn't resist constantly coming back to *FITB* and *TTEOTE* and pulling a song or two off them. I was in denial and then one day I woke up and smelt the coffee..."These are awesome!" Every song on these two releases is a winner! *Forward Into Battle* will always be my favourite for many reasons. There's a moment just after the intro song *Forward Into Battle* into the opening chords of *The Final Conquest* when Pinch powers through those trademark drum fills and the fast tempo snaps in .The circle pit was INVENTED for that very moment!! The blend is perfect in that record. Of course we can play it better now and our gear is a higher standard but that was a special thing we did back then and when I see the love from people in the audience the world just gets better. It's good to know that there are many friends out there and a lot of love for the band.

Adie: Oh yeah for sure. *To The Ends Of The Earth* and *F.I.B* certainly do for me. They were the two records that changed things, They are still very listenable. Very proud of those records.

MM: I heard a story a while back about copyrighting the band's that is the English Dogs, name, and why it can't be done because of an issue with the monarchy and have never been sure if it's true or the stuff of urban legend. So, is it true? Can you not legally copyright the band's name because of the Queen, and if so, can you share the story of how you found out with us, or is it just a load of old bloody nonsense?

Gizz: There is no problem with registering the band name because we've done it but if we wanted to register the name at companies' house then we would come against that problem. Also I think the name was registered many years ago by a dog breeder! You will come up with opposition registering any name like that. The same happens with the word "Royal" and other similar. I do recall it was linked with Monarchy and old laws. There really is some truth in it!

MM: What's your favourite English Dogs story? Every band has one, one that they tell late at night when the last drinks are being served and the lights are dim... Come on Gizz; tell us the English Dogs story...

Gizz: There's a few late night drunken tales to tell but I always enjoy telling people that Metallica phoned us up from the MFN offices as we were about to finish a day of recording on the *Where Legend Began* sessions and we arranged a meeting down the local pub and went back to their hotel . James was listing all the songs of ours he liked, Kirk was laughing at this hilarious pic of us in Kerrang that had us sticking our head through cuts made in a huge roll of red paper, they played us a cassette of Spastik Children and we showed Cliff Burton this mad trick where we pushed down on his head while counting to a hundred and then lifting him to the ceiling with one finger each. It's one of those mad "mind over matter" levitation tricks. Cliff bumped his head on the ceiling and we were all in stitches. Then there was the gig where Stuart West who was playing bass in the Dogs in the 90's, did a dump in a butter dish and placed it amongst the buffet. It was great watching people pick from the buffet and stare at this turd in disbelief. They were literally thinking "That cannot be what I think it is ..." and we are like "Yes it is!!!!"

Adie: There is a story that involves a hotel cleaning lady in America, buts that's all I'm saying.

MM: You're all in different bands as well as the English Dogs, so do you want to tell all the folks out there what you chaps get up to when you're not crossing over and thrashing out with the English Dogs?

Gizz: I have a band called The More I See, we're signed to Earache Records and we're currently on our fourth album titled *The Disappearing Humans*. We have three official singles up on YouTube for you to view, the latest one being *The Eye That Offends* which was filmed on the set of Star Wars in Tunisia which was a very unique experience. We're touring the UK in November 2014.

Pinch has The Damned of course who never cease in their popularity and they are always touring Ryan and Craig are in a band called ….wait for it - The Thing With Two Heads. That should tell you a thing or two.

MM: One for you Gizz and I have to know. Will Wardance and The Desecrators ever get back together again, will their records ever see the light of day on CD and will you ever write and record more music with either, or both bands?

Gizz: I get asked regularly about whether I would consider re-recording the Wardance material and it is possible. If I was going to do it though I would be with The More I See guys (James, Drew and Harri) as it would be an utter logistic nightmare to do such a project with the original guys. Not so the same with The Desecrators who reunited in 2011 and played a fantastic show. I'd be up for another gig with them, why not? I wouldn't want new writing or recording. Just a bit of live fun with old mates.

MM: What are your touring plans for the English Dogs? Your schedules must be a blooming nightmare to work around and out given your other commitments, so will there be a tour or two? What's next for the English Dogs?

Gizz: TOURING, I CANNOT WAIT!!!!! Beginning with the USA. I cannot tell you how hungry we are for this. Ready? You cannot be readier!

Adie: Well once the album is out and other commitments are sorted, then yes, we will be looking to tour and are looking to play anywhere in the world that will have us, including the UK

Originally published in the Mass Movement Crossover Special, July 2014

EXCEL

Excel is back! These three words will have many old school punks and metal heads jumping for joy. The history of the band, from their humble beginnings with a few demos and tracks on the illustrious *Welcome To Venice* compilation, to their untimely demise has been well documented over the past two decades. What's more important now, is that the book of Excel has been reopened with another chapter, yet to be written, about to begin. Debut album *Split Image* will get an amazing reissue to get that circle pit, Venice-style, going again. MM caught up with bass player Shaun Ross, and got the in's and out's about, and the lowdown on, Excel in 2014.

Interview by Martijn Welzen

MM: Southern Lord are about reissue *Split Image*, the previous reissue of which was on Rotten Records which was released in 2000. Why is it time to give it another release?

SR: Our contract with Rotten Records had long expired and *Split Image* had not been released on vinyl since 1987. With vinyl becoming such a popular format again in recent years, we felt that it was long overdue.

MM: Will this version be different from the one Rotten Records did? And, will *The Joke's On You* also get a proper overhaul?

SR: Yes, it's very different. Even though a new CD version will be available, this Southern Lord release of *Split Image* will be emphasizing the vinyl reissue. Southern Lord has spared no expense in the packaging, it has good amount of new material, and it'll be priced very reasonably. We'll be following up the release with live shows too, which we didn't in 2000. And yes, *The Joke's On You* is next.

MM: Feels like this time around, you're much more involved with the reissue. Didn't things works out as well with the 2000 version?

SR: It's been great working with Greg Anderson at Southern Lord, he let's us be as involved as we want to be. We've worked together producing the definitive version of this release. The 2000 CD version was fine, at that point it had been unreleased for 13 years and it served its purpose. 14 years later, we've decided to reissue it again, this time on vinyl too.

MM: Very often your hear about bands having problems getting the rights to their own music back for a reissue on another label. Seems like you have the copyright thing firmly in hand, right? And the new reissue will also be done from the original tapes?

SR: Like I said previous contract had long expired which allowed us to move forward and sign with Southern Lord. Yes, the upcoming Southern Lord reissue of *Split Image* has been remastered from the master tapes. We just received the vinyl test presses, it sounds really good!

MM: Can we also expect some extra surprises and bonuese? I read that you'll be releasing the *Personal Onslaught* demo on tape again, that will, unlike the previous reissue, also have a vinyl version. Will the latter also include all the bonus tracks?

SR: Yes, it'll include 2 LP's, a 7" (first 1000 copies), a gatefold cover with unseen alternative cover art, 34 page booklet, 11x17 poster of the complete Michael Seiff artwork. That contains the *Split Image* LP, *Sonic Decapitation*, *Personal Onslaught* and *Refuse To Quit* demos as well as the *Welcome To Venice* and Thrasher Skate Rock comp tracks. There's 5 alternative versions of different songs that have unavailable since the mid 80's. Only the first 1000 vinyl copies will include everything and then it will be all available digitally.

MM: And what about *Seeking Refuge,* the record that is often overlooked? Will that ever see the light of day, again?

SR: We're not planning on reissuing it. If there was a demand, maybe. We're basing our reunion on how we started in the beginning, as a metallic hardcore punk band. We enjoy playing our original style that we're best known for the most.

MM: Now that the release, of *Split Image*, is upon us, have you also revisited the album? How do you personally think the songs have stood the test of time? Will the sound of the reissue be tweaked a little to match today's standards?

SR: We started writing *Split Image* in 1985 so some of the material and the recording style is bound to sound dated in 2014, I think it represents that era well though. The producer of *Split Image,* Randy Burns, produced some classic LP's of that era (First S.T., *Seven Churches, Scream Bloody Gore, Peace Sells* etc.). It's definitely in his style of production. It's been remastered to today's standards and when playing the songs live now, we're able to modernize them some by how we play them.

MM: You've played again in New York recently. Does that mean you're actually a band again? Can we expect (extensive) touring and possibly even new music? Did you also put the focus of your set list on *Split Image*?

SR: Yes, we just played NYC, we've played two smaller warm-up shows in L.A and we'll be going to Sao Paulo, Brazil for the first time this October. We' re a band again. As much as we'd like to tour extensively, we have more responsibilities then we did when we were younger. If there's a demand for us to play somewhere, we'll do our best to get there. We're looking to book more shows for 2015. We're also working on new material with the new line-up as well. As You can see most of our live set now is from the *Split Image* LP with a few songs from *The Joke's On You*.

MM: Who is currently in the band, and was it easy getting the band back together again? Were you all equally as excited, and who's idea was it originally?

SR: The current line-up is Dan Clements (vocals), Alex Barreto (guitar), Mike Cosgrove (drums) and myself on bass. We're all really excited to be playing these songs live again. We grew up writing and playing this music so when we're not, it feels like something's missing. It was Alex's idea. Alex Barreto (Hard Stance, Chain Of Strength, Inside Out, Statue etc.) contacted me in 2011 and brought me out of 'retirement' for a HC project he had called Fraud. I had met Alex a few times in the 80's and we'd been familiar with each other for years. When we couldn't put together a solid line up for Fraud, Alex had the idea to putting together an Excel jam to see how it went. It went really well and we've working on rebuilding the band since.

MM: How does it feel knowing that your first two albums, are now considered true classics of the genre, while in the '90s they didn't really get the praise they deserved?

SR: It's really cool if some consider our albums classic. We were just 80's latch key kids in a bedroom trying to write the best music we could, we had no idea we'd being having this conversation in 2014. There are albums that I have listened to religiously for 20-30 years, so I can totally appreciate if there's people who feel that way about Excel. We don't think that our first two albums were under appreciated, things changed in the 90's and the change wasn't in our favor. We're really happy that our first two albums are being reissued now in a time when fast, heavy music is here to stay. If we want to release a proper follow up to *The Joke's On You* now, we still can.

MM: Thrash and crossover are both in the spotlight again, and so many bands cite 'the Venice Sound' as an influence. How does that make you feel? Did you ever feel you were creating something special at the time?

SR: It's an honor to have had an influence on anyone with what we've done in the past. It's really cool how these genres have grown over the years. Not just crossover, there's so many different sects of punk, thrash, HC etc and a lot of really good bands. It makes coming back challenging, to remain relevant and interesting to the newer generations. At the time, we were just living for the moment. Being a little kid going to early 80's punk shows, I do remember thinking that it was cool that we finally had a scene to call our own. I think that there's many aspects of the mid to late 80's punk, thrash, HC scene that are considered influential now, it's really cool to look back and to know that Excel was able to be a part that era.

MM: Are there also any new(ish) bands playing crossover that you follow? Or have you wandered into other musical-territories over the years?

SR: Yes, some of the newer bands that I like are Antichrist, Infernöh, Herätys, Green Beret, Paranoid, Power Trip, Martyrdöd and Think Again. They're not necessarily 'crossover' bands but still punk, thrash, HC etc. We still listen to all the bands that we've always considered 'classics' as well.

MM: Does the 'Venice-scene' actually still exist? It was always about you guys, Suicidal and Beowulf... and maybe No Mercy. Are you all on speaking terms, or have you lost contact now that many have also left Venice, even to other parts of the world?

SR: A Venice scene still does exist, I don't know too much about it now. Dan has lived there his whole life, he was the only member of Excel from Venice. Mike Muir put Excel on the *Welcome To Venice* comp and then helped produce our first LP. We played a handful of shows with the bands from the Venice scene but we were able to become an independent band, doing our own thing, pretty early on.

I've been in contact with a few guys from those bands recently because we're working on a documentary about the artist Ric Clayton for the Museum of Contemporary Art. Ric was the bassist of No Mercy and has done quite a bit of of influential art for all of the bands you've mentioned. Last year we put together Ric's first solo art exhibit here in Los Angeles.

MM: When looking back towards 1983 / 1984 what was so special about that time, and especially about Venice? How did that typically hardcore, yet incredibly groove laden, sound come about. It was totally different from what Bad Religion where doing at almost the same time, not that far away...

SR: 1983/1984 was time special time for us because that's when a lot of the punk bands that were influential to us were active, putting out albums and playing shows in Los Angeles. Bands like Discharge, Crucifix, GBH, BGK, Jerry's Kids, SS Decontrol, 7 Seconds, Stalag 13 and Necros. Then in late 1984, early 1985 we were exposed to metal bands like Slayer, Trouble, Exodus, Death and Possessed. All of that had a major impact on Excel's direction. As much as we were influenced by these bands, we wanted to be as original as possible. We always tried to mix slow, mid tempo and fast riffs within songs with unpredictable time changes the best we could. That's how our sound came about.

MM: I often wondered what influence skateboarding, and possibly surfing, had on the music. Did that influence the groove or rhythm in some way?

SR: In 1979 my father and I started skating regularly at the Marina Del Rey Skatepark, I was 9. This was the home of the Z Boys. This is where I first met Dan. It was a very special time and place for us that we still hold in high regard. This era and skateboarding in general heavily influenced us as individuals and as the band. that we became.

MM: As with all different genres in the hardcore, metal, punk realm, the pure, youthful, energy is very important. Isn't it hard keeping up that energy so many years down the line?

SR: The energy is very important to us. It's not that hard for us, we all keep a pretty active lifestyle and we enjoy doing this. We give it our all when we play live.

MM: The original *Split Image* release was in 1987, the Rotten reissue in 2000, the Southern Lord one in 2014. Where do you see the legacy of Excel 14 years from now? How long does music have to be around, you think, to truely be called 'timeless'?

SR: It's hard to say if Excel will be considered 'timeless'. I think the era that we represent will always be recognized to some degree and it would be cool to be a part of that history.

Originally published in the Mass Movement Crossover Special, July 2014

LUDICHRIST

If I was forced to pinpoint one band that epitomized Crossover, it would be Ludichrist. They were a thrash tour de force, a Hardcore powerhouse and a band who weren't afraid to experiment with hip hop and jazz, incorporating both into their songs with a fluid ease that left their contemporaries floundering in their wake. Following their reunion shows at Black'N'Blue Bowl in New York, MM finally managed to corner front-man Tommy Christ for a long overdue chat about the Crossover champions…

Interview by Tim Cundle, Tom Chapman, Ian Pickens & Mark Freebase

MM: All things have a beginning, a middle and an end, so let's start at the beginning… When, where and why did Ludichrist get together and first become a band.

Tommy: I was jamming in a band with a few friends. We rehearsed in the back of some haircutting place. I met Al and Mark there. They were working on a couple of projects. One was a melodic hardcore thing, and the other was the heavier Ludichrist thing. Their melodic singer wouldn't work for the Ludichrist material, so I joined up with them.

MM: What were the early days of the band like? Stylistically, like the Crumbsuckers, you guys were pretty far removed from the established NYHC sound and attitude. So, how difficult was it, establishing yourselves in the NY scene, getting shows and getting your name out there…?

Tommy: It actually wasn't difficult, but it did take a lot of hard work and some time. We played some crappy shows on Long Island for a while, at one of which we met Glen, and he joined the band. Once we recorded our demo, things picked up a lot. It was selling in local record stores, getting good reviews in zines, and it got our foot in the door for our first CBGB hardcore matinee.

MM: Talking of which, the band's name, Ludichrist, I've always assumed that it was a play on words that combined Ludicrous with Christ, and that the later part of the name came directly from you. Is that true, or just a wild guess…? How did you end up being called, and becoming known as, Tommy Christ? And which religious moniker came first, yours or the bands?

Tommy: Al and Mark went to Catholic school together. They had the name Ludichrist picked before I hooked up with them. When I picked a name for myself, I took my name from the band name in a moment of Ramones-esque inspiration.

MM: What do you remember most about the very early days of the band? Any favourite or funny stories from that time that you can share with us so that all the folks out there can maybe get an idea of what Ludichrist was like in the beginning….?

Tommy: Unfortunately my memory sucks. Some images from the early days…Writing in in Al's basement at the very beginning. Playing a gig with Horror Planet (great band) and stealing Glen from them. Playing our first show outside the NY area at a karate studio in South Carolina. Playing the basement at the old Anthrax in Connecticut. The beginning was pretty cool. Just trying to write, record, get our demo out there and get shows.

MM: How did you guys end up signing up with Combat Core / Combat? They were pretty big players in the scene at the time, and I wondered if signing with the label, helped raise the bands profile? Was it all sweetness and roses with the label, or were there rough times as well?

Tommy: It raised our profile a lot. It got us recognition throughout the US and Europe. We were able to tour extensively in both places. Our demo was good. It got Hilly at CBGBs to get us to do one of their live *Off the Board* albums, and it also got us signed to Combat. Overall the experience was good. Was a little rough at the beginning. A guy named Steve Sinclair signed us. He was okay, I guess. But money was tight and it was hard to get them to do a lot. We did work with some really good people there too. Eventually Howie Abrams was doing a lot there, and he was great.

MM: Lyrically, you used a lot of satire and humour in order to try and emphasize and exaggerate the subjects you were focusing on (*Government Kids*, *Young, White and Well Behaved*, *Blown Into The Arms Of Christ* etc.), and it always made your lyrics stand out for me. While other bands were being deadly serious, there was this imaginary wink and a sly grin behind your songs... I guess what I'm trying to say is, did you do this on purpose and how important was, and is, a sense of humour to the band and to you as an individual? Do you think music as a whole is too serious? Why?

Tommy: Too me, a lot of Hardcore lyrics were too heavy handed. Al had written the lyrics to a couple of the early songs, like Big Business. I was more into saying something, through storytelling, or satire or both. It's just more interesting to me that way, and it's better than being clubbed over the head with a message. I was really into Kurt Vonnegut at the time, and I think that inspiration showed in songs like *Zad*.

MM: Whose idea was The Monkees cover? What made you guys originally start playing it and did, and do, you play any other covers.

Tommy: I don't remember whose idea it was. We did a few covers. I think Johnny B Goode we did live. I can't remember what else. Once we became Scatterbrain, we did tons of covers live.

MM: How did the whole *You Can't Have Fun* thing come together, how easy was it to get Eddie, John, Roger and Chris into the studio with you and what do you remember most about recording the song?

Tommy: We were friends with all of them. I thought it would be cool to have "guest stars" on a song. I basically remember being in the room with them telling them what to do, which took about two minutes. I also remember all of us in the room with tons of other people recording the background vocals. Sorry, no cool story's I'm afraid...

MM: I have to ask about Chuck Valle. He's one of those guys that people still talk about and no-one has a bad word to say about him. What was he like? Chuck's senseless death hit a of people hard, and I'm guessing it had a profound effect on you guys as well, and I've always wondered if, even though he wasn't in the band at the time, if his passing was one of the reasons why you guys didn't get back together before your reunion shows in 2007...?

Tommy: He had been out of the band for a while when he was murdered. Chuck was a great guy. One of those kind of guys that got along with everyone. We saw each other every now and then after he left the band, and we were glad to see each other and always had a good time. I can't say that about some other ex-members. His death didn't have anything to do with us playing or not playing reunion shows though. I had no interest in playing any shows, until I saw the Crumbsuckers reunion. It was great and it got me psyched to do one.

MM: Were you aware that you helped pioneer and were one of the spearhead bands of the Crossover movement when you started playing, or did that realization hit you later? Why do you think the whole crossover thing fizzled out only to remerge nearly twenty years later? And... What do you think of the new breed of crossover bands? They in the same league as the pioneers, or are they still playing in the minor leagues?

Tommy: I think we realized we were different than a regular hardcore band. Don't think we were conscious of spearheading any crossover thing. I think we were conscious of doing something new by adding rap, jazz, classical music, etc. to our sound. I don't listen to too much new hardcore music. Like anything else, some are good at it, and some aren't.

MM: How do you think the band changed, as far as musical, personal and professional levels are concerned, between *Immaculate Deception* and *Powertrip*?

Tommy: It changed in two ways. First, the talent level increased dramatically. Paul is a great guitar player, and Dave is a ridiculously excellent drummer. So, our capabilities to play different things in different ways expanded greatly. Second, it brought in new influences, which became our writing. For example, Dave was into progressive rock. Stuff like the Dixie Dregs, while Paul brought in some classical training, along with classic rock and guitar virtuoso stuff.

MM: Do you feel that Ludichrist got its due credit for the part they played in helping establish and develop crossover? Not just in terms of metal and hardcore, but also the way you incorporated jazz and hip-hop into your music? Or do you think the band was side-lined by history...

Tommy: We were probably sidelined. Not sure why. We didn't look hardcore. We didn't look metal. We were from Long Island instead of New York City. Our lyrics were weird. Our music was different. Who knows?

MM: What do you remember most about your original, and first, European tour? Do you remember the bands you played with or any of the shows in particular?

Tommy: I don't know if it was our first tour, or if I'm mixing up tours, but some things I remember from the early days. Playing with Erosion. Very cool guys who made fun of American beer, calling it "chemical wasser". And they were right, but If I could see them now, I'd tell them that today's American beer kicks German beer's ass! I remember staying at the squats along the Berlin Wall. Totally cool experience. I remember being taken to an Italian

prison under the cover of machine guns, because they thought we were terrorists. I remember how amazed I was that the kids were so aware of important issues and how political they were. I remember playing a show in Germany when in the middle of one of our songs, the WHOLE place cleared out. It turned out they all went to chase some Nazi skins out of town. I remember the Stegmund Void's Austrian Eye Flick. And I have images of some totally cool people we met, hung out with, stayed with, and got to know. It was a really great experience.

MM: How did Ludichrist end up becoming Scatterbrain? Do you think there was a movement of bands branching out and doing the same thing at the time, like 24-7 Spyz, Murphy's Law, Token Entry (to a lesser extent) etc.?

Tommy: We weren't sounding like Ludichrist anymore. The new stuff we were writing was getting farther away from hardcore and metal. You could kind of see the beginnings of that with a song like *This Party Sucks* on the *Powertrip* album. Plus we had two new guys in the band (Guy Brogna and Mike Boyko) It felt like a new band, so we made the switch. I don't think it was part of a movement. For us, it felt like a natural progression. I'm sure we alienated a bunch of Ludichrist fans with the switch.

MM: And going full circle, how did you, personally, first become involved in the NYHC scene and what initially attracted you to it? Are you still a part of the scene, or do you still think of yourself as being a part of it? Or have times changed, and have you moved on? And if so, what changed and why did you move on?

Tommy: First, I fell in love with the music. In high school I was into bands like Hot Tuna and the Grateful Dead. I also liked heavier rock and some metal. After high school, someone turned me on to some college station in Florida, where I was living for a couple of years. First hardcore band I heard was the Dead Kennedys. I loved the aggression, anger and intelligence. For a kid who grew up on classic rock, finding out you could write songs about hanging your landlord was a revelation. Once I moved back to New York, I started going to shows. That was the second thing that made me fall in love with the scene. Small, intimate shows where the bands hung out with the kids and loaded their own equipment and shit like that. I still go to shows sometimes, but can't really say I'm a part of the scene. I go to see bands I like and hang out.

MM: What's the state of play with Ludichrist after Black'N'Blue Bowl? Is there going to be a tour? And, is there a slim chance, a remote possibility that you guys might even make a new record...?

Tommy: We've been playing a couple of shows a year for the past couple of years. Doubt there is a tour in our future. Maybe a week long thing on the East Coast here or a week or so in Europe, but only if someone/a promoter pursues us. We're not averse to playing, but none of us seem motivated enough to do the work of organizing it! We've been talking about writing, but haven't done anything about it. Seriously doubt we'd do an album. A digital download or two, or an EP might be in our future at some point, but don't hold your breath.

Originally published in the Mass Movement Crossover Special, July 2014

ROTTING OUT

Being an old school guy, there aren't that many newer bands that I'm inclined to get behind, maybe it's because I'm jaded, cynical or maybe it's because part of me thinks that I've seen it all before. Or maybe it's because they lack creativity, originality, passion and energy. Whatever the reason, it just feels like a lot of new bands don't have the same drive that used to be such an important ingredient of and driving force behind the scene.

So, when a band seemingly appears out of the blue and completely blows my mind, for me, it's a big deal. Rotting Out are one of those bands, and they did exactly that, they fried my brain with their hard as nails, catchy as hell Venice inspired HC that's part Suicidal Tendencies and part Pennywise.

They're an insane ball of energy, fury, passion, anger with songs that make you want to sing-a-long and slam your guts out, and they're the best damn thing to emerge from the LA underground in a long time. I shit you not. I caught up with singer Walter Delgado (who is one of the friendliest, most open, honest and sincere guys I've had the honour of interviewing) for a chat about punk rock, Los Angeles and Rotting Out...

Interview by Tim Cundle

MM: So I guess the best place to start is the beginning: when where and why did you guys get together?

WD: The band got together in around 2007. We're from a place in Los Angeles called San Pedro, it's just by the harbour. It's kind of a ghetto at the bottom of the hill there, then as you go up the hill it's kind of middle class then up at the top its upper class and all that good stuff. We all got tired of hearing bands that weren't really appealing to us at that time, so we thought let's put something together that sounded like stuff we grew up listening to Black Flag, Suicidal Tendencies and stuff like that - something that would sound a bit like what we really admired, with that grit and tone to it as it did then, when I was about seven. There were the five of us some of us were from the Valley and some of us from Compton. We all met each other through shows.

MM: Is there any significance to the band's name; it sort of has a death metal ring to it?

WD: Rotting out? We were very, very – being from California, from the west coast of America – we were very proud of the bands that came out in the run up to our adolescence like Black Flag, Circle Jerks, the list goes on – Dead Kennedys and all that good stuff – but we were looking for a band name that would remind people of the West Coast. So we were looking through the band the Descendents and we noticed Rotting Out, and it sounded kind of poppy and very much the kind of attitude that we were looking for so we thought let's go with that. So we were pretty much named after the Descendents' song.

MM: To me you guys sound like a glorious old school collision of Suicidal Tendencies, a bit of Excel with a bit of Beowulf thrown in..

WD: Oh yeah. A lot of Suicidal Tendencies. That was pretty much our much our major influence, in the era of the self-titled album and the *Freedumb* album. Those two records from the '80s and '90s were pretty much our two big inspirations in staring this band.

MM: You've got that sort of Venice Beach thing going on.. I mentioned Excel and Beowulf and No Mercy; it's nice to hear that style again…

WD: You mean that whole Venice attitude? When we first got started people would give us shit for wearing our own merch... People would say it was so arrogant and snobby; but when we grew up we were watching bands that were doing that all the time, Suicidal would do it, Pennywise would do that, people in No Mercy or Black Flag would do that and these were bands we grew up with and thought were cool. This is what we wanted to be like. We wanted to keep it like what we loved when we were kids. Eventually though everyone in the scene started doing it as well, which was pretty awesome and makes you proud of what you do. So the attitude had a big influence on the way we write and kind of the style that comes with the band, from the sound to the way we present ourselves as a band.

MM: You seem to wear your heart on your sleeves in your songs, almost like they're a cathartic release. Some of the lyrical subjects you pursue… Drug addiction in *One More Kiss*, gang culture in *Stabbed*, the search for identity with *No Clue*… Do you find it helps, sharing your emotions through the lyrics?

WD: Absolutely. Everything I've written has been because I have to get it out because it's too emotionally exhausting to think about and handle. Not once did I ever write a song where I tell people what they should be doing or what I think people should do with their lives, that's not our place. But every song that we've written is a true story, something that's happened in my life. I feel that reality has nourished me and whatever has happened in my life, it's something I can learn from and grow from to make things better. So everything I've written has been about a relative or a friend, a situation I've been in and didn't know who to handle like *Stabbed*.

People will hear *Stabbed* and think "Who's stabbing his father?" – No, not necessarily. That was a position I was put in and the whole message of the song was my mother looking at me like I was my father. That song was me turning into my old man, turning to violence; becoming the worst to defeat the worst. At a young age you don't understand anything but survival; things like self-control and being the higher person, more level headed didn't concern me so I did those actions. Finally my mother would look at me like I was a disappointment being like him. It was like: "Look what he did to you, what he turned you into". You don't understand those things when you're a kid. It's when you get older and you think like "I should have held back, I should have done something else" but what can you do in that situation? What would you do if that were you? When you're in that situation you don't really know how to accept your emotions; they are so fresh and so new. It's so scary sometimes that you don't know how to react, so you just really have instinct and most of the time that's violence.

The song *One More Kiss* that was about my father's addiction to drugs; how he just threw away his whole family, his children. How he didn't realise the sacrifices until it was too late. He would lie to himself so much until he was sent to jail and he couldn't lie to himself any more. He had to face up to the mistakes he had made, and all too often we don't realise those mistakes until it's far too late. It's not saying this person was wrong or what's right or what's wrong. I just tell it like it is. These things happen. These are everyday people just like us.

MM: I wanted to ask you about *Verbal Risk*. What's the song about? And have you thought about singing en Espanol more often? Spanish always seems like a much more emotive and demonstrable language and as such, much more suited to punk rock and Hardcore…

WD: Yeah. *Verbal Risk* was… When I was growing up, any time an adult, my mother – let's be clear I come from a Mexican community, I was born in a Mexican community – so whenever any parent would get mad, they would turn to their native language. They would always yell at you in their first language. They would always shout "What are you doing? Wait till you get home, you're in real trouble" and I always thought these were real words, genuine words, whether it was anger or love, they were so mad they had to resort to not even caring if you could understand them it was just the only way of getting it out.

I kind of thought about that when I was writing this song. The song is mostly about people who think they can their mouths and say whatever they want saying that 'opinion is opinion' when that isn't the case, sometimes opinion is more like insults and dragging peoples' names through the mud. There are repercussions for what you do and what you say; remember that. You are responsible for what you say whether it's online, in person, on stage, in the back of the room where no-one can hear you. You are responsible for what you say whether you think you're right or wrong, you're responsible.

MM: Do you think you'll write more (songs) in Spanish?

WD: I pick and choose. Whether it will be just a line or two or a whole song it will depend on whether it sounds right and feels right. I never try to force anything into a song, that way I will end up hating the song and we'll end up having to re-do it. Usually it's just on a whim whether I think it will sound better or more powerful in Spanish.

MM: How do you think the band's grown between *Street Prowl* and *The Wrong Way*?

WD: *Street Prowl* was scary actually. We had never released before, so we were like "Oh man, I hope we have one or two songs that people like. At the time we had literally written the whole record and our singer at the time he left, he just left and we suddenly had no lyrics. I was playing bass at the time but we thought that we ought to keep it just between us so I had a go at writing some lyrics but I had no idea of what I was doing. I'd never really written lyrics from my own perspective so we were very much feeling our way and working out what works and what sounds good. Some of the better songs were ones that were written so last minute that we thought they would never make it onto the album, but when we played them people liked them and we kept them for the record. It was a very amateur attitude.

Then when it came to *The Wrong Way*, it was very different. We knew what we were doing and what we wanted from the record so we knew where to focus and how to write. I was a lot more confident, my voice was a lot stronger; it was beefed up, it was a lot fuller a lot grimier and stronger than on the first record and I thought it sounded better. So I was quite pleased with that. I felt like that was what I'd been looking for the whole time. I knew how to control my voice, how to yell longer and harder and which key to do it in.

MM: Keith Morris once sang about being a product of his environment; how much influence do you think Los Angeles has had on you as a band?

WD: Oh it's absolute. Everything we are is because of Los Angeles. A lot of people don't like LA, it's like an attitude, there's a lot of attitude, a lot of lip you get a lot of glares and stares. Because most people will know that it's usually where you're at rather than where you're from. Even if you're from Los Angeles. I always just liked that. It keeps you on your toes, very sharp all the time. When people come here they want to go to Hollywood, they want to go to Beverley hills and they want to do it comfortably. When you're born here you tend to like it more, to appreciate that attitude. These things are just so organic to the city that it just kind of grows and grows to itself and that attitude will save you. Even the violent stuff.

I'm definitely a product of my environment, grew up in the projects. I saw people shot and just die right there in front of me, and I couldn't go to school because my front porch is a crime scene you know? Things like I can't ...At first, the first time it was like "Holy shit I never heard of this happening; I've seen it in movies but I've never heard of it in life. That was in my face. I've seen someone overdosing, I've stumbled across dead bodies in the street. One thing that happens in LA is there are car accidents all the time and you see this body just mangled from a semi. It becomes everyday life. Not because it's okay, just that these are my surroundings and this is what, over time makes you a little bit more numb to the crazier things in life.

I got stabbed when I was 18 – you might think wow, I've never been stabbed in my whole life that must be crazy – but you know what, it sucked. You can't go round complaining like, that you had it so bad or whatever, this is where I'm from, this why I am who I am. This is why our sound is the way it is because of who we are, where we've come from, what we've been through, the shows we've been to, the people we've admired or the people we've hated

MM: Los Angeles is regarded as the spiritual birthplace of Hardcore, as far as punk rock is concerned. What do you think the real legacy of Los Angeles punk rock and Hardcore is?

WD: I completely agree. I feel however that at one point or another it got taken to New York, and New York took it to its own. Where we had Black Flag and Excel, Adolescents, Descendents, all that good stuff but in the 1980s in New York they kind of took it to their own and a whole new thing happened in New York. I have a lot of respect for New York and their Hardcore scene. A lot of my favourite bands came from there; Cro-Mags, Breakdown, Side by Side, these were all bands that I was fucking stocked on as a kid and thought was really cool.

I grew up and was listening to Nerve Agents in 8th Grade and someone said to me that I should check out Youth of Today and I thought "Holy shit this is fucking sick". So as much as it is from Los Angeles, I would definitely want to recognise that it's owned by New York as well. Both have long strong legacies in their own way and I think that's fucking great.

MM: What does Hardcore mean to you?

WD: Hardcore is more about a sense of community; being realistic about what you do in life. There is nothing wrong with making good money; but if you go around and your with a band and part of a community, and you go around, flashing your name around saying you're a Hardcore band, you're Hardcore but you're not in town and you're not supporting the local bands, you're not promoting new bands or other bands in general – rather you're just trying to get yours when it's your turn to shine – then you can just fuck off. That's very disrespectful to the scene and to the people who supported you on the way up there. And people will see you; they will see through you and recognise what you are. Community is more than where you come from; it's also your family, your friends, people in general just like that.

People are like "Whoa, you broke straight edge, you're a fucking sell-out"; I see that as "Hey you're awesome but that just isn't for you any more" which is absolutely fine. When you're young you get into all kinds of situations and you don't know how it's going to affect you. Making that decision at a really young age might seem like a good idea at the time but you may find that it doesn't work for you and that's okay. But that doesn't mean you go round trashing shows because when we used to go to shows it was way better than what it is now; or hardcore isn't what it used to because you're some old geezer and you think you've outgrown this thing, because you're some old geezer. You left because it wasn't right for you any more, perhaps it wasn't so important which is perfectly fine...

MM: I'm the old geezer, I'm 42 years old and I've been going to shows since I was 14, so it's a long time for me...

WD: You should know better than anyone then. If you leave then that's perfectly fine but don't leave and think the golden age was only when you were here. You know "I was here when fucking Warzone came through, that was Hardcore, that was the best fucking show you'd ever go to". So for him then Warzone was the best moment, but for somebody else it might be the Bad Brains, it's just an on-going cycle. If you can't appreciate that then you can just fuck off man, nobody wants you here.

MM: What's the strangest thing that's happened to you guys as a band so far?

WD: We got padded down in Brazil by the cops who thought we were a Christian band because we didn't have any drugs on us. They padded us down and were like: "There's no drugs! Are you a rock band? Are you a Christian band?" we just said "Yes sure". We were surprised because we thought people in America have it rough, but there are other countries out there that have it a lot worse than we do. We once got caught in an ice storm in Texas. We couldn't get the van to move at all. There was no traction; nobody had any chains because no-one was expecting an ice storm. What other things? My guitarist broke my hand, I broke my hand during the middle of a tour.

We stomped out a security guard one time – that could have been handled a lot better. There was this security guard, he was working the stage, and I totally respect that, I've worked that job in clubs myself. Usually when kids get on stage you push them straight off, or push them over to the side, but it was our last song and one of our fans, a kid who can't weigh more than a buck twenty, a long-haired kid you know? He came back stage and was gonna come on, but this dude - he was literally 6'4", just a heavy dude, just fat, probably twice my size pushing 300lbs – and he grabs this kid and puts him in this choke hold. There are certain ways that you grab a kid if you're a security guard – but this guy's choking this kid and pulling his hair at the same time. I'm like "It's okay, relax, chill out let him go" then he tackles me with his elbow – gives me an elbow in the face – and I thought "Okay that's it you've broken the wall down, now we're good to go". As I was swinging at him, literally mid swing I notice that our guitarist has already put his instrument down and is swinging at him at the same time, hitting him just before I did. So this guy got blindsided by the guitarist then I just smashed him in the face. So we were just stomping on this guy and we got pulled apart and my shirt tore. There was a big argument outside with the promoter, the guy who owned the show, the security people about what happened on stage, but this guy was literally abusing this kid and everyone saw it too. I said to the guy that if he wanted to go down the street and into the alley and sort it out there that was fine. I didn't want to just hit the guy I wanted him to understand why we reacted the way we did. Apparently he was infamous for doing that. Some kid from the show came up to me and said "I'm glad you did that to that guy because he's always beating up on the kids". Like I said to the guy: "The reason we fucked you up is because you acted like a fucking bully. You'll bump into some people who will tolerate it. There are people who are a lot more violent than we are so you better watch out. Don't come to a place like this and beat up on 15 year old kids. You're going to fuck up eventually, someday somebody's big brother is gonna come down and fuck you up big time. I know it's a hard job but you've got to try to be a professional about these things." I'm the first to admit that we over-reacted when we did what we did, but you've got to understand that I'm not just going to sit there and watch this dude harm this kid.

MM: What's your rule number one, your guiding principal?

WD: If it stops being fun, don't do it.

Originally published in the Mass Movement Crossover Special, July 2014

SCHEISSE MINNELLI

Sorry State Of Affairs, Scheisse Minnelli are a very appropriate band for the shape our planet is in. You'd expect Scheisse Minnelli to spit pure bile at an unsuspecting audience, but that's not the case, as you also can feel fun, energy and enthusiasm in everything they do. It's not always easy though finding middle ground between a happy life and to know about, and care for the world. As Samuel McGuire explains...

Interview by Martijn Welzen

MM: I received *Sorry State Of Affairs* around the time of the EU elections. Seems like a rather fitting soundtrack to the shape of Europe today. Are you influenced by current affairs in Germany or Europe?

Sam: As a resident of the Germany and therefore the EU I am constantly affected by the current affairs. It is an odd experience living it all through a foreigners perspective. I have to pay all the same taxes and follow all the laws, yet I am not allowed to vote in the elections because I am not a citizen, just a permanent resident.

MM: Is Frankfurt also important as far as your ideas about the world are concerned, as the city is becoming the banking centre of the Euro-zone more and more...

Sam: Yeah Frankfurt is a banking hub. People think a bit more of London or Zurich but in the end Frankurt is just as important in the banking industry. You can see the power with the amount of high rises going up daily and the new ECB building that casts a large shadow on the Ostend Skate-park. It is harder and harder for an average person to be able to afford to live here. The bankers and the other industries around it are driving up the prices of the rental market and other markets are following suit. The city has many evils living and breeding in it, but on the other hand it is also very multicultural and that makes me feel really at home.

MM: At the moment when the economy is in shambles, the political parties to the far right and left are gaining momentum, and there's the fear the situation in the Ukraine will explode, there seems to be a good breeding ground for punk and hardcore bands, just like there was in the Reagan / Thatcher era. Have you noticed some sort of upswing in interest in these styles? Are more people interested in having, using and listening to an angry, yet conscious, voice?

Sam: I like your comparison, but the Reagan era was a bit different. The average person, in the US at least, was thriving on the surface. The middle class boomed in theory, taking out large loans and spending like crazy to show their consumer power. It was the youth in that era rebelled against the grown-up's that were trying to get them to conform and follow a lifestyle more akin to the 50s that the 60s or 70s, while doing cocaine behind their children's backs. So the HC and Punk bands gave the teens and other rebels not only an outlet but information on what was really going on.

Today due to the internet and other media's people just have access to more information and don't really need someone to tell them about the evils of Obama or Putin, they have that information at their fingertips. We are don't have someone to unite against that was as evil

as Reagan. People are too scared to put Obama down due to his race and people in American and in Western Europe are too detached from Russia to use Putin as their pansy.

MM: I 'm curious about why the nightmares are from Hessen and the dreams are from California? Is that linked to 'the grass is greener on the other side'? Is there a country / place in the world where dreams do come true?

Sam: Those headings are not meant to say that Hessen sucks and California rules. I have a love hate relationship with both parts of the world. I, like many people, can't seem to find the right place to live and fit in. You just have to make the world around you better and work it out you the best you can. At the moment Frankfurt is a really good place for me. I miss Cali but everytime I go back I also remember why I left, though I love it very much and miss the beach like a mofo. Hessen is not bad at all. Actually it is a really beautiful area. Many ex-pats and Germans like to talk shit about Frankfurt. They all love living in cities like Berlin, Hamburg or what have you. I love those cities too. One big problem is that is those cities are overrun with hipsters. There are also hipsters here in Frankfurt but they are far and few between and they are mostly in Bornheim, a part of the city I just avoid and therefore I rarely have to deal with hipsters.

A funny sidebar: when I has young in California we had a special nickname for the metal heads. The dudes with the leatherjackets with the Slayer patches and such. They were always down with the skaters, we got along with them due to both coming from clicks that were rejected by the 'cool' kids. We called them Hessians. Haha. Now I live in Hessen, guess I am sort of a Hessian now, minus the leatherjacket.

MM: The guy on the cover made me think about two things; 1) Drinking can make you forget, but 2) You have to face the hangover eventually. Seems very appropriate to how 'we' treat the world too. It's all party and consumerism now, but we will have to pay the price in the end. Did you intend the cover that way?

Sam: The cover has to be left to the interpretation of person that sees it. I don't wanna pigeon hole the meaning at all. That being said I really like your take on it for sure. The world seems to going through the party-consumerism-hangover-we-ruined-the-world phases on a regular basis in both short and long term. It is so hard to find a perfect balance. Sometimes I am at the supermarket and I just think, there is really nothing here I can buy with good conscious but I do have to eat. The same goes for technology and clothing.

MM: When listening to *Sorry State...* I sometimes get the feeling you're trying to get away, you want to be ignorant, but you just cannot shut your eyes to the problems in this world. Is there always this conflict? A line like "Wanna live a life sedate" seems to emphasize that...

Sam: Escape is an important part of life in my opinion. If I had to be in this 'reality' at all times then I would just flip out. Clarity is also very important. I believe that clarity and escapism should both be dealt with in moderation. Too much of either leads to bad things.

MM: Still when a song like *Memory Lane* comes along you also realize that not everything used to be better, right? What do you miss from your youth, and what don't you miss at all?

Sam: What I miss from my youth is the disregard for everything. The lack of real stress. I don't wanna call it ignorance, but I guess the lack of the knowledge I have now. I think I know too much sometimes and that can also be a bad thing. On the other hand I not miss that, I love learning and growing. It is a catch 22. It is all true, knowledge is power but ignorance is bliss. Sometimes I wonder how I was so mad as a young man and how at sometimes I feel so content as a jaded old man.

MM: To me the toughest lyrics to write would seem *Cycle of Abuse*. How important is it to touch on such a heavy subject for the band? And why this particular subject?

Sam: This subject is important on so many levels. I think people really need to understand how much children are affect by their surroundings and the poeple that they are most in contact with. I have no children. But I see it on a regular basis. One of my oldest friends who I grew up with listening to punk, skating, drinking, going to shows with and listening too all these great bands with great messages is a great example. His father passed away but he carries his father's political beliefs which were very conserative. I wonder sometimes if he was listening to the lyrics of the bands we loved or not. I love him but we depart strongly when it comes to politics and he has a child now, who is now in high school. I just wonder where the childs beliefs will fall. I hate to say it but more often than not they fall with those who had the most influence on them.

MM: I was a bit scared asking you any questions at all after having read *Lost In Translation*, is that song about a particular subject, or do you just hate interviews in general? Are you happy you're not playing in a well-known band? The more people know you the more distorted your words will become...

Sam: I have just been misquoted and misunderstood so many times it is just ridiculous. I was quoted as saying my mother lives in Germany but I don't visit her!!?!! That is just bullshit. Her cousin lives in Aachen but I don't get to see her often, it is almost three hours away! Other mistakes include I never finished University, I was in the the military, I fought in Iraq, among others, all wrong. It seems to happen mostly with interviews that get translated although I have done the interviews in both German and English thinking one or the other would help avoid misunderstands, wrong. Lets just say I am happy this interview won't be translated. Or will it? haha

MM: Besides journalists twisting words around to their own benefit, you also have fellow musicians who can be very insulting and competitive. Is that what *Wasted Talent* is about, or is that about a talented artist, not doing things to his (or her) ability?

Sam: Your second guess is right. It's about people that end up wasting their lives aways on drugs instead of getting out there and playing in bands. Wasting talent that I wish I had. Not only is that a waste for them but for all of us that would get to hear them and see them play. I sadly know too many lost souls like this especially in the US.

MM: As beer is an important part of what the new album is about, what brand it your preferred brew? How has you beer consumption changed over the years, I can imagine getting older also means not having a party with plenty of beer every single night anymore...

Sam: The beer we drink in Germany is very region based. It's not like I can throw a brand name out and then everyone knows it. The beers here are only sold like 100km from the brewery to keep the beer fresh and allow thousands of small breweries to thrive. I love Schlappe Seppel from Aschaffenburg. And since I have moved to Frankfurt I have become a Bindings fan too.

I don't drink anywhere near to as much as I used to. I am more of a weekend warrior, though since I am not a normal 9 to 5 Monday thru Friday worker, the weekend comes on different nights of the week. On tour I seem to fall back in the hard boozing though.

MM: Anything really important the world has to know about Scheisse Minnelli, but I forgot to ask?

Sam: We are just stoked to still be around after 10 years and countless shows and tours and too many guitar players. We now have Mikey on board and we are really stoked on this line up. It really captures the sound that we all have in our heads. Don't be surprised when a few more new releases pop up. We are currently a song writing machine. Hope to see you all on the road.

Originally published in the Mass Movement Crossover Special, July 2014

GARY NUMAN

It's not every day you get the chance to put some questions to a musical legend and bona fide pop star so when the opportunity arose to interview Gary Numan I jumped at the chance. His latest album *Splinter* is a fascinating record - dark and brooding yet featuring some incredibly catchy songs and of course starring *that* voice - unique and instantly recognisable. And whilst it would be easy for Gary to rest on his laurels and play it safe, this record is the latest in a long line of releases that sees him pushing his boundaries and developing a style that continues to inspire. Funnily enough for an artist who was pivotal in creating cold electronic music that side-lined emotion and humanity, in interviews his personality and humanity shines through and so it was a real pleasure to put some questions to the man.

Interview by Tom Chapman

MM: Your latest album, *Splinter*, has been a good number of years in the making, and I understand those years were not an easy journey for you; how did you feel when you completed the recordings?

Gary Nervous mainly, although, because of my illness, I didn't spend all of the 7 years between *Splinter* and the previous album actually working on *Splinter*; I was worried that the album wouldn't be able to live up to the expectations that inevitably build during such a long gap. But, the reaction to it has been amazing; far better than I dreamed of.

MM: If you had recorded and released this a few years earlier, how do you think it would have sounded?

Gary: Hard to say; so much of it comes from the experience and damage done by the depression so, if you take off a few years but keep the depression it would probably sound the same. But, lose the depression and you would likely have quite a different album.

MM: I am surprised at how heavy the album is. Was it a conscious decision to create something as hard and, at times, dark sounding?

Gary: No, *Splinter* is just the latest in line of a series of much heavier albums that started back in 1994 with *Sacrifice*. Add to that the illness and it becomes a very natural progression from what I've been doing for the last 20 years. It is dark though, I can't deny that.

MM: You have Robin Frinck from Nine Inch Nails playing guitar on the album; did he have much of an influence on the sound? Is this a collaboration we will get to hear again?

Gary: The album was pretty much finished when Robin got involved so he didn't add to the feel of it, but he certainly added some beautiful detail to it. We're very good friends and near neighbours these days so I hope he gets involved again. He's a great player. What with Robin and my regular guitarist Steve Harris playing some brilliant stuff on *Splinter* I think, for an essentially electronic album, it has some incredible guitar moments.

MM: I often imagine music in terms of film soundtrack and the video you have made for *Love Hurt Bleed* seems to work exactly like that, as a haunting soundtrack for a short horror film. I could even imagine songs like Splinter or Lost being put to a David Lynch/ David Cronenberg directed road movie; is creating soundtracks something you would be interested in?

Gary: Very much so, in fact that's a big part of the reason for my moving to Los Angeles in 2012. I've done one movie score already and I hope to do many more.

MM: The *Splinter* world tour is a big project; has it taken you to places you haven't visited before; and are there any places on the forthcoming UK dates that you haven't played before?

Gary: Yes to both. I've been touring *Splinter* for about a year now and it's taken me over much of the world, to some places I've not been before. Poland for example was an exciting surprise. Amazingly it's going to a few places in the UK I've not visited before as well, I really thought I'd played everywhere you could play in the UK by now.

MM: What can fans expect from your set? For me the visual aspect has always played a large part in your style and music - are you putting on a big show/performance at these smaller UK dates, or will you let the music do the talking?

Gary: We can't put on a 'big' show as the stages can barely fit the band themselves but we're still bringing a sizeable light show. It looks quite spectacular actually in these smaller venues.

MM: You're also playing a show at Hammersmith Apollo in November, this sounds like it will be quite an event. Do you have any special plans for this particular show?

Gary: Many; it will be the final show of the entire Splinter campaign, my most successful for decades, so I intend to make the night as amazing as possible. Special production, lights, more songs, whatever it takes to make it memorable for everyone involved. We're filming it as well.

MM: I read in an older interview that your wife now tours with you; do you now take your whole family on the road with you? If so, it must be an exciting time for the children and, if not, you must miss them like hell ...

Gary: I don't take the children on the road full time as they are all at school but they do come out whenever possible. I hope when they are older that they will tour with me, perhaps be in the band. They can all sing really well and Raven, my eldest, is already becoming quite the piano player. And yes, I do miss them very much when I'm away. It's the one big negative side of touring, but everything else about it is great so I'm not grumbling.

MM: Now that you are based in the California, what is it like when you come back to the UK? Does it make you nostalgic or does it simply confirm that you made the right decision to relocate?

Gary: I love my life in Los Angeles, simple as that I'm afraid. No disrespect to the UK but when you have beautiful weather everyday life opens up in a way that you can barely recognise, after spending over 50 years of my life sheltering from rain, damp and cold it's a very welcome change. Obviously I miss many things about the UK but I still think I made the right decision, for me, my wife and for my children.

MM: Besides California, is there anywhere else that you could be tempted to call home?

Gary: Australia. I love Australia and I love Australians. Again, great weather [mostly] and fun, friendly people.

MM: I saw on your twitter feed that you actively promote Peta tweets. What is your interest in that area and what message are you trying to get across to your twitter followers?

Gary: Just trying to help animals in my own little way; I'm not vegetarian so I'm aware that it would be somewhat hypocritical of me to re-tweet everything so I concentrate on certain areas; animal testing, cruelty, zoos, Sea World, whaling, recreational hunting, things like that. One day I hope to become vegetarian but I have a weird diet so it's easier said than done. At the moment I'm a 'meat reducer'.

MM: Following on from the previous question - music and ethics/politics; do they or should they mix? Or do you choose to keep them very separate?

Gary: There is no reason at all why they shouldn't mix but it's not something I incorporate into my music. I leave that to people far cleverer than I who understand the complexities of politics and feel knowledgeable enough about it to write songs with political messages and opinions.

MM: Finally, when can we expect the follow-up album to *Splinter*?

Gary: I start writing it in January 2015 and expect it to be released in the Spring of 2016.

Originally published in Mass Movement #40, July 2014

LESS IS NEVER MORE - MORE OR LESS

About a decade and a half ago Keith Tyson, a conceptual artist and childhood friend of mine (who would later go on to win the Turner Prize), invited me to one of his shows. It was in a boutique gallery in a trendy part of West London and the place was filled with just the sort of preening, pseudish individuals you'd imagine attending these sort of events. Many were artists themselves and paraded about the gallery with a sense of overweening entitlement and a desperate need for attention.

After admiring Keith's work for about half an hour and drinking a little too much of the complimentary wine, I fell into a conversation with a group of people. It was one of those earnest, self-regarding conversations about the nature of art and the role it plays in everyday life. The sort of conversation I'd had with many first year art students back when I used to hang out on campuses to score free drugs and sex. Frankly it was boring me rigid (and in all the wrong places).

To liven up the conversation I decided to change the topic. Cutting a floppy haired public school boy off in mid-sentence I blurted: "Never mind all that, what do you reckon to Arsenal's chances next week?" The young man looked down at the ground, shifted from foot to foot and sheepishly admitted that he didn't know anything about football. The other people standing around in our little circle looked uneasy and confessed to knowing nothing about the sport either.

At that point there was a lull in the general hubbub of conversation and I heard a loud, boorish and rather drunken voice shout: "Don't know anything about Football? Don't Know Anything About Football?! What are you QUEER?!!" As the Gallery Owner escorted me to the door, under the glaring displeasure of everyone else present, I realised the voice had been mine.

As I wended my way back to the tube station it occurred to me that, as a then bisexual man who knew less about Football than Amanda Knox knows about being a considerate flatmate, my utterance made me, without any doubt, the single most pretentious person in that gallery. If not the whole of West London. I can never be accused of not taking things to their excess.

Which sort of leads me to theme of this month's column. Namely, the joys of excess and how much I'm growing to hate the phrase: "less is more". It's one of those platitudes that people constantly trot out like an unchallenged piece of wisdom handed down through the ages. This sage proclamation is applied to endless situations as though it's a sure fire argument winner that no one could possibly question. "Ah yes, but as they say 'less is more'," says someone, and that's it, conversation over, game set and match to the self-satisfied asshole with the smug grin. With this column, I beg to differ however. If I'd drunk *less* at that party all those years ago, I wouldn't have made *more* of a fool of myself.

One of the things that annoys me about this ludicrously overused phrase is the rather chilling air of Orwellian doublethink that it has. It's a bit like the three Party slogans from *1984*: "War is Peace, Freedom is Slavery, and Ignorance is Strength." Less after all is the very opposite of more. We don't tell people "ah yes, but low is high" or "fat is thin". So why are we obsessed with telling ourselves that is 'less is more'? It's not, it's less, otherwise it wouldn't be called less it would be called more.

I may be sounding a little anal and literal here but, as a writer, language and the uses to which it is put, are of tantamount importance to me. 'Less is more' is exactly the sort of thing that a Politician says before applying swinging cuts to much needed public services. It's the excuse of the chief executive of a company that's making big cuts to the workforce, not because it will necessarily improve efficiency in the long term, but because it will give a short term boost to profit. Moralistic old ladies use it to justify their campaign against revealing female fashions, as though they want to paradoxically give women more sex appeal by making them less sexy. It's a term that's inextricably bound up with different forms of repression. It's repressive because, as Orwell pointed out, it involves you having to hold "two contradictory beliefs in one's mind simultaneously, [while] accepting both of them".

Try telling a single parent whose hours have been cut, while their bills have gone up, that 'less is more' when it comes to feeding and clothing their family. Alternatively, try telling a lover who no longer wants to see you because you turn them on *less* that you're actually *more* attractive to them. You can point out to them 'less is more' as smugly as you want, but it won't save your relationship.

Like all moronic platitudes of course, there is a little kernel of truth hiding within the overused phrase. There are situations where it is preferable to have less of something. In prose fiction for instance, it's better to use a few choice details when describing something than to overladen the story with endless descriptive passages. This is because with every descriptive detail you add, the reader is forced to redraw the mental picture they have formed of either your characters or their setting. This in turn distances them from the action and pushes them out of the story. Today's readers don't tend to respond well to pages and pages of description. This doesn't mean that *less* details are *more* details however. We've already established that you don't want *more* details. In this instance it means *less* details are *better*.

When it comes to horror the phrase 'less is more' is constantly trotted out. Considering that horror is supposedly a genre that sits on the bleeding edge of all that is forbidden and taboo, this seems eminently ridiculous to me. If less really is more, why do we pay extra to buy the director's cut or the uncensored version of a movie? Surely if less were actually more we'd be paying a premium to see a shorter movie with *more* things taken out of it. We'd be praising the censor for finally revealing the director's true vision by slicing his film to ribbons.

Horror is the genre of excess. One of the things I love most about horror is the way it always pushes at the boundaries of taste. It forces us outside of our comfort zone in order that we begin to question what truly is and isn't acceptable in all areas of life. The *less* we do this in horror fiction, the *more* likely we are to turn out something mediocre.

All of which leads me to my new book *Stuck On You* That's right, your dear old Uncle Jasp has got another book out. In this case it's an Ebook novella. If you don't read Ebooks, fear not, it will be coming out in paperback as the lead story of a new collection of my work later in the year. As you've quite rightly guessed by now, everything I've said so far is one long preamble aimed at selling you my new book. You may be wondering why I didn't have *less* preamble and get to the point *more* quickly, but that would rather contradict everything I've said above wouldn't it? What's more, if you've gotten this far and see that there's much *less* to get through till the end of the column, then you're *more* likely to finish it aren't you.

The phrase 'less is more' could not be applied to *Stuck On You* in any way whatsoever at all. *Stuck On You* is as excessive as it gets. I can honestly promise you, with my hand on this recently severed heart, that this novella will be the guiltiest pleasure you read in a long, long time. It's a story that takes you way beyond the boundaries of everything that's acceptable and just keeps on going.

You'll laugh, you'll cry, you'll hurl and all the while you'll be unable to remove your hand from the front of your pants. Could you ask anything more from a work of fiction? Trust your Uncle Jasp on this, you know it makes sense.

Here's what my concerned publisher Crystal Lake Publishing had to say about it:

"Warning! Do not buy this book, gentle reader…

No really, we mean it. Move along, click away from this page and go look at some Dino porn instead. We're not kidding. The only reason we published it is because award winning author Jasper Bark has got some serious dirt on us. Honestly, there's no other reason to put out something this depraved.

This is the sickest, filthiest and most horny novella you're likely to read this year. It will turn you on even as it turns your stomach. Think you've seen everything there is to see in horror and erotica? Think again! Just when you think this story can't get any lower it finds new depths to plumb.

Why are you still reading this?! Oh God you're going to buy it aren't you? You can't help yourself. You're going to click on that purchase button and download this little bad boy.

Well don't say we didn't warn you…"

Jasper Bark

Originally published in Mass Movement #40, July 2014

THE FIGHTING DEVIL DOGS
THE FORERUNNER TO DARTH VADER

In my opinion, there are two things that make *The Fighting Devil Dogs* (1938), a fairly interesting serial to watch: a giant, flying wing and the villain, who is known by his enemies as "The Lightning." Remember his name from my previous article? He's the guy that inspired George Lucas in his creation of the menacing character Darth Vader. Who knows for sure whether or not George really did use his image as a blueprint or was it merely a coincidence? If you've already watched this serial, then you can decide for yourself. But it really doesn't matter too much because both villains want to rule either the world or, in Darth Vader's case, the universe.

As far as chapter plays go, *The Fighting Devil Dogs* is a weak entry of the genre. There's really nothing special about the storyline: two "jarhead" marines do their best to destroy The Lightning, while he attempts to destroy all those who oppose him. Again, it's a popular chapter play theme of good verses evil. The serial itself relies a lot on stock, wartime footage and the use of two economy chapters as filler. Basically, it's a way for people who missed a few chapters to be brought "up to speed" by repeating past episodes. It also is a way for the studio to save money by not having to shoot additional scenes.

In this particular chapter play, we have two heroes: Lt. Tom Grayson and Lt. Frank Corby, played by Lee Powell and Herman Brix respectively. The story opens in Shanghai, where both lieutenants help rescue innocent victims from an air raid. Shortly afterwards, the two men are assigned to a post in Lingchuria (is there such a place?) to locate American soldiers who are said to be stranded there. When they arrive at the post, they discover that everyone there is dead with no clues as to what or who killed them. Grayson discovers that one of the deceased victims was in the process of writing a letter addressed to an Ambassador Lin Wing in San Diego

Lt. Grayson then orders some of his men to search the upstairs of the post for possible survivors, when, suddenly, a strange sound is heard coming from outside. Grayson and Corby run from the post to investigate the origin of the noise, and they see large bolts of lightning falling from the sky and striking the exterior of the post. As the building begins to burn, Grayson attempts to save his men from inside the rapidly, deteriorating structure, but it's too late to rescue them from the blazing inferno.

The two men return home, where Lt. Grayson faces court-martial charges based on his fantastic tale of how his men died. The members of the court-martial (which include Tom's father, Colonel Grayson) fail to believe the lieutenant's story, that is, until he produces a letter from Ambassador Lin Wing pleading the court to contact him immediately. When contacted by phone, Lin Wing begins to tell the court that he has certain important papers which the United States government must see. The papers speak of who's behind the destruction in Lingchuria as well as future plans to wreak havoc throughout the world. Of course, before Wing can finish his story, The Lightning mysteriously enters the room and shoots the ambassador with a handheld ray-gun that spews an electrical charge of death. On the other end of the line, the court-martial officers hear Wing's last words of, "The Lightning," before he dies.

When they investigate Wing's house, they discover his body and an open wall safe. Lt. Grayson also notices some ashes near the wall safe and concludes that they could be the remains of the same papers that Wing referred to on the phone. The men then take the ashes to the laboratory of Professor Warfield for a closer inspection. For the lack of information from the studio writers, it is unclear as to the significance of the ashes. What is significant, however, is that The Lightning thunderbolts Professor Warfield's laboratory, killing several scientists and Tom's father, Colonel Grayson. Curiously, Warfield is absent.

With the murder of his father as his chief objective, Tom is now bound and determined to eliminate The Lightning and his cohorts. By the way, The Lightning's lead henchman is an actor of very small stature by the name of John Picorri. Picorri made several chapter plays, always as a villain's handyman.

The serial continues with more and more mass destruction brought about by The Lightning and his band of misfits and ends with his demise aboard the flying wing, the details of which are unimportant. I have to say that although I love The Lighting's outfit, and his very cool flying wing, the serial itself is only marginally enjoyable. First of all, even though The Lightning wears a great outfit to conceal his identity, his voice is obviously that of Professor Warfield. It seems that Republic Studio paid more attention to the big picture with great special effects that they ignored the smaller details. At any rate, the villain and his fantastic flying wing are both worth the price of admission, but that's about the extent of my praise.

The two protagonists are merely there to obstruct The Lightning's insane quest for world domination and not much more. Powell's portrayal of Lt. Tom Grayson is rather "wooden" as he more or less reads his lines rather than to act. Oddly enough, he died as a marine from alcohol poisoning after having fought in the Battles of Tarawa and Saipan during WWII. The details of his death remain rather sketchy. As for Herman Brix, he later became known as Bruce Bennett and went on to have a pretty successful film career. Earlier in his life, he won a silver medal at the 1928 Olympic Games for both the indoor and outdoor shot-putting events. His good health (and great genes) allowed him to live to be almost 101 years old.

As for the special effects, the Lydecker brothers were experts at creating an extremely believable flying machine. To augment their effects, they made larger, scale models   (about ¼ scale of actual size) than most studios and filmed in natural light instead of using studio lights; thus, the illusion of the wing as a real airplane is amazing.

All things considered, I give *The Fighting Devil Dogs* a six out of ten, and most of that is due to the villain and his flying wing

Doug Crill

Orignally published in Mass Movement #40, July 2014

GARY DANIELS

If you're a fan of martial arts cinema or action thrillers (and let's face it folks, most of us are), then you'll be more than aware of Gary Daniels, the fats kicking, hard as nails actor and ex-MMA fighter and legitimate cinematic heir to Chuck Norris' crown. Following the release of *Misfire* Mass Movement caught up with Gary via a crackly Vietnamese phone line to talk about his career, *Misfire* and more…

Interview by Tim Cundle

MM: What originally made you want to be a martial artist and what made you want to retire when you were so successful?

GD: The reason I originally wanted to be a martial artist was because when I was a kid I used to enjoy reading Marvel superhero comic books, to the point where I really wanted to believe there were real superheroes running around. Then when I was 8 years old I saw *Enter the Dragon* and saw Bruce Lee for the first time and for me it was like he was a real life superhero. From then on I wanted to be him; I knew what I wanted to do with the rest of my life, I wanted to be involved in martial arts and I wanted to make movies. So I grew up studying movie arts and got into kick boxing, but I was always training to be a pretty martial artist and I wanted to be effective as a player. So I got into kickboxing, and then, it's not like I decided to retire, it's just you get into films and you get to the point when - in order to fight you have to train; you have to put a lot of hours in to train and stay in shape. You just can't put in those kind of hours when you're working on a film to train. Also back then I wasn't making any money kickboxing, the films were making me a lot more money.

MM: So how did you get your initial break in film and TV?

GD: I moved to Florida and got into acting while I was in Florida. In truth it was one of the reasons I moved to America, because I wanted to get into the industry. The opportunity came up through my kickboxing promoter, who used to bring fighters over, and then take us over to California or Florida. I chose to go to Florida first and got involved in some acting classes there. I started doing some commercials, had a part on *Miami Vice* and a few other shows; then this guy from the Phillipines saw me training and said that if I went over to the Phillipines he could make me a star. So that was really my start, out in the Phillipines, then I returned to America and it built up from there really.

MM: *Misfire* really feels like an old school action film; was that something you were aiming for or was it a happy and fortuitous coincidence?

GD: I wasn't really aiming for that, I'm not really conscious of time, that I'm doing a film like the 80s or whatever. It's all about the script really. There are a few good scripts out there but the budgets these days have been lowered so much since the eighties that you can't put as much action into them as you would back then, and it was the same in the nineties. Nowadays we get some really great scripts but the budgets aren't there. In the end this really affects the schedule; you don't have as much time as you might like to pull the scenes together. It's a real shame actually because of the piracy and the DVD market not really being there any more, it really has an impact on the budgets, which means tighter schedules and shooting in cheaper locations. I never really went out for that eighties look, if it turns out that way then I don't really have a problem with that as long as people enjoy the film.

MM: Cole is incredibly reminiscent of John Booker in *Good Guys Wear Black*; he's got the same kind of intensity, drive and determination. This got me thinking: how do you go about building a character like that, bringing him to life on the screen.

GD: A lot of it's to do with the writing. If it's really well written there's not a lot I have to do. If it's badly written then I have to do more work myself and work out what parts of me I have to bring to the character. The Cole character was written pretty well so a lot of it was on the paper, so it wasn't too difficult to pull together. The writer knows me pretty well and we've done lots of work together before. So he understands the way I work, and it was written for me so it was very easy to play that character.

MM: What was the general mood like on set? Was it a relaxed atmosphere, or was it focussed and concentrated?

GD: The production company and the crew down there are absolutely fantastic. I've worked with them once before and am working with them again shortly. We all know each other really well and the atmosphere on set was really relaxed. They are like family, very easy going, very humble, and it's surprising because a lot of time on a lower budget film like this the schedules are so tight that things can get really tense and stressed. It wasn't like that on this film. The director on this film was a very relaxed guy and that's usually where it starts really in terms of atmosphere on set; where we filmed in Mexico was a really laid back as well which contributed a lot.

MM: How would you sell the film to its potential audience?

GD: It's a quiet, tense action thriller. It builds slowly with the characters and the story. The action comes out of the story. It's a slow burn thriller.

MM: In your career to date; apart from *Misfire*, which film is your favourite?

GD: That's a tough question, because a lot of it is to do with the experience you have making the film rather than the end product really. It could be to do with where you were shooting, or the people you worked with, so it's really hard to day which is my favourite. It could be *Rage* or *Riot*, there is so much action in those films and we have so much fun making them. It's like *Expendables*, with such a great cast, and working with Sylvester Stallone was fantastic. *White Tiger* was a great experience too, they had such a great crew it was a really good atmosphere.

MM: I was going to ask you about *Expendables*; how does it feel to be part of the biggest film franchises of the 21st Century so far. Did you know at the time you were making it that it was going to be as big as it was.

GD: I'd heard about the cast, and a cast like that had never been put together before, and you hear about it and you think you'd love to be involved in something like that but you don't think it will happen. Then a friend of mine who was working on the film called me and said "Stallone wants to meet with you" I couldn't believe it. So I got to meet Stallone, and I had a twenty minute meeting with him; a film like that is a once in a lifetime opportunity really - although I've done two of them now – it was an honour to be part of it.

MM: What's next for you now Gary now that Misfire is out?

GD: *Misfire* sold really well, so they immediately funded another project with the same writer and the same production company to work with me, called *Rumble*. We shot it down in Mexico again. Lots of gun action and chases, a lot more action than *Misfire*.

Originally published in Mass Movement #41, November 2014

DICK BRIEFER'S FRANKENSTEIN

If you're a regular reader of this column then you're obviously a person of taste and intelligence. You might also have noticed by now that, although it's ostensibly a column about Horror Comics, I tend to go off on tangents as often as an ADHD toddler in a 'Shiny Things' factory.

This month however I'm going to narrow the beady eye of the column not only to Horror Comics but to one individual horror comic creator. I know that many of you might have turned up simply for the knob gags and the celebrity fisting anecdotes, but sometimes this column has to do exactly what it says on the tin. Especially if the tin says 'shut up and get to the fucking point'.

And The Point Is ...

This month's column is all about the comics genius of Dick Briefer. Seconds after I typed that last sentence the phone rang. It was a friend of mine who's a noted comics journalist. He asked what I was writing and when I told him it was a piece about the comic creator Dick Briefer he said: "Who? Isn't that like a porn star's name?" Which pretty much sums up why I'm writing about Briefer for this column.

Dick Briefer is one of the most sorely neglected writers and artists who've ever worked in comics. Sixty years ago his work would sell close to a million copies and now hardly anyone has heard of him. This is an incredible shame as he's fast becoming one of my favourite creators from the 40s and 50s.

Like many comic greats, Briefer started his comics career working for the now legendary Eisner-Iger studio, that supplied comics to many of the New York publishers during the boom years of the Golden Age. Over the years he wrote and drew cowboy stories, crime comics, fantasy shorts and science fiction strips. Like every American comics creator of his time he also drew a lot of super hero comics. Writing and drawing as Dick Hamilton he created for Novelty Comics and under the pseudonym Dick Floyd, it's believed, he wrote and drew The Adventures of Pinky Rankin for the Daily Worker, the organ of the American Communist Party. My personal favourite of all the superheroes that Briefer worked on is the the son of a Native American Chief, who trained as a lawyer but now fights corporate American corruption as a costumed avenger in order to uphold the rights of the First Americans.

However, if Briefer is remembered at all these days it is for creating what many argue is the first on-going horror comic for Prize Comics, namely Frankenstein. Possibly inspired by the 1940 midnight revival of Universal's Frankenstein movie from a decade before, Briefer convinced his publisher that, as the character was in the public domain, it would make a great on-going series. He updated the story to a modern setting and redesigned the character to avoid any legal action from Universal.

Two decades before Jack Kirby and Stan Lee unleashed the Incredible Hulk on the world, Briefer's Frankenstein was a rampaging behemoth, unleashed by an unwitting scientist, persecuted by the authorities and fighting sometimes against and sometimes alongside teams of superheroes. Briefer's creation was a lot more terrifying than the Hulk though. He never transformed back into a man and he tore scores of innocent bystanders apart without any conscience, simply to torment the man who created him.
Eventually the monster was brainwashed into hating Nazis and was co-opted into the fight

against Hitler. Then at the end of 1945, when the Nazi menace was quashed, Briefer's hideous monster underwent one of the most remarkable transformations a comics character has ever undergone. Briefer convinced Prize comics to let him reinvent the monster as a cutesy kid's character who had whimsical and somewhat surreal adventures. Hailed as the 'Merry Monster, he was given his own comic which quickly became a runaway best seller and sold out every issue This was Briefer's favourite incarnation of Frankenstein and I have to admit it's mine too. It's obvious from the looser, more fluid and cartoony art, as well as the madcap stories, that Briefer is having a ball. Imagine if you combined Charles Addams' gothic sensibility with Al Capp's kooky satire, then threw in Walt Kelly's whimsy and Carl Banks' storytelling and you're still nowhere how good these stories are.

Seventeen issues later, sales had fallen and Prize Publications shelved Frankenstein. Two years later EC comics were doing amazing business with their horror titles and the newsstands and drugstore spinner racks were groaning with Horror Comics from every publisher in the business. Not wanting to be left behind Prize resurrected the character this time as a gory horror comic, with Briefer once more handling the art and writing. Even though Briefer was, by all accounts, beginning to tire of the character, he once again excels in stories full of grim invention and genuine terror.

More than twenty years before Marvel revolutionised Horror Comics with on-going titles like , , and their own , all of which featured a monster as the main protagonist, Briefer proved himself ahead of the curve with the most anarchic antihero in horror comics. For many of Briefer's select band of devotees, this is his best run on the character and the stories remain fresh, inventive and frightening to this day.

Sadly the comic finally came to an end in November of 1954 after 33 excellent issues and three totally different incarnations, each one the brainchild of a unique and gifted creator with a genius for reinvention. Even more sadly, after the scandal of the Kefauver hearings and the introduction of the comics code authority, Briefer left comics altogether to work in advertising. Unlike other masters of the medium who left at around the same time, such as Will Eisner and Gene Colan, Dick Briefer never returned. Frankenstein remains his last will and testament to comics. But what a testament!

Briefer was one of the many cartoonists of his era who threw wild dreams and raw ink onto Bristol board pages, in a constant race with an ever demanding deadline. However, few of Briefer's contemporaries blazed quite such a trail. He remains the first pioneer of four colour fears and an unsurpassed master of mirth and the macabre.

If I've inspired you to go and search out some of his work (and I hope I have), yours first stop should be Yoe Books and IDW's brilliant . This is a beautifully produced book that includes stories from every one of Briefer's three different interpretations on the monster. There's also from Idea Men Publications.

And if you hunt all that down and you're left begging for more, then don't worry. Renowned writer Monstrous Martin Powell and indie fave artist Notorious Nik Poliwko are bringing back the monster in an for Dark Horse Comics and Sequential Pulp.

Remember you heard it here first.

Jasper Bark

Originally published in Mass Movement #42, March 2015

WELLY ARTCORE
(ARTCORE FANZINE / FOUR LETTER WORD / VIOLENT ARREST)

In a scene where many people come and go over the years, there are some people who are constants. I first met Welly in the late eighties in Autonomy Records in Cardiff and bought my first copy of his zine Artcore shortly after. Twenty five years later and he's still doing the zine and an active participant in the Hardcore scene. Mass Movement caught up with Welly for a chat about Artcore and his recent uptake of the vocalist slot in the wonderful Violent Arrest.

Interview by Ian Pickens

MM: Introduce Yourself…

Welly: I'm the new vocalist for Violent Arrest. The other guys are Steve 'Baz' Ballam on guitar, Ed Varney on the bass and John Millier on drums. I will be your host today, hope you're sitting comfortably.

MM: People familiar with the band will have noticed the departure of vocalist Steve Hazzard; has he jacked in music completely?

Welly: I think so. The time comes for everyone I guess. I don't think there was any animosity, he just wanted to stop.

MM: You've had a long association with VA – having handled the artwork on quite a few of the bands records/CDs and released the split 7" with Endless Grinning Skulls as part of Artcore Zine #31 so was it an easy decision to join as vocalist?

Welly: Oh yeah, Baz phoned and I said yes. I'd seen Ripcord play back in the eighties, and in the nineties the first tour for my old band Four Letter Word was with Spite that featured John on drums and Steve Hazzard on Vocals, so the connection goes back. I've done all the design work for VA bar one; the Criminal Record double 7" on Grave Mistake, and John did that one and did a great job.

MM: Would you agree that your previous bands (Four Letter Word and State Funeral) leaned more towards the melodic side of punk rather than VA's Hardcore sound? Have you altered your delivery or vocal style to fit the music or have the band altered their musical style?

Welly: Four Letter Word was definitely 'melodic' punk, but it was the nineties so now people seem to think we were pop punk, when in reality we just thought we were copping Stiff Little Fingers and The Ruts for the most part. State Funeral was a short lived thing. We were definitely going for a Hardcore sound, and I wouldn't say it was 'melodic', at least that wasn't the intention. To answer the question though, I have approached the vocals for Violent Arrest in keeping with their sound, I didn't want to alter anything at all, and they haven't altered their approach to the music. If it's different, then it's due to the dynamic of the different members. I didn't try to sing at all, I just belted it out as hard as I could in the studio, to try and keep it sounding the same.

MM: Do you guys get jaded by continued references to your former bands?

Welly: One of the reasons I finished my old band Four Letter Word after twenty years was because being in a band long term can sometimes feel like everything you do gets compared to one or two things you did at the beginning, and it can all end up being a bit of a strait jacket. But as for VA; I can't really speak for the other guys, but pretty much all their bands have played the same stuff with different names and slightly different line-ups. I doubt they care, and they have never gone out there peddling covers of their old classics or 'reformed' their old names for tours, and that speaks volumes really. It's refreshing for me to do this band, as after what I said above, that doesn't matter to me now, so I don't care.

MM: VA have covered the Jags and Mau Maus; surprising choices given the band's sound – are there any more covers planned or are they more spontaneous choices?

Welly: Spur of the moment I think. I don't think everyone can agree on most stuff, so when it happens it's just spur of the moment. Those guys wanted to do the Mau Maus so we just knocked it out. We've only played it a few times. We did a BGK cover for a couple of gigs too.

MM: Are the lyrics down to you or a group effort? Both *'The Game is Rigged* and *Degradation Street* certainly seem your style of writing. Do you feel lyrics have become increasingly marginalised in Punk and Hardcore?

Welly: All mine I'm afraid. The VA back catalogue I think is pretty much all John's work I think. It has been said that political lyrics are passé in punk rock now. I think that all changed with the rise of pop punk in the nineties, and then that whole 'emo' nonsense. A lot of new people came into it then with different motivation. It was the first time 'success' was attainable in punk rock since the old '77 days, and a bi-product of all that was commercialisation and a move away from political messages. Popularity is easier to attain if you just play to the widest demographic, and the knock-on effect twenty years after all that is you don't hear as much overtly political punk rock now. I think this takes away something from it.

I know there aren't any rules, and it's important to retain a sense of humour. But there's a difference between then and now in that in the old days non-political bands tended to goof off and be comedy punk, whereas nowadays it's more songs about feelings and staring up your own arse, and this is no different from mainstream pop content as far as I can see. And I think what carried punk rock beyond the seventies and through the eighties was *because* of the social conscience. It felt like a 'mass movement', that change was possible, and that it was protest music of some description, in all its guises. But now it's more a disparate collection of bands and labels seemingly competing in not much more than a marketplace, and there's a lot of music and vinyl but not a lot of anything to say.

MM: Was the intention always to make this release a split between the last stuff recorded with Steve and the first stuff recorded with you – kind of a bridge between old and new?

Welly: Nah, it was because there were only eight songs on the last record, so rather than rip people off pressing it onto CD, the band and label waited for the next session to put out a full CD. In the interim, Steve left and I joined, so you get both sessions which include the split 7" tracks from the last session I put out as well. The fact that it's a different vocalist is purely coincidental.

MM: The title of the new album is *Life inside the Western Bloc* - do you feel people in the West are in denial about the lifestyle they are participating in daily? Are you pessimistic about humankind's chances of making any real, lasting change towards equality and freedom?

Welly: The title is a reference to propaganda and how the perception of 'freedom' very much depends from where you're viewing it and through what lens. In that sense, yes we are in denial. Humanity collectively and selectively turns a blind eye to a lot of things, from what is done in our name, what is done in order to preserve our 'lifestyles', even when they threaten us existentially as a species.

The basis of our dominant system is of limitless growth from limited resources, this in itself should be enough to see that we're on a collision course with our habitat. The systems of hierarchy that we live under create an order of things whereby individuals are absolved from personal responsibility, in the name of furthering the aims of their macro corporate regimes. The aims of course being more profit at any cost and more return for the rich.

Key tools of this is the aggressive seeking of absolute influence and power over of what is left of our corrupted political institutions, reversal of social gains for the poor, and the absolute transfer of public wealth to private profit, paid for by the poor and its labour. Another weapon in the corruption of power is the corruption of the media, and hence the propaganda we receive in order to stay true to the course of the capitalist mission, and the propaganda to which the title relates.

It should be fairly obvious to all, that all of this is counterproductive to humanity. And you only have to look at the modus operandi of the rich, the banks and corporations that control, and seek to control, to see that there is no future in it. But because this is the dominant paradigm of our age, and therefore the narrative of the blanket propaganda we receive, there is also very little chance of humanity pulling out of the terminal velocity we find ourselves in.

Thus, as mass inequality and climate damage worsen in the furtherance of these goals, we are only going to see an acceleration of the above in the future, as the rich and powerful will only seek to somehow insulate themselves from the end result of their ideology, by amassing evermore wealth and power. So yes, bar a mass uprising of millions of confused, misinformed, frightened and purposefully isolated people, the prognosis is not good. If there is hope, it lies in the proles.

MM: Does *"Punk deserve to die when it becomes another stale cartoon"*?

Welly: I've thought for a while that maybe it could benefit from ripping it up and starting again, but then this is quickly followed by the next thought, which is 'what would replace it?' And punk rock is an idea, and you can't kill an idea. Not only that, but it is an idea that distils music, art and the ideas that surround it, down to a point of perfection. So you can't destroy it, all you can do is take part or sit back, and either way enjoy the show and hope that subsequent generations do something interesting with it, which I think they will.

MM: Have the band had many opportunities to play live; I caught the set with Negative Approach and it was pretty visceral and tight but haven't seen any other gigs advertised since then. Do you feel the advent of Social Networking has had a negative impact on gigs? Is flyer culture dead?

Welly: VA will play when we can, as long as we can fit all in around other aspects of our lives. We're playing Leeds in a week, and then it'll be whatever else comes along. Social networking has had an impact on a lot of things, but gigs? I don't know. I do know that I stopped putting gigs on, as in 15-20 years we went from 200 people turning up, to struggling to reach 40, and therefore pay the bands. Maybe that was my fault, maybe it was trends, who knows. Either way, I figured it was time to step aside.

Flyers have taken a downturn in the wake of the internet, but then again, the whole 'gig' thing has changed. A lot of touring bands seem to have handed operations back over to 'big promoters' or people with making money in mind. And some people seem content to buy their overpriced tickets and go to the professional rock 'concerts'. Stand, applaud and file out past the merch stall. Each to their own, all I know from experience is the local 'support' bands play for free, and usually get scammed for selling tickets in the process. It's a bullshit 'business' model I want no part of.

On the plus side, there's a really healthy underground DIY scene, but it's not just one big punk rock scene anymore though is it? It's a load of styles all claiming 'punk' to enjoy the benefits of a 'network', but a lot of the time working against each other. Way back, you'd have one or two DIY promoters and one gig a month, an 'event'. Now we're spoilt for choice. There was one scene and all the styles of bands would play, that's the biggest change for me, but times change. I'm not particularly interested in turning up for four bands who all want to sound like Screeching Weasel and everyone dresses the same. We need more weirdos on the bill, and in the audience, at gigs put on by weirdos.

MM: A lot of eighties Hardcore bands have resurfaced over the past few years – which is great for, ahem, young whippersnappers like me who never got the chance to see them, but do you feel it's all a bit nostalgic and/or money motivated?

Welly: I think we've got to a point where it doesn't really matter. Take what you want and make of it what you will. There's always going to be nostalgia and money motivation, but ultimately I think from the bands' perspectives, it's more often than not more to do with reaching a point in life where you look back and realise what defined you and the friends you were in a band with, and having some sense of unfinished business.

Back when most of these bands were around they weren't popular, and it takes thirty years for the world to catch up with most things. There were very few of us around then as fans and participants of this very underground music. A lot of these bands were nothing more than legend. You didn't get to hear them for years sometimes. The records were actually rare, and not just a click or a pay cheque away. There weren't any books out, and no documentaries.

What was achieved with limited means was amazing. No-one even knew what other people looked like before the bands showed up y'know? Fast forward to the present day, and there's good and bad, and people sometimes tend to play it safe when they get older, regarding sleeping in hotels with big riders and dealing with industry promoters, but I'm never likely going to be in the position where people ask us to reform our old band for X amount of money, so who am I to judge? Show up, or don't, it no longer seems to matter.

MM: Stepping away from the bands for a moment, a lot of people in the punk scene will be familiar with you from Artcore zine – it must be one of the longest running print zines, if not *the* longest running print zine, in the world by now? Do you still enjoy doing it? Are people more apathetic towards zines than they used to be? How has the internet affected zines and the wider Punk/Hardcore scenes? 'Artcore til Death'?

Welly: I started in 1986, and Maximum Rock'n'Roll is the longest running by far, followed by Trust and Suspect Device. If I didn't enjoy it, I wouldn't do it. It's definitely not the wads of cash (laughs). It is my 'voice', and a creative outlet, and however small, to me that's still better than a homogenised voice on the internet. Shout above the noise.

As for the net, it has definitely changed the relationship between people and information in all spheres. The challenge is to offer something that can't be simply absorbed in a quick internet fix. Part of the problem is everyone thinks everything is free via the internet. Of course, it's not 'free', it's simply a case of transfer of power. As in, if you read a 'zine' or blog online, regardless of where it's hosted, you're paying some global corporation for your internet time, and you're also invariably seeing adverts. By buying a print zine, there's either no advertising, or it's invariably for some DIY label, so you're helping keep some small printer in a job somewhere, and helping keep the zine going as the money will just go into more zines, as there's no 'profits' to be had apart from the creative satisfaction.

Artcore 'til death? No idea. Some issues don't do so well, and it has its up and downs, and it's definitely diminishing and getting harder to justify doing a print run, but I have no interest in putting it on the internet or jumping ship to some kind of 'music journalism'. So that said, I guess I'll keep going, and if you notice there hasn't been one for a few years, I've probably stopped. Thirty year anniversary next year though, let's go!

MM: Do you find it frustrating when bands don't bother replying to interviews they've agreed to, or do you philosophically shrug it off?

Welly: Sometimes it's frustrating. I think it says a lot about the change talked about above, that bands would not bother with FREE advertising for their music in a print zine. I guess I tend to shrug it off in that I shrug off the bands from there on. There's a few I can think of who I liked their music enough to want to have them air their opinions in print and pay for the privilege by printing it, who've let me down, and it basically leaves me disinterested in their music, and I no longer support them by buying it. A lot of the time I don't bother listening to them anymore. Not out of bitterness, just in the sense that they've revealed their true nature and I lose enthusiasm.

MM: You also do a lot of artwork for labels and bands; what or who inspires your artwork? Do you work in any other mediums than ink/paper?

Welly: I think the inspiration is either there or it isn't. All I wanted to do since I was a kid was design and write stuff. I used to make illustrated story books, writing lyrics and making handmade record covers when I was about ten and in junior school in the late 70s. So this is probably an outlet I was going to gravitate towards, and discovering the underground Hardcore punk scene in the eighties just blew the world wide open for me.

It was a revolution of music but also the mind and I feel privileged to have been involved in some small way.

After school, I got a place doing graphic design in a print college. This was in 1987 and they had these amazing new machines you could print text on called Apple Macs. This whole thing of course was so I could furiously cut and paste fanzines and record covers. While I was at this college, I was lucky enough to do the paste-up art for the records of local bands like Cowboy Killers and Life Cycle. After this course, the art college gave me a spot on a higher course. Of course I was in the dark room making halftones, and typing up interviews on the Macs with the likes of Spermbirds and C.O.C. for the zine, as well as making record covers for local bands like Slowjam.

I work primarily in print design for record and CD sleeves, fanzines, flyers and t-shirts. I don't do web 'design' apart from a site I maintain. Nowadays design work is all about internet design, I'm not interested in writing code, it's not 'design' to me, it's maths. As to what inspires the artwork? I have no idea. Outside of one or two labels, I never get asked to do much. Maybe people think it's expensive or something (or the art is bad - ha ha), as I've had comments in the past about how I 'make a living out of punk rock', but nothing could be further from the truth. So if anyone out there has seen my work, and needs any help, get in touch, there isn't an 'hourly rate'. If you look up Welly (2) on the Discogs website, you'll see a lot of what I've been up to for the last thirty years. I like to keep busy, drop me a line.

MM: What's next for you Welly?

Welly: I've always said; don't plan and you won't be disappointed, so I guess we'll just wait and see what comes down the pipe.

MM: Final Comments or Parting Shots?

Welly: Thanks for the opportunity to air my thoughts here and thanks for your support.

Originally published in Mass Movement #42, March 2015

MANHUNT OF MYSTERY ISLAND
THE SWASHBUCKLING VILLAIN WITH AN ATTITUDE

Okay, so this time I may have cheated a little bit. That is to say, the villain of this chapter play (Captain Mephisto) has the ability to switch his identity back and forth using a weird transformation device, So, loosely speaking, you could consider that to be a superpower. As I have stated before, the purpose of this entire series is to study only those heroes and villains who have no extraordinary, physical advantages. Which means, they cannot possess the power of personal flight, demonstrate unusual feats of strength and so on. They may, however, be able to conceal their identities by wearing some type of disguise and use various gadgets and devices to accomplish their nefarious goals (in the case of the villains), but they themselves are mere mortals with ill intentions.

In this particular serial, the villain is one of four gentlemen who has the power to change from a mortal being into a ruthless, legendary sea captain when the need arises. The transformation device is a large, spark-filled spinning wheel that is attached to the back of a chair. The trick is, the audience never sees the front of the person who is being transformed; therefore, as with most chapter plays, it's anyone's guess as to the villain's true identity. Now for the basic storyline.

An island resort area, known only as Mystery Island, is located somewhere in the Pacific, and it is owned and operated by four gentlemen. It is believed that a famous scientist (Professor Forest) and his assistant are being held captive somewhere in the general area. Forest had the blueprints for a revolutionary device (another made-up chapter play creation) known as a radiotomic transmitter that can power all types of mobile vehicles, including ships and airplanes, from a central location. He secretly gave the blueprints to another one of his colleagues (Spencer Harvey, a well-known Civil Engineer) and helped him to escape the island aboard a ship to the mainland. Stop right there. If the professor helped his colleague to escape, then why didn't he try? Ask the writers. Once there, Harvey was to deliver the prints to the professor's daughter (Claire), who works for a famous criminologist by the name of Lance Reardon.

With the dwindling supply of natural recourses an ongoing concern, the professor's device could be of great value. Of course, if the blueprints were to fall into the hands of some unscrupulous individual, the consequences could be disastrous. On a side note, I find it interesting that even back in 1945, the scriptwriters were aware enough to know that someday in the future there may be a shortage of natural resources. Imagine that.

At any rate, Claire hires the famous criminologist Lance Reardon to help locate her missing father. Using his unbelievable skills of logic, Reardon narrows the search for Professor Forest down to three locations, one of which, is Mystery Island and that's where their search begins. But before they can leave, Harvey is shot to death just outside the door of Reardon's laboratory by two of Mephisto's henchmen. Fortunately, he had the blueprints on his person, so they are now safely in the hands of Claire and Reardon.

Back on Mystery Island, Mephisto finds out that his henchman (Brand) failed to retrieve the blueprints. However, Brand assures the captain that Harvey was killed before he could tell anyone where his two companions were being held prisoner. Not totally convinced,

Mephisto tries to pressure Professor Forest and his assistant into completing the radiotomic transmitter by telling them that Harvey was killed before he could tell anyone about their whereabouts.

But the wise professor knows that any threats directed towards him would be foolish, since he is the only person capable of completing the transmitter. Still, Mephisto warns Forest that he had better not try to stall in completing the assignment or else there would be consequences. What Mephisto doesn't realize, is that the professor has created an attachment to the transmitter that can produce a stream of jet vapor, capable of burning through the walls of their laboratory dungeon, a detail which is later put to use.

Using his transformation chair, Mephisto changes his identity back to one of the four owners, and he arranges a stay at the resort for Claire and Reardon in the hopes that he can do away with the two of them. It cracks me up to think that Mephisto has the ability to change his molecular structure enough to assume the shape, structure and size of another person, yet he is unable to figure out how to design a radiotomic transmitter. How much harder could it be for such a genius?

From this point on, the story incorporates Reardon's brilliant detective work to discover Professor Forests' whereabouts and to expose Mephisto's true identity. The chapter play is loaded with plenty of Republic-style fistfights and precarious situations, but the true focus is on which one of the four gentlemen is the real Mephisto.

Actor Richard Bailey, whose acting skills leave much to be desired, plays the part of Lance Reardon. Combine his incompetence as an actor with the way his character is written, and it makes for a very dull hero. He is certainly no match for the villain's panache. One of the reasons why Bailey was chosen for the role is the fact that he is very similar in size and build to the great stuntman Tom Steele.

Speaking of stuntmen, it might be of interest to know why most of the actors and stuntmen wore some type of hat, usually a fedora, especially during the many fight scenes. It was used as a clever device so that a stunt double could replace the actor leaving the audience unaware of the switch. The hat was somehow attached to their heads so it couldn't fall off, especially, when the action was "hot and heavy." Today, with the use of DVD players, it's easy to stop the action at any given point and see that a switch has been made. By the way, Professor Forest does manage to burn a hole through the dungeon wall in order to escape, only to be trapped by one of Mephisto's henchmen. At least that's what the writers tell us.

As for the villain, my all-time, favorite bad guy, Roy Barcroft, portrays Captain Mesphisto. Of the many "B" westerns and chapter plays that Roy made, I chose this particular role because of his grand ability to act the part of the bad guy without going "over the top" in character. His performance is as smooth as silk even though his intentions are wicked. He is most definitely at the top of his game in this performance as the swashbuckling Mephisto.

Complete with everything that a pirate should ware, Mephisto is the epitome of ruthlessness. He commands his henchmen with only the expressions on his face and some cleverly chosen threats as warnings should they fail to do his bidding. Sure, he can mix it up with his fists (although I'm not positive if Barcroft did all of his own stunt work), but it's his sheer, magical ability to deliver the dialog in such a nonchalant fashion, while at the same time, conveying a message of, "don't even think of screwing with me," that makes his character so cold-hearted.. He is totally believable.

He was only fifteen-years old when he enlisted to fight in WWI and was wounded in action somewhere in Europe. He then drifted from job to job before he finally discovered that he had an interest as an onstage actor. Originally, he used this experience to improve his speaking ability as a salesman but, over time, he made his way into the motion picture industry and signed a ten- year contract with Republic Studios. It was at Republic that he did the bulk of his work in serials and "B" westerns, almost always a villain. Those who knew him personally said he that was one of the nicest persons in Hollywood, despite his wicked onscreen characterizations.

Manhunt of Mystery Island concludes with the usual fistfights, only this time, the villain knocks Reardon unconscious and plans to transform him into the dreaded Captain Mephisto. Why, do you ask? Remember that one of the four owners is Mephisto and, during the chapter play, the captain has eliminated two of the gentlemen. That leaves two suspects remaining, and from there I'm going to leave you hanging in true chapter play fashion. If you want to know what happens, then you'll have to watch this very entertaining serial. On a scale of one to ten, I give this one a nine.

Doug Crill

Originally published in Mass Movment #42, March 2015

ROGER MIRET
(AGNOSTIC FRONT)

If we're going to talk about New York Hardcore, then we have to talk about the Godfathers of HC, Agnostic Front, and with their new album, *The American Dream Died* due for release on April 7th, the timing couldn't have been more fortuitous. So, on a cold, windy evening in February, and via a transatlantic phone line, I sat down to talk to Roger Miret about the bands new record, the old days in New York, the gradual erosion of our civil liberties, police violence and the unifying power of Hardcore…

Interview by Tim Cundle

Photographs by W. Craig and Todd Huber

MM: So, when the did the American Dream die Roger? Or did it never exist? Was it just a construct, a lie designed to sedate the masses…

Roger: Well, I guess I'd go with the latter. What I'm trying to do is give people something else to look at, a chance to see it the same way I do. The media always lies and tells you the stuff they need to tell the masses in order to make you follow like sheep. I'm just trying to tell you, people, that everything that this country (USA) has stood for, it's constitution, is coming to an end and events are shaping it to the point where it will eventually become a police state. You know, you may not think that it's true, or you might think it's far-fetched, but hey, that's the way I look at it and I'm presenting my view…

MM: You just mentioned the evolution toward a police state, which forms the backbone of *Police Violence* on the new record, so is that song inspired by personal experience and your day-to-day dealings with the police, or the more recent revelations about the widespread use of horrific and inexcusable violence by police forces across America…

Roger: That song is inspired by something that we have today the police didn't have years ago. You're from England, right? I lived in London for a while and I saw camera's everywhere, and back then, that was the only way to capture what was going on, and this stuff's been going on forever. But now, thanks to the technological age that we live in, people can break out a phone camera and record cops do anything that's illegal. I'm not talking about all cops, I'm just talking about the cops who are going beyond the boundaries of what they're supposed and entitled to do, and illegally beating people. And you know what I'm talking about we've seen it all over the world, and that's what that song's really about, the standards that they think they have. And they have the best prosecutors and defence on their side, so it's hard to convict these people even with that kind evidence. You know why? Because they don't want to have the lawsuits that'd follow a conviction or whatever, that's why. I'm not talking about the people who throw things at, or attack, the police because if you're going to do that, then y'know, what are you gonna do? It's obvious what's going to happen. I'm not talking about that, I'm talking about the cases where there's nothing going on and they suddenly start choking people, or beating them and in some cases end up killing them and that kind of violence has to stop, y'know what I mean? And now in this digital world, they can't get away with it. I remember, when I was living I London, someone got murdered (*I think Roger is referring to the Jean Charles De Menezes case – Tim*) and you could see it unfold, his movements, street by street, and then he got on the tube and…

MM: Do you think that the police should held to a higher standard of behaviour and accountability given their office, the fact that they're armed and what they're employed to do...

Roger: I feel like they should. They should know better, they took an oath. They're being paid by us, to protect and serve us and now they're breaking that oath and the law and they're getting away with it. They should be held accountable for any crime they commit. If you're going to act like a criminal, you should be prosecuted like a criminal. You shouldn't be treated any differently just because you've got a badge, y'know what I mean?

MM: It almost seems like, these days, that the Police have a new set of bosses, the corporations, executives and politicians rather than the citizens who employ them (through taxation). Do you think that they think that there's one law for them and another for the rest of us?

Roger: Absolutely. I think that they think that because they have a badge and they know how to cover each other's backs they can do and they've been doing it for years. You read about these things, they plant guns on people, they plant drugs on people, anything they need to do to make it look like a crime that they had nothing to do with, they'll do it. But, I truly believe that there are good cops out there, cops who really do care. So when does that type of (police) corruption happen? I don't know, but there are cops out there who don't care and whether they're on a mission for themselves or whatever, they just don't care. They hate people. I mean I know shit happens, and if you throw something at a cop, you'd better expect repercussions, just like if you throw something at me, you'd better expect repercussions. I understand that. But when they get caught doing wrong and get away with it... I mean the word sees it, we see what's going on and they still get away with it. That's the anger that I'm talking about.

MM: That anger, it flows through this new record, which is sort of like a fusion of *Victim..*, *Cause..*, *Liberty...* and *One Voice* and has that eighties and early nineties energy...

Roger: Yeah, you're right. This is the easiest record that we've ever done, collectively as a band. We knocked it out in four days, it was really cool. We worked on these songs for a year, a good year and a half, but there was a session which I call the 'CBGB's Matinee Session' which has all those crazy, fast songs, those were presented to the band at the studio. I'd written those on my own, with my buddy Rich Labbate, we do The Alligators together, and he helped me and my drummer for The Disasters (***One of Roger's other bands – Tim)*** and we demoed these songs and presented them to the band and then they nailed it. I wanted to capture that chaotic, almost sloppy and a little bit off feel of *United Blood* and *Victim In Pain* which we did, which was really cool. So, half the record was done with the metronome on the anthemy, classic feel stuff and the heavier songs and the other half was nuts. Just hearing the song, you have two or three takes to get it, do it, put some aggression and whatever you've got into it, give it, kill it. That's just how it was...

MM: Yeah, it sounds incredible. First time I put it on, it took me straight back to 1987...

Roger: I'm glad it did that and I think that our older fans, and even some of our newer fans, will appreciate it. That's where Hardcore comes from and it's like a history lesson being retold and repeated again, and it's like I've always said, if you're going to get into something, learn about it, go back to its roots and find out about it. This goes back to the roots ...

MM: Sticking with the new record, and a theme touched on in *Reasonable Doubt*, do you think that as a society, we'll ever seen true equality between all men and women regardless of the position that they're born into in society and the role that it enforces on them, or will there will always be division and inequality caused by wealth, class and position?

Roger: Do I feel like there'll ever be a sense of equality with the people who govern us? No, I don't think there will be. The problem is... The minute greed comes into play, especially corporate greed, it's over. They'll do whatever it takes, and by any means necessary to ensure they get what they want. One of my favourite artists, Bruce Springsteen who I've always thought was a great songwriter and one of my favourite lines by him goes "Poor man wanna be rich, rich man wanna be king and a king ain't satisfied 'til he rules everything", which says everything. And we're just little tokens to them, they don't give a shit. That's why they start all these meaningless wars and create all this shit, it's all the agenda of someone higher up, we're just numbers to them. We're just population, they don't care, they can do away with us because there's millions of us.

MM: And *Never Walk Alone* seems to revolve around the idea of unity in the Hardcore scene, do you still think that's something that's....

Roger: Yes, and it's funny because when I first started talking and singing about it back in the *United Blood* days, it was a lot smaller, it made a lot more sense, as it was basically twenty, thirty people and then it started growing and growing, and now you look at the scene and it's huge, so does the idea work now on a much bigger scale? At our shows, yes it does, and I see it. I see people of all different races, religions and sub-cultures of our culture, getting together in a room and enjoying themselves. And I've always said that we need to stick together and unite because there's a whole world out there that doesn't understand us and doesn't want to hear our voice, because that causes and creates problems for them, so we need to unite, come together and fight oppression. That's what it's always been about for me and with a song like *Never Walk Alone* it's almost like a pride song like... You know that song that Liverpool FC song? *You'll Never Walk Alone*? It's like that. New York Hard Core is really responsible for putting Hard Core on the worldwide map, and for me, that's really what it's all about, getting out there, seeing it and putting this unity on the map. If it wasn't for NYHC, none of this would have happened, which is why I asked my brother Freddy from Madball, Toby from H2O and Lou from Sick Of It All to sing it with me on the record, because together we're like the four NYHC bands that have made an impact worldwide, singing about this.

MM: When did you first realise that Agnostic Front wasn't just a New York band anymore and that your music had reached out and struck a chord with people all over the world and how did it make you feel....?

Roger: It was amazing because I never thought that there was anything outside of New York City, and to be honest with you I never knew there was anything outside of New York State until I went to prison (laughs) and then I was like 'Oh shit, New York is pretty big' especially when they started throwing me around everywhere. I was pretty ignorant, I was living in New York City and thought that New York City was the only thing there was pretty much. Then I went on our first tour of America and I thought "Wow, this is really cool and it's really big" it was awesome, and then we going to Europe for the first time and I was totally amazed by the love that people had for the band and it was just...Amazing. Then it got even further and we started going into all the Eastern Bloc countries and I remember the first time we went into Russia and I met a kid there and he brought along his *Cause For Alarm* record and he told me

he went to prison just for having that record, just for listening to that record and it meant so much to him just to meet me and... You know what I mean? Wow, the impact that this music, and what I have in general with my band is incredible and I'm very grateful for everything. There've bene many times when I've sat back and wondered 'Why am I doing this? Is it pointless? Where am I going?' I don't have a retirement plan, I never went to high school, I never went to college and then you meet these people, like that kid and you feel so good about what you're good about what you're doing. I guess my purpose in life was to be here to help people fight oppression in... You won't believe the countless times I've heard people say 'If it wasn't for you I would have been dead' and 'If it wasn't for you or my life would have gone completely wrong' and it feels great. It's rewarding, it's in my heart and that's all that matters.

MM: Back to the record... *A Wise Man*. Who was the wise man? And do the things that he told you back then still ring true today?

Roger: Absolutely. *A Wise Man* is a magical song for me, because it's very much like our album *One Voice*. A friend of ours, Ricky from Backfire had presented us with this song and said "Hey I think you guys should have it because it sounds like a *One Voice* song". And when I heard it I went: Whoa it really does. I wrote the lyrics to it, the band put their flavour to it and then I had Matt Henderson, who was one of our guitarists on the *One Voice* record come in and play on it. Lyrically, its content is about an old friend of ours who kind of watched us grow up in New York City, whose name was John Noone. He was an old Italian guy who protected us from all the insanity and all the stuff we used to do. There is a classic story, I was trying to park the band van and I guy snuck in and took the parking spot when we'd left so we went round the corner, I grabbed an axe, Vinnie grabbed a bat and Carl grabbed a brick; and we just, in broad daylight on Houseman St., which is unheard of, axed the car like a can opener all the way round. Vinnie put in every window, Carl broke all the lights and there was one more person (I can't remember his name) stabbed all the tyres. We went on a roof and watched the guy come back out. John Noone would see us do stuff like this and say "Hey guys it's hot out here right now, wait two or three days then come back out." He kind of taught us the way of things. He was an old Italian guy – very Mafioso and this song ties into that.

MM: Again, back to the album and the song *Enough is Enough*. Do you think it's every citizen's duty, as it states in the Declaration of Independence, to overthrow a Government that doesn't work for its people and stand against unjust oppression? Or do you think people have forgotten this is their right and do you think it will ever happen?

Roger: I believe so. I think things have gone so far in this country.... I mean they don't even teach cursive in schools any more. I have this crazy theory, call me a conspiracy nut or whatever, that in twenty or so years from now, when some kid looks at the constitution they are not even going to be able to use it. They will say "What is this crazy thing?" and if they can, they will start to erase the history books because it's not the first time it's been done, the history books have been erased before. It's been done for centuries. That's what this album speaks about, especially in the intro when it talks about all our constitutional rights being stripped away. And the way the media works in this country is they will tell you whatever they want you to know, but they are working for their own political groups; they are working for the Democrats and the Republicans.

It's hard to find any true independent media, I listen to a lot of RT news and I listen to a lot of the BBC to find out what's going on in America, and I listen to a little CNN but they can be a little biased at times, rather than the regular American news.

MM: On *Old New York* you talk about how you miss the old city. So how has New York changed as a city?

Roger: It's like a foot to a coin, you know what I mean? The old New York that I miss, the city that I write songs about... If you listen to my first album *Victim in Pain* and then you visited New York City, you'd be like "What's this guy on about? This guy is crazy – it's beautiful, it's safe it's nice; back then it was dangerous and it was this element of danger that helped to create these great bands and great artists. There was an element of nastiness to the city that's now missing in a lot of these newer bands and artists, that don't have the same grit, the same edge. I'm talking about the New York City you probably see best in a movie like *Taxi Driver*, which is why we use a clip of that movie in the song; because it describes that New York. The New York City you go to today is bullshit; it's safe, it's nice, which is great for the tourists but at the same time it's ripping them off because if you try to get a hotel there it's going to cost you $300 for a night. It's ridiculous, but it is what it is...

MM: in *Test of Time* you talk about what you've learned from the past and how it relates to whom, and where, you are today. What, if anything, do you regret?

Roger: I don't know, regrets are a hard thing. There was probably a different path I could have taken, I don't know if I regret anything because everything has led me to where I am today. I've had hard times in my life, I've been incarcerated, I've lived on the streets, I've lived in abandoned buildings, but that that was the stuff that led me to where I am. Do I wish that other people lived, or live like that? No, of course not. That's why, with my other band Roger Miret & The Disasters I have a song about all these people that think it's cool to dress, or look like they're impoverished or even live in poverty when they don't need to. There's nothing cool about poverty. I lived in poverty, I had no choice, I lived in the ghetto, but I didn't know it was the ghetto because I was just a kid. Looking back at it now, it was completely normal for me, but it's dangerous and there's nothing cool about it.

MM: Staying on point and following a similar theme, what do you attribute Agnostic Front's longevity to?

Roger: Being genuine, being honest and being real. You know people have heard all sorts of stories and myths about us, but when actually come out to a show and meet the band, they see that we're genuine and real and who doesn't want to be a part of something like that? You want to be a part of something that's fake or something that's real? I think people catch on to that really quickly with us and they want to associate themselves with something that's real.

MM: You mentioned the stories and rumours that people hear about AF, so are there any that you've heard that stand out for you that are so ridiculous they just make you laugh...

Roger: Absolutely, I can't remember all of them. We've been accused of all sorts of stuff, even racism, which is totally ridiculous. I mean, first of all, I'm Latin and I grew up poor, living amongst all kinds of people, different races and religions which led to me being able to get along with anyone and everyone and that's why when I talk about unity, I really understand it. I hate being Pidgeon-holed and being accused of being something that I'm not, like being anti-gay, which I'm most definitely. I mean, I lived in New York City, I didn't live in a fucking cave, I've seen it my whole goddamn life. I have relatives who are gay, what do I care? As long as they're in love and they're happy, why should I care about anything else? People always try to put stuff on me and say that I said this or that or interpret something in the wrong way or for their own benefit, but that's the nature of the hater and I don't focus on haters, I gravitate toward people who are genuine and real like myself. These people, all they want is their noise to create a little buzz for something else. Have I done bad things in my past? Have I done things, that like you mentioned before, I regret as a teenager? Probably.

MM: But we all do though, we all do stupid things when we're young. That's part of growing up...

Roger: Yeah, we all do. If you ever want to read my "diaries", just pick up any of the Roger Miret & The Disasters albums because I can write stuff there and feel like I'm not under a microscope y'know? True story from when I was a kid though, I threw a garbage can through a McDonald's window on 6th Street and 1st Avenue in broad daylight, because I was totally against that corporation and everything they stood for. But that was '81 or '82. Would I do that today? No, because I know about the camera's and how they watch your every move, but what I would do is go there late at night with a tube of glue and put some of that in the lock, give 'em a hard time when they try to get back in. Did I do stupid things? (Sighs) Yeah...

MM: But, we all did, that's just the way of things...

Roger: And you're an idiot if you think that you didn't, you know what I mean? Some people are so elitist and politically correct that they think they didn't. But you know what? I'll be completely honest with you, the scene when it was created, when punk rock began, there was nothing cool about being politically correct, the whole politically correct thing was incorrect. That's a strong statement right there... And that's this whole thing came from. Eventually with all the rules and shit you had to go through, people want to Pidgeon toe you into something, which is just completely ignorant.

MM: Talking about the beginning of the scene and where it all came from, I've just read Tony Rettman's book, *NYHC: 1980 – 1990*. Do you think that paints a much truer and more accurate portrait of the NY scene than Steven Blush's *American Hardcore* did?

Roger: They're both really good books, but they're both really different books. Tony's is more super-intensive about New York and it's got way more information about the New York scene and the other one is a much broader examination of American Hardcore as a whole. That being said, I prefer Tony's book, because I'm enjoying it more a perspective as it takes me back there. I'm finishing my book off too by the way...

MM: Whoa, wait a minute. You're writing a book?

Roger: I've been writing a book since... Jesus, 1998. I lost it two times, once during the attacks on the World Trade Centre and another time after that due to all the file corruption and shit on my computer. I finally teamed up with a guy called Jon Wiederhorn who helped Scott Ian finish his book, and he also helped what's that guy from Ministry...Oh yeah, Al Jorgensen finish his. We've been friends for a while and he was just like 'Roger, just let me help you finish that book' so I've teamed up with him and given him all the information that I have. We do these intense interviews and go back and forth and stuff and it's scheduled to be released at the end of this year. So, who knows? It's really intense, it's an in-depth story about my life. About coming to America as a Cuban immigrant, living in the harsh area's I did, my abusive upbringing as a child, coming into the NYHC scene and my life in it...

MM: Who's publishing it?

Roger: Well, right now, it's at a couple of places, but Jon is hoping to go with a publisher that he works with a lot, Da Capo, but we don't know, because there are other offers on the table. But y'know, I'm excited that it's coming out after all these years. I've talked about it on a couple of records, and people were always asking 'Where's your book?' and life in general, touring, having children again in 2007, I thought 'You know what, I'm never going to finish this thing' and so I thought, I'm just going to team up with Jon and finally get it finished and out.

MM: You guys reunited the *Cause For Alarm* line-up at Black'N'Blue last year. So, do you have any plans to do that again, or was it just a one off?

Roger: That was just a one off, two nights only. We do these special things once in a while, we did the one off for *Victim In Pain* years ago, so the next one I guess, in a few years, will be *Liberty And Justice* if that happens, or maybe *One Voice*.

MM: How were the shows?

Roger: They were great. I didn't get to practice with the band, so the minute I arrived in New York... I live in Arizona now, I've been living here for nine years, as soon as I arrived in New York I went to one rehearsal and I was like, 'Wow', we played the songs and it sounded vital. It was magical man, they were magical times. Even with the 'Victim In Pain' line-up I didn't get to practice with the band except for the one night before, but as soon as we hit the stage, it feels great, it really does.

MM: I'm sorry Roger, but I have to ask you this. You were very nearly in the Cro-Mags weren't you?

Roger: I was asked to join the Cro-Mags and sing for them, yes.

MM: So why you'd turn the gig down? I'm just curious is all...

Roger: Well, y'know... Me and Harley were friends for a long time, but deep down inside I knew that I could never be in a band with Harley because we're both the same kind of person. We're both leaders and eventually we'd just butt heads. I played bass for the Cro-Mags first show when Eric was the singer and Paris was on guitar and Harley played drums. That was the Cro-Mags first ever show, we'd just jammed out five or six songs really quick and *Victim In Pain* has just come out at the time and I was really into doing Agnostic Front, so I was really doing the Cro-Mags as a favour to Harley and at the time I was working on another band with Petey Hines, and it was a whirlwind thing as everybody was playing with everybody and it didn't really work out. The only thing that came out of that was that Petey eventually became the drummer for the Cro-Mags. It is what it is and that band has got its own history and its own dealings and they put out a phenomenal record in *Age of Quarrel*. You can't take that away from them. I was also asked to be a part of S.O.D, but I passed that on to Billy Milano because that wasn't what I was about. It was a joke but y'know, I'm not a jokey kind of guy.

MM: What's next for Agnostic Front? Because the albums out in April, yes? What about touring?

Roger: Yeah, the album is out in April, and then we're doing three sets of touring. I know that Europe isn't in the first, but it might be the second or the third as they're still being booked. I'm hoping it's more toward the Third as that's happening in the Fall, bit whatever it is, it is. I don't tour as much as I used to because I have a family and I want to be able to spend as much time as I possibly can with them.

Originally published in Mass Movement Presents: NYHC, July 2014

ANDY WEST
(KILL YOUR IDOLS)

I've written at length about Kill Your Idols in other intros for this issue of MM. Suffice to say the band remains one of my all-time favourites, and I have been lucky enough to tour with them on numerous occasions. As always tour life has its ups and downs, and KYI certainly had their fair share of both, but whatever life threw at them, they always remained absolute gentlemen and a pleasure to be around. Vocalist Andy was no exception to this, so I was more than happy to get his feedback for this NYHC special. Take it away Andy...

Interview by Tom Chapman

Photograph(s) by Angela Boatwright

MM: When did you first become aware of the punk/Hardcore scene and in particular NYHC?

Andy: Well when I was in high school and still a hippy/dead head type guy someone gave me Angry Samoans *Inside My Brain* and Descendents *Milo Goes To College* They were so interesting to me. No record label that I'd ever heard of, or that looked "real" and the music and lyrics. At that time Zappa was like the most shocking thing I knew because of all the curses and stuff. I remember just staring at the back of the Angry Samoans record wondering what kind of people were these? It still took a few years for me to really seek out more and go to see bands but those records really had an impact on me.

A few years later I was going through a bad breakup and looking for something new or different. A friend of mine who was also a hippy had come from the Hardcore scene and even though he wasn't into it anymore he still loved some of the stuff he knew. So anyway he dragged me to a Circle Jerks show. Again, I was so fascinated by the people and scene, The angry, aggressive, but not violent, dancing and everything. So I started to check out some of the bigger bands like Exploited, GBH, etc. I'd go and I remember wondering, "where do these people go when there's not a show" and stuff like that. I'd be real gung ho on it, but the shows were few and far between, so it's like the feeling would fade. At one of those big punk shows though I was handed a flyer that said "Hardcore matinee" it was at CBGB's and was Bold Gorilla Biscuits I don't remember who played but that was it, I was hooked. It was more a crowd of "normal" people, You know, not so much the Mohawks, liberty spikes, etc. And more personal, just everything about it blew me away. I remember seeing the guys from GB just walking up to the show. That alone really blew me away!

MM: Who were your peers that were around you when you started your hardcore journey?

Andy: I had no peers then (laughs). I literally went to shows alone the first few years. Once in a while if it was a bigger show my best friend (the hippy who took me to the Circle Jerks show) would go. And rarely I could drag one of my other friends along. But none of them got it like me. Not one. Honestly it was an amazing time. By going alone I'd absorb everything. Every band, zine, flyer, every other kid I'd see at all the shows. I didn't know any of the gossip or rumours or anything. It was so pure, exciting and really just what I had been looking for.

MM: Does "NYHC" as such still exist in your mind today?

Andy: Of course it does. I can't claim to be right in the middle of it as I once may have been. Or even really on top of it, as far as what newer bands are making a splash and all. But I know full well it's something that's very important to a lot of people. And for sure there will always be a new crew of kids to carry that torch.

MM: What were some of the magical factors that made the scene in its heyday what it was for you?

Andy: It's kind of hard to say, the whole thing was magical to me. The sense of unity and everyone knowing each other. The breakdown of the band/audience barrier was huge. It's like what I got into earlier, I was alone usually so I really absorbed everything. I didn't hear or know about all the rumours and "beef" and all.

Originally published in Mass Movement Presents: NYHC , July 2014

CHAKA MALIK
(BURN / ORANGE 9MM)

Burn was a flame that shone very brightly around 1990. Their debut EP on Revelation and contributions to a couple of classic Hardcore compilations *Forever* and *Rebuilding* put their name on everyone's lips. As with many explosive Hardcore acts, the initial fire raged for a short time only, before the band drifted apart and band members went onto acts that were part of the next wave of New York Hardcore - Die 116 and Orange 9MM.

But from the embers arose new flames, and the previously unreleased *Last Great Sea* and *Cleanse* records surfaced many years later. Now almost out of the blue Burn have been announced as special guests for the 2015 Black N Blue Show in New York, so it felt like the ideal opportunity to get the lowdown from Burn frontman Chaka Malik himself...

Interview by Tom Chapman

Photographs by Adam Tanner, Sean Cronan & Tom Chapman

MM: Let's go back to your roots, which part of New York did you grow up in, was that where you started discovering the music?

Chaka: I grew in Queens, born in Woodside in Astoria. There were some people that hung out locally but generally most of the engagement was happening in downtown, the lower east side of Manhattan, around the CBGB's area. This was around 86, 87.

MM: What were the bands that really inspired you at the time?

Chaka: SOIA, Absolution, bands like Side By Side. I was also into a lot of the oi bands. I was into Black Flag, I was into Last Resort. I liked the 4 Skins, The Business. I also liked Vice Squad, I liked the punk, you know, Cherry Red Records stuff.

MM: What were your early memories of going to Hardcore shows in the city - was it a frightening experience? Was it good fun? What was the atmosphere like?

Chaka: I guess, one thing I can recollect, when I was walking from my apartment to the train, I had like a nervous feeling in my stomach. I don't know what it was, it wasn't fear. It might have been anxiousness, excitement. But I know that when I got outside of CBGB's there was definitely a tangible feeling. I don't know if it was good or bad. All truth be told, there was some fright, there was definitely a lot of energy. There was a lot of physicality, a lot of angst being released. People say you could cut the air with a knife, it was definitely that kind of thing.

MM: Was it a welcoming place, or did you have to prove your place - were people accepting?

Chaka: I guess there was a bit of both. I mean, I used to dance pretty aggressively, and there were misunderstandings that occurred with different people and that got worked out and ended up in friendships. I don't think there was a prove your ground type mentality - maybe in the pit there was, but it wasn't really something that translated to just standing around outside of CBGB's. I don't recall being singled out or something like that but I know that in the pit, if you were dancing, I remember seeing like a couple of guys who were not psyched that I was dancing this aggressively. I remember things like that.

MM: From being a person attending the shows, was your first step towards getting more involved and putting out the New Breed compilation?

Chaka: I guess it was, right? I was friends with the kids that looked more kinda like me, black or Latino or something like that. I was friends with the nerdier kids at school, I was friends with the jock guys. I was always the kind of person that got along with people and that lent itself to... Hardcore is structured in a sense that if you can create something that is worthwhile, people will purchase it and support it, and that allows you to move up - not the rungs or something, but become more visible. I think that... Being an interesting dancer, maybe that lent me some kind of notoriety. So when me and Freddy decided to do the comp it was kind of a natural progression. It was like, what do you have to offer? Being in a band, or you're someone that can silk screen shirts, or you know somebody at the venue. Everybody does their part and at that time I guess my part at that time ended up with me putting out that compilation.

MM: Do you remember any of the bands that you were especially involved with on that comp?

Chaka: I would probably give Freddy a lot of the credit for pulling a lot of the bands together. I think he had been interviewing bands by then and had established himself as a resource of some kind. He did most of the legwork, my major focus was doing the artwork, getting the cover done, doing a couple of pages for Absolution and the credits page, some in-house mastering and trying to get the different songs from different sources. Bands had recorded with almost no budget in some cases - I think we put up some money for Absolution to record. Getting the music to sound like music, and doing the duplicates, one by one at my house. It was a DIY thing in the true sense of the word, a multi-dimensional experience and having the booklet really helps it.

MM: Then you put Burn together. How did that happen?

Chaka: I became friends with Gavin - there was a bit of a graffiti tie-in there too, and, working at the health food store and being around musicians. I'm pretty sure it was Gavin's idea to be honest, but I could be wrong. It was myself, Alex Napack, John Cruickshen and Gavin and we started rehearsing.

MM: For me when Burn arrived at an interesting time, you had the tail end of the bands like SOIA moving onto bigger things and you had the more underground stuff happening at ABC No Rio. Did you fit more in between those scenes?

Chaka: Yeah, oddly enough... You may or may not know this, but the first time we played live, Sick Of It All was kind enough to let us play four songs before them, and then our first full set was at ABC No Rio. In a weird way you've kind of answered your own question! It was a combination of influences and this is where I won't take credit for the new Breed comp musically, but with Burn we had multiple tastes and multiple influences that we were bringing into the genre.

MM: I think Burn was a little different, less formulaic, as at the time the NYHC sound was a marketable sound, so you had bands across the globe doing it....

Chaka: There's some truth to that statement, because the New York sound is so good, it makes sense to copy it. It's like pizza. The recipe for pizza it's frickin' amazing so why not, if you can, open up a pizzeria and people are gonna come. That's a testament to Hardcore, and bands like AF, Sick Of It All, Madball, Cro-Mags, Bad Brains to some degree and Murphy's Law, the bands that really put that sound on the map.

MM: How did you hook up with Revelation?

Chaka: Alan was actually playing in Quicksand, and through Walter they had already recording a seven inch, and Alan was like "Jordan, hey I'm playing in this band Burn" and sent him a tape, and Jordan was like "Record as many songs as you like and I'll do an EP or an album" and so we ended up doing an EP.

MM: It came out at roughly the same time as the Quicksand EP...

Chaka: It was in the same kinda era. I think that kinda marked the next step for the post-Hardcore thing.

MM: Before Burn split, what would you say were the highlights of the band?

Chaka: We a lot of great shows in Boston. We played the Channel with Agnostic Front and then there was the show with Sick Of It All and Boogie Down Productions at the Marquee. That was a great show, probably one of the illest cultural shows I think as it helped in seeding the whole street music kinda thing. At that time "moshing" was so different - some of the dudes that were with BDP's entourage got tight because they didn't understand what people were doing, people we bumping into them. Now everyone knows what it is and either mock it or join in but to them I think it looked like a skirmish or something. That goes to show how early it was in terms of urban culture, because after all, Hardcore is urban music.

MM: Was there much of a tie-in with Hardcore and hip-hop, or was that show the exception?

Chaka: Well, graffiti is the great equaliser. It was before the internet you could see - and now I sound like an old ass man, and I don't care - if you saw a black dude, a white dude and a Chinese dude together, you knew they were writers. At the end of the day it's art and that's what art does. That's why people go to art school to hang out. No disrespect to people who go to art school because that's amazing, but you always hear people in bands say how they met at art school. I wish I had gone to art school, who knows what I would have been! Something about art and music and the way they tie into each other, can be powerful in terms of opening doorways and sharing ideas. It's like the pre-internet internet right? The key is, often you have communities made up of people that look just like each other, but when it's made of people that don't look like each other, that's where your point of view becomes uniquely interesting to me.

MM: Okay, getting back to Burn, it felt to me that no sooner had you started up, then you had split and there were bands like Orange 9MM and Die 116 on the go. Did Burn break up before their time?

Chaka: I've been asked this question in the last couple of interviews! I think the people in the band are very individualistic, I think Gavin is very individualistic and very creative and able and I felt like I'm like that too. When you have people that are that way, and you're having a difficult time finding a drummer to replace Alan and Alex ends up not wanting to play in the band .At a certain point you're like you know what, I think I'm going to do my own thing, it's just a natural reaction to the round peg not fitting in the round hole.

MM: With Orange 9MM was the aim for that to be a continuation of Burn, or to explore new musical horizons?

Chaka: New musical horizons without a doubt.

MM: The sound moved on and you attracted the major label interest...

Chaka: What's interesting is we had major label interest with the existing sound, and I think what happens is... You go to California and you work with Jane's Addiction's producer and all of a sudden you forget what your first and last name is, you forget where your hind end is and basically making a record that sounds like something else.

Instead of making our record I think that we ended up making somebody else's record and that was the beginning of the undoing. I could play you the very first song that Orange 9MM demo'd at Don Fury's studio and it sounds very much like the EP that was recorded a few months later. We got a record deal a couple of months after that and we went out to LA and all of a sudden... You learn from an experience like that.

One of the things that I know now as an adult is... Let me give you an example. I record my own music, and when I record new songs and that reminds me of a song that I recorded five or ten years ago, and that's because as a person I have a sound. The more that you can recognise that you have a sound, the more successful you can be. Look at a band like the Rolling Stones or any of these bands that basically kept doing themselves. You have success, your fan base comes in and comes out, new people come in, old people go out, old people come back in again, it's like that intertwining, continuous figure of eight pattern. That's the natural progression of any manifestation, you keep doing what you know how to do. I mean, Apple makes innovative products that look really cool and push the boundaries of technology. If Apple came up with something that didn't do those things people would be like okay, what is this? I think that's what we did with Orange 9MM. We didn't stick to the script. We didn't let ourselves just do "us", We tried to do somebody else and tried to be a different band because we were under the influence of people. I'm not saying anybody forced us - nobody forced us.

MM: Do you wish you could change that?

Chaka: No! Because that's fruitless. What I do recognise now, and I'm glad I'm having this conversation with you. It's like you know what dude, you are who you are at the end of the day. Not that you can't grow and change - you have to grow and change, you have to improve, but at the basis of who you are. Maybe my voice gets more... Maybe I'm able to sing more in tune, maybe I'll be able to scream louder, maybe I'm able to scream softer, but it's still my voice.

But if I try to sound like somebody else it's like I'm not in my real house, I'm not in my comfort zone. People grow accustomed to things. You have friends because they are comfortable around you, but when you do something crazy they're like why did you do that? I'm no longer comfortable around you and you have to say, "Well okay, this is why that happened..".

MM: With the music you're making now, is it a solo sort of deal? What kind of set-up do you have?

Chaka: (Pause) I'm basically working solo, I have invited one friend of mine - a singer that you guys know but I'm not going to say his name because I don't want to as I don't want to jinx it and I'd rather let it happen than talk crap, to guest with me on a song. The new thing that I do is called Ghost Decibels. One of my friends described it as Goth... It's really gothic, meets some R&B influences, meets some hip hop and electronic type influences. I really like Goth, new wave type music.

MM: Is there anything out there for people to listen to?

Chaka: I'm debating that. I'm considering putting out a cassette tape, just to be weird and have people not be able to play it (laughs). Maybe that's counter-intuitive, maybe not, but then I'm also like, there's so much music already out there what's the point of releasing stuff, just so there's one more MP3 on Soundcloud?! Let me ask you - you're in a band right. You record music, what do you do, you put it on Soundcloud, what are your expectations?

MM: Well I'm old fashioned, I want to see that on vinyl, on 7" or 12" record rather than just on a virtual platform...

Chaka: I kind of live somewhere between that. Let me tell you this - when you buy software from a store, you get a big box. You don't need that big box, but they give you that box with a nice illustration on it, because people like physical crap. I wanna feel like I'm getting something tangible. I'm spending a couple of hundred bucks on this piece of software, give me a frickin' box! Don't just put the CD in a sleeve. And that's how I feel with music. Give me a package, I want a package. I want some pictures, maybe some writing, I want some thoughts, give me something. Seed me, help me understand this experience.

When I was a kid I used to listen to my parents' records. They had everybody - Jimi Hendrix, The Doors, Aretha Franklin and all kinds of jazz. I used to sit down and put the headphones on and open up the gatefold. I loved gatefold records, I would listen to a gatefold record more just so I could open up the gatefold and look at all the things included. That's my relationship with music, there's an audio component and a visual component. I want to feel the record and the cardboard that it comes in. I want to be able to smell the cardboard!

MM: And with MP3's and Soundcloud, that kind of thing is great for hearing new bands but it doesn't have the same feeling for me...

Chaka: I agree. Let me ask you this - let's say we meet in person and I say Tom I really wanna thank you for this interview, before I go what are we gonna do probably?

MM: We'll shake hands...

Chaka: Exactly. We solidify the moment, and that's what's missing for me. And you can't appreciate music, on a deeper level without that handshake upholding the MP3. There's too much content. How do you take your music from being just content, to being something that someone can experience and continue to experience in a unique way. For me, after a full day's work I feel good if I got something done, if I don't get anything done I'm almost confused, like is the day over? What did I do today? I feel like music is the same thing - if I record something just to put it out on the internet that almost feels anti-climactic to me.

MM: Okay, let's get back to the present - you guys (Burn) are playing a show - how did that happen?

Chaka: Actually my friend Sasha is the one that basically was like you guys should play (***The annual Black n Blue show held in NYC - Tom***), and there was no resistance from me, I was like, okay let's make it happen! It was a very weird thing, it was almost like when your mom finally says yes to you going to the party at the weekend with your friends and you're like "I can't believe she just said yes, is she drunk or something?" But it was very easy.

Originally published in Mass Movement Presents: NYHC, July 2014

FREDDY ALVA

NYHC has experienced many different waves and had more than one golden age. For me one of the prime eras was the birth and early days of the ABC NO Rio scene. Bands like Born Against, Citizens Arrest, Go! and Rorschach had a gritty rough sound, compounded with a strong DIY ethic and positioned themselves as an alternative to the CBGBs scene which had suffered from violence at its shows. One of the labels at the forefront of that scene was Wardance records, operated by Freddy Alva.

Freddy had also released the incredible *New Breed* compilation tape which featured some of the best material from the likes of Absolution, Raw Deal, Beyond, Outburst and Fit Of Anger, and so many other raw, talented bands. Freddy is still around, releasing music and literature under the Wardance label as well as writing some great columns for , so it was a real pleasure to catch up with with and get his take on the world of NYHC.

Interview by Tom Chapman

MM: I remember seeing the *New Breed* compilation come out and then some great releases on Wardance records, what were your first steps towards getting involved in the NYHC scene?

Freddy: I got into the scene through some High School friends that had a band called Occupied Territory. That was in 1985 and I went to my first Hardcore Matinee at CBGB's. By the following year I was fully engrossed, attending concerts at the Pyramid Club, buying demos, singles and albums at Some Records and making friends with kids in my neighborhood of Queens, which at that time, was a hotbed of HC related activity.

MM: How did you go about putting the New Breed tape together? There's quite a variety of bands on there? Am I right in thinking Chaka from Burn helped you out?

Freddy: The New Breed compilation was an extension of my fanzine, of which I did one issue. I became friends with Chaka through hanging out in the same circles and I proposed we do a venture together which became "Urban Style Records" and the compilation tape was the first and only release on that.

The variety of bands on the compilation reflects all the people we knew that had bands, everything was through word of mouth, there were some people that we asked to be on it. Others heard about it through mutual friends and asked to be on it, everything came about in a very organic fashion. I used the cut and paste skills from doing fanzines to put the booklet/tape cover together. Chaka was in charge of "production", which meant equalizing all the demos we received onto one master tape. This was accomplished on his double cassette deck which also served as our dubbing factory. I would say the compilation had a domino effect on Chaka to get Burn started as the musicians he asked to play with him later on, he got to know through assembling the tape.

MM: Whilst that release is a total DIY effort, various bands on there soon went onto record for bigger labels, at the time how did you feel about that? Were you happy for the bands or did you feel like you were a stepping stone for them?

Freddy: I think the only band that went on to a "bigger" label was Raw Deal, when they changed their name to Killing Time and signed to In Effect Records. All the others that managed to put records out did so on DIY labels like Combined Effort, Blackout, Wreckage. I felt excited about all the bands that put records out & think that the compilation helped, in a small but significant fashion, as far as getting their name out there. I don't think they considered being on the comp as a rung on the ladder to bigger and better things. We were all in this together and would have gladly done anything to promote this amazing music that meant everything to us.

MM: How do you feel about the various bootlegs and reissues that have come out over the years, are you glad the songs lived on, or do you wish people had left your work alone?

Freddy: I was all for the bootlegs, even if done shoddily, they still kept the name out there for the succeeding generations of NYHC enthusiasts. Cover versions of songs on the comp by younger bands also helped keep the memory alive. I've tried to compile over the years a list of cover versions of songs on the comp done by other bands and there are dozens of them. At last count, Outburst's *The Hardway* seemed to be leading the pack, as there quite a few of them but one of the coolest tributes I ever saw was a European tape compilation done in like '08 called *Pressure Release- Europe's New Breed* which, as you can tell, is a direct homage with contemporary bands sounding like the Some Records demo scene circa '87-'89.

MM: A couple of years afterwards you had the emergence of the ABC No Rio scene, what got you involved in that world? What were the factors there that made it special?

Freddy: When ABC No Rio started in 1990, about 2/3rds of bands on the comp had broken up. The scene had grown considerably larger, violence was at an all-time at the CBGB's matinees. A lot of people I knew from hanging out with just a couple of years previously, were moving on with their lives. Whether that involved going to college, joining the service, having kids or getting into "Indie Rock" or its successor: Alternative Rock. Change was in the air and almost overnight, a new scene sprung up at ABC No Rio. The Hardcore Matinees started there by Mike Bullshit were to be an alternative to what was going on in the "regular" NYHC scene with an emphasis on political/personal issues, non-commercialism and zero tolerance for violent behaviour. Highly idealistic and naive thinking at times, but that's what made the early days at ABC No Rio so special. I honestly don't think I would have stayed involved with Hardcore if ABC No Rio had not started. I would have probably just grown out of the dominant NYHC scene, moved on to "Post-HC" bands or simply drifted away like a lot of my peers. What happened at ABC No Rio in 1990 was a sort of rebirth for me as far as why I got into HC in the first place in '85.

MM: Did you keep involved in the "other" side of the scene with bands like AF, GB, SOIA etc or were they two completely separate worlds?

Freddy: I kept a peripheral interest in what was going on in that world, but honestly, I wasn't into what AF, SOIA or GB were doing musically by then. I also wasn't into what was becoming the dominant "chugga-chugga" mosh metal sound in NYHC. This was kind of ironic because a lot of those bands claimed being influenced by stuff on the New Breed comp. In my view, it was a case of the followers not being as enticing as the originators. There was definitely different scenes by then: The bigger standard NYHC one, ABC No Rio and the Squat Or Rot shows/bands; which was a different beast all together.

MM: Are you still involved in the ABC side of things?

Freddy: I haven't been actively involved with ABC No Rio since I stopped booking shows there in late 1991. The successive collectives that took over did an amazing job of maintaining and expanding the club to the extent that besides having shows there is also now: a zine library, photo/shirt screening work stations, activist workshops plus a ton of other worthily activities going on at any given moment.

MM: Can you tell us how you ended up working with some of those great bands on Wardance records?

Freddy: I have to say I lucked out. A couple of guys that played in bands on the New Breed comp started up Citizens Arrest and quickly became one of the ABC No Rio "house bands". They put out a ferocious nine song demo and Matt Domino from Infest expressed an interest in doing a 7" with them. Matt couldn't do it for whatever reason so they asked me if I'd be into doing it. I figured how hard could it be and that's how Wardance started. The next releases happened in the same fashion: I was friends with the people in Rorschach, Hell No and 1.6 Band. They played continuously at ABC and I wanted to document them. Luckily for me, it was just a matter of being at the right place and time.

MM: After the initial brutality of bands like Citizens Arrest, Born Against, Rorschach, the next wave of those bands were much more experimental, Hell No, 1.6 Band, Young Pioneers etc, was there a conscious move do you think to "grow out of" Hardcore?

Freddy: I would say that Rorschach and Born Against also moved on to more experimental sounds by the time they recording their second LP's and I'm sure Citizens Arrest would have some expanded their range had they not broken up in '91. I always dug Hell No's blend of Am Rep style riffs with Hardcore, Young Pioneers take on lo-fi punk and 1.6 Band's incredible musical skills that put them in their own category. I don't they were consciously trying to grow out of Hardcore but more like to trying to experiment and push the boundaries of the genre while staying rooted in its essence. Of course if you were to compare what they were doing in '93 as opposed to what was considered Hardcore in '83, it would not sound the same at first, but upon repeated listenings; the basic Hardcore fury and spirit is still there. It's just being manifested in an updated & musically proficient manner.

MM: What caused you to stop doing the label and, ultimately, to recently relaunch it?

Freddy: I put out my last release in '94, a 7" by a Peruvian band called Futuro Incierto. Except for them, all the other bands I'd released had broken up. I stopped going to ABC and Harcore shows in general. I got seriously involved in relationships, did a lot of traveling and finally buckled down to go to school full time by '98. I followed what was going on in Hardcore land vicariously through friends for the next ten years until in '08 an old friend of mine offered to finance a vinyl and CD reissue of the New Breed compiltion. That kicked off Wardance's return and since then I've averaged about a couple of releases per year.

Whether it be 7"s, LP's, Tapes or a book, the main impetus is still the same: put out material by friends whose work I admire. Trends will come and go but it's my friends output that continues to inspire me.

MM: Looking back, it seems most people have come full circle and the older faces from those scenes seem much happier talking/ working together on music projects. I mean in the early 90's I wouldn't have expected to be seeing someone from Wardance records writing about Dmize or Madball...

Freddy: Well, it's actually not so strange to see me talking about somebody like Dmize. I went to High School with their singer, knew him and the drummer when we all followed Occupied Territory, the band I mentioned at the beginning of the interview. I love their demo and they played like the third matinee at ABC No Rio in 1990 plus we all grew up in the same neighborhoods so we go way back.

I think time allows for retrospection and what might have looked like opposing factions back then, was really just different ways to express ourselves within the wider Hardcore /Punk culture. People would be surprised to know who was friends with who back then and now. I think NYC has always been an all-inclusive, big enough place to hold divergent views kinda place and the NYHC scene reflects that outlook.

MM: Is NYHC still alive and well, or has it become a museum piece that gets showcased in professional books, art galleries and eBay?

Freddy: NYHC is alive and well, both as a "brand" and a functional entity. It's probably bigger worldwide than ever. The recent documentation of its early days via books, articles, films etc., only adds to the canon and builds upon an ever growing reputation. The continued success of bands like SOIA/Madball, allows a spotlight to be shined on lesser known bands and recordings that got over looked. For example: the never released Antidote related High & Mighty 7", the post- Agnostic Front/pre-Nausea band Sacrilege and their unreleased LP. There are tons of other as deserving reissues being churned out on a regular basis. I don't think NYHC has become a museum piece. A lot of the originators are still around and putting out new material. As long as contemporary bands continue to cite this scene as an influence and maintain the same sonic arc. This music will keep on being relevant to newer fans that might not have been around during the scene's genesis but are willing to continue and expand upon the enduring blueprint.

MM: A lot of bands broke up with only and EP or demo to their name - which bands do you think would have put out incredible records had they carried on?

Freddy: Oh man, I could go on forever with a list! For starters, all the 1st generation bands that only put out 7"s. Bands like Antidote, The Abused, Major Conflict, Urban Waste, No Thanks... Wish they'd all recorded more stuff during that era. Also, demo only bands like The Psychos, Kreig Kopft, YDL (w/English Nick) or undocumented ones like MOI, Irate, Frontline, Bloodclot, Mr. Softee, Shok. Bands from the New Breed compilation that I wish had done records: Collapse, A-Bomb-A-Nation, True Colors, Our Gang, Under Pressure, Fit Of Anger... Bands from the early ABC No Rio days: Antiem, Insurgence, Slaughter. Last but not least, I wish Absolution had stuck around and done a proper full length back in 1989, same goes for Burn!

MM: Following on from that are there some hidden recordings which bands made that never saw the light of day, any buried treasures or holy grails you'd like to see released?

Freddy: Well, I wish that Krakdown/NY Hoods split LP had come out, not sure if it was ever recorded. The first Token Entry LP with Anthony from Killing Time singing is another "lost" recording that should see the light of day. Sacrilege (AF/Nausea members) recorded a 7" in '85 and only a couple test pressings exist somewhere. There are rumours of Straight Ahead studio recordings post "Breakaway" 12" floating around. A-Bomb-A-Nation recorded an LP with a different singer sometime in '89. There is also supposedly a 12" lacquer cut for The Psychos, but I've never been able to confirm that. There is also a legendary LP by The Icemen, but no one really knows. It's funny the stuff that pops on the regular, so I wouldn't surprised to see some unknown gem seeing the light of day in the near future.

MM: I know you write a lot and interview various characters from the scene then and now, do you want to tell us a bit about what you do - which zines/ websites you write for etc?

Freddy: My current writing "career" started as an offshoot of a blog called Quixotic Dreams, which I started in 2012. One of the pieces I wrote, called "The Hispanic Impact in NYHC", got some attention and the guys from the No Echo asked to run it on their site. That got a really good response and other sites like Cvlt Nation reposted it. I've done about twenty articles since 2014, mostly for No Echo, as well as a couple pieces for actual ink and paper fanzines like *Not Like You* & *Chiller Than Most*. I really enjoy writing, whether it's stuff on NYHC, Peruvian music, Graffiti related or doing interviews. This stuff literally writes itself and I'm fortunate that there's an outlet for it and people dig it. I'll keep doing it 'til I run out of inspiring topics to cover.

MM: When did you first become aware of the punk/hardcore scene and in particular NYHC?

Freddy: I first became aware of it freshman year of high school in 1984. There were several NYHC types at my school, people like Joe Bruno, who roadied for Murphy's Law and sang(briefly) for Armed Citizens. By sophomore year I'd be hanging out with a couple of guys from Occupied Territory (OT) they're the ones that really introduced me to NYHC scene.

MM: Who were your peers, did you find it easy to get accepted into the Hardcore world?
Freddy: The guys from OT were, for the most part, Latino kids into Hardcore. That made it easier for me to fit in, we all came from similar neighborhoods in Queens and Brooklyn. By extension, hanging out with the OT "posse" was a great gateway into the scene. It was cool seeing "friendly" faces at CBGB's matinees as sometimes it could get a little confrontational if you happened to often the wrong person/crew. Being connected with them made my entry a lot smoother and I'll always thank them for inducting me into the scene.

MM: What do you think it is about New York as a place that shaped the sound and style of the scene?

Freddy: The incredibly varied multicultural aspect of NYC played a big part. Sure, other cities had as diverse ethnic populations but the urban layout and the efficient mass transit system made it easy for kids from wildly different socioeconomic backgrounds to congregate on the epicentre of the scene: Manhattan's Lower East Side. The NYHC sound reflects the experience of kids that grew up in NY's five boroughs, as opposed to their suburban Hardcore counterparts. It's rougher and more street oriented as befitting the concrete jungle that shaped it.

MM: Does "NYHC" as such still exist in your mind today?

Freddy: Yes, it most definitely does. As long as people from the genre's inception & subsequent generations continue to put out worthwhile music (and there's quite a few of them!), this music will still be relevant. I'll continue to write about and put out records by people that fit this criteria.

MM: What were some of the magical factors that made the scene in its heyday what it was for you?

Freddy: The whole getting involved and contributing instead of just being a passive spectator is what's always made this so special for me. I've been involved with just about every aspect of the scene. From playing in a band, doing a fanzine, putting on shows, been a roadie, done a record label, being involved with running a Hardcore/Punk record store. Some of these things I've done better than others, but no matter, being actively involved in something you believe in always gave me a sense of fulfilment.

MM: For you, what was the Golden Era?

Freddy: The heyday for me was anything that occurred between the years of '81 to '93. There is actually very little that I don't like musically between those 12 years. Of course I'm biased and this is not knocking anything that came out after '93 or currently. If you take into consideration all the shows/record stores/fanzines and releases that occurred within that time frame, the heyday of NYHC is clearly evident during those dozen golden years.

MM: If anything spoiled the scene, what do you think it was?

Freddy: I don't think you can pinpoint one thing that spoiled the scene. Whether one think it was violence, drugs, commercialism, high real estate, metal etc. It's inevitable that a youth based subculture will change or peter out once it's participants grow up and move on. NYHC experienced that but curiously enough, a good amount of old timers stuck around and maintained the same level of commitment as the rank and file got younger. NYHC did quite well for itself and it continues to thrive and adapt to changing times.

MM: Although a lot of the HC crowd are purists, the NY scene had a close relationship with metal bands and sounds and the accompanying big labels and music biz. Was that a good thing or a bad thing for you?

Freddy: I think a lot of good things came out of the Metal influence in NYHC. I think it would have run out of ideas if it hadn't incorporated Metal into its repertoire. I loved the crossover stuff that bands like Leeway, AF and the Cro-Mags started doing. I disliked the bigger labels attempt to market NYHC via Metal aesthetics. So in a nutshell, dug the music but hated the business side of it. This same scenarios was played out it '91 with "Alternative" substituting Metal as the flavor of the month.

MM: Scenes go through cycles and have their highs and lows, were there any particular low points for you?

Freddy: The low point for me was not really being involved between '95 to 2007, but that was through my own choice. I didn't really listen to too much HC throughout those years but I took the lessons that I learned during my time in the scene and applied them to school/career. Sometimes you get so involved in a meaningful pursuit that you need to take a step back and re-evaluate what drew you to that object in the first, lest one burns out. So this is a bittersweet low point that allowed me come back recharged and renewed.

MM: How can you explain to the outside world how the NY scene worked. How could you have YDL and Nausea appearing together on records for example?

Freddy: Everybody was, for lack of better adjectives, united and strong back then. Outsiders might be puzzled by people from opposing ends of the political spectrum hanging out together and appearing on the same compilation. That's just the way things were back then. There were people into both Nausea and YDL, such as myself. Whether a band had punks/skinheads/straight edge/, the only thing that mattered was the music. With the hindsight of more politically correct point of views, this might seem like a lame explanation, but I'm not trying to sugar-coat anything. People are not so one-dimensional and in NYHC, as in the world at large; things are never so clear cut and easily digestible.

MM: There are lots of figureheads and popular characters in the NYHC scene, surely there are also unsung heroes? Who would you like to mention as having made a big impact on the scene without necessarily getting the recognition that others have?

Freddy: The people that immediately come to mind are figures like Tommy Rat (Trip 6/Warzone). I remember seeing him at Pyramid club shows in '86, at CBGB's matinees in '88 and at Abc No Rio in '91. He also went as far back as the A7 shows in '82. I never saw him with an ounce of jaded attitude, no "I'm so old school" mentality whatsoever. So it's people like that whom I tip my hat off to. They may have done popular bands and were around since way back but never let that get to their heads. Others along the same lines are: Nausea's first singer Neil Robinson, Combined Effort records honcho Dave Stein, Ralphy Boy from Squat Or Rot....in short, "lifers" that rolled up their sleeves and continued supporting the scene long after their peers had faded away.

MM: For first time visitors to New York, is there anywhere you recommend they visit, that still captures the spirit of the city?

Freddy: I would recommend first time visitors to yes, of course, do the obvious landmarks. Once that's out of the way, do non-touristy things like: Take the #7 train all the way out to Main Street Flushing and walk around the area. Take the ferry to Staten Island and catch the Bus or train that goes down Bay Blvd to the south shore. Get on #1 or #3 to Fordham Road in the Bronx. Take the D to Brighton Beach Brooklyn and go to Totonno' s, the best pizza in the universe. Go up to the Cloisters on the upper west side of Manhattan, by 207th St., coincidentally where Raybeez grew up!

There are still tons of great, undiscovered spots in NYC. Ask a local that's lived here for at least 30 plus years where to go. Enjoy your visit to NYC's off the beaten path.

Originally published in Mass Movement Presents: NYHC, July 2014

GARY BENNETT II
(KILL YOUR IDOLS / SHEER TERROR / BLACK ANVIL)

I remember seeing Gary play guitar for Sheer Terror at the With Full Force festival in 1998, After they played Gary gave me a cassette featuring a couple of songs from his new band Kill Your Idols. I have loved the band ever since, with each of their many releases hitting the mark. As well as KYI, Gary has flexed his musical wings more recently with the bands Deathcycle and Black Anvil...

Interview by Tom Chapman

MM: When did you first become aware of the punk/Hardcore scene and in particular NYHC? Was Long Island a part of the scene or its own thing?

Gary: I became aware of Cro-Mags, SOD, Ludichrist, and Crumbsuckers about the same time. It wasn't really until I started going to shows a year or two later that there was such emphasis on bordersBut yeah, the NYHC bands had their thing.. The LI bands at that time mostly tried to be a part of the NYHC thing. It was easier, I guess. Later on, LIHC was finally something to take pride in because there actually was a scene and real venues.

MM: Who were your peers, and did you find it easy to get accepted into the Hardcore world?

Gary: Getting into Hardcore was a rite of passage. I didn't cut my long hair right away. Skinheads would fuck with you, but once people started to recognize you and you made some friends, it was easier. NYC shows were actually easier because no one seemed to focus on hair. I know it wasn't always like that, but by the time I got involved, the redneck skin-head thing was on LI, not in NYC. On LI, it was metal heads shaving their heads and still being numb-skulls. NYC was more liberal by then.

MM: What do you think it is about New York that has shaped the sound and style of the scene?

Gary: You have to be hard to survive in NY, as cheesy as that sounds. Poor people struggle, but it's not easy to get rich here either. You have to be very intelligent and competitive to make it here. Even the middle class self-made suburban guy has to be a hard ass to make it. All around, everyone is just mad and on edge all the time. So the music is hard, as a result.

MM: Does "NYHC" as such still exist in your mind today?

Gary: Yes, it does. The torch is carried by younger people, but the original NYHC are still around, a lot of them. Look at Vinny Stigma! He's the grand-dad of the whole scene. If I'm still running into guys like that regularly, it's there.

MM: What were some of the magical factors that made the scene in its heyday what it was for you?

Gary: It was new and exciting, and dangerous. I'll never forget seeing SOIA at CBGBs to only 30 people. Sheer Terror opening for MOD and Paul Bearer bawling out the entire club. The Nihilistics playing half a song and then fighting everyone in the front of the stage, and then chasing everyone out... The first time I saw Leeway and they were SO FUCKING HARD that I was actually frightened at first. That was real energy. Rest In Pieces too...Breakdown... Those bands were as heavy as any metal but much more gritty.

MM: Although a lot of the Hardcore crowd are purists, the NY scene had a close relationship with metal bands and sounds and the accompanying big labels and music biz. Was that a good thing or a bad thing for you?

Gary: I love metal, I love punk, Hardcore.. I love rock and roll. Being "punk" is sort of an oxymoron. Little Richard didn't call himself a "punk", but think about being a flamboyant black guy way back then and having to deal with the cultural set up in those days. "Punks" today just start a band and take for granted what being a rebel really is. Musically, for me, it's a perfect fit. I got into a lot of Hardcore bands that opened for metal bands. Those were great shows. There were fights. I never understood that. Most of the skins and punks back then WERE metal heads a week earlier. Stupid.

MM: The sound also got very close to metal at times did you appreciate that or was that more a dilution of the pure NYHC sound?

Gary: I wouldn't say it was a dilution. Think of it this way, Blondie was a part of the punk scene, and they went on to be more commercial. Ramones were always Ramones. But you're not gonna tell me Madball is diluted because the guitars are heavy.. That's just stupid. Don't matter if the guitar is fuzzy or if it sounds like Van Halen. It's the attitude.

MM: Scenes go through cycles and have their highs and lows, were there any particular low points for you?

Gary: The Long Island scene is at a low point because there's a lack of smaller, DIY venues. Bands keep playing the same rock clubs that force them to sell tickets to play. Bands from Long Island do better to play in Brooklyn or NYC now. There's a couple of exceptions to what I said, but there's no PWAC. Basically.

MM: Over the years there were some big divisions in the NY scene, as people have gotten older are those divisions still there or have people got closer with age? I'm thinking of the CBGB's scene vs the ABC No Rio more DIY scene for example.

Gary: That division is less evident these days, but I guess it's still there, somehow. I think people realized what they lost when CBGB was actually gone. I also think the older people get, the more tolerant and "live and let live" they become.

MM: There are lots of figureheads and popular characters in the NYHC scene, surely there are also unsung heroes? Who would you like to mention as having made a big impact on the scene without necessarily getting the recognition that others have?

Gary: Brendan Rafferty of SFA. There's others, for sure, but I want to make mention of him in particular. Brendan was a huge factor in both the NYHC scene, as well as the more DIY aspects of it. People forget that the early NYHC scene was very DIY. Those bands got huge and it just became less DIY for them because they had the juice to sell out bigger places. Brendan had a lot to do with both ends. SFA is one of my favourite NYHC bands. The band as a whole is largely unsung.

MM: Would the NY scene have worked in another city?

Gary: Every city has its own charm. But the answer is no. Maybe Detroit is similar.

MM: You guys have always loved your metal - how did the concept of Black Anvil come about?

Gary: Raeph, Paul, and myself always talked about one day taking it to the next level and doing a full on metal band. Not only did we want to challenge our skill level for writing, but we all started with metal and never stopped loving it. It's all we listened to on long van drives during KYI tours. I had always imagined it would be like Dio era- Sabbath or Judas Priest. I wanted a singer like that. Paul and Raeph were more into black metal than I was.. I liked a lot of it, but not like them. They were into finding new stuff, where I sorta left off at Venom, Bathory, and Celtic Frost. I like Immortal, Emperor, Mayhem. Paul got me into Funeral Mist and some next level shit like that. Around the time KYI was ending, Celtic Frost made their comeback and released *Monotheist*. That record, and the return of CF, was my biggest inspiration to do what we always talked about. We already had Deathcycle going, which was heavier Hardcore, like Godflesh mixed with doom.. So we had a darker approach to writing going and we just decided to fully embrace that.

MM: Has the band become more successful than you expected?

Gary: Definitely. We started as a studio only band. We practiced our songs for a year before recording, then we decided to try playing a show. Our first show was with WASP on Long Island, and we destroyed. So we took more gigs. People liked it right away.

MM: How did you attract the attention of Relapse? That's kind of a big deal!

Gary: Dave Witte of Municipal Waste brought us to Gordon's and Rennie's attention at Relapse. Also, a friend of mine that I've known since childhood was working in marketing for Relapse, Pat Egan. He was like "Oh shit, that's my boy Gary's band " Next thing you know, they came to a show, and we had a meeting over dinner a week later. Pat was older than me, he was a neighborhood friend that got me into lots of metal early on. He passed away a couple of years ago. He was a popular guy. His wake was like a concert, it was mobbed.

MM: Would you say the Black Anvil sound has evolved over the years?

Gary: Yes, we try hard to keep evolving. Some of it is natural, but Paul and Raeph especially always have new ideas for sound in mind. I just write heavy riff after heavy riff. Those guys are good at shaping into something more thought out.

MM: You are touring and playing the metal circuit now, what are the differences between that world and the hardcore world?

Gary: In some ways it's very similar, and in other ways it's VERY different. But at the end of the day, the goal is the same. We play as hard as we can, and the audiences have their own ways of showing their appreciation. The energy of the crowd is important in both spectrums, whether they mosh and dive, or just yell and fist bang, and head bang. Although a Black Anvil performance is definitely more about our own inward perspective. It's more about us, ha!

MM: Does NYHC play a part in Black Anvil's sound or approach to doing things?

Gary: NYHC plays a part in everything we do in life. It's our tribe. We definitely aren't trying to be these different people. We have grown, and expanded our horizons as people, as anyone should. We don't try to set out to be a "crossover" band. We are definitely a black metal band. But I guess we can't deny our influences. Cro-Mags and AF are just as important to me as Sabbath and Celtic Frost. People say they hear it in our sound. Lots of people, actually, so. Why argue? It's not important to debate. The lyrics and the idea behind it is clear to us. Morgan from Marduk said "You guys are definitely a black metal band... From NY." I think that was a compliment, so, I'll take it, because we also aren't trying to copy Darkthrone like tons of US black metal bands do. I think live, we bring it like a NY band.

MM: Does Black Anvil play Hardcore shows or do you strictly aim for a metal crowd?

Gary: We've played shows with HC bands. We don't get asked, typically. Personally, I've always loved GBH and Hellhammer just the same. I can't expect everyone to feel the same way. But we have many supporters who liked KYI and have supported ANYTHING else we've done, collectively. Those people turn up at metal shows to see Black Anvil. I'd play with Madball if they asked us. Not sure if we'd go over well. Maybe! But all the members of Madball are friends and supporters of ours. Real recognizes real.

Originally published in Mass Movement Presents: NYHC, July 2014

EDDIE SUTTON (LEEWAY)

Back in the mid-eighties, when the whole Crossover was beginning to take shape in the rest of the US and Europe, it had already solidified itself, and taken root, in New York thanks to the Crumbsuckers and Leeway. And while the former burned brightly and briefly, Leeway went from strength to strength, their live shows thriving on the aggression, energy and raw fury of HC, while their records embraced the technicality of metal, effortlessly fusing it with the speed and power of HC.

They were originality personified, a bruising powerhouse of everything that was good about both metal and HC, and to this day their legacy remains steadfast, and their music sounds as fresh, vital and original as it did when they first hit the ground running three decades ago. I caught up their vocalist and all round nice guy, Eddie Sutton while he was booking and planning the Eddie Leeway Show's first European assault, for a chat about HC, Leeway, overcoming addiction, his past, his present and his future and this is what he had to say...

Interview by Tim Cundle

Photographs by Jammi Sloan York, Mosh Front, Jimmy Ferrari, Philup Flashpoint Muri, Ed Esposito and Lou DiBella

MM: Which came first for you Eddie, Hardcore or Leeway?

Eddie: Hardcore has always been a lifestyle for me but Leeway is what I've become known for. Leeway was a way for me to show what I can do vocally and express who I am later on in life. Hardcore to me wasn't really about a sound it was a lifestyle. For me, a female vocalist like Anita Baker can be Hardcore because she puts her whole soul into what she does. Even though Hardcore is known as a very brutal and abrasive sound, it's really all about passion and heart and being yourself. It's become the phenomena it is today through a lot of hard work and some very determined fans.

MM: How did you get into Hardcore Eddie? After all, nobody's born a punk rocker...

Eddie: I knew punk rock, but I moved to New York City the same night that John Lennon was shot and killed (Dec 8th 1980) and within 6 months I was learning about Hardcore bands in my neighbourhood; Hardcore was the new sound, the new term for this music. I think American punk really started around 1979/80 but I don't think American Hardcore really became what is it is now known to be until about 81/82. The sound was starting to be organised around 80/81 and by 82 we really knew what Hardcore was all about.

MM: So you sort of fell into it?

Eddie: Well that's how it was, y'know? That was the music and the sound that was around. I met the guys Kraut who were the first major band in New York to put out a Hardcore single and a full length record. I learned from them about DIY ethics, then one of the first shows I ever went to I got to see the Bad Brains, and HR just holed up by his van and started talking to people and being really cool. Then there was Gary, their guitar player, who was becoming a hero of mine, who I could just talk to, sit together and hang out. That was an incredible experience for me, rather than idolising a rock star that I couldn't even get close to. And the music speaks for itself: the energy and passion that's in it. You get to sing along with the band, sweat with the band; it is what it is, that's why everybody loves it so much.

MM: So what were the early days of Leeway like? Did you have a vision that you guys were going to inject a metal vibe into the music...?

Eddie: We did have an idea of what we wanted to do. Obviously AJ and I were fans of the music, you know, fans of the bands. But at the same time we grew up listening to Sabbath, and there was the Van Halen of the seventies, so we wanted to bring all that stuff together. I like to call it a Reese's Peanut Butter Cup – y'know what I mean? You bring together the peanut butter and chocolate... And in 1983 when Metallica's *Kill 'Em All* album came out, and everybody heard the riffs and everybody wanted those riffs in with the Hardcore energy and the Hardcore brutality. That's what we were trying to do as we were learning our instruments and we were learning our roles within the band, but we were always determined and practised more than any other band did in New York at the time. That's why the Hardcore paid off and we started getting noticed within about a year and a half, two years – because we started getting really good shows.

MM: Was it difficult for you guys to fit in with the more traditional Hardcore scene at the time, because with the metal in the sound – there was you and the Crumbsuckers - pioneering in New York City?

Eddie: We weren't really outsiders, because we'd already been doing shows for four or five years, so we didn't really have that abrasive transition like New Jacks or New Beats did: showing up with long hair and not knowing anybody - they'd be getting their ass kicked. We didn't have that problem because we were already down, if you know what I'm saying. It was easier for us. I mean, we weren't a traditional Hardcore band by far, but we strived to do more... We weren't just satisfied being a Hardcore sounding band, Hardcore was the element and the passion of it, but we wanted to do as much as we possibly could musically which is why we broadened our horizons

MM: I know a lot of folks credit DRI and Corrosion of Conformity with starting the whole crossover thing, but I always thought it was more of a grass roots thing started by you guys, the Crumbsuckers, and to a lesser extent the Cro Mags and that second Agnostic Front album. So at that stage, 85/86 did you realise you were at the forefront of something that was going to make musical history, and that you guys were a pioneer of it.

Eddie: No. And I think anybody who tells you that is full of shit. I've got to be honest with you on that. We were just doing what we were doing, man, we were just coming from the heart and shooting from the hip that was it. It just turned into something magical which is why Leeway are still being talked about thirty years later.

MM: So do you think Leeway got the credit that you deserved, do you think you've ever been short changed?

Eddie: You know what, maybe we were at times, and I did feel bitter about that, but the fact that we still have a new generation of fans twenty five years later, that's where our success came from and that's what mattered because we've stood the test of time. I don't feel that way anymore; I feel very blessed and humbled to know that a kid who is half my age or younger can actually relate to something I did twenty five years ago. That's just an incredible thing to me and I'm humbled by it.

MM: Do you think that the New York Hardcore scene that you guys grew up in could possibly happen today or do you think the city has changed too much?

Eddie: No that time and space is over. I'm not saying good bands can't come out, but I don't think they can create a scene that changed things the way that New York Hardcore did for American Hardcore itself. I don't think that's going to happen again, I think that time and opportunity is gone.

MM: The Leeway records have just been reissued haven't they?

Eddie: Yes the first label to reissue them was in Brazil, then Reality records is releasing them for the US and Europe. It's really so we can bring the releases to people at a better price. They should be out soon. The band isn't together but I'm looking to go out doing shows under the banner "The Eddie Leeway Show". I'm doing exclusively the UK this summer; I have shows booked in in Manchester and Leeds, then in the Autumn I hope to come back and do a full tour including the mainland and all around.

MM: Is there any chance of a full blown Leeway reunion or is that just never going to happen?

Eddie: I can't really answer for the other guys. If it's going to happen it will probably be in another year. I think the other members, we have our frustrations and thoughts about how things have turned out. Let's not kid ourselves; every band out there is a dysfunctional family. They just want to get sorted at times. I know AJ and Pokey are out playing at the moment and doing really well, and it's probably an easy gig for them, so it's probably not a good time for them.

I myself am enjoying that we have a whole new generation of fans, and going out to do the Eddie Leeway show because it gives me the opportunity to play Leeway with friends. When you play with friends and you don't have that band mentality, you're just having fun and having a good time playing; and I can do stuff that I've recorded with other bands as well. I'm one of those guys who does not believe that a singer has the right to go out with new musicians and call it the same band. To me that's lying to your audience. So I'm not going to go and get new musicians and then take it out and call it Leeway because that would be lying to my fan base, that's my opinion. So I call it the Eddie Leeway show because that's what it is: Eddie Leeway out with friends, playing some songs. I'm not out on this ego driven thing to go as a solo artist, but if I have the opportunity then why not? TruthandRights is another thing I'm very passionate about; I'm very close to putting that out as a full length as well, so there are lots of things I'm looking forward to doing on my own as well.

MM: I was going to ask you about the TruthandRights record.. It's been in the pipeline a while now hasn't it?

Eddie: Yeah. I know people really appreciated the *Greenlight* EP we did, so we do have people waiting on the full length and it's going to be worth the wait. It's important for me too to show people that I can write songs just as strong today as I did as a kid. I still have the same fire and passion. For a vocalist to that is quite a challenge. Not many people can achieve that, so I'm hoping to achieve that and be one of those rare individuals.

MM: With your song writing now, surely the added maturity and life experience will bring an extra edge to it...

Eddie: You know, that's what a sensible man would do, those who don't have the same challenges in their lives and can stay the same person. I'm a broken neck survivor, I'm blessed to be recovering from drug addiction, I've been able to control the depression that I've grown to live with and I also do volunteer work, I'm a home help aid; I do a lot of different things, as well as advocate for patient rights. This is the human being I grew up to be. So having this opportunity again to go out and perform for a whole new generation is incredible for me. I don't take any of this for granted the way some people might and I just want to go out and do it right. If that means going out with Leeway, or going out with the Eddie Leeway show I'm just going to do it, I'm going to go out one way or another. It's just the way it is.

MM: You mentioned that you were a broken neck survivor and had been through drug addiction. I'm assuming it was opiates...?

Eddie: Yes it was. It seemed I needed something to slow down. Most people seem to need something to get them up and going and sadly it is very prevalent in our music scene, it has been for a long time. And I know this is nothing new in any music scene in the world, it doesn't have to be Hardcore, it could be dance music, it could be hip-hop; I'm sure there are classical musicians who have a problem or two as well. This is just the reality of it. It's just there. Some people take it to mitigate a pain, some people just like the party atmosphere and get caught up. I'm no angel, I'm still a big cannabis and weed fan and I think I always will be, until my lungs fall out. The other stuff I really try very hard to stay away from.

You know, once in a while I'll have a drink but that's it . It's just not something I enjoy doing anymore – forget about cravings, I just don't want to do it anymore. I count myself lucky as there is many a person had sleepless nights because of this disease and it's a hard thing. It's very sad and prevalent in our scene and I try to be open to people who come and ask for help and things like that, and that's kinda how I became involved with patient rights over the years. And with my own treatment too; there are a lot of people in that area that're afraid to speak out so I try to encourage them to speak out for themselves and to be a voice for the others as well. Not only is it an ongoing problem but the system needs to change, the care needs to improve in order to help others. The patient needs to step up and try to help in that processes.

MM: Do you think decriminalisation would help in that process?

Eddie: Sure, sure. We give people tickets and arrest them for driving under the influence but it seems like drug addiction is not only a great way to seize assets, but also to ruin peoples' lives through imprisonment. And I'm not just talking about the kingpins who get rich off of other people's suffering, I'm talking about the drug addict who gets caught in this vicious circle just to survive, so they have to deal drugs, then their whole lives are destroyed; their families are destroyed. Decriminalisation is a very important thing. I know it's not an easy thing. You can start with legalising marijuana though across the board then tackling these other problems so that they can be changed. But the war on drugs is good money so why are they going to change that policy, it's how they get paid. That's when you start looking on your authority figures as the biggest racket in the game. You know, I'm no angel, never have been, never will be, but I just feel blessed to be where I am now and able to see my music reissued and getting to be a part of this again, whilst in my own life being strong enough to help others. It's a beautiful thing.

MM: Do you think the "positive mental attitude" that goes along with Hardcore helped you to get through your addiction and rehabilitation from being injured the way you were?

Eddie: In some ways, yes. But I also think that being hard headed, it took my recovery a little longer than it could have been. I think being enlightened to Hardcore music helped me to be more open minded, and I educated myself to my particular disease. So it's a pro and con, but thankfully Hardcore gave me a way to think and question authority so that I can have the clarity what's for real and what's bullshit. I'm just trying to use that vision to do what I can to help people nowadays. I survived this and I can use that to help others. If I can't use this to help someone else then I'm not being part of the 'core I'm being part of the problem.. That's how I see it. I'm not some ra-ra protester, but I do know there are some core issues out there that need to be changed that are literally killing people, programmes themselves are not there enough to give people the help that they need yet, and without getting too much up on a soap-box about it I'm just trying to do my part. Doing this reminds me every day how lucky I am to be out of that life and that helps me to fly straight if you know what I mean.

MM: What's your favourite early memory of your involvement in the New York scene ?

Eddie: It's come up a few times over the last few days, one of the first times I ever saw the Bad Brains. Gary Miller, Dr Know, literally pulled up outside two plus two which was Houseman St and 2nd St and just started bullshitting with everybody. Coming from the seventies, life and being a kid in the seventies, we saw arena rock bands and these guys were gods, you couldn't reach out to touch them they wouldn't talk to you, you were inferior creatures to them. But Gary and Doc, they'd stand right there hanging out, bullshitting, talking and being genuine; not just saying what's up and hanging out for the sake of hanging out while they waited to go on, they were genuinely involved. This guy was just as bad ass as any other guitar player I'd ever seen, but he was getting down with the kids. That's something that never left me.

Whenever there is a fan, or someone who appreciates Leeway or any of the music I've been a part of I try to give them my full attention; and I learned that from Gary. That's something that I never forget. I always try to remember that. I'm not a rock star, I'm just a guy who got very lucky in this music scene and got to be a part of a thing that's intergenerational, and now I have to teach to the next generation that we were all freaks and outcasts. All of us. When we joined this thing it was about no trends, no conformity; but sadly elitism started creeping through the cracks and now we have trends and we have conformity and I don't see that changing any time soon, especially since the music has become global over the last couple of decades, but we can try to maintain our beliefs and we can try to teach them to the next generation. Hopefully these ideas will stay within this thing of ours. I don't expect everybody to follow this rule but if most do it will keep this thing of ours pure.

Originally published in Mass Movement Presents: NYHC, July 2014

JORDAN COOPER
(REVELATION RECORDS)

Some things just belong together. Cheese and crackers, Starsky & Hutch and Revelation Records and NYHC. Born in, and to support, NYHC, Revelation epitomises and embodies the energy, vitality and spirit of the scene it emerged from, and for me at least, no other label has managed to capture the imagination of successive generations of HC kids in the same way that Revelation has, and continues to do. I caught up with Revelation head honcho Jordan Cooper to talk about Hardcore, Revelation and New York...

Interview by Tim Cundle

MM: So, how did you discover Hardcore, or more accurately, the NYHC Jordan? Were you already a punk / Hardcore kid or was it the New York scene that drew you in and set you on the path that you're still on today?

Jordan: When I lived in NY my friends were listening to Black Flag, Dead Kennedys and some other stuff like that but at the time it was presented to me as "crazy" or "funny" and that didn't interest me enough to look into it much. When my family moved to Connecticut to be closer to where my mom worked, I ended up in the same school as Ray Cappo. He introduced me to Negative Approach, Minor Threat, SSD and a lot of the NY bands like the Abused, Agnostic Front, The Mob, Cause For Alarm, Antidote, etc. It was those bands that made me realize that it wasn't all just a poke in the world's eye, but that it was its own culture and that it helped people play music and express ideas that were their own and that weren't going to be heard elsewhere. I don't remember a particular moment or decision about it, but at some point that was just something I wanted to be a part of.

MM: What was, and is it about the NYHC scene that appealed to you? What do you think made the scene so special in its formative years, and during what many people consider to its "golden age", that is 1982 through to the mid-nineties?

Jordan: Most of the shows I went to in the early-mid-eighties were at the Anthrax in Stamford, Connecticut (which is about 40 miles north of NYC). In NY, I went to shows at CBs and the Pyramid and a couple of the bigger venues in NY and also in New Jersey, Rhode Island, Boston and places in between. I feel fortunate to have seen a lot of the shows I did in NY. I think the NY scene's main appeal to me was that it was big, had a lot of great bands and people, and it was pretty inclusive (from my point of view at least) of bands and people from outside the city. There was the reputation of NY being a rough scene and the famous bit of writing on the wall of A7, but I generally had positive experiences at the shows and the out of town bands that I saw there seemed to feel the same way. NY was a crazy place in the early 80s and I think that's reflected in the Hardcore scene that formed there.

MM: At the same time there were plenty of other scenes starting, coming into the their own and slowly developing in the US, so why do you think the New York scene, arguably more than any other, resonated with so many people around the world? What do you think made the New York scene unique and led to it having the impact that it did at the time, and continues to have to this day?

Jordan: It probably had something to do with the mix of people and the way the bands formed, broke up and evolved. It obviously led to a lot of bands that connected with people all over the world.

MM: Everybody who was a part of the NYHC in the eighties seems to have a favourite venue, one that holds special memories for them. Which was yours and why?

Jordan: I loved the Anthrax, which was in Connecticut, but in NY CBGBs was obviously it. The sound was great and it was historic even back when the first Hardcore Matinees were happening. I never went to A7 or some of the earlier places that had Hardcore shows in the city.

MM: Scenes invariably revolve around bands, but how much of an impact do you think zines, like *The Big Takeover, Tse Tse Fly* and later *In Effect* had on the NY scene? What kind of impact and effect do you think they had, and have, on the scene overall?

Jordan: Zines played a big part in the scene. They communicated about things you knew about that might help shape the way you thought about them, and more importantly clued you into things you didn't know about.

MM: And sort of sticking with a similar theme, and veering away from bands, how important was Some Records to the development of the NYHC scene? Why?

Jordan: Some Records opened up at a really important time for Hardcore. It was right around the time crossover was happening and after Revolution Summer. Duane helped bring Hardcore fans and bands together.

MM: Almost everyone seems to point to the Bad Brains as the band that focussed the collective energy of the emergent scene, and the band that kick started the whole thing. Do you think that's true? Which band do you think spear-headed the movement and why?

Jordan: The Bad Brains were already legends by the time I heard them. I take people who were influenced by them at their word. They were amazing and I don't doubt anyone who says they inspired them. Reading Tony Rettman's new book, a lot of credit is also given to the Stimulators.

MM: Without NYHC there would be no Revelation Records would there? Populist urban HC legend has it that Revelation, was started to release the first Warzone record. Is that true? And, if so, what made you want to release that Warzone record enough to start a label? Was Raybeez the heart of NYHC, and how did his passing (in your opinion) effect the NY scene as a whole?

Jordan: That's true that Rev started because Ray and I wanted to release a Warzone 7". We (or I at least) didn't think it was going to be a label beyond that one record. Then we came up with the idea for the compilation and then Ray started talking to more bands and the ball just kept rolling. I didn't really know Raybeez until we started working on their 7", but he was obviously part of the "old guard" being in Agnostic Front, friends with Jimmy from Murphy's Law and being a part of that early NY scene. It was a shock to everyone when he died and it definitely had a profound effect on those who knew him and cared about him and everyone who was affected by his music.

MM: Talking of Raybeez, do you have a story about Ray, one that always makes you smile whenever you think about it that you could maybe share with us?

Jordan: There isn't a particular story I can remember, but I was always struck by how well he could relate to people even if they were different from him. His personality and voice were so distinctive, I can remember both clearly any time I think about him. I didn't know him really well, but any time Warzone played or he was working at the Ritz or Pyramid, he seemed genuinely happy to see you there.

MM: So, in the beginning, how did you choose the bands that you wanted to release records by? What made the first five bands (not including the West Coast's No For An Answer) you released special for you?

Jordan: It's hard to remember specifics at this point. Ray (Cappo) was in Youth of Today and had a clear vision of what he wanted the label to represent I think. But for both of us it was primarily a way to document the resurgence of Hardcore we saw happening at the time (particularly in NY which is where Ray and Youth of Today were based at that point). Every record was a different process, involved new people and getting to know them and how they worked also learning new things about getting things done logistically.

MM: Did you ever think, in your wildest dreams, that you'd still be running Revelation twenty eight years after your debut release? How, if at all, do you think that both yourself and Revelation have changed, both personally and as a business, in those three decades?

Jordan: No, I didn't think so, but I also didn't realize how fast twenty eight years would fly by either. I've changed quite a bit over the years, Revelation a little less so, but no complaints at the moment, just lots more to do!

MM: Which show from the classic NYHC days do you remember most? What was your favourite show from 'back in the day' and why was it your favorite?

Jordan: I can't say that I remember a lot of shows vividly anymore, but the first Cro-Mags show (at CBs in 1984) had a big impact on me. It was the first time I'd heard them and I knew nothing about them, but I knew that they were playing something that was Hardcore in the style that I wanted to hear but also adding their own twist to it. This is around the time that Ray and Porcell were beginning to talk about wanting more bands to play raw Hardcore and not liking some of the changes/progression etc. that was happening at the time. The Cro-Mags seemed to me to fit that bill pretty well.

MM: What do you think the best thing about NYHC was, and is? Why? And, what do you think the worst thing about was... And still is?

Jordan: For me it was the music and the energy. I never lived in the city at the time I was going to shows so I wasn't really part of the family like Ray, Walter and everyone else, but I still felt at home there. I guess the worst thing was seeing people come to the bigger shows from outside the scene and think it was about picking on the one punk looking guy in the pit or just fighting in general. NY could be a rough place, but to me NYHC is about music, not violence.

MM: Do you think something like the NYHC explosion could happen again, or did the whole thing happen because of a combination of unique factors – people, location and time. Could that HC lightning ever be captured in a bottle again?

Jordan: NYHC is still evolving and for all we know it could be bigger tomorrow than it was whenever it seemed biggest to anyone. But yes, anything can happen. Music changes and scenes change and the next big thing would likely pass under my radar at this point.

Originally published in Mass Movement Presents: NYHC, July 2014

SEAN TAGGART

Black Flag had Pettibon, the DKs had Winston Smith, Septic Death had Pushead and NYHC had Sean Taggart. Taggart's cartoon style became as synonymous with NYHC as the bands themselves, with two of the mid-eighties classic Hardcore/Crossover albums - Agnostic Front's *Cause For Alarm* and Crumbsucker's *Life Of Dreams* - featuring his instantly recognisable artwork. No feature on NYHC would be complete without a chat with its seminal artist. Ladies and gentleman – the straight talking Sean Taggart...

Interview by Ian Pickens

Photographs by Freddy Alva, Clockwork Records & Steven Yu

MM: Introduce yourself...

ST: My name is Sean and I have a 36D bust and my cock is 10" uncut. I like cling film and turpentine.

MM: How and when did you become in involved in the NYHC scene?

ST: Pretty much when it evolved. I was happy for the US' response to the second British Invasion. After all the Pistols and the Clash were my Beatles/Stones. A chance to be the "new" Punks, so to speak. The first generation the Ramones and the Heartbreakers seemed so far removed from us kids at the time. I'm still a huge Dead Boys fan by the way...

MM: Were you aware of the impact those mid-eighties NHYC bands were having outside of NYC, even to the extent of having fans in small villages in Wales, UK?

ST: I kinda did. By the time that shit was happening there was a fairly strong worldwide scene. I literally could go to any hick town see some funny looking kids and immediately be "down". I never tested this internationally but I knew folks from all over the world back then. Y'know - face to face, not digitally.

MM: Agnostic Front's *Cause For Alarm* and Crumbsucker's *Life of Dreams* which you did the artwork for, were two of the most popular NYHC/Hardcore records of the time over here, and the artwork was particularly appealing – I remember talking to you a few years back and telling you how we used to doodle artwork from both onto our folders and books at school; did you imagine your art would reach people so far removed from their origin?

ST: With good reason! Those were great records man. I knew it was possible 'cos I liked underground shit from all over as well. I hunted that stuff down, but it's weird, flattering and humbling when it happens to you. Oh yeah and GREAT!

MM: Those were the first pieces of your artwork that most people would be aware of, but had you been creating artwork for the NYHC scene prior to that? Were there any record releases featuring your work before the Agnostic Front/Crumbsuckers covers?

ST: I did a 7' for Armed Citizens, they changed the cover to a photo at the last minute but the back cover and the insert were mine. Actually the back cover was a jam with a fellow artist by the name of Danny Hellman, an amazing talent in his own right... AC (not Anal Cunt)

ended up using the front cover art for some posters. A few other little things here and there, nothing that stands out.

MM: *What other bands from that era did you provide artwork for? Did you do any commissions for bands outside the US? Are you still creating artwork for bands in the NY or wider Hardcore scenes?*

ST: Pushead invited me to do a piece for Thrasher Magazine (the skateboarder mag), Pus is one of the greatest supporters for all things underground. In the late 80's he was instrumental in getting me started as a full time professional artist. Damn! For Murphy's Law I did flyers, stickers and a beer mug (hey Jimmy I'm still waiting!). Uncle Al - the original guitarist and artist for the band, whom I can't praise enough. Not only did he write the best songs for ML, he was/is a great artist! He can draw circles around me; completely overlooked in my book. Carnivore, two LP covers and a couple of flyers – *Retaliation* was a fuckin' great record. Whiplash's *Power and Pain* (which I also named!). I did stuff for PMS which later spun off into a really great Metal band Wench. I did a lot of work for GIANT Studios - a rehearsal space for virtually every NYHC band. I still do work for HC bands on occasion, but y'know it's not the same.

MM: *Were there any bands that you really wanted to create artwork for but never got the chance?*

ST: Black Sabbath!

MM: *What influences or inspires your artwork - music, people, politics, social issues, history? What mediums do you enjoy working in?*

ST: I'm essentially a cartoonist - so I tend to favour distortion and extreme types of things and characters. Also anyone who is sincerely trying to do their own thing, Rashan Roland Kirk, Daniel Johnston, Jack Kirby, Keith Haring, Vaughn Bode, Lee Quinones to name a few. Politically I'm mostly apolitical but I admire Malcolm X, The Black Panther Party, A.I.M (American Indian Movement) - people who are willing to sacrifice themselves for their people. If only mainstream officials had the same commitment.

MM: *More than twenty years on and people are still really enthusiastic about the NYHC scene; why do you think that is? What was it about the scene that resonated with people outside of NY? How has the scene changed over the years? Many bands (Caught In A Trap and Agnostic Front for example) have written songs saying that the clean-up by Mayor Guilliani killed off the city; do you agree? Would it be possible for the style of Hardcore that developed in seventies and eighties NYC to happen now?*

ST: I blame Giulliani and the TV show *Friends* for the ruination of my home town. So Giulliani is basically a boot licking dog for the super wealthy with delusions of grandeur! I could write a three thousand word essay on him easily. Feckless, clever, cunt. *Friends* on the other hand is a somewhat eccentric viewpoint. Hear me out. First let's get one thing straight, it's the out of town mother fuckers that ruined the city – *Friends* and Giulliani are just the catalyst. The ass fuckin' fuck-tards come here from all over the US of A, not to become New Yorkers, but to have shit just like home and like what they saw on *Friends*. Here's what they saw: One - no black people, in fact no-one of colour! That right there is FALSE! Two - that any tool from the 'burbs can fit in and everyone's going to see how "wonderful" they really are. False! Three - that you can get a nice apartment; leave your doors unlocked, and just pop in on your super great friends that live in your building. False! Four - you don't have to bust your ass just trying to make ends meet. You guessed it -FALSE! So, unfortunately the result is that NYC is now more like *Friends* than, let's say *Taxi* (a sitcom from the late seventies set in NYC)

That's the how and the why of NYC's current state of shit. I was hoping after 9/11 the city would return to normal, but sadly the roaring tide of rich, vapid people was too great to quell. Fuck.

MM: You have had quite a bit of input to Tony Rettman's recent book *New York Hardcore 1980-1990* both as a contributor and in participating in Press Release interviews; have you known Tony since 'back in the day'; do you think the book is an accurate representation of the scene during those years? Are we all looking back on this period with middle age nostalgia?

ST: I haven't gotten a copy yet so I can't say. But no I've only gotten to know Tony in the last few years; he's the generation that came after me. I read his previous book about the Mid-West HC scene *Why Be Something That You're Not?* and I loved it. I'm sure it had some blurred memories and nostalgia. I enjoyed it and felt like I got some insight into a scene that I admired, but knew virtually nothing about.

MM: In the book you highlight the issues some people had with the NY scene being perceived as getting more attention and press than other HC scenes, and you attribute this attention to NY being one of the World's media capitals; do you feel that the NYHC scene was misunderstood by other HC scenes? MRR's beef with Agnostic Front seemed to alienate the NYHC scene even further; do you think this helped to foster that feeling of 'All For One and One For All' in the NYHC scene.

ST: Well let's just say, in the states everybody's got an axe to grind with NYC 'cos were the best, and we know it and they know it too! I'm sorry your town sucks. Don't blame me I didn't set it up that way. I don't know what it's like to live in a place where you have to drive ten minutes to do anything. I don't know what it's like to live in a homogenous society where everyone has the same background as you. I don't know what it's like to live in a place filled with endless fast food joints and strip malls. Or live in a place that's never heard of art or read a book or questioned the news on TV. I don't know about that, that's re-fuckin-tarded, USA-tard shit that SHOULD be rebelled against. NYC is to me the ultimate manifestation of the American dream and the rest of the country has no fuckin' imagination.

MM: In Stephen Blush's *American Hardcore* you were quoted as saying that "the whole swing to the right in New York" was down to Paul Dordal (famous NY Skin who wrote the words for the Murphy's Law song *California Pipeline*); so was there some truth to MRR's claims or was it simply that he was one of the first punks/skins to show support for the Republicans; do you think there was an element of hypocrisy that the Ramones weren't singled for attack by the punk/HC scene even though Johnny was openly Republican?

ST: Paul was, and probably still is, a very charismatic and smart guy. He's grown as a human, I'm sure. I think he was both being reactionary to the failed, hypocritical, politically correct leftist movement. That, pragmatism, and perhaps a little Punk contrarianism. You should ask him to weigh in on this -'cos I'm not him. Tell him I sent youse. I'm curious to hear what he has to say about all this. Also I mentioned him specifically in the book -'cos with these things, the focus is always on the music alone. Giving short-shrift to the social phenomena as a whole.

I know the characters involved and they're too self-involved to fess up to things outside of their own "legend". Sorry, no one's perfect. As for the Ramones I never thought of them in any context other than being a punk band. Funny, irreverent, shocking (for their time) and aggressive.

MM: Do you feel the crossover with Metal that happened in the mid-80s had a negative effect on the NYHC sound or Hardcore in general? Was it simply an obvious progression along with the influence of Hip Hop on the scene given NYC's 'Melting Pot' of cultures?

ST: It was good for NY in general but it was the death knell for a decaying rock'n'roll subculture. I love metal, but it's an eater of musical souls. Just about every cult form that I love has been ruined by metal. Hardcore, Hip-Hop, Goth, Industrial even Psychobilly! It's the fuckin' AIDS of music!

MM: At a push who would you choose as the definitive NYHC band and the definitive NYHC release?

ST: The Cro-Mags demo tape, definitely not the record! Same goes for Murphy's Law. I don't know what went down at Profile but those two bands recorded slammin' stuff over at Jerry William's and then what gets put on vinyl is this flaccid shit. C'mon! Murphy's Law at that time were the fuckin' best live band. That record should have rocked

MM: Final comments and parting shots?

ST: Thanks, it was a real treat!

Originally published in Mass Movement Presents: NYHC, July 2014

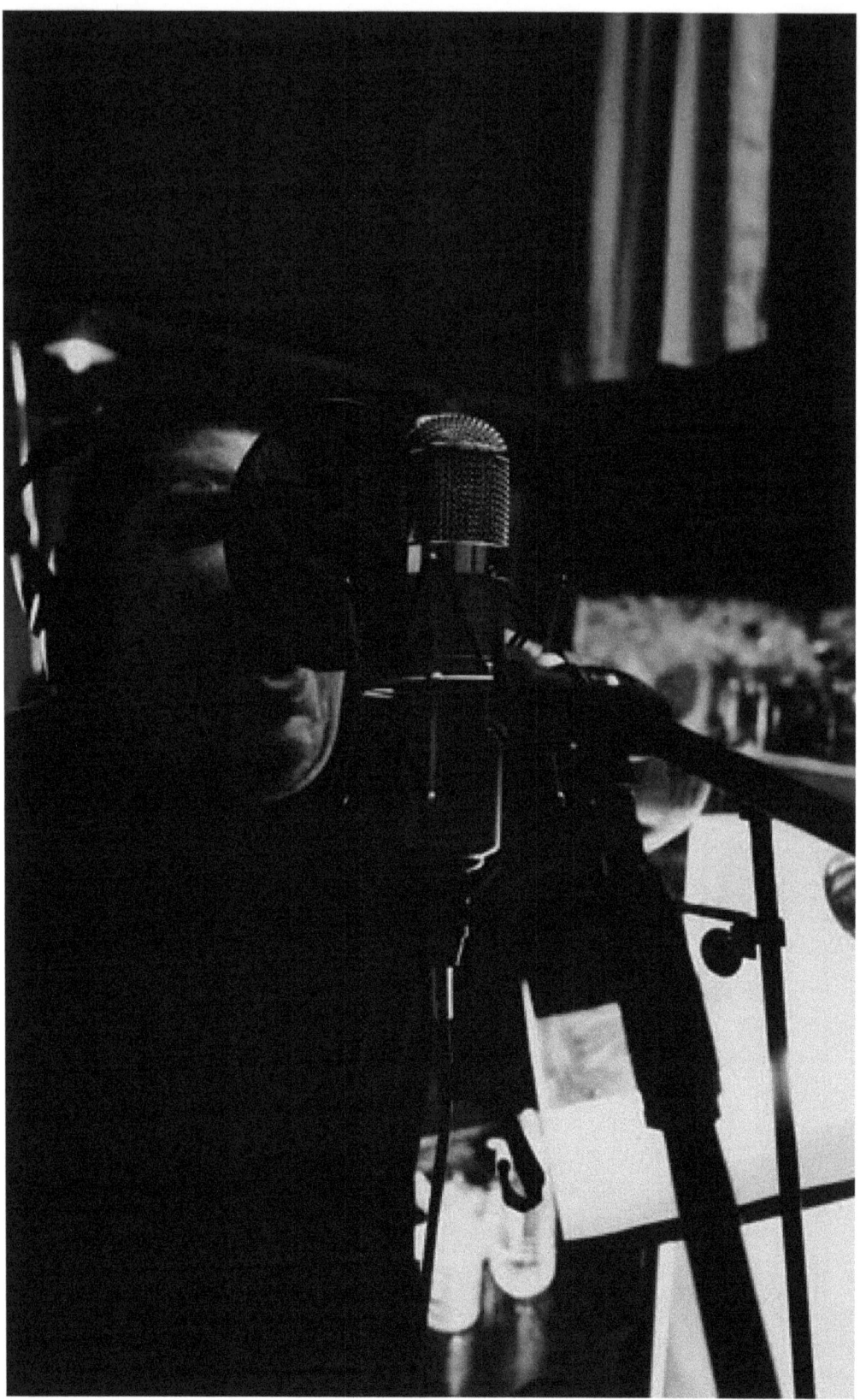

PAUL BEARER
(SHEER TERROR)

For me, the quintessential NYHC band has always been Sheer Terror. The moment I heard 'em on the *Where The Wild Things Are* compilation (on Blackout Records), I was sold. And even though they walked their own path and were never beholden to anyone, to me (and many thousands like me), they, more than any other band, were, are and always will be the true heart and soul of NYHC. Which, when it came time to putting this special together, meant only one thing. That we'd have to include 'em. So, ladies and gentlemen, boys and girls, without further ado, it's my honour to present to you, Sheer Terror and their most excellent singer, leader and frontman, Mr. Paul Bearer…

Questions by Ian Pickens and Tim Cundle

Interview by Tim Cundle

Photographs by Jammie Sloan York & Carl Gunhouse

MM: Why did you get Sheer Terror back together?

Paul: A friend of mine was going to Japan and I had never gone, so it was just a way of going to Japan I'd never been….

MM: That's as good a reason as any…

Paul: We did the "This is Hardcore" festival about a month before as a warm up then went to Japan; and I realised I was enjoying it again, which I hadn't in a long time. I had a really good band, a bunch of really great guys who got what I wanted and understood what I was going for. So I asked them if they wanted to try writing some songs and they said "We kinda already did"! So I was like: Alright, alright. It just felt right and I'm glad that I did it. I really didn't know if I was going to enjoy doing it again, but I did. It wasn't like I was trying to walk away from the Hardcore scene, but playing that kind of music wasn't what I was feeling like I wanted to do at the time.

MM: You once sang "I couldn't Care less about the Lower East Side" so would it be fair to say that you've always been a bit ambiguous about the New York Hardcore scene?

Paul: I just wasn't into that whole "We're all in this together" thing… I just didn't feel it. It was like a lot of people singing "Lower East Side Crew" and in all honesty, none of these people are from the Lower East Side. There are very few people who can claim they grew up on the Lower East Side: Vinnie Stigma and Harley, because he was always travelling round with his mom and when they weren't in Europe they were living down there; but all these other people they were from Queens or Brooklyn and they gravitated down there because it was cheap and you could get away with almost anything down there. But really no-one's from the Lower East Side apart from old Ukrainian and Polish people and Puerto Rican's….

MM: Talking about that, did you guys ever feel at odds with a lot of bands who were about during that time, talking about positivity and unity and Sheer Terror just, y'know… weren't. Did you ever feel out of step with the scene you were part of?

Paul: Oh big time, big time. I'm not going to say it wasn't a conscious thing either because I really didn't like a lot of the bands and I didn't like a lot of the stuff, it almost seemed forced to me, that whole unity thing. I just didn't feel it and it almost seemed like it was unity, but only on their own terms. I didn't agree with their terms, I didn't care for their bands; I didn't care for their message. There was a lot of attitude being thrown around at the time and I was just: "Fuck you then – I'll be over here… You guys, run along, do what you gotta do.. I'll be over here".

MM: How did you get involved in the Hardcore scene then, as it doesn't sound like something you'd naturally gravitate towards?

Paul: It was the music really. It was the music. There were some early New York bands: The Abused; The Nihilistics and Urban Waste that I really liked a lot. It was the music, DC bands, Boston bands, New York bands, West Coast and European bands that I really liked. I just really liked the music. Everybody else was peripheral. I knew they were there, but I really didn't pay attention to them.

MM: When you started the band back in 1984, did you think you'd still be doing this thrty years later: touring and releasing records?

Paul: Well I didn't really know what the hell I was going to do the next day. I hoped to. I always hoped to be doing something with music, as it was something that was in me from when I was a little kid. It was always about music. Luckily I latched on to it and took a run at it rather than thinking it was never going to happen. That was the whole beauty of Hardcore and punk rock, it was like "Why not?" and thank God for that because otherwise who knows what the hell I'd be doing right now. I'm always going to be doing something with music whether I'm making a dime off it or not. It's in me; I guess I'm stupid that way!

MM: A lot of people outside of New York and outside of the US became aware of Sheer Terror through the *Where the Wild Things Are*; how much of a game changer was that for you?

Paul: It helped. It got the band's name out there more. But in the mean time we had an album out, even though it was poorly distributed and on a German label which made it difficult t to get hold of; you couldn't just go out and buy it. So we'd go out and play shows, and we'd play our entire set and people didn't really know any of the songs and then all of a sudden, we'd play *Cup O' Joe* and they'd be like "Oh my God *Cup O' Joe*!!" and they would go nuts for one song. It was like being a one hit wonder without the accolades.

MM: The band as a whole always said there was a lot of Celtic Frost in your sound, but you've always been kind of critical of the whole metal crossover thing in Hardcore. Were you just being contrary or do you genuinely dislike metal?

Paul: I didn't. I never grew up as a heavy metal fan. That was Blake and Neuman. Those guys loved Celtic Frost. I like Black Sabbath and the rock and roll thing, and Motorhead of course, but that's rock and roll. I like the rock and roll stuff that people sometimes consider to be heavy metal. I was never a metal guy. I like the first two Venom albums because they are sloppy as hell and really crazy. I like Saxon too, but they, again are rock and roll. I didn't like metal people; when I was a kid, walking round in boots and braces in high school and even though these guys were the same as me, poor white trash, because they have an Iron Maiden patch on their jacket they were the enemy. It was almost like they were looking down on me.

MM: So your perception hasn't changed over time then?

Paul: I mean, I'm still not a fan, not really. I like the more rock and roll stuff like AC/DC and Rose Tattoo. And UFO, I love UFO.

MM: So Dave, your old drummer, his musical taste didn't rub off on you then?

Paul: You know, he wasn't even like a metal guy. He was a glam rock guy. He played on a Law and Order record... He was one of those guys! I mean his favourite drummer was Bonham, which is kinda cool I guess, but apart from that, he liked a lot of crap. A lot of eighties hair rock, so you couldn't even call him a metal guy. I don't think he even owned a Slayer record, but you know, neither do I so... But yeah he was into eighties hair rock or whatever the fuck that was.

MM: Do you think it was inevitable that the New York Hardcore scene would develop the way it did, with the influx of metal that was personified by bands like Nuclear Assault which brought the whole crossover thing to the forefront?

Paul: You know, Nuclear Assault... John and Danny were really cool. They were just white trash metal kids who found out about Hardcore and came to the shows. They never pretended to do anything or be anything they weren't; they were nice guys, a thrash band, and came to all the shows. I actually worked with them in a warehouse for a while and they were really cool, really nice guys. What bothered me – and not just in New York, but everywhere else as well – when bands started out, they were punk or Hardcore or whatever, then you start learning how to play your instruments better, but why does it mean that just because you can play better you have to be "metal"? Why does that have to be the logical next step? Why can't you just get better at what you're doing? That's what I didn't understand: why did it have to be fucking heavy metal? Why don't you just play Hardcore or punk and play it better than you did before? Why heavy metal?

MM: One of the reasons you are held in such high esteem is your depictions of life and calling things exactly how you see them. Has that ever got you into any trouble over the years? Have people ever got the wrong idea about you?

Paul: Here and there. People might want to come up and question me on some stuff and I'm sure I've probably got some enemies out there, I have no idea, but do I care? But, nothing drastic, and now, thanks to the internet, everyone has something to say without even showing their face.

MM: Yeah it's not like in the old days, when you'd actually have to front it out and say something to somebody's face...

Paul: Exactly. There's plenty of frigging loudmouths on the internet. That's what they like – shooting their mouths off... anonymous, anonymous and anonymous. They can all suck a dick and die. They're nothing. I just laugh at them, they're ridiculous. But yeah, you know, people will come up and ask about it, but it never ends in a fight or anything like that, we just talk...

MM: A lot of people consider Sheer Terror to be the very definition of a New York hardcore band. Do you think they are right? Why do you think so many people (especially from rural areas) identified so strongly with the New York scene more than any others?

Paul: A lot of the bands, especially in the mid-eighties, we'd get out and we'd go touring; because in the early eighties nobody from New York was really getting out and doing any touring, it was all the California bands. Bands from DC and Boston would come through, and occasionally we'd get bands from England and Europe, but we never thought we'd be able to do anything like that. So when the New York thing hit and the bands started touring, getting out there and going further and further... Most people have this idea of New York, the mystique of the city: dirty, gritty, full of people, and of course when the bands were out there they were talking New York up a lot more than it is and it was. And yeah it was dangerous and there was a lot of stuff going on in the city back then; so if you're in the middle of America, like Ohio or something, then the war stories come out so there was a lot of exaggeration and a lot of embellishment went on. Yeah so a lot of stuff did happen, but if you're talking to a kid from a farm who has never even seen a Puerto Rican then... Forget about it (Laughs)

MM: Would you agree with Roger from Agnostic Front who thinks that old New York is done and dusted, dead and buried, mainly due to Rudy Giuliano's zero tolerance policies? And how do you think the New York of today compares to the New York of the eighties?

Paul: Yeah, it is dead to a great extent because they keep tearing down the old and building up all this new crap. Any personality and any history are just being trod on. All these new buildings going up for the rich; and although they talk about rent control at 30-40% nobody can afford to live there. You're not going to get a whole city full of rich people. It's not going to be rich, rich, rich, because rich people want exclusivity. So you've got all these gigantic empty buildings, pushing people out when they've got nowhere else to go, then you get all these hipsters, college kids – whatever the fuck you call them, I don't know – they come in and it's almost like they are homesteading. They bring their whole organic thing and it's like... Fuck you. The neighbourhood was there before you and maybe it isn't what you like but it's what people had. They come in almost like Christopher Columbus discovering this new place and trying to change it. Yes, you change it for you but you'll be gone soon – these aren't the kind of people who are going to put down roots and raise families.

It's like in every science fiction movie you see these days. When the aliens come down to the planet, they take everything; use up all the resources but then they leave. That's what these people are like. What are you going to do? You know I'm still here because this is where I friggin' live. I've tried living other places, but it didn't work out. I'm a New Yorker and I plan on being here the rest of my life but you never know what happens. But I'm not going to pick up and go to fucking California like other people do, who are like "It's dead so I'm leaving..." Fuck you, don't let the door hit you on the way out then... You were here when things were worse, and now you're leaving? Fuck you. California can go to hell too, because it's like every 1970s sitcom or television show in America. What broke up the family? The job offer in California. Then everybody's all sad and like "Ohhh, we're gonna miss you, we're so sad to see you go" which only proves to me that California is full of a bunch of fucking retards who can't take care of their own shit, so they outsource it to people from New York.

MM: Tony Rettman's book – do you think it paints an accurate portrait of what the New York scene was like back then?

Paul: Yes, I guess. I really like the early part. He did a good job of compiling it, especially the old interviews with bands like the Simulators and Heart Attack. The really, really early days, I think that's handled really well, but then the rest of it, the majority of it is like the Youth Crew stuff. Really lot of it. Me and Mike Judge, after all these years we talk finally, no reason we didn't before, we just never really did. I'm not saying we're friends or anything but we talk. But Jesus Christ there is a lot of him in that book – which is fine – but do we really need a four page article on Mayhem and Straight Ahead? The bands didn't really do that much. It starts out great but then seems to go more into the bands that influenced Tony. That's fine and dandy, it's just tilted towards that way a little more. There is like two pictures of me in there and Tony is a nice guy, but as for Sheer Terror, in all honesty, we only really get a paragraph. The chapter that we're in is more about Blackout Records and fucking Outburst. But whatever...

MM: That was my one main criticism of the book, I don't think Sheer Terror were featured enough...

Paul: The book will do what it will do and people will read it. It's nicely put together and it's nicely compiled. It started out good but then it became more and more about how Agnostic Front and the Cro-Mags invented sliced bread.... (laughs)

MM: One of our writers spoke to Sean Taggart recently and he asked about the hostile attitude of people outside of New York toward the New York scene at that time. And Sean said "In the states, everybody has an axe to grind with New York because we're the best. They know it, we know it..." Do you think that's true?

Paul: I don't know, honestly. The best at what? The best at making a bunch of noise and jumping around on each other's heads? Whoopeeeee. I think a lot of people had that attitude towards New York because we're dirtier. They'd come in from the suburbs, like DC or whatever and they would see the punk rockers drinking and hanging out or whatever... then it's like "go the fuck back to Marbelhead Massachusetts But when they were here, they didn't have an attitude. We wanted to see them because we enjoy the music but they weren't giving us that attitude from the stage, it wasn't like that. It wasn't until they left and got together with their friends that they would start to talk shit. But who cares? We did have problems. We weren't the brightest people in the fucking world, but who is? We were trying to have fun and find out what we wanted to do. We were like 13, 14, 15 years old. What would you expect from us?

MM: *Standing Up...* Have you been surprised by the reaction to the new record?

Paul: For the most part it's been positive which is always cool. There 've been a couple here and there talking about the new production and how they are not used to it – whatever the hell that means. I don't know what that means. Are we supposed to record a record and make it sound like a piece of shit from 1985? I don't understand that. The new production? That's your fucking problem? Get over yourself. That and a few reviews I've been sent from Europe, some of the non-English speaking countries, and I go to the Google and use the translate thing which is always fun. But it's like some of these people; I just want to smack them. They give a positive review of the record then call me a fat bastard on top of it. It's like "ugly fat man singing!" and I'm like: Jesus Christ pal! (laughs)...

MM: Yeah, because what' that got to do with the price of butter?

Paul: Exactly, and it's like: Who the hell are you? I want to see a picture of you. Yeah I'm overweight but I'm not obese. What the hell? (laughs) But that's how they talk to you over there, some of these people. In Germany, I just want to smack some of them. They'll come up to you, and you'll be having a nice conversation and suddenly they'll be like: (adopts German accent) "So you're new record is shit? And you're like: what? What the hell is this? (laughs) get the hell away from me! (laughs)...

MM: Are you going to do any more touring off the back of this record?

Paul: Yeah we've just done three dates in Germany and one in Rotterdam and then we've got some stuff in the US and what not. We want to come back to England. The guy who brought us across last time is busy doing his own thing and said he could only sort us out for September. I asked for sooner, but he is busy on the Temples festival, but we definitely want to come back over there and maybe play the Rebellion fest which is in Blackpool, so that I can get so see some of the bands I can't get to see at home.

MM: Is there going to be another record?

Paul: Most definitely. We're screwing around with songs right now and there will probably be an EP before we do an LP, but then again you never know, it depends how things go. There will most definitely be another record without a doubt. I love doing this, I love the guys in my band and I'm going to keep doing this till the wheels fall off.

Originally published in Mass Movement Presents: NYHC, July 2014

TONY RETTMAN

Having done a fantastic job in covering the Detroit Hardcore scene from 1979-1985 in *Why Be Something You're Not*, Mass Movement was pretty stoked to discover author and scene chronicler extraordinaire Tony Rettman had written a history of the NYHC scene between 1980-1990. With the book being everything we hoped it would be, and acting as a trigger for this Mass Movement NYHC special, it would have been rude not to speak to the man himself.

Interview by Ian Pickens

MM: Hi Tony, thanks for taking the time out to talk to us...

TR: No problem. We're in the middle of a historic snowstorm right now in New York. So, doing an interview will be a fun way to kill time as I'm snowed in with a case of beer and too many downloads of Schoolboy Q mixtapes.

MM: I'm guessing you've been very much in demand since *NYHC 1980 -1990* was released?

TR: When the book initially came out in the first half of December 2014, my life was pretty hectic. There was a quiet time there right after Christmas that I really relished. But now that the second printing is coming back in the next few weeks, so I'm starting to feel the wave building again.

MM: What's the response been like to the book? Have you had a lot of feedback from outside of the US?

TR: The response to the book has been great thus far. Totally unexpected on both mine and Bazillion Points' end. We've received huge support and interest from the Core Tex Store in Germany and the Straight and Alert distro in France. Plus, you see chatter on Facebook and Instagram from all over the world.

MM: Let's go back to your origins in the NYHC scene; how and when did you first become involved?

TR: I grew up in central New Jersey, so I wouldn't feel right saying I was truly 'involved' in the NYHC scene. I came into NY here and there to buy records and see shows. But I started doing a fanzine at the age of 16 named Common Sense with a guy named Tim McMahon who you might know from the bands Mouthpiece, Hands Tied, Triple Threat, Face the Enemy, etc. You might also know him as a part of the Double Cross website. We pretty much covered/interviewed a ton of NYHC bands in that 'zine. Some of them included Youth of Today, Sick of it All, Gorilla Biscuits, Alone in a Crowd and a few more. So, that's about as close as my 'involvement' goes. But I was a huge fan of the stuff as soon as my brother brought home Agnostic Front's *Victim in Pain* in the summer of 1984. The combination of the looks of that record and the sheer brute force of it totally knocked me out.

MM: Have you always leaned towards the journalistic side of things? A chronicler of events so to speak?

TR: When my brother started taking me to shows in the summer of 1984, I really took a liking to buying fanzines at the shows. They were cheaper than buying a t-shirt from a band or anything, so I bought them. I just thought they were cool and when I was 14 I decided I wanted to do one on my own.

Since then, I've always did 'zines whether they about Hardcore or Psych Rock or whatever. Now, thirty years later, I'm still doing what I did as a kid. I guess it's just on a larger scale.

MM: As the scene began to develop and started to crossover to the metal crowd in the mid-80s, were you conscious of its reach outside of NYC and the US in general? How aware were the bands of the controversy that the crossover with metal was causing?

TR: That whole summer of '84 when I started going to shows, the influence of Metal was just starting to rear its head. I remember seeing east coast Hardcore bands embrace it and then I saw Suicidal Tendencies in September of that year and they were going the same route. Pretty soon, you had COC wearing Slayer shirts and DRI re-doing their songs with a Metal flavour. Later on, those English Dogs records came through; as did the Discharge records. It was then my tiny mind figured out this wasn't an isolated thing.

I was very aware of the controversy the crossover thing was causing. I myself was not a fan of it as a kid. The music of a lot of those bands was cool, but the lyrics and vibe was something totally alien to me. Hardcore to me was a music with a message and all Metal had were songs about Satan. In the rear-view, it's pretty obvious the crossover was something that needed to happen to keep the Hardcore scene going. It helped 'both sides'. Bands like Nuclear Assault and Metallica started to write lyrics of worth and some Hardcore bands were almost better as Metal bands than Hardcore bands!

MM: What was it about the NYHC scene that made so many people outside of the city identify with it?

TR: I think with bands like Agnostic Front, Cro-Mags, etc. people maybe didn't really identify with it, but they dug the gritty, street vibe those bands had. I think it became something kids wanted to latch onto in the late 80's with the Youth Crew thing. People all over the world really took to that vibe and identified that as NYHC more so than other stuff.

MM: As you've documented in your book the NYHC had several different stages in its development from those late seventies/early eighties almost pre-Hardcore bands like the Stimulators and the Mob through to the more metallic nineties bands – do you have a particular favourite period and if so why? If pushed who would be your definitive NYHC band?

TR: Like most people, I'm very infatuated with the '82 to '84 scene that revolved around the A7 Club. The *United Blood* era of Agnostic Front, The Abused, Cause for Alarm, Urban Waste, Antidote, etc. is super intriguing to me. That music has such a primal sound to it compared to the other stuff that was going on around the country at the time. But having said that, I still have a deep interest in the Youth Crew element of the late 80's just because it's such a juxtaposition to the '82 A7 scene. How did it go from chains around the waist and fighting in the street to nice clean high tops, handing sandwiches out to the homeless and singing songs about your friends? It's sort of perplexing. Definitive NYHC band to me would be Agnostic Front. Like I stated above, my gateway into NYHC was *Victim in Pain*. Since I wasn't from NYC, seeing them for the first time was a real myth busting moment. Staring at these pictures of them on that record and in crapilly Xeroxed Hardcore 'zines made them out to be these tattooed superheroes almost. So to them in the flesh combined with the physicality of their crew was amazing.

MM: Why did you decide to stop at 1990 rather than continue up to present day? Is there a Volume Two in the pipeline?

TR: I stopped at 1990 because, honestly, that's around the time I checked out of the Hardcore scene for a time. That era holds my interest and it's the one I can write about with a bit more confidence. That's not to say bands that came after that are bad. If anything, those are the bands people truly identify NYHC with.

People have asked about a Volume 2. It could happen for sure. But I think I need a little breathing room for now. The book took up almost 2 years of my life and I'd like to get some semblance of normalcy back into my life.

MM: One of the things I picked up on reading *NYHC 1980-1990* was a distinct absence of the kind of score settling that featured a lot in Stephen Blush's *American Hardcore*; given the inevitable (and widely publicised) uh… communication breakdowns between certain members of the NYHC fraternity, was there a conscious decision to exclude any negative comments? Were you concerned that people might accuse you of re-writing history or maybe viewing it through rose tinted glasses?

TR: I definitely went in with the mind-set that I wanted to solely concentrate on the music and bands and exclude the other stuff people like to go on and on about in regards to the NYHC scene being violent, etc. I'm personally sick of reading about it. Music is my number one interest. If you want to read about all the well-publicized beefs in NYHC, go to your laptop and look it up. It's all there.

I have heard second hand that some have complained that I did put together a book that doesn't cover the 'real' NYHC scene that revolved around violence, etc. But like I stated above, I wanted to put together a book about the bands, 'zines, record labels, etc. that made up the scene. There's nothing written in stone saying my book will be the be-all/end-all book on NYHC and I certainly don't fucking think it is! If someone who was there first hand wants to do a book that includes such things, they're obviously free to do it. I was coming at this as a fan with respect for what these bands and people accomplished.

MM: One of the things I liked about the book was that you featured not only the band members from the scene but also artists such as Sean Taggart, zine writers such as Jack Rabid, record store owners such as Duane Rossignol, not to mention the clubs and promoters that played such an significant part in NYHC; was it important to you to present a wider picture of the scene and not just the usual musicians angle?

TR: Yes. As a kid who wasn't in a band, I looked up more to 'zine editors than musicians. People like Wendy Eager from Guillotine, Jack Rabid from *Big Takeover*, Gary who did *Tse Tse Fly*, etc. were the people I admired. They took everything in and reported on it with great enthusiasm and they all had great memories of that time. Sean Taggart's artwork defined NYHC in the 80's and there was no way you could exclude him from the proceedings. I don't think Duane from Some gets the recognition he deserves for being a lightning rod for all that happened in the later 80's era of NYHC. A band like Sick of it All who tour the world to this day got their start by dropping off their demo at Some. The way he pushed all these legendary bands was super important in the grand scheme of things.

MM: One of the most poignant parts of the book was the section on Reagan Youth and Dave Insurgent – did you know Dave personally? Do you think that Dave's demise was a factor in the development of the Straight Edge scene in NYC as opposed to an alignment with the Boston/DC scenes? Did the influx of Krishna thought play a part?

TR: I never met Dave, but saw Reagan Youth once. That's about far as that goes. Dave's demise had nothing to do with the influx of Straight Edge in NY as far as I can tell and the Krishna influence was in the NYHC scene even in the early 80's due to people like John Joseph, Louie Rivera, Keith Burkheardt, etc.

MM: Were the different factions in NYHC ultimately a positive or divisive development? As an outsider, to me NYHC seemed more open than other HC scenes to outside influences, in musical and cultural terms, such as the impact of Hip Hop on both the music and fashion of the NYHC scene.

TR: New York in general is a melting pot of cultures and people, so it was inevitable that things would cross-pollinate. Hip Hop and Hardcore were two no-bullshit forms of music coming up at the same time that most people refused to comprehend, so they had an immediate connection. But I think Mark Ryan from Supertouch should really be credited as probably the first Hardcore kid to really take in and embrace Hip Hop culture and bring it into NYHC.

MM: How do you feel about bands such as the Crumbsuckers and Ludichrist reforming after so many years? Do you feel the NYHC scene is in safe hands with AF, SOIA and Madball amongst others, still commanding so much respect worldwide and releasing consistently strong albums?

TR: I personally have no issues with any bands re-forming, putting out new music, playing the same old music or whatever. If the demand is there and they're into what they're doing, it's all fine by me. There's probably so many kids that are excited to see bands they thought they'd never see. We have Altercation re-forming for an upcoming book release show and I'm so frickin' psyched! I never got to see them back then and their demo is one of my all-time favourites, so I'm there on the same level as some kid who never saw Judge or The Crumbsuckers, etc.

NYHC is in more than capable hands with the bands you mentioned. They live it and will continue to until all that's left is cockroaches on the earth.

MM: Stepping aside from NYHC for a second - why did you decide to document the Detroit Hardcore scene between 1979-1985 first?

TR: The scene from the early 80's in the Midwest revolving around the Necros, Negative Approach, Meatmen, Touch & Go Fanzine, Violent Apathy, etc. is something that I've been infatuated with since I was a tiny kid. But unlike the NYHC scene, I never got to witness it. By the time I was going to shows, Negative Approach had broken up and the Necros and Meatmen were hardly what they were in the early eighties. I don't mean that in a qualitative sense; just they weren't like...burr headed dudes in boots anymore, you know? So, there was always this sense of mystery with that scene with me. *Touch & Go* Fanzine was always filled with these juvenile in-jokes that I wanted to know the answer to. I wanted to know who all these dudes were hanging out behind Negative Approach's amps in the photos on their 7". All this dumb shit haunted me throughout my life. So, when the opportunity came up to explore that, I took it. I wanted to get the mystery out of the way first, then I went onto NYHC which was part mystery, part my everyday knowledge.

MM: Do you see parallels between the two scenes? Detroit seemingly sat more in the Boston/DC camp in the NYC /DC rivalry?

TR: I can see a parallel between the two places that the crucial early eighties Hardcore shows happened in Detroit and NYC. Both were illegal clubs situated in the shittiest parts of both towns. But I think that's where it ends. The Midwest people definitely had an attitude coming to New York just like the DC people. Maybe they had a chip on their shoulders? Who knows? I wasn't there.

MM: Could you see yourself documenting any of the West Coast Hardcore scenes?

TR: I think those scenes have been very well documented so far. They don't need my help. Although I think books about sole bands from that early era of Southern California would be interesting. That's a road that could be cool.

Originally published in Mass Movement Presents: NYHC, July 2014

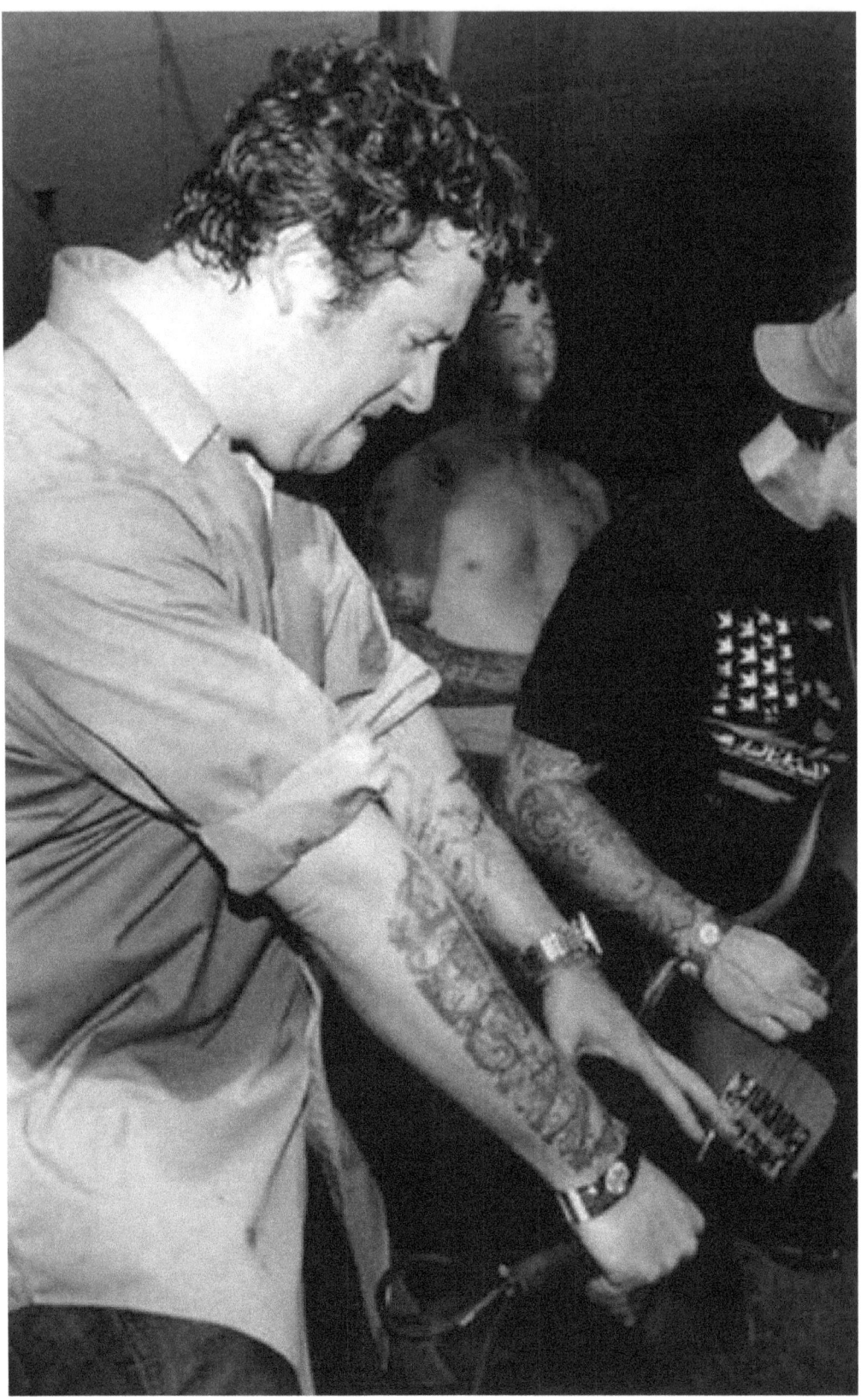

RICHIE BIRKENHEAD
(UNDERDOG / YOUTH OF TODAY / INTO ANOTHER)

Underdog. They've been one of my favourite bands since I first managed to lay my hands on *The Vanishing Point* around a quarter of a century ago, and at this point in my life (more than four decades in and counting), I can safely, and categorically, state that they will almost certainly occupy the same place in my musical affections until I shuffle off this mortal coil.

Hell, I even named the magazine after one of their songs. As such, I figured that we couldn't do an NYHC special without featuring them and after a little to-ing and fro-ing, I managed to get in touch with singer and all round good guy, Richie Birkenhead for a chat about NYHC, Underdog, Youth Of Today and Into Another…

Interview by Tim Cundle

MM: Were you always aware of, or into music, or did your interest in music begin with punk rock and Hardcore? Has music always been a part of your life?

Richie: I was born into music and art. My mother, Susan Birkenhead, is a brilliant lyricist and composer. Many members of her extended family were/are artists, musicians and songwriters. I spent much of my childhood sitting underneath my mother's piano while she played. I started playing various instruments and singing as a child.

MM: When, where and how did you become aware of the NYHC scene? Was it something that you immediately gravitated toward or did it gradually draw you in over time?

Richie: As a teenager In the early eighties, I was into the rockabilly/psychobilly scene. I played guitar and sang a bit in a band called the Bel Airs. I was always downtown, playing shows and going to shows featuring bands from all genres. In the winter of 1981, a couple of friends from high school and I went to a Bad Brains show at Max's Kansas City and I was blown away by the experience. I started seeing hardcore bands whenever I could at places like CBGB, A7, Great Gildersleeves. Another friend from high school was in The Young and the Useless, and I would go to their shows whenever they played. Hardcore just really connected with me emotionally at that point in my life.

MM: Was it the idea of the scene and everything that it represented, or the music that initially attracted you to NYHC? What was it about both that you found appealing? What made you want to be a part of the scene?

Richie: It was the fact that it felt more genuine, more visceral, more dangerous than anything else. It was the only TRULY underground music scene. I was also drawn in by the bands themselves. I was a huge Agnostic Front, Murphy's Law and Cro-Mags fan. To my mind, Harley, Jimmy, Roger and Vinny are the founding fathers of NYHC. They were larger than life on stage and off. I loved many other bands in that scene, too, including the Nihilistics, Kraut, The Mob, Reagan Youth… Too many to list.

MM: What do you remember most about when you first discovered Hardcore? Everyone has a first show... What was yours Richie? Do you want to tell us about it?

Richie: As I mentioned previously, it was the Bad Brains at Max's. What I remember most was the way the way people reacted. The slam dancing. It gave me goose bumps. I'll never forget it.

MM: What, in your opinion, makes a scene? Bands or people, and what do you think made NYHC (in the eighties and early nineties) so special? The music, or the people involved? Why?

Richie: In the same way that it can be difficult to describe an aesthetic or the ethos of a great city, it's hard to define what really makes a "scene". In the case of NYHC, I'd say it was a coming-together of people who were, to varying degrees, misfits - kids who were on the margins and alienated from the boring mainstream, carrying around a lot of pent-up aggression and a burning desire to say and scream a few things. Along with that, you have the music, the haircuts (or absence of hair), the boots, the sneakers, the clothes, the shows, the lingo...

MM: Sort of following on from the above question... All scenes have a focal point, a band that starts it all, that fires the imagination of those around them and spurs them into action. Which band do you think was the initial locus of the NYHC scene and why were they thus?

Richie: If I had to single out one band, it would be Agnostic Front. They embodied and symbolized the scene. By way of DC, you get the Bad Brains. Technically not a New York band, but hugely influential here and definitely a "part" of the New York scene. As far as the individual New Yorkers who started it all, it was the aforementioned Harley, Jimmy, Roger and Vinny.

MM: Given the stories of street kids, runaways and squats that have always seemed to form the core of the NYHC scene, the NYHC scene always seemed pretty tough, and at times incredibly violent, was it really like that? Did you see any of that stuff, the violence and fighting, or has it all been blown up and exaggerated over time?

Richie: It was really like that, but mostly because the scene was centered around what was then a very violent neighborhood - the Lower East Side. NYHC kids, generally speaking, did not go out and start fights. The violence was much more a result of the fact that they were protective of one another and did not take shit.

MM: Ask any Hardcore kid in the world about CBGB's and they'll automatically know what you're talking about... So, what was about CB's that made it so special? What was it about the matinee shows that made them the stuff of legend? What's your favourite CB's moment or story, and can you share it with us?

Richie: The Ramones started playing CB's in 1974. It was the punk Mecca. The place resonated and vibrated with the spirit and essence of punk rock. Of course, it didn't hurt that CB's looked like a bombed-out homeless shelter covered in graffiti. The matinees there felt like magic. They used to remind me of movies like *The Warriors* and *The Wanderers* — every faction of the scene coming together. Peace punks, skins, skaters, straight edge kids, kids high on dust... all one family for an afternoon.

MM: What is about NYC that made its scene so special? I mean, there were hundreds of scenes starting everywhere, so what do you think it was, and is, about the New York scene that meant that kids and people everywhere around the globe could identify with, and immediately feel a connection to, it?

Richie: Most other Hardcore scenes around the country sprang up in college towns and were intertwined with university culture. The scene in New York - despite the fact that New York is home to Columbia, NYU, etc. - was entirely separate, and largely (although not completely) comprised of working class kids and lower class kids – even kids living in squats and living on the edge of survival. I believe that's a huge reason for the more genuine, gritty, harder sound of New York hardcore. The fact that the music made by NYHC bands touched people everywhere is due to the same things that made people love Black Sabbath, Pete Seeger and Billie Holiday: Music and Poetry made by people who genuinely suffer and struggle tends to make a much broader connection.

MM: When did you first realise that the NYHC scene was starting to blow up and was becoming a musical force to be reckoned with around the world instead of being confined to the limits of its point of origin? How did that make you feel at the time?

Richie: I don't recall a particular point in time when it dawned on me. I do remember being aware of the Cro-Mags, Murphy's Law and Agnostic Front becoming gradually more and more popular around the world and that made perfect sense to me.

MM: Okay, I wanted to ask you about your bands... So, let's start with what I think is one of the three definitive NYHC bands (hey, I named the mag after one of your songs, so y'know, I think you guessed I was a "bit" of a fan), Underdog. What's been, up until now, your favourite Underdog moment or story, the one that always gives you a warm glow inside whenever you think about, or remember it?

Richie: I have so many great memories. I'll pick one: We had a friend, roadie, driver, all-around-everything called Big Lou. Nicest guy on the planet, built like Bruce Lee on steroids. We were playing a show somewhere and had to stop mid-set because a bunch of asshole skinheads showed up and started picking on and hurting smaller kids on the dance floor. The biggest skinhead started screaming, "Who wants to fuck with me?!" over and over and Lou walked up and knocked him out cold with an open-hand slap. Then a riot ensued. Pure gold.

MM: And, what was your favourite Youth Of Today moment or story? What's your one, over-riding, perfect memory of being in YOT?

Richie: I have incredibly fond memories of the rehearsals and writing sessions leading up to the recording of *Break Down the Walls*. There was an amazing camaraderie between us. We laughed like crazy, got out a ton of rage and aggression. It was really special. It also really cemented my friendship and musical connection (which continues to this day) with Drew. A particular on-stage moment that sticks out is a show where there was some altercation beforehand and a few fucked-up people were making threats of violence against us. In a spontaneous reaction, we decided, instead of playing *Time to Forgive*, to play it in its original form, as *We Just Might*. The place went insane.

MM: And, the same with Into Another? Up until now, this moment, what's been your favourite Into Another moment, show, story, record etc. that you've experienced while being in the band?

Richie: Into Another is the band I have the deepest creative connection with. The lyrics I've written and sung in that band are, by far, my most candid, cathartic and personal. My most cherished memory is playing *Without a Medium* (a song I wrote for a friend who died, and a song we very rarely played) for a kid who had lost someone very close to him. After the show, he thanked me with tears in his eyes and I thanked him with tears in mine. Then we sat on a curb and shared our stories. It was a vivid illustration of how baring your soul through pencil, pad and guitar can eventually reach across thousands of miles and move another soul. Incredibly humbling.

MM: Do you think something like the NYHC explosion could happen again, or did the whole thing happen because of a combination of unique factors – people, location and time. Could that HC lightning ever be captured in a bottle again?

Richie: Something like it, possibly; but it will never happen again in exactly the same way. New York is far too gentrified, sterilized and stripped of much of its soul. A subversive subculture couldn't naturally form and grow in the same way it did in the early '80s. The world has become so homogenized by the digital age that regional culture is almost extinct.

MM: Is the scene still the same as it ever was, or has it changed and evolved over time? How do you think it's changed and have those changes been positive or detrimental to the NYHC scene as a whole? Do you miss the old days? What do you miss most about them?

Richie: Of course I miss the old days, but isn't that always the case with any previous generation? I don't pretend to have my fingers on the pulse of the NYHC scene today. I leave that to those who make up today's scene and drive it. I have nothing but respect for them. What I miss the most is the feeling of being part of something special, something real, something important, something dangerous.

MM: What do you think the enduring appeal of NYHC is? And what do you think its lasting legacy is, and will be?

Richie: The enduring appeal is the thoroughly unpretentious, pissed-off, gritty honesty of it all. Its lasting legacy will be that it symbolized the ultimate do-it-yourself sub-culture.

MM: What's happening with both Underdog and Into Another at the moment? Do you have any touring plans? What are the chances of seeing new records from either or both bands?

Richie: Into Another will release a 5-song E.P. next month. We plan to do some touring and follow with a full-length in the near future. Underdog plays a handful of shows every year. Next one will be at Saint Vitus (Brooklyn) in May.

MM: If there's anything that you'd like to add Richie, now would be the time…

Richie: Be kind to human and non-human animals, and to the planet we share. Thank you.

Originally published in Mass Movement Presents: NYHC, July 2014

ACID REIGN

Although the US dominated the heady days of Thrash in the mid-late 80s, the UK also produced some of the most popular and enduring bands of the genre – Onslaught, Reanimator, Xentrix and the Square-danciest band of them all – Acid Reign. With the band 'Rebooted' by singer Howard 'H' Smith, Mass Movement find out if the joke is still on them.

Interview by Ian Pickens

MM: First of all thanks for taking the time out to talk to us H, much appreciated.

H: My absolute pleasure. Thanks for asking.

MM: This incarnation of Acid Reign is being called a Reboot rather than a Reformation, could you clarify the difference for the hard of thinking?

H: Well this started out as a reformation of the *Obnoxious* line up in May 2013. Slowly but surely, one by one and for varying reasons the other guys all dropped out. When Hollywood decides to bring back an old favourite and update it they call it a reboot so I thought "If it's good enough for Hollywood its good enough for Acid Reign". In the band with me are Paul Chanter, Marc Jackson, Pete Dee and Cookie.

MM: There have been calls for the band to come out of hiatus/retirement for years; why did you decide the time was right to re-launch AR now?

H: Well as described above it's taken a while. The initial spark was Kev suggesting playing some shows in 2015 to celebrate the twenty fifth anniversary of *Obnoxious*, two years on and this is where we're at. Kev is still involved in the background and will make the odd guest appearance when schedules permit.

MM: Lots of Punk/HC/Metal bands seem to be reforming – do you think it's because we're all hitting middle age and having a crisis?

H: Not a midlife crisis as such, I just think it's about the time that people start to take stock of their lives and look back on their youth. Whether that is because their own kids are about the age they were when they were going to gigs and drinking three times their body weight in cider I don't know. It's all about the "N" word, nostalgia.

MM: You must have been pretty stoked by the amount of reaction the band were getting on Social Networking sites; were you surprised that so many people were still interested in the band?

H: Hell yes! I guess it ties in with your last question a bit too. The biggest surprise has been how positive the response has been. I was genuinely expecting more "It's just H and some blokes" but it's been overwhelmingly positive.

MM: What are your favourite memories from the first incarnation of the band (my personal ones were watching you in St. David's Hall in Cardiff with Nuclear Assault and Reanimator in 1988 I think? And also the fact that I was wearing my Moshkinstein t-shirt when I first met my now wife).

H: That was a cool gig, I remember Kev having a go at the bouncers and we refused to continue playing until they were removed as they were kicking the shit out of kids coming over the top of the pit. As soon as we got off stage the venue manager summoned Kev and I to the production office where we were informed we would never play the St David's Hall again. Kev turned around and said something to the effect of "Does it look like we want to play here again?" he was still fuming. That's very cool about your first meeting with your wife; see how we traded stories there? There are so many cool and not so many cool memories it's too hard to name them. I could go on for days!

MM: With Garry Jennings and Adam Lehan going on to Cathedral and Kev Papworth-Morgan taking up the Flymo in Lawnmower Deth, did you ever feel like carrying on musically at that point or did the stand-up comedy have more appeal?

H: I did carry on musically. I moved to Newcastle and joined a band called Strange Thing. Did that for two years played a show with LD and The Beyond plus some other local stuff and did two demos. Two weeks after ST split I moved to London to do stand up. I had thought of doing it after AR split but decided to give music one last shot. Stand up had been at the back of my mind since before AR to be honest it was something I was always going to do.

MM: Are you still performing as Keith Platt - Professional Yorkshire man? Are there any similarities between fronting a band and delivering stand-up?

H: Of course! AR isn't fulltime; I'll be doing way more gigs as Keith than I will be with AR per year. Apart from both of them taking place on a stage in front of people the similarities end there. Totally different.

MM: How did the new guys become involved in the Reboot? Have they brought something new to the mix?

H: Paul has been there since 2013, he was going to be involved with the reformation as back up for Kev who is on the road a lot as he crews for bands (mainly BFMV). He also played *Motherly Love* on stage with us on the *Jokes On Us* tour in 1990 and we've remained friends. Marc was recommended by Jeff from Onslaught, Pete by Si from Annihilated and Cooky comes via way of Kev so all nice and incestuous.

MM: Cooky also plays in the Black Sabbath tribute band Children of the Gravy – any thoughts on resurrecting the Sabbath Medley in AR?

H: (Laughs) Good knowledge and a great question. We all went and saw him play the other week in Swansea as we were recording the new song in Cardiff and it was great; a proper show. Their singer does a hilarious Ozzy impression. No plans for reviving the medley though.

MM: You personally host a Metal podcast called *Talking Bollocks* right? Do you feel that these newer forms of media (Facebook, Twitter, Podcasts etc.) have replaced the old 'Tape' Trading/Fanzine ways of communicating with each other? Do you see any negatives in the newer forms of communication?

H: I do and thanks for plugging the world's ONLY comedy metal podcast! Yes definitely they sure have, It's a mixture of both good and bad. I don't miss tapes that's for sure I hated those fucking things! I spoke with Chad Arnold the other day founder of Global Thrash Assault and he got into AR because he saw Joe from Gamma Bomb wearing an AR shirt in one of their videos on YouTube, that's no different to me buying the first Suicidal Tendencies record because Scott Ian wore their shirts all the time. The downside is not confined to metal but society in general and that is that we communicate so much in written text that actually talking is taking a back seat and that is a shame. On our soon to be launched website that section of our site is called Anti-Social Networks, see what we did there?

MM: Has the online response been mainly from older fans from the eighties and nineties, a new generation of Thrashers or an even mixture of both?

H: Both. The music has carried on without the band and reached people all over the world. The music didn't spilt up in 91' it kept on touring via the internet and has gone to some far flung places, we've been approached to do a South American tour for fuck sake! There are plenty of thrashers out there both young and old that didn't get into us or see us back in the day so it will be cool to get out there, meet old friends and make new ones.

MM: Candlelight Records released *The Apple Core Archives* last year, which is pretty much a comprehensive discography of everything AR ever recorded; are you happy with the way it turned out? What has the response been like?

H: Very happy and I think the people who bought it are too if the Amazon reviews are anything to go by. The response has been great, sales modestly impressive for a first release in twenty fiv years and no band to support it, Candlelight seem happy enough anyway so that's as good a sign as any.

MM: If you had to pick a favourite AR song what would it be and why?

H: Not what I would call our best song but my own personal favourite is *Creative Restraint*, because it all came together beautifully and to me still sounds as good today as it did back in the day. I love it, there are some great grooves and it's so heavy and got a bit of everything.

MM: You've been recording new material in South Wales, I know its early days yet but are you able to tell us anything about this new material?

H: Just one song *Plan Of The Damned* will be coming out as a taste of what this line up is capable of then it will be on with the nostalgia tour. After that we'll see what next.

Originally published in Mass Movement #43, July 2015

I WAS SATAN'S SLAVE TO THE MUSIC!

Horror fiction and heavy metal go together like a fist fuck and five star lube. Many horror fans have a weakness for doom laden power chords and a dark driving beat and who can blame them given the things they read and watch. Everyone knows that the Dark Lord's had all the heaviest tunes since the dawn of time, and occult subjects slip as easily into death metal lyrics as a priest into a choirboy's cassock.

In fact, the long association between horror, metal and the satanic arts goes right back to first painful contractions of metal's birth. In the late 60s and the early 70s the so called 'Age of Aquarius developed a noted . The Stones gig at Altamont had driven a stake through the heart of Woodstock's dreams of love and peace and the permissive society began to embrace Crowley's dictum that 'Do what thou wilt shall be the whole of the law'. Along with his dictum (stop sniggering), many were also embracing Crowley's magickal practices. The popular bookshelves were dominated by Dennis Wheatley and his authorial acolytes, cinema screens were infested with a slew of satanic movies including *The Devil Rides Out* and exploitation classics like and the tabloids were stuffed with tales of swinging suburbanites who'd shifted from wife swapping to full on satanic orgies.

Rock music was in a strange hinterland at the end of the 60s, psychedelia was busy spinning off into a variety of nascent genres including heavy rock and prog. With all the black magic in the air at the time, it stood to reason that sooner or later various brave and thrill seeking musicians were going fall under its beckoning spell. The little scene that sprung up around this music has been fascinating me of late, so I'm going to devote the majority of this month's column to it. I know this is technically supposed to be a column about horror comics but I long ago abandoned any illusions of keeping to just that subject, so you'll have to bear with your Uncle Jasp as we descend into the swinging and subterranean scene known briefly as Occult Rock.

The first stop on our dire descent is a group known as Black Widow, who very nearly had Black Sabbath's career (more on that later). Hailing from Leicester they began life as a rather mediocre blues and soul outfit with the teeth-gnashingly perky name of 'Pesky Gee!' Even though their name sounded like the sort of catch phrase used by a faded comedian who would later be indicted for crimes against nature, they actually managed to get a record deal and put out an instantly forgettable album called *Exclamation Mark*. According to their flautist the name of album was an accident that came about when their manager phoned the record company to complain they kept forgetting to spell their name with the 'exclamation mark', sadly that's the only interesting thing that can be said about the album.

When the album failed to set the charts alight, the band changed their name to Black Widow and began to hang around with , Britain's self-proclaimed 'King of the Witches'. Mostly forgotten today, Alex Sanders was a household name in the sixties and seventies, appearing often in the papers and on the television to pontificate on all manner of occult subjects from the right time of the month to slit the throat of your goat through to the correct temperature at which to serve human blood to your coven, he even released his own album .

Under Sander's tutelage the band began building real occult secrets into their music and lyrics. They also developed a stage show steeped in ritual, that culminated in the mock sacrifice of a naked virgin. Little England was horrified, bishops were wheeled out to fulminate and warn the young of the dangers of black magic and the queues formed around the block for Black Widow's shows.

Their single *Come to the Sabbat* was tipped for the number one spot but was subsequently banned by the BBC and their psychedelic/proto-prog album Sacrifice peaked at number 34 in the charts, but continued to sell well for a long time afterwards.

They were singled out for even bigger things in the States, but their tour coincided with the Manson family furore and their satanic reputation led to a countrywide ban. To fill all the dates that had been booked, their management were forced to turn to the only other band on their books, the aforementioned Black Sabbath. The rest, for Sabbath, was history. Black Widow subsequently dropped all the occult paraphernalia but their career slowly dwindled, they recorded four more album to decreasing sales and split up at the beginning of the seventies only to reform briefly in 2007.

Here's a film of them in their heyday, that was shot for a German TV station. I can only imagine how that was announced to the viewers at the time: "Coming up we have the weather and then a delicious Wiener Schnitzel recipe from Frau Helga, but first some crazy British rockers sacrificing a virgin ..."

While Black Widow dabbled and flirted with the occult, the American band Coven lived, breathed, ate and even shat their satanic beliefs. They are also the band responsible for introducing the s to rock music, which, if nothing else, should guarantee them a place in metal history. Their highly charismatic singer Jinx Dawson was a twin whose sister died in the womb. She was raised in her parent's secret society to study opera and the occult, but rebelled against them and formed a rock group in the late sixties with guitarists Chris Neilsen and Rick Durret, drummer Steve Ross and bassist Oz Osbourne (no relation, but coincidentally they did also release a song call *Black Sabbath* and Black Sabbath were dubbed "something like England's answer to Coven" by Lester Bangs when they first toured the States. Later, enraged at Sabbath stealing their image, Coven daubed inverted crosses in human blood on Sabbath's dressing room doors in Memphis).

Coven had a lot of success on the touring circuit playing with bands like Alice Cooper, Vanilla Fudge and Jimmy Page's Yardbirds. Given Page's later interest in Crowley and the supernatural, it's interesting to speculate whether his occult leanings began in his months on the road with Jinx and company, who would hold black masses back stage before every performance. Their stage show was said to be jaw dropping its high point being the crucifixion of a Jesus-look-a-like roadie and then the inversion of the self-same giant cross to which they'd nailed him, no wonder the Alice Cooper band were purportedly scared to death of them.

In 1969 they signed with Mercury Records and released *Witchcraft Destroys Minds & Reaps Souls* which is actually a pretty good gothic psych/proto metal album. It culminates with the 13 minute track 'Satanic Mass' which is a full and authentic depiction of a black mass, complete with chanting, incantations, bells, chimes and other sound effects. I wonder how many hippies dropped acid and put it on the turntable, only to find the Goat of Mendes's blistering hoof coming down hard on their trip.

The album did really well initially but fell foul of an article in Esquire magazine entitled *Evil Lurks in California* that linked Coven and their music with (yep you guessed it) the Manson Family slayings yet again. The unwanted publicity caused Mercury to pull the record and cancel upcoming tours. Coven rallied though, when two years later director, actor and activist Tom Laughlin asked them to record the track for his indie movie . The film was a huge hit and the single topped the charts in 1971 AND 1973.

The renewed interest led them to release two more albums, the eponymous *Coven* and the excellent *Blood on the Snow,* neither of which achieved any chart success. Jinx apparently carried on a slew of torrid affairs with everyone from Jim Morrison (was there any female in the 60s he didn't bed?), Queen's Roger Taylor and even Charlie Chaplin (no really). Coven's many other near brushes with renewed success included turning down producer Neil Bogart's offer to become a "made up costume band called 'Kiss'" (Gene Simmons and co. bit his hand off instead) and starring in an unreleased horror film called *Heaven Can Help* in 1990 for which Jinx and drummer Ross also wrote the score. Coven's cult status slowly grew over the decades and in 2008 they released a new album *Metal Goth Queen-Out of the Vault* which included a number of rock dignitaries from bands such as Deep Purple, Steppenwolf and Jethro Tull.

One last claim to fame of which Coven can boast is very probably shooting the first ever music video. This little devilish gem was shot by Disney Studio's of all people, in 1974 to promote *Blood On The Snow*

There were other notable bands of this time who chipped away at this same satanic seam for inspiration, Italy's Jacula and for instance, Germany's and Britain's acid folk maestro's . However, I've already gone on at length, so I'll maybe save them for another column on the same subject, if you're interested leave me a comment below.

Although I mentioned earlier that I wasn't going to write about horror comics for this column I fear I may have spoken too soon, because your dear old Uncle Jasp has a new graphic novel out. It's a horror/crime mash up called *Bloodfellas* that's an homage to the pre-code crime and horror comics of the nineteen fifties such as Tales from the Crypt and Crime Doesn't Pay. TIH's own described it, on this very site, as "epic in both scope and design ... definitely one for your collection!" Set in 1930s prohibition era America, the elevator pitch for Bloodfellas would be "The Walking Dead meets Boardwalk Empire". I know you've heard this a million times before but this really IS a reinvention of the zombie genre, this is the undead as you have never seen them before.

So don't delay, buy it today! If you're not 100% thrilled with your purchase I will personally come round to your house and perform a Death Metal Black Mass stark bollock naked by way of recompense.

Trust your Uncle Jasp on this, you know it makes sense.

Jasper Bark

Originally published in Mass Movement #44, November 2015

NIGHT BIRDS

It's one of those bands Mass Movement was created for. There's just no denying that Night Birds are the sonic storm we aspire to be with our magazine. Having recently signed with Fat Wreck and giving us *Mutiny At Muscle Beach*, Night Birds have again taken a serious step towards punk rock domination. Frontman Brian Gorsegner was more than happy to offer us a Nightbirds update…

Interview by Martijn Welzen

MM: You're looking back towards the early days of punk(rock) on *Mutiny At Muscle Beach*, how did you get in touch with the old bands of the seventies and eighties? Did you discover that on your own of was it the case of an 'older brother'?

Brian: No, I had to learn the hard way. Lots of trial and error. The Clash and Ramones were early finds for me, thanks to their songs that would get 90s airplay like *Rock the Casbah* and *I Wanna Be Sedated* respectively. And then your bound to hear a Minor Threat cover, and you buy the Minor Threat discography, and then you learn about the early days of Dischord, so you need to seek out these bands called Teen Idles and SOA... And then you realize the singer of SOA was the same guy who was one of the singers in Black Flag! And then you learn about SST and Husker Due, and the Minutemen and then you see these old show flyers where they are playing with Flipper, and that guy is wearing a Verbal Abuse shirt... You get the idea. Discovering punk is so cool cause it just spiderwebs all over the place. And there's just so much great shit. To think there's still so much rad shit I've yet to discover blows my mind. And I got into punk just before the internet. A time when there were still Misfits songs and recordings that were very hard to come by. And the Decline of Western Civilization was something your friend had a 3rd generation dubbed VHS of. The internet is cool in that regard, all this rad shit is just accessible.

MM: What drew you to that particular sound?

Brian: It's just the best. Aggressive songs that can still carry a tune and melody, that's it for me. Bands like the Damned, Dickies, Naked Raygun. That's my favorite stuff.

MM: I find it very interesting that you are not only looking towards a different time in music, but also have lots of Californian influences. How does that go down in New Jersey?

Brian: Hey, we have a shore too! And we're madder. We have seasons, so we are bitter grumpy people. We love those West Coast melodies and just do em with out own twist.

MM: And now you've also signed with Fat Wreck, in 2013, known for it's upbeat, mostly Californian bands. How did this all come about?

Brian: The Fat folks all appreciate the classic stuff we're rooted in. Mike has Crucifx and Lewd logos tattooed on him. We just sound crankier then some of their other bands cause we're from out East, most of their other bands are West Coast. We approached them back then about doing the *Maimed for the Masses* EP. They have a built in fan base in places like Australia, Japan, Brazil; all these places that are sort of bucket list places for us to go. Plus their distribution is so great. That's what we were after, and we started talking to them and they were all so down to earth, and down to let us do things our way. It was a no brainer. We're so anal and particular, I drive em crazy. They love it.

MM: What have you noticed as the biggest difference between Grave Mistake records and Fat Wreck Chords?

Brian: Mostly the stuff I just mentioned above. Alex at Grave Mistake rules, and does everything he can for his bands, but twenty five years of experience and a solid reputation of always treating everyone right goes a long way and offers a few things a "newer" label cannot.

MM: I am wondering if you in that matter also notice a difference in the way questions for interviews are being formulated? Does it also feel like a fresh start in that aspect? Do you have to answer a lot of who is who, and when did you start out questions again?

Brian: Yes, funny you should ask, I thought about that the other night. A lot of people go into it like we're a brand new band, but we've been a band six years already. But it's cool, makes sense we'd be on some different peoples radars, that was the point of working with a new label in the first place.

MM: With the title *Mutiny At Muscle Beach* Dead Kennedys came to mind, while the cover reminded me of *Walk Together, Rock Together* by 7 Seconds. Is that all a coincidence or are you also being influenced by the words and imagery of the bands of the eighties?

Brian: Yeah all our old classic favorite bands inspire us in all kinds of ways, of course. I think the aesthetic of all those early bands is so cool, and when you're a kid the way a record cover looks can be as impact-full as the songs on the record. I remember staring at the cover of *Plastic Surgery Disasters,* or *Damaged,* and just thinking it was fucked up looking and so rad. Still to this day I will overlook records at the record store if the artwork sucks. That stuff is important to me.

MM: History, music like music goes in waves, or circles. Are we in that aspect also living in a same sort of atmosphere as the eighties. Seems like the cold war paranoia is really flaring up again? Is that also an influence on your music in some way?

Brian: Yeah, maybe. Let's wait and see if Donald Trump becomes president, that should make for some really good punk rock.

MM: Many of your songs seem to rebel against the rat race we live in. Are you just signaling this or are you also offering an escape? Obviously playing in a band is a good escape, but that's not for all of us.

Brian: Everyone needs something. My parents never had a hobby and they were always cranky. If you don't wanna start up your own band then paint, or take up karate, plant a garden... I dunno, find some sort of creative outlet. That's pretty important to me, I'm not looking to speak for everyone. But yeah, I'm a poor person with a shit job who works my ass off to make it all work. Gotta have some sort of an outlet.

MM: Your lyrics seem to be timeless, in the aspect we're always struggling with power, greed, religion and politics. To what extend does it bother you that humans never seem to change, and your words will never be outdated? It does make for good metal / punk bands though....

Brian: It bothers me a lot. I used to think most people were good and there were some bad mixed in. I don't feel that way anymore. I think the majority is bad, and finding the non scum is getting harder and harder. It's a shame really.

MM: I often wonder to what extreme a band is willing to go to get the music / message out, without having to compromise on said music / message? Fat Wreck is a proper punk label, but would you possibly sign with a major? Or have your video played on MTV / mainstream radio? Where's the line you drew in the sand?

Brian: No we wouldn't sign to a major. It's 2015, the music industry is dead, no ones going to be offering us a million dollars anytime soon. We take it all on a case by case basis. A couple years ago MTV wanted to use our song *Prognosis: Negative* as the opening credits to some new cartoon with Will Ferrell as a surfing monkey. We said no. It sounded lame. We wanna do stuff that we don't think is lame. The best part about working hard with your band is being able to be proud of your records, and shows, and tours. I don't want that to be tarnished. But at the same time we do want people to hear our music, and sometimes that means doing weird shit. But not all weird shit is evil.

MM: One of your songs is *Off The Grid* something you hear quite a lot about in an era we all 'need' to be connected by wifi and social media. Is that a burden to us, or possibly you personal? Would you like to be living off the grid?

Brian: Sometimes, but other times I don't mind. So much good and bad come with something like that, I think it's difficult to make it a black and white subject. Being hardline against that stuff is silly, like my Dad, but putting your whole life out into the world like some fish bowl is also weird. I guess it's just a matter of a finding a balance you can live with. No one is forcing you to check this shit.

MM: What can we expect from Night Birds in the near future? Extensive touring across the globe? Any unexpected places you're going to pop up?

Brian: We wanna go weird places, but nothing set in stone yet. A fun US tour is in store for March 2016, and Europe again in April. For the rest of this year we have some shows coming up with the Dickies and Negative Approach. Stoked!

Originally published in Mass Movement #44, November 2015

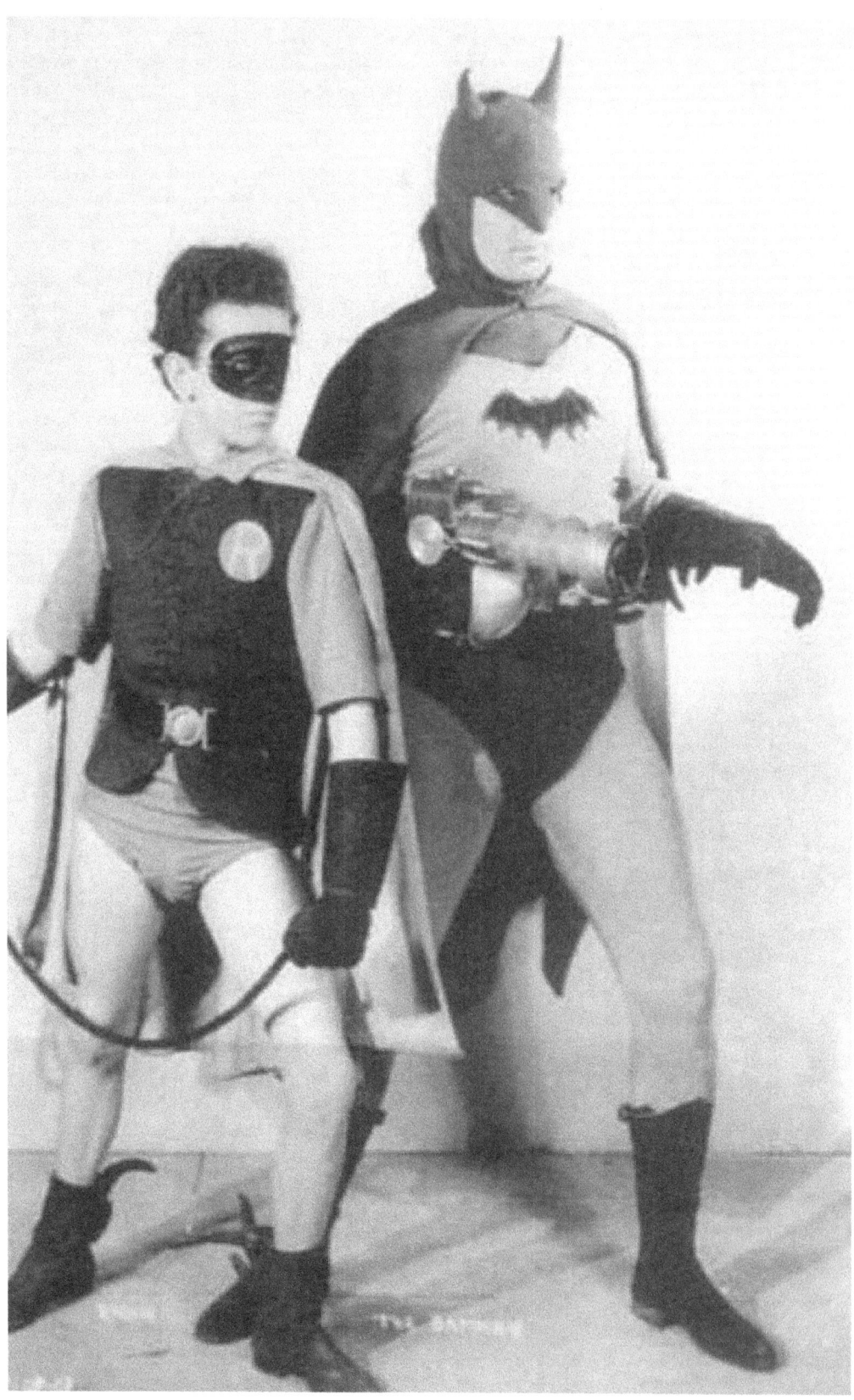

THE BATMAN
A WARTIME SUPERHERO

The Batman: A Wartime Superhero - My favorite serial

Hands down, *The Batman* serial (1943) is my all-time favorite chapter play. I can't even begin to count the number of reasons why, but I'll do my best. First off, you have a serial where both the hero and villain are equally as entertaining, similar to the *Captain Midnight*/Ivan Shark relationship that I wrote about earlier. Just in case you're wondering, this chapter play is the first appearance for the "Caped Crusader" and his sidekick Robin, so Columbia Studios refers to him as "The Batman." This serial is not to be confused with the later Batman and Robin chapter play in 1949.

Ok, now for the principals: Lewis Wilson is the lead and Douglas Croft as the "Boy Wonder." Together, they oppose their nemesis, the Japanese archenemy Dr. Daka, played by the well-known character actor J. Carrol Naish. All three characters are worth the price of admission.

The Batman wears an ill-fitting costume with very large ears and sports somewhat of a paunch (his utility belt covers most of it). Robin, on the other hand, is diminutive in stature with an almost "Shirley Temple-style" curly top. There is no Batmobile, no Batplane or Bat-boat, merely a Cadillac convertible in which the dynamic duo uses the backseat to change into their famous outfits. It's interesting to note that, over the years, their basic wardrobe really hasn't changed much, only updated to appear a little more "slick and shiny." Remember that the character of Batman has no superpowers.

Before I begin to dissect the storyline of this chapter play, it must be realized the time period in which it was made. Without making this explanation too much of a rah-rah, let's kill the enemy-type of pep rally for the Allied forces, the fact remains that the Japanese did attack America at Pearl Harbor, and we were at war with all of the Axis Powers, Japan among them. This is to address what some readers might consider to be racial slurs directed against the Japanese that can be heard throughout the chapter play. But considering the fact that you can't change history, certainly not by censorship, the remarks are appropriate for the times. What happened, happened, and that's all I have to say about it.

Therefore, the basic storyline involves Dr, Daka and his network of spies, who operate behind a Funhouse façade: the inside made to resemble a cave-like motif. The various members of Daka's inner circle are former "captains of industry" who have somehow been, as Daka states, "dishonored by America's corrupt form of government." His main objective is to establish the roots for a "New World Order" on American soil. According to Daka, the order would destroy the democratic forces of evil in the United States and bring about the liberation of the enslaved people of America. Wow,

To do so must require complete and total obedience to Daka's agenda without question. Failure to comply would result in the loss of the individual's personal will to resist by turning the subject into a zombie.

Those who are willingly involved in Daka's nefarious plan would ride the Funhouse cars and exit at a certain location inside the cave. At that point, they would be allowed to enter Daka's so-called office, complete with a stature of Buddha, by placing their palms at a certain spot on the cave wall. This, in turn, would activate an image of the palm print on a screen inside of Daka's office, and he would allow the person to enter by pushing one of two buttons located underneath his desk. The "other button" is reserved for a different purpose. It's your basic example of fingerprint ID. There you have it, simple and to the point.

The story begins with the prison release of a former, honest industrialist (Martin Warren), who had been wrongly accused of some undisclosed crime. He is to meet at the prison gate with his niece (Linda Page) and driven home. Unfortunately for Martin, he is intercepted by some of Daka's men and taken to the Funhouse headquarters.

Seated behind an impressive and ornate desk, Dr. Daka is surrounded by several of his cronies, who sit in rapt attention as he outlines his nefarious plans for world domination and the destruction of America. His cronies have all been "hand-selected" by Daka himself based on their expertise in various fields. Martin is offered a position to join the organization but refuses to cooperate; thus, he is to be stripped of his will and turned into a mindless zombie. This is where the real fun begins.

Daka leads Warren to a basement laboratory that is filled with various, electrical instruments similar to Doctor Frankenstein's set-up. The device used to gain control of the individual's freewill is a ridiculous looking, glass-encased helmet with wires attached to its top. Martin is held into what appears to be an electric chair so that the helmet can be lowered over his head. Then, Daka throws a switch and watches in glee as the "zombafacation" (don't bother to look it up) process begins. Within minutes our unlucky friend has successfully been transformed into an obedient servant of the evil-minded doctor. On a side note, the zombafacation process can be reversed, a fact that is played out in the final chapter.

The writers also came up with another interesting apparatus that Daka uses to dispose of those individuals who refuse to cooperate. It's a hidden, trapdoor device located on the floor of his office, which can be activated to open whenever Daka pushes "the other button" underneath his desk. Waiting below is a pit of hungry alligators ready to make a meal out of the unfortunate soul who happens to be standing in the wrong place at the wrong time. Whenever someone tries to flee, Daka sees to it that the person never leaves the room alive.

The character of Daka is a straightforward, albeit, biased representation of a Japanese spy due to the many anti-Nipponese references made throughout the serial. Basically, the script is very careful to paint him as a vicious, evil-minded servant to Emperor Hirohito and the "Land of the Rising Sun". Naish's exaggerated portrayal of him only adds to the character's sadistic nature, but it is somewhat tempered by his comical, "over-the-top" performance. As a villain, you don't love to hate him, but instead, you hate to love him. After all, you're not supposed to like the enemy, right? The fact is, he is downright hilarious to watch. His overzealous desire for the total annihilation of a corrupt and unjust United States is unmistakably enunciated by the fiery, anti-American dialog. It's clear that he hates the enemy.

As for his opponent, *The Batman* is equally as hilarious to watch for many of the same reasons. As scripted, he is the comical savior against the shifty-eyed villain. He and Robin are almost totally inept in their attempts to defeat Daka, but somehow they manage to be victorious.

The chapter play continues to entertain the viewer with an abundance of laugh-filled endings that can only be described as hilarious.

Like so many other Columbia serials, the emphasis is designed to generate laughs rather than the more serious approach used by Republic and Universal Studios. However, I'm sure that to a youngster from that era, it was dead serious stuff. Again, this is my all-time favorite serial, so it has to be a "ten" in my book.

Doug Crill

Originally published in Mass Movement #44, November 2015

SIAMESE FIGHTING FISH - PAGE 20

M M 32

ALSO IN THIS ISSUE:

CANNIBAL CORPSE
NAPALM DEATH
CHRISTOPHER
FOWLER
LAGWAGON
EMILY BOOTH
PILGRIM
DANNY DYER
FREEGASE
KISSIN' DYNAMITE
SOIL
PAUL RENNA
ANTERIOR
ANDY ANDERSEN
HUNTRESS

FINAL PRAYER
SIMON GUERRIER
CONTRAST THE WATER
SCREEN DAMAGE
THE DUNGEON'S MASTER
COLUMNS
FEATURES
REVIEWS
...AND MUCH, MUCH MORE!

M M 33

Also featuring:

JFA
James Lovegrove
Exumer
Damn Vandals
Ignitor
Unearth
Dr Living Dead
Rival Sons
John Dorsey
Teenage Bottlerocket
Black Breath
Royal Thunder

Killing California
Klaus Luley
Justin Melkmann
Hard Resistance
The Dungeon's Master
Screen Damage
Features
Columns
Reviews
...And much more...

34

- Therapy?
- Ensiferum
- Steve Niles
- Lucy Davis
- Strife
- Wintersun
- Charlie Higson
- History Of The Hawk
- Fear Factory
- Goodtime Boys
- The Sword
- Eric Brown
- Bison BC
- Michael Biehn & Jennifer Blanc Biehn
- Trail Of Murder
- Tony Parker
- Thorun
- Karma To Burn
- Gareth Powell
- We'll Go Machete
- Coelmus,
- Features & Much, Much More...

35

- Bad Religion
- Dropkick Murphy's
- Neal Adams
- Snuff
- Six Feet Under
- Valve Rider
- Pat Mills
- Testament
- Chris Wollard & The Ship Thieves
- Bafflegab Productions
- Hierophant
- Gama Bomb
- The Mervyn Stone Mysteries
- Ays
- Lordi
- Dead City Records
- Snake Charmer
- Screen Damage
- Injured Eyeballs
- And Much, Much More...

MM 36

featuring:
• D.O.A. • Fading Bliss •
Jeff "Swampy" Marsh • Voorhees • Sterling Gates • Gimp Fist • Joe R. Lansdale • The Bunny The Bear • Maya Plas • In This Moment • The Sick Livers • Paul Magrs • Night Birds • Michael Alan Nelson • Alpha & Omega • James Tynion IV • Vatier • Bai Bang • Hardress • I.D.O. • Thirty Six Strategies • D-A-D • Battlecross • Shining

...and much, much more plus features, columns and reviews...

MM 37

BAD SAM

BL'AST!
Out Cold
Phil Mall
Jesse Damon
Thai Mahal
Victo Chino
Adjudgement
Onslaught
Salq
Gregg Hurwitz
Symphony Of Pain
Tyr
Harvest Impulse
Death Angel
Robert Venditti
GWAR
Toxic Shock
Toby Hadoke
Matthew Pritchard
Castles
And much more...

38

BIOHAZARD - LESS THAN JAKE - RED FANG - WAYNE SIMMONS - FUNERAL FOR A FRIEND - CJ RAMONE - VINCENZO BILOF - SATAN'S WRATH - MATT FITTON - FM359 - ZODIAC - RHAPSODY OF FIRE - LIBBY MCGUGAN - AND MUCH, MUCH MORE

Briggs & Barnes talk Holmes

39

RICHIE RAMONE

ARTILLERY
CAUGHT IN A TRAP
GUSTAVO DUARTE
COKAS
GIUDA
CRYSTAL VIPER
NEAL ADAMS
VERNON G. WELLS
VANISHING POINT
JAMES MAXEY
TRUTH CORRODED
KEVIN LUCIA
KAIJU RISING
INJURED EYEBALLS
SCREEN DAMAGE
AND MUCH MORE...

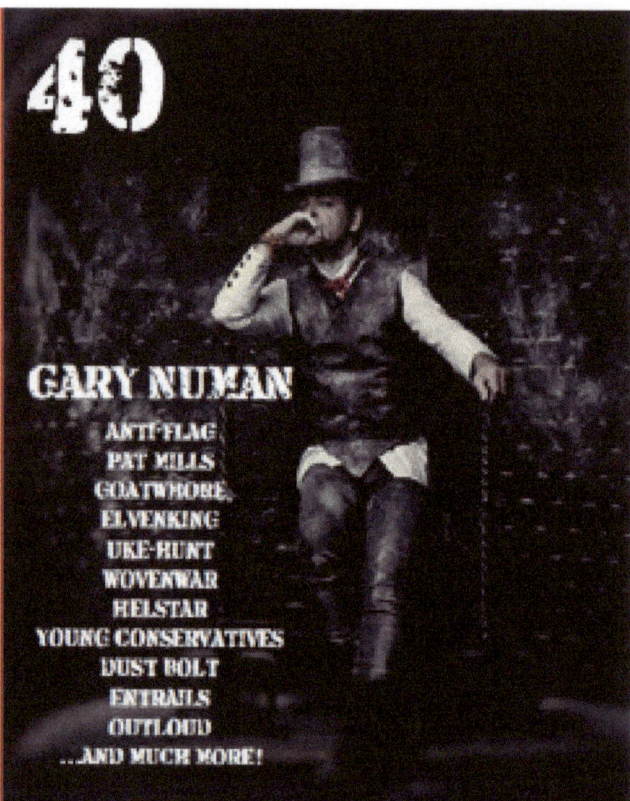

40

GARY NUMAN

ANTI-FLAG
PAT MILLS
GOATWHORE
ELVENKING
UKE-HUNT
WOVENWAR
HELSTAR
YOUNG CONSERVATIVES
DUST BOLT
ENTRAILS
OUTLOUD
...AND MUCH MORE!

41

AT THE GATES

THE DESTROYERS, CAVALERA CONSPIRACY, ALEC WORLEY, REVOCATION, CRIPPER, GARY DANIELS, EVERGREY, COLUMNS, FEATURES AND MUCH, MUCH MORE...

42

Ensiferum

VIOLENT ARREST, BLACK STATE HIGHWAY, DENIAL FIEND, EDENS CURSE, GRUESOME, EVIL INVADERS, LOYAL UNTIL DEATH, YORKSHIRE RATS, MORDRED, MOTOR SISTER, WINDSOR DRIVE, COLUMNS, FEATURES AND MORE...

43

Onslaught

ARMORED SAINT, AHAB, BISHOPS GREEN, THE F.T.W, ACID REIGN, THE SICK LIVERS, BURNING POINT, SIBERIAN MEAT GRINDER, PYOGENESIS, WELCOME TO ICELAND... AND MUCH, MUCH MORE!

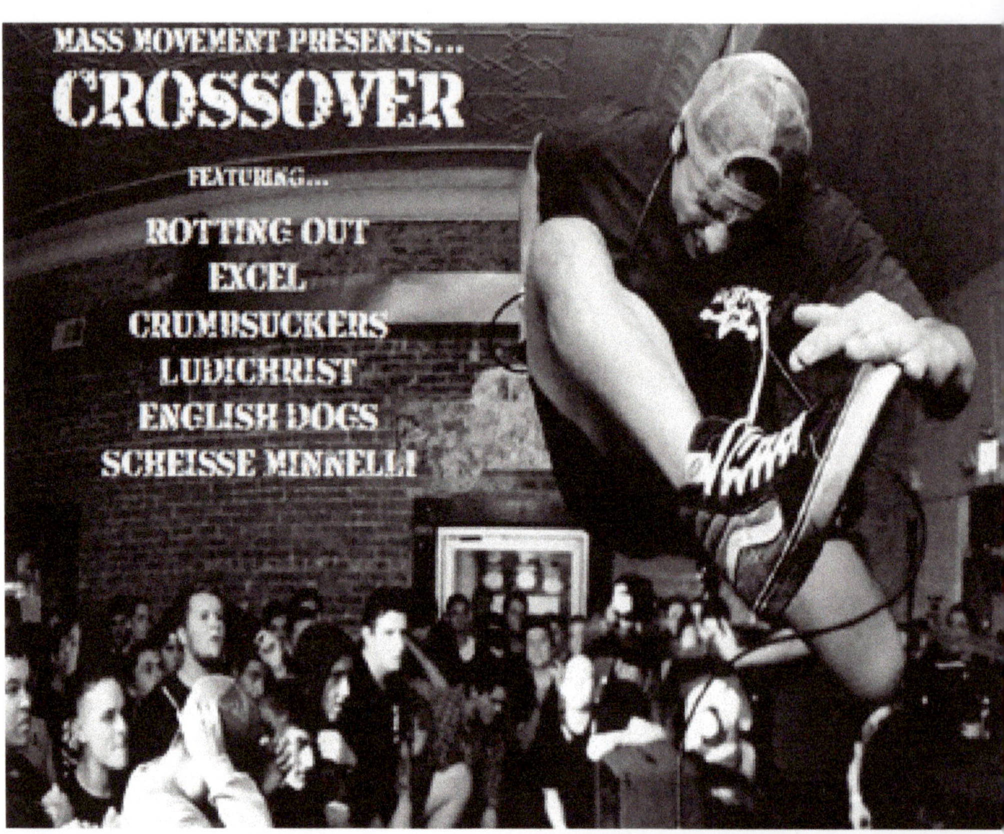
MASS MOVEMENT PRESENTS...
CROSSOVER
FEATURING...
ROTTING OUT
EXCEL
CRUMBSUCKERS
LUDICHRIST
ENGLISH DOGS
SCHEISSE MINNELLI

MASS MOVEMENT PRESENTS...
N.Y.H.C.
WHERE THE WILD THINGS ARE...
AGNOSTIC FRONT, SHEER TERROR, AWKWARD THOUGHT, UNDERDOG, LEEWAY,
SEAN TAGGART, REVELATION RECORDS, CHAKA MALIK, TONY RETTMAN, FREDDY ALVA
MIKE D. LORENZO, GAVIN VAN VLACK, ANDY WEST, RON GRIMALDI, GARY BENNETT II...

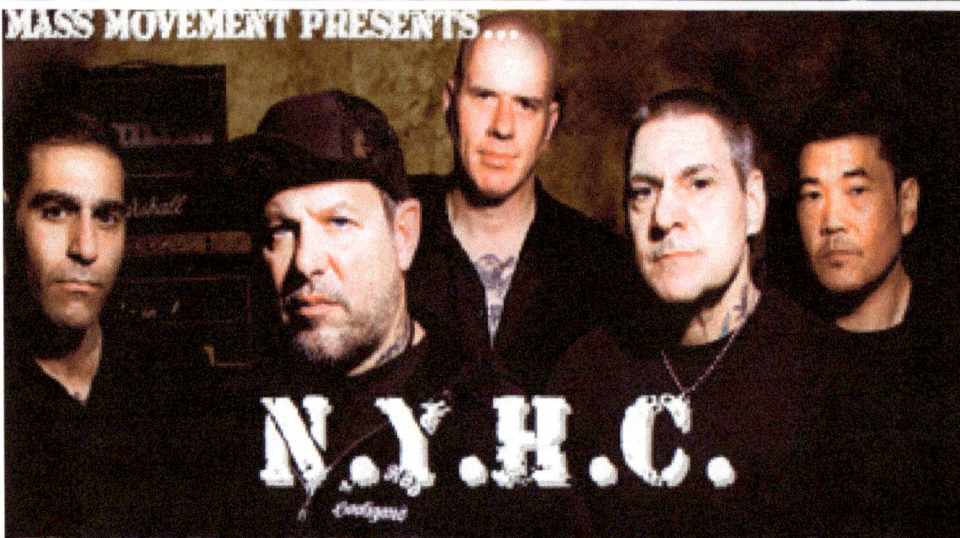

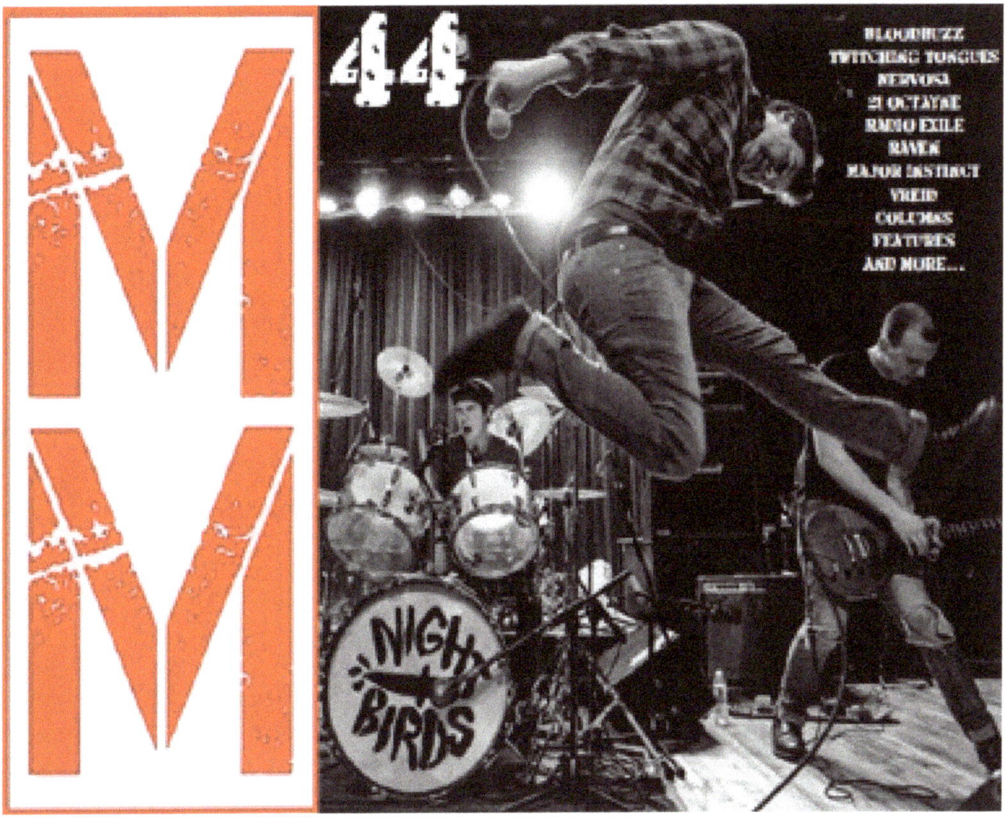

MM 44

BLOODBUZZ
TWITCHING TONGUES
NERVOSA
21 OCTAYNE
RADIO EXILE
RAVEN
MAJOR INSTINCT
VREID
COLUMNS
FEATURES
AND MORE...

MASS MOVEMENT

With thanks

Mass Movement Magazine was brought you by Liam Ronan, George Tabb, Doug Crill, Tim 'Bunky' Davis, Tom Wilding, James McLaren, Brady Webb, Steve Scanner, Martijn Welzen, Jason Thomas, Marv Jolly, Ian Pickens, Tom Chapman, Pete Williams, Jethro Kamba-Wall, Leigh McAndrew, Jim Dodge, Ian Glasper, Mark Freebase, Kai Woolen-Lewis and Tim 'Mass Movement' Cundle

Dedicated to the memory of James McLaren, Dave Brockie, John Sicolo, Eric Brockman, Paul Spragg and Jason Sears. Until the next life. Slainte

Thank-you Andy Turner, Vique 'Simba' Martin, Chrissie Yiannou, Mosh Knockout, Johann at Reflections, Nanette & Wiebke (Fat Wreck Europe), Delphine Victory, Simon & Nita Keeler and Bill 'Doctor Strange' Plaster for believing in Mass Movement from the beginning - if it wasn't for you folks, we wouldn't be here today , Nathan Bean, Sophie Francois, Chris Andrews, Tom Chapman, Ian Pickens and Tony Fyler the current Mass Movement crew, Alan Wright, Rhodri 'Poggles' Dawe, Adam Caradog Thomas, Rachel Evans, Everyone at Earth Island Books, Engineer Records for sponsoring the Mass Movement podcast, Anna Hinds, Leanne Toy, Ross O'Brien, Jonathan Evans, Matthew Davies-Kreye, Neil Randle & Bang-On Brewery, Michael Davies, Welly Artcore, Gavin Gates, Darrel Sutton, The Legendary TJ's (the spiritual home of Mass Movement), Simon Phillips, Dean Beddis, Wayne 'Pig' Cole, Alexandros 'Alex' Anesiadis, Richard Torres, Marcus 'Mivvi' Davis, David 'Dog' O'Grady, Will Pywell, Dark Horse Comics, Titan Books & Comics, Turnaround Publishing Services, DC Comics, Epitaph Records, Bafflegab, Revelation Records, Big Finish, Fat Wreck Chords, Asmodee Games, Black Library, all the incredible bands, writers, artists, wrestlers, film makers that we've been fortunate enough to meet and interview during the last two and something decades, the labels, publishing and PR folk who rose above and beyond the call of duty when called on and last, and most importantly of all, my long suffering and (most of the time) understanding family (Emma, Siobhan and Ma) whose wisdom, guidance and help mean more to me than they will ever know - none of this would have been possible without you.

About Tim Cundle

Tim Cundle stumbled into the punk scene sometime in the mid-nineteen eighties and his life has never been the same since. Having worked as riflery instructor and drug counsellor and studied both English Literature and Behavioural Science at University, he decided his career lay down a different path and, having written for local newspapers since he was fifteen, did what most aspiring writers do. He became a journalist.

Currently the editor of Mass Movement Magazine, he has also contributed to, and written for, Doctor Who Magazine, Big Cheese, Fracture and many other publications. A lifelong geek and Disney, Star Wars and comic book fanatic, he spends far too much time obsessing over obscure Hardcore and Crossover bands, playing Dungeons & Dragons, reading genre literature, devoting himself to television shows and films that most people would consider to be puerile, recording and presenting the Mass Movement Presents podcast with his partner in audio crime Chris Andrews, drinking too much coffee, indulging his passion for craft beer and watching Professional Wrestling and Ice Hockey.

After "singing" for two Hardcore bands, Charlies Family Crisis and AxTxOxTx, he now considers that chapter of his life to be closed and the chances of him doing the band thing again are slim to non-existent. However, just like Sean Connery, Tim learned a long time ago to never say never again, so who knows? You may see him on stage again. But you probably won't.

The Best of Mass Movement: The Digital Years Volumes I & II are the result of a crazy five year period that saw Mass Movement reluctantly enter, and make its mark on the digital age. They are a testament to Tim's enduring love of the written word and the underground and capture the essence of a magazine and website that celebrated, and continues to champion, punk rock and geek culture.

Tim lives in a small, sleepy Welsh village with his wife Emma and daughter Siobhan and keeps himself busy by working on his upcoming books and Mass Movement, which takes up far too much of his time. He dreams about muscle cars, Disney World and disappearing to live in a small cabin in the wild woods of Tennessee.

MASS MOVEMENT MAGAZINE VOL 2 AFTERWORD

True story.

I'm writing this in the middle of the Coronapocalypse. I may have a mild dose myself, I certainly have a lot of the symptoms, but not the ones that are most talked about. There's currently no way to tell because it's next to impossible to get tested in the UK at the moment.

I'm a little under the weather and not working at full capacity. That would normally be fine, but I have to finish the second draft of a 180,000 word novel, that's now a year overdue. On top of that I have a bunch of other commissions that are imminent this week. I've also promised Tim I would write an afterword for this second volume of articles from Mass Movement Magazine. That's okay, though, I really like Tim, but I only had a couple of hours in my schedule to skim through the volume and write the afterword.

So, as I'm flicking through the pages, I find this volume has articles on hardcore and death metal legends, it covers horror comics, obscure pulp characters, movie serials from the 30s and 40s and a whole load of other things I'm obsessed with and, before I know it, six hours has passed and I'm still reading. You probably had exactly the same experience.

However, you might not have come to an article headed "What Makes Comics Scary" and thought to yourself: who f***ing cares! You may not have read the opening line and thought: who is the asshole that wrote this? I did though. And then I flicked to end of the article to see who'd written this s*** only to see my own byline! I didn't bother to read the rest of this article I just cringed and skipped ahead to the next one.

You see, I'd completely forgotten that by this point in the Mass Movement story (2013), I'd started submitting articles at Tim's invitation. I've written thousands of articles, reviews and opinion pieces over the last three decades and I honestly don't remember them all, sometimes with good reason. As I said above, this is a true story and those were my genuine thoughts. But I also thought to myself: Never mind, this is the best of MMM, at least there won't be any more features by me.

So, imagine my embarrassment to find there were more features by me, and some of them contained photos of me dressed like an asshat! But I could at least content myself with the thought that the internet is full of photos of me looking like an asshat, so in that respect, at least, this volume is nothing special.

What does make it special, and what made writing for MMM so crucial, was the editor and driving force behind Mass Movement – Tim Cundle. His enthusiasm for the music, the comics, and the films he covers spills over in every conversation you have with him. It comes across in the emails he sends, the articles he writes, and every facet of the magazine he publishes. That's why I ended up writing so many articles for him.

It's also why I ended up losing so much time to this volume. And I'll bet it's why you did too. You have Tim to thank for that. And so do I.

Jasper Bark

May 2020

www.ingramcontent.com/pod-product-compliance
Ingram Content Group UK Ltd.
Pitfield, Milton Keynes, MK11 3LW, UK
UKHW020246240426
12048UKWH00026B/1630